2/04

ALSO AVAILABLE FROM CONTINUUM:

Brooker:

Batman Unmasked

Klock:

How To Read Superhero Comics and Why

Leymarie:

Cuban Fire

McMahan:

The Films of Tim Burton

O'Keefe:

Readers in Wonderland

Shipton:

A New History of Jazz

Dr. Seuss: American Ic

DR. SEUSS:
AMERICAN ICON

Philip Nel

NEW YORK • LONDON

2004

The Continuum International Publishing Group Inc
15 E 26 Street, New York, NY 10010

The Continuum International Publishing Group Ltd
The Tower Building, 11 York Road, London SE1 7NX

www.continuumbooks.com

Library of Congress Cataloging-in-Publication Data

Nel, Philip, 1969–
   Dr. Seuss : American icon / by Philip Nel.
      p.   cm.
   Includes bibliographical references.
   ISBN 0-8264-1434-6 (hardcover : alk. paper)
   1. Seuss, Dr.—Criticism and interpretation.   2. Children's
literature, American—History and criticism.   3. Children—Books and
reading—United States—History—20th century.   4. Seuss,
Dr.—Appreciation—United States.   I. Title: Doctor Seuss.   II. Title.
   PS3513.E2Z787   2004
   813'.52—dc22
                                                    2003024443

Table of Contents

List of Illustrations and Credits

Dedication

To Dr. Seuss, Sesame Street, *and my parents,*
for teaching me to read

Acknowledgments

For their advice and assistance, I would like to thank Leith Adams, Roger Adams, Rebecca Alexander, David Barker, Jerry Beck, Linda Brigham, Herb Cheyette, Jay Clayton, Charles Cohen, June Cummins, Bill Dreyer, Chelsea Eckert, Greg Eiselein, Bill Ellis, Phyllis Epps, Richard Flynn, Joanne M. Gangi, Sally Gray, Jerry Griswold, Gloria Hardman, Charles Hatfield, Michael Patrick Hearn, Michael Heyman, Daniel Hirsch, Sara Kearns, Julia Mickenberg, William Moebius, Judith Morgan, Neil Morgan, Thomas E. Murray, Larry Rodgers, Kevin Shortsleeve, Rob Suggs, Jan Susina, Brian Tessier, James Wadley, Helen Younger, Marc Younger, and Karl ZoBell.

For invaluable research assistance, my thanks to Lynda Claassen of Mandeville Special Collections, Geisel Library, University of California at San Diego; Sarah I. Hartwell, Joshua D. Shaw, and Edward Connery Lathem of the Rauner Alumni Library, Dartmouth College; Mona Bradley and Maggie Humberston of the Connecticut Valley Historical Museum; Heather Haskell of Springfield Art Museums; and Cari Williams, my diligent researcher here at Kansas State University. For their prompt and thorough response to my query about children's literature statuary, thanks to these members of the child_lit listserv: Karen Beil, Jackie Corinth, Jane Cummiskey, Phyllis Danko, Ellen Donovan, Rodney Elin, Richard Flynn (again), Diane Foote, Nick Glass, Alison Hendon, Michael Joseph, Diane G. Kerner, Jameela Lares, Sharon Levin, Ellen Loughran, Leonard Marcus, Doug Mitchell, Sharon Morris, Linda Sue Park, Barbara Tobin, Judith Ridge, Jane Stemp Wickenden, and Pam Yosca.

Thanks also to Kansas State University's Interlibrary Services Department for filling my many requests for books and articles, and to the Seattle Public Library for loaning its volumes of *Judge*.

Special thanks to Chris Donovan, Lauren Ash Donoho, Rita Moore, Alisha Young, Regan Romanoff and the staff of the Hotel del Coronado, where part of this book was written. Thanks to Matt Dunne and Sarah Stewart Taylor of Hartland, Vermont, for putting me up when I was doing research and writing at Dartmouth.

ACKNOWLEDGMENTS

For funding my research, thanks to the National Endowment for the Humanities for an NEH Summer Stipend; to Kansas State University for a University Small Research Grant; and to the Mona B. Webb Foundation.

An earlier version of Chapter Two was published in *Mosaic* 34.2 (2001); an earlier version of Chapter Five was published in *Cultural Studies* 17.5 (2003). Taylor & Francis has requested that *Cultural Studies'* website be mentioned, and so here it is: <http://www.tandf.co.uk/journals/routledge/09502386.html>. Thanks to both journals for their editorial suggestions, and for allowing the work to be reprinted here. Thanks also to the organizers of conferences at which earlier (and shorter) versions of each chapter were presented: Children's Literature Association Annual Conferences (2002, 2000), Biennial Conference on Modern Critical Approaches to Children's Literature (2003), American Literature Association Annual Conference (2003), Kansas State University's Annual Cultural Studies Symposium (2002), and the South Atlantic Modern Language Association Conference (2002).

Last but most, a generous helping of thanks to Karin E. Westman, for her advice, love, and support.

How to Read Dr. Seuss

I n Springfield, Massachusetts, you can shake hands (or paws) with
the Grinch, the Lorax, Yertle the Turtle, Horton the Elephant,
Thidwick the Big-Hearted Moose, the Cat in the Hat, and Theodor
Seuss Geisel himself. Bronze sculptures of these characters and their
creator greet visitors to the Dr. Seuss National Memorial. Lark Grey
Dimond-Cates, the sculptor and Geisel's stepdaughter, said of the sculpture garden she designed, "I want people to leave taking Dr. Seuss's
work a little more seriously. . . . I think a lot of people take Dr. Seuss's
work lightly—it's fluff, it's cute. If you sit down and read his books
carefully, they have so much more to them" ("Springfield Celebrates
Seuss").

This book takes as its premise the notion that Dr. Seuss's works
have much more to them, and that they are worth taking seriously. One
reason for taking them seriously is that Dr. Seuss is more than an author
of popular children's books. Dr. Seuss is an American icon. He is an
icon because "Dr. Seuss" stands for more than just the author's given
name of Theodor Seuss Geisel. "Dr. Seuss" represents children's literature, nonsense poetry, energetic cartoon surrealism, and the process of
learning to read. Seuss is also distinctively an American icon. Though his
works have been translated into many languages, he is universally known
only in the United States and much less recognized abroad.

Famous enough to have his own public memorial, Seuss has gained
an honor given to very few authors of children's books, although to
considerably more characters. For example, in London, you can find
statues of Paddington Bear, Winnie-the-Pooh, and Peter Pan. A statue
of Robin Hood stands in Nottingham, England; statues of Pinocchio
appear in Milan and Collodi, Italy; statues of Huck Finn and Tom Sawyer
look out from Cardiff Hill in Hannibal, Missouri. New York's Central
Park has Alice in Wonderland; Chicago's Oz Park features Baum's Tin
Woodman; and the Boston Public Garden has Robert McCloskey's ducks

from *Make Way for Ducklings*.[1] Even when their characters become monuments, many creators do not. Statues of Hans Christian Andersen are in Copenhagen's Rosenborg Garden and in New York's Central Park, which also has a statue of Mother Goose (if she can be considered an "author"). Stockholm's Tegnerlunden Park includes a bronze statue of Astrid Lindgren. Though not always thought of as a "children's author," Charles Dickens and his character Little Nell have statues in Philadelphia's Clark Park.[2] And there are statues of Mark Twain in Hannibal, Hartford, Los Angeles, and Elmira (New York). The proliferation of Twain statuary notwithstanding, only a small number of children's authors are revered enough to become memorialized as statues. So, then, how does Dr. Seuss end up in the company of Hans Christian Andersen, Mother Goose, Astrid Lindgren, Charles Dickens, and Mark Twain?

On May 31, 2002, when the Dr. Seuss National Memorial was dedicated, many people tried to address precisely this question. Former First Lady Barbara Bush wrote to praise Seuss for doing "so much to promote children and parents reading together. [. . .] Through rhyme and wit and brilliant drawing, Dr. Seuss brought the beauty of language to life." If literacy is one answer, another may be money—not only Seuss's commercial success, but the money required to build such a monument and the tourism revenue that Springfield hoped the memorial would bring in. During his brief speech, Springfield Mayor Michael Albano alluded to the 6.2 million dollar cost of the memorial park by asking, "I think this is a good use of taxpayer dollars, don't you?" The hometown crowd applauded. As he introduced the mostly Democratic politicians on hand to speak that day, David Starr, one of the co-chairmen of the Dr. Seuss National Memorial Committee, joked that it's "ironic to ask Ted Kennedy to unveil an elephant." It may be ironic, but it is hardly surprising: a third reason why Dr. Seuss may merit a monument is that his books appeal to people from a wide range of political perspectives. Democratic Congressman Richard E. Neal called Seuss "one of Springfield's great sons," and invoked the activist spirit of Seuss's books by reminding us that "he stood against bigotry and he was patriotic." In his remarks, Senator Kennedy further developed theme of Seuss as activist-patriot. Standing near a statue of Horton, the senator said, "Horton is a very special elephant," and went on to name *Horton Hears a Who!* as his favorite Dr. Seuss book because it teaches us that "we should all be compassionate to others," even if we cannot see them or others do not like them. He particularly enjoys that "it is the smallest Who that saves the day." Growing up the youngest in a family with two older brothers, Kennedy explained, "I've always had a soft spot for that little Who who had a hard time finding his own voice." He paused, and added wryly, "Of course, a lot has changed since then."

A lot has changed in the century since March 2, 1904, when Theodor Seuss Geisel was born at 22 Howard Street in Springfield. In 1906, his parents, Theodor Robert Geisel and the former Henrietta Seuss, moved the family to 74 Fairfield Street, where Ted and his sister Margaretha grew up. Ted Geisel, who lived to the age of 87, grew up with the twentieth century. He became "Dr. Seuss" during Prohibition. He first adopted "Seuss" as a pseudonym in 1925 during his final semester at Dartmouth College. Then, in 1927, nearly three decades before Dartmouth gave him his first honorary doctorate, he added the "Dr." to "Seuss," creating the pseudonym he began attaching to magazine cartoons in the 1920s and 1930s.[3] In the late 1930s and during World War II, Dr. Seuss became a propagandist, writing political cartoons for *PM* and co-creating the *Private SNAFU* cartoons for U.S. troops. In the years after the war, his books addressed the major issues of the century: civil rights in *The Sneetches* (1961) and *Horton Hears a Who!* (1954), environmental conservation in *The Lorax* (1971), and the Cold War in *The Butter Battle Book* (1984). The postwar baby boom and the country's concern about children's literacy led Seuss to write *The Cat in the Hat* (1957), *Hop on Pop* (1963), and *Green Eggs and Ham* (1960). In these and other "Beginner Books," Seuss answered Rudolf Flesch's question *Why Can't Johnny Read?* by creating lively, fun primers designed to make Johnny (and Susie) *want* to read—unlike the bland *Dick and Jane* primers that seem designed to make children want to do anything but read. Indeed, of *The Cat in the Hat*, Seuss says, "It's the book I'm proudest of because it had something to do with the death of the *Dick and Jane* primers" (Cott 25). Given his success in teaching children to read, it is not surprising that, of all the many different things he did, Theodor Seuss Geisel is best known for his children's books.

According to Herb Cheyette of Dr. Seuss Enterprises, "One out of every four children born in the United States receives as its first book a Dr. Seuss book" ("An Awfully Big Adventure: The Making of Modern Children's Literature"). He is not exaggerating. In 2001, *Publishers Weekly* ran a list of the all-time best-selling hardcover children's books, based on publishers' U.S. sales figures through 2000. Seuss has sixteen in the top 100 including: *Green Eggs and Ham* (at number four), *The Cat in the Hat* (9), *One fish two fish red fish blue fish* (13), *Hop on Pop* (16), *Oh, the Places You'll Go!*(17), *Dr. Seuss's ABC* (18), *The Cat in the Hat Comes Back* (26), *Fox in Socks* (31), *How the Grinch Stole Christmas!* (35), *My Book About Me* (40), *I Can Read with My Eyes Shut!* (58), *Oh, the Thinks You Can Think!* (65), *Oh, Say Can You Say?* (85), and *There's a Wocket in My Pocket!* (93).[4] No other single author comes close. In the top twenty, Seuss's nearest rival is J. K. Rowling, whose *Harry Potter* novels have four spots to his six. In the top 100, Seuss's closest competitors are Beatrix Potter and Carolyn Keene, who hold five spots each—with Potter's *The Tale of Peter Rabbit* at number two. If we include all 189 books with sales of over 750,000 copies, Seuss's nearest rivals are Richard Scarry, who makes seven appearances, and Sandra Boynton, who makes six. However, when one includes all 189, the number of Seuss's books with sales in this range rises to twenty-six, a figure that represents less than half of Theodor Seuss Geisel's published works.[5] Finally, were we to re-order the list in terms of number of books sold, Seuss would again be at the top, with the two Potters—Harry and Beatrix—at a distant second and third, respectively.

Beatrix Potter hit on one of the reasons why Seuss was so successful, in a letter she wrote to Anne Carroll Moore, the influential children's librarian of the New York Public Library. Thanking Moore for sending her a copy of *And to Think That I Saw it on Mulberry Street* (1937), Potter called the book, which was Seuss's first,

> the cleverest book I have met with for many years. The swing and merriment of the pictures and the natural truthful simplicity of the untruthfulness. I think my own success was largely due to straight forward lying—spontaneous natural bare-faced! Too many story books for children are condescending, self-conscious inventions—and then some trivial oversight, some small incorrect detail gives the whole show away. Dr. Seuss does it thoroughly! (84)

Potter identified one cause for Dr. Seuss's popularity: he does not condescend to his readers, but instead treats them with respect. As Seuss told an interviewer in 1985, "I think I can communicate with kids because I don't try to communicate with kids. Ninety percent of the children's books patronize the child and say there's a difference between you and me, so you listen to this story. I, for some reason or another, don't do that. I treat the child as an equal" (Georgatos). His ability to communicate with children as equals earned him many adult fans, including Clifton Fadiman, whose review of *Mulberry Street* Seuss could quote verbatim even near the end of his life (Morgan and Morgan 84). In the *New Yorker* of 6 November 1937, Fadiman wrote, "They say it's for children, but better get a copy for yourself and marvel at the good Dr. Seuss's impossible pictures and the moral tale of the little boy who exaggerated not wisely but too well."

Such positive notices and brisk sales notwithstanding, it took twenty years for Dr. Seuss to become an icon of children's literature. Though he published a dozen children's books between 1937 and 1956, Dr. Seuss does not appear among the best-selling children's authors until the late 1950s. In Alice Payne Hackett's *Best Sellers* compendia (*Fifty Years of Best Sellers*, *Sixty Years of Best Sellers*, etc.), Gene Stratton Porter dominates the best-selling children's books for 1895–1945, with *Freckles* (1904), *The Girl of the Limberlost* (1909), and *The Harvester* leading the list. The *Boy Scout Handbook* (1910) and *Girl Scout Handbook* (1916) lead the best sellers for 1895–1955, followed by Baum's *The Wonderful Wizard of Oz* (1900), *Freckles*, *Girl of the Limberlost*, and Evelyn Willis Duvall's *Facts of Life and Love for Teen-Agers* (1950). Dr. Seuss makes his first appearance in the list for 1895–1965. In this list, the top four are Baum, Duvall, and Porter (*Freckles* and *Limberlost* again), but Seuss is not far behind because, following the publication of *The Cat in the Hat* in 1957, his popularity had taken off. In November 1958, the *New York Times Book Review* published a list of "Children's Best Sellers" covering the past year's sales of children's books, and Seuss had four in the top sixteen: A. A. Milne's *The World of Pooh* (1957) was at number one, followed by Seuss's *Yertle the Turtle* at number two, *The Cat in the Hat Comes Back* (1958) at seven, and *How the Grinch Stole Christmas!* (1957) at eight. In Hackett's 1895–1965 list, Seuss ranks among the all-time best-selling children's authors, with *The Cat* and its sequel at nine and fourteen, respectively, followed by *One fish two fish red fish blue fish* (20), *Green Eggs and Ham* (22), *Yertle the Turtle* (34), *Hop on Pop* (36), and *Dr. Seuss's ABC* (37). For the 1895–1975 list, Dr. Seuss is the undisputed leader, holding all top five spots with, in descending order, *Green Eggs and Ham*, *One fish two fish red fish blue fish* (1960), *Hop on Pop, Dr. Seuss's ABC* (1963), and *The Cat in the Hat. The Wizard of Oz* and E. B. White's *Charlotte's Web* get sixth and seventh place, while *The Cat in the Hat Comes Back* does exactly that at number eight. Since then, Dr. Seuss has remained the most popular children's author in America (figure I.1).

The baby boom and Seuss's Beginner Books—*The Cat in the Hat* and his descendants—established Seuss as an icon of children's literature. As Flesch wrote in 1959, "A hundred years from now [. . .] children and their parents will still eagerly read the books of a fellow called Ted Geisel, popularly known as Dr. Seuss." He added, "I predict that Dr. Seuss will emerge as one of the great classics of this era. In 2059, children will still hoot with joy" when they come across one of Dr. Seuss's books. There is yet another half-century before we can know if Flesch's prediction may prove accurate, but several of Dr. Seuss's books have already become classics, and others may shortly follow. Though such claims will always be somewhat subjective, a list of classic Seuss must include: *And to Think That I Saw It on Mulberry Street, The Cat in the Hat, How the Grinch Stole Christmas!, Green Eggs and Ham, One fish two fish . . . , Hop on Pop, The Sneetches, Yertle the Turtle* (1958), *The Lorax,* and both books about Horton. Few would argue if we were to add *The 500 Hats of Bartholomew Cubbins* (1938), *Dr. Seuss's ABC, Fox in Socks* (1965), and *Oh, the Places You'll Go!* (1990). Individual readers will certainly have their own canons of Dr. Seuss classics, but these are certainly some of his best-regarded books.

What many readers may not know is that Dr. Seuss's status as eminent creator of children's literature is the *second* phase of his iconicity. In 1928 he created "Quick, Henry, the Flit!", a campaign which would first make him an icon of advertising (figure I.2). For the January 14 issue of *Judge,* Seuss drew a cartoon in which a knight remarks, *"Darn it all, another dragon. And just after I'd sprayed the whole castle with Flit!"* As the story goes, the cartoon was spotted by the wife of an advertising executive whose firm handled the account for Flit insecticide. She asked her husband to enlist Seuss to write ads for the Flit campaign, and, as they say, the rest is history (Morgan and Morgan 65). The campaign was so successful that Flit remains one of the primary ways in which Dr. Seuss is remembered. As Robert Cahn writes in his 1957 profile of Seuss, "'Quick Henry, the Flit' became a standard line of repartee in radio jokes. A song was based on it. The phrase became a part of the American

Figure I.1. Seuss signing books at Dartmouth, 1962

Copr. 1935 Stanco Inc.

Dr. Seuss

"He says 'Mama', and 'Papa', and 'Quick, Henry, the Flit'!" *(Adv.)*

Figure I.2. "Flit" advertisement by Dr. Seuss, 1935

vernacular for use in emergencies. It was the first major advertising campaign to be based on humorous cartoons" (42). Even today, the line continues to appear in the most unlikely of places. In Don DeLillo's *Libra* (1988), one character refers to the campaign: " 'Quick, Henry, the Flit,' Robert said" (40). In the *New York Times Magazine* of July 1, 2001, William Safire's "On Language" column invoked the Flit ads in its title, "Quick, Henry, the emollient!"

"Quick, Henry" and Seuss's roots in advertising may have been one reason why some in the children's literature establishment initially did not like Dr. Seuss. In her essay, "On Beyond Zebra with Dr. Seuss" (1989), Rita Roth reflects on why American educators resisted Seuss, starting by asking herself why she did not at first see Seuss's stories "as 'literature.' " Though Roth now admires Seuss, when she began teaching elementary school in the late 1960s, she felt "puzzled and annoyed by the strong preference [her] students showed for Dr. Seuss." However, she says, "there was no way I could ignore their enthusiasm as they read and reread *The Cat in the Hat* nor their foot-dragging as they approached the basal reader." It seemed clear to her then "that Dr. Seuss, like comic books, provided a frivolity that was not appropriate for school. 'Let the children read Dr. Seuss at home,' I thought, 'not in my class-room' " (Fensch 142). In singling out Seuss's "comic book" style of art and "frivolity," she has identified why some critics thought his books to be non-literary. That is, while cartoons and whimsy may be fine for selling Flit, such stuff is not what serious, high-quality literature is made of, is it?[6] As a children's librarian replied when Roth asked her about Dr. Seuss's books, "Dr. Seuss? Oh, we hide Dr. Seuss . . . well, not really. We keep him over there on a *special* shelf. . . . We'd really rather they read something better—something more like A. A. Milne" (142).

When Seuss's works were published in the United Kingdom, English critics, too, disliked them, and for many of the same reasons. In 1963, well after Dr. Seuss's works had become popular with American children (if not with all of their teachers), the *Junior Bookshelf*, a British publication, expressed some disappointment that any Britons might enjoy Dr. Seuss: "There is much in the books to make some of us reluctant, for most of the pictures are downright ugly and the texts are often tiresome and sometimes vulgar. [. . .] Compared with Lear and Carroll he seems madly common, slick, unmemorable, and yet Lear seems no better to some people" (Dohm 324, 329). Despite her misgivings, the article's author did admit the appeal of "something alive and kicking" in Seuss's work which "might make the good doctor prove the all-American Lear" (329). A dozen years later, Myra Barrs, a British admirer of his work, speculated on why Seuss took so long to catch on in Britain, identifying some of the same qualities: vulgarity, ugly pictures, and American-ness. Barrs noted that Seuss's books "are brash and noisy; nothing could be more unlike the beautifully tasteful, colour-washed picture books that [. . . are] universally admired. The characters, too, are indefinably vulgar, and the style, for some people, overpoweringly American" (21). Perhaps, she mused, the books' "American voice" is the reason for Dr. Seuss's appeal to many children. She has a point. Seuss's characters do not speak English. They speak American and they speak it with great gusto, often announcing their enthusiasm with a generous helping of exclamation marks. Titles like *Scrambled Eggs Super!* (1953), *I Can Lick 30 Tigers Today!* (1969), and *Oh, the Thinks You Can Think!* (1975) are brash, American, and slangy. And that's why we like them.

Given many teachers' insistence that their students use standard English, Seuss's fondness for American slang may have contributed to the impression that his style is "vulgar." If so, such a judgment would be unfortunate, because Seuss's use of nonstandard English helps to give his work its distinctively American voice. In *If I Ran the Zoo* (1950), Gerald McGrew announces, "A zoo should have bugs, so I'll capture a Thwerll / Whose legs are snarled up in a terrible snerl." *Snerl* sounds like *snarl* as it might be pronounced by person from central Appalachia (eastern Kentucky). And *The Sneetches* begins, "Now, the Star-Belly Sneetches / Had bellies with stars. / The Plain-Belly Sneetches / Had none upon thars." People from the Ozarks also might pronounce *theirs* as *thars*, but as the sociolinguist Thomas E. Murray points out, even if these pronunciations of *thars* and *snerl* cannot "factually be linked" to a particular region of America, "they do both connote a sort of rural, lower-class, uneducated speaker." Seuss's language has also been influenced by the vernacular of American advertising. Peter T. Hooper promises us "*Scrambled eggs Super-dee-Dooper-dee-Booper.*" In *The Lorax* (1971), the Once-ler proclaims, "And, for your information, you Lorax, I'm figgering on biggering / and BIGGERING / and BIGGERING / and BIGGERING, / turning MORE Truffula Trees into Thneeds / which everyone, EVERYONE, *EVERYONE* needs!" Words like *snerl*, *thars*, *figgering*, *biggering*, and *Super-dee-Dooper-dee-Booper* may not be "proper" English, but their slangy playfulness gives Seuss's language its verve and energy. Seuss's willingness to experiment with words—even if that means breaking the rules—is one reason that his books are so fun to read.

Perhaps because neither fun books nor children's literature have been considered subjects for serious study, thorough critical analyses of Dr. Seuss are a relatively recent phenomenon. Lewis Nichols concluded his 1962 profile of Dr. Seuss by gently poking fun at the very idea of Seuss scholarship:

> One further note, this directed to those writers of dissertations and theses on Dr. Seuss. On the table in his hotel room were these objects: One copy of *Live and Let Live* by Ian Fleming; one folder of delicacies offered by Room Service; six partly used folders of matches; two bars of chocolate; one large pear. Dr. Seuss could make something of this. Can the scholars? (42)

In the four decades since Nichols's article appeared, prejudices against Seussian studies have diminished, but it has taken some time for such attitudes to change. Judith and Neil Morgan's *Dr. Seuss and Mr. Geisel*, a superlative biography, appeared in 1995. At that time, the only book-length work of literary criticism was Ruth K. MacDonald's *Dr. Seuss* (1988). With the notable exception of Richard Minear's *Dr. Seuss Goes to War* (1999), a well-researched analysis of Seuss's political cartoons, there have been no other substantial book-length studies of Dr. Seuss.[7] There have been many more analytical articles and chapters: if we include personal essays, essay-reviews, and editorials (as I have, in the bibliography at the back of this book), Dr. Seuss has inspired about seventy pieces of literary criticism, although admittedly some are of a better quality than others. A particularly striking feature of Seuss criticism is that almost no one writes more than one article on Dr. Seuss.[8] This fact suggests that Dr. Seuss attracts few specialists: someone will say his or her piece on Dr. Seuss, and then move on to a new subject.

Despite the paucity of Dr. Seuss experts, we can at least construct an overview of Seuss scholarship, charting the development of a body of criticism (at this point, those readers uninterested in children's-literature scholarship may wish to skip ahead three paragraphs). To date, the major areas of inquiry have been politics, gender, psychology, art, folk and fairy tales, and whether or not Seuss's books liberate the child reader. The two articles from the 1950s, by Lorrene Love Ort (1955) and Rudolf Flesch (1959), are notable primarily for their enthusiasm. As Flesch writes, "What exactly is it that makes this stuff immortal? I don't know. There is a something about it—a swing to the language, a deep understanding of the playful mind of a child, an indefinable something that makes Dr. Seuss a genius pure and simple." Flesch's words were soon adopted as blurbs for the back covers of Dr. Seuss's books. The first essay to move beyond praise and offer a fully developed analysis of Seuss's work is John Bailey's "Three Decades of Seuss for Dr. Seuss" (1965), a five-page article that assigns Seuss's work to three distinct periods: an early period (1937–1947), a highly inventive "middle period" (1947–1957) and the "crass marketing approach" of the work since then. In the 1970s, when children's-literature scholarship was beginning to establish itself as a discipline, central subjects of inquiry at last began to emerge. Barbara Bader includes Seuss in her comprehensive study of children's literature (1976), the same year that Thomas Burns publishes the first essay to consider Seuss as an icon of popular culture, a subject that has gone largely unexplored since then. In *Down the Rabbit Hole* (1971), Selma G. Lanes advances the idea that Seuss's books help to liberate the child, and thereby establishes a central topic of Seussology. Although Michael Steig (1983) and Joseph Zornado (1997) would argue that Seuss's books instead encourage children to repress their imaginations, scholars usually take a position closer to Lanes's, including, notably, Betty Mensch and Alan Freeman (1987), Rita Roth (1989), Tim Wolf (1995), and Shira Wolosky (2000). The 1970s also introduces gender and fairy tales into the critical discussion. Though written in a tongue-in-cheek style, Emily Stong's "Juvenile Literary Rape in America: A Post-Coital Study of the Writings of Dr. Seuss" (1977) paves the way for Alison Lurie (1990), Wolf (1995), and Jill Deans (2000). Roger Sale (1978) and Jill P. May (1985) first consider Seuss's work in the context of fairy tales, but the subject receives its fullest treatment in essays by Francelia Butler and Mavis Reimer (both 1989).

The publication of *The Butter Battle Book* (1984), Seuss's fable of nuclear proliferation, inspired intense interest the politics of his work. While Ruth B. Moynihan is the first to address this subject (if briefly) in "Ideologies in Children's Literature: Some Preliminary Notes" (1973), the controversy surrounding *Butter Battle*'s publication led to many substantial analyses of the subject during the 1980s and since then. Roger Sutton's "Children's Books: Yooks, Zooks and the Bomb" and John Cech's "Some Leading, Blurred, and Violent Edges of the Contemporary Picture Book," both essay-reviews published in 1987, consider *The Butter Battle Book* in the context of other politically engaged children's books of the 1980s, such as Raymond Briggs's *The Tin-Pot Foreign General and the Old Iron Woman* (1984), David Macaulay's *Baaa* (1985), and Judith Vigna's *Nobody Wants a Nuclear War* (1986). For Sutton, Seuss's book is overly simplistic; for Cech, *Butter Battle* compares favorably with its peers. The most insightful piece on the subject may be Mensch and Freeman's "Getting to Solla Sollew: The Existential Politics of Dr. Seuss" (also 1987), which clearly influences Roth's 1989 essay. In the 1990s, politically minded critics produced several eco-critical readings: Lisa Lebduska (1994), Ian Marshall (1996), and Suzanne Ross (1996) each investigated how effective *The Lorax* (1971) may or may not be in promoting environmental conservation.

In addition to eco-criticism, gender, and politics, Seussologists of the 1990s devoted their energies to art and psychology. Though Steig may be the first to place Seuss on the psychoanalyst's couch, Zornado, Wolf, and, more recently, Louis Menand (2002) all probe the subconscious desires of Seuss's work. Seuss's artwork drew the attention of Richard Marschall in his introduction to *The Tough Coughs as He Ploughs the Dough: Early Cartoons & Articles by Dr. Seuss* (1987) and Perry Nodelman in *Words About Pictures* (1988). Following Nodelman's lead, Paul G. Arakelian (1993) and Maria Nikolajeva and Carole Scott (2001) examine the relationship between Seuss's words and pictures. Several public displays of Seuss's paintings perhaps did the most to draw attention to his artistic skills. An exhibition of Seuss's artwork inspired John Cech's "Pictures and Picturebooks on the Wall" (1991), and the publication of *The Secret Art of Dr. Seuss* (1995) led me to write "Dada Knows Best: Growing Up 'Surreal' with Dr. Seuss" (1999). In identifying the major critical approaches to Dr. Seuss, I have of necessity skipped some very interesting essays—such as Chet Raymo's fascinating "Dr. Seuss and Dr. Einstein: Children's Books and Scientific Imagination" (1992)—because they fell outside of developing scholarly trends. (Any curious readers may wish to consult the "Literary Criticism" section of the bibliography, which is fully annotated.)

13

Dr. Seuss: American Icon approaches its subject from six perspectives—poetry, politics, art, biography, marketing, and influence—because I consider these to be the defining features of Dr. Seuss's work. Chapter One, "U.S. Laureate of Nonsense: A Seussian Poetics," offers the first extensive analysis of Seuss's verse, locating Seuss among the great purveyors of literary nonsense. In the next chapter, "Dr. Seuss vs. Adolf Hitler: A Political Education," I argue that World War II transformed Seuss into America's first anti-Fascist children's writer, and inspired him to write activist books like *Horton Hears a Who!*, *The Sneetches*, *The Lorax*, and *The Butter Battle Book*. "The Doc in the Smock," my third chapter, establishes Seuss's place in art history by identifying the influences he synthesizes in his unique artistic style. Chapter Four acts as an interface between the Seuss people know and the Seuss people do not know, examining the adult and adolescent sensibilities behind the popular children's author. "The Disneyfication of Dr. Seuss: Faithful to Profit, One Hundred Percent?" asks whether the posthumous licensing-and-merchandising bonanza detracts from or adds to Dr. Seuss's artistic legacy, and finds answers at the intersection of aesthetics, commerce, and the law. The final chapter, "The Cat in the Hat for President: Dr. Seuss and the Public Imagination," investigates the ways in which Dr. Seuss has become intertwined with defining myths of America. In its study of Seuss's influence, Chapter Six concentrates on a topic which recurs throughout the book.

Finally, a brief note on method: while the precepts of American Studies and Cultural Studies underwrite this book as a whole, I have allowed the analytical method of each chapter to develop from its particular approach. No chapter draws exclusively on a single methodology, but the dominant method in each is as follows: Chapter One (Formalism), Two (Historicism), Three (Art History), Four (Biographical Criticism), Five (Cultural Studies), and Six (American Studies). Now, having summed up how Seuss has been read and having suggested how I think we might read him, it is time to conclude the introduction and begin thinking about poetry, the subject of Chapter One. Or, to borrow a couplet from an early draft of *Oh, the Places You'll Go!* (1990), "Whether your name is Binxbaum, Trilby or Monk / It's Full steam ahead! may you never get sunk!"

Chapter 1

U.S. Laureate of Nonsense

A SEUSSIAN POETICS

When they dedicated the Dr. Seuss National Memorial Park in Springfield, Massachusetts, everyone used couplets. Describing the tourism that the memorial park might bring in, Acting Governor Jane Swift observed, "As the third largest industry in our little state, / it provides jobs for people and makes our economy great." Senator Ted Kennedy spoke of "Seuss and his Cat with that jazzy big hat / Not to mention the books that we've all got down pat." In other words, when we think of Seuss, we think of poetry—we even *imitate* his poetry. But he isn't often recognized as a poet.

After *And to Think That I Saw It on Mulberry Street* was published in the fall of 1937, Anne Carroll Moore wrote, "The verses have a rhythm and swing born of familiarity with good nonsense verse." She was the sole reviewer to focus on Seuss's poetry.[1] Other reviewers, who focused more on the pictures, accurately anticipated how critics would perceive Seuss. As one critic wrote more recently, the "very special fantasy of Dr. Seuss lies primarily in his visual creation": "his language [. . .] is not nearly so unusual and inventive" (James Steel Smith 314). This chapter will ignore the visual (which is discussed in Chapter Three), in order to focus on the often overlooked language of Dr. Seuss. Of the roughly seventy critical articles or chapters on Seuss, only three offer any sustained analysis of his poetry: Don L. F. Nilsen's "Dr. Seuss as Grammar Consultant," a five-page essay published in a 1977 issue of *Language Arts*; Evelyn Schroth's "Dr. Seuss and Language Use," a three-page article published in a 1978 issue of *The Reading Teacher*; and portions of Francelia Butler's insightful "Seuss as a Creator of Folklore," published in a 1989 issue of *Children's Literature in Education*. Ruth K. MacDonald's *Dr. Seuss* (1988), the sole book-length critical-study to consider all of Seuss's work, presents some insights into his poetics, though it vacillates on the question of whether Seuss's verse should even be *considered* as poetry (9, 16).

It is odd that relatively little attention has been paid to Seuss's poetry because, of the forty-three books written and illustrated by Dr. Seuss, all but four are in verse. If we add books illustrated by others, books written under another name, books co-authored, and books published posthumously, then the total number of books rises to sixty-five, all but *five* of which are in verse.[2] Within those five prose books, the language frequently veers towards the poetic: in both *The 500 Hats of Bartholomew Cubbins* and *Bartholomew and the Oobleck* (1949), King Derwin's magicians chant in verse; the former book introduces assonance, in phrases like "the Yeoman of the Bowmen," and the latter, alliteration, in people "flopping and floundering" in oobleck. Indeed, Seuss often joked that he couldn't speak in prose at all. In his 1978 address to the American Booksellers Association convention, he began, "As everyone present undoubtedly knows . . . / due to a prenatal defect in my nose . . . / (which seems to get worser the longer it grows) / I am completely incapable of speaking in prose" ("Small Epic Poem, Size 3 1/2 B"). Seuss could speak in prose, of course, but he so preferred verse that he used it for almost all public speaking.[3]

Rhythm

Seuss's particular style of verse is one the most distinctive things about him. Seuss has become the unacknowledged U.S. laureate of nonsense poetry because elements of his style have caught on, and one such element is rhythm. According to a story he told often (albeit with variations), the rhythm of a ship inspired *And to Think That I Saw It on Mulberry Street*, Seuss's first book for children. Seuss said, "In the fall of 1936, while aboard the *S. S. Kungsholm* on a long rainy crossing of the Atlantic, I amused myself by putting words to the rhythm of the ship's engine. The words turned out to be *And to Think That I Saw It on Mulberry Street*" (Seuss, "Dr. Seuss" 112). While we cannot know whether the ship's engine really chugged in anapests, that's the way that Seuss claims to have heard it: "And that is a story that NO ONE can beat / When I say that I saw it on Mulberry Street!" (figure 1.1). The meter of the smaller "Beginner Books" varies more widely, but all of the larger-sized Seuss books rely upon a similar rhythmic pattern, using mostly anapests and often introducing anapestic feet with an iamb. In *Horton Hatches the Egg*

Since poetic terms are not part of most people's vocabulary, here are a few definitions, beginning with four common **feet** (∪ represents an unstressed syllable, and / represents a stressed syllable):

iamb = ∪ / (The adjective is "iambic.")
anapest = ∪ ∪ / (The adjective is "anapestic.")
trochee = / ∪ (The adjective is "trochaic.")
dactyl = / ∪ ∪ (The adjective is "dactylic.")

When these feet recur in a regular pattern, you can measure a poem's **meter**. If each line contained three anapests, then the verse would be in anapestic trimeter. If each line contained five iambs (as Shakespeare's tend to), then the verse would be in iambic pentameter. In other words, the name of a metric line comes from the number of feet it contains:

monometer = one foot
dimeter = two feet
trimeter = three feet
tetrameter = four feet
pentameter = five feet

And so on.

Figure 1.1. A few poetic terms, adapted from M. H. Abrams' *A Glossary of Literary Terms,* Sixth Edition (1993).

(1940), Seuss's second book in verse, Horton's "I *meant* what I *said /* And I *said* what I *meant* . . . / An *el*ephant's *faith*ful / One *hun*dred per *cent*" twice repeats the pattern of an iamb followed by three anapests (emphasis added).[4] *In Horton Hears a Who!*, Horton's "A *per*son's a *per*son, no *mat*ter how *small*" reprises that meter. And Yertle uses it in lines like "I'm *Yer*tle the *Tur*tle! Oh, *mar*velous *me!* / For *I* am the *ru*ler of *all* that I *see!*" (emphasis added here, too). Pick your favorite Seuss book and you will find this pattern of iamb followed by anapests—a pattern also found in the first, second, and fifth lines of many limericks.

These anapests—and Seuss's meter more generally—lure readers into a pattern that keeps them reading. It's fun to be carried along by the rhythm of the language, a characteristic which Seuss exploits when he completes an end rhyme on the following page. Seuss introduced this page-turning strategy in *Horton Hatches the Egg*, at the moment when Mayzie confronts Horton, demanding the return of her egg: "Poor Horton backed down, / With a sad, heavy heart. . . ." The page ends. Turn it, and the rhyme completes: "But at that very instant the egg burst apart!" Seuss returns to this device at the climax of *Thidwick the Big-Hearted Moose* (1948), when the hunters have cornered Thidwick and he remembers, "Today was the day / Thidwick happened to know . . ."—now, turn the page—"*that OLD horns come off so that NEW ones can grow.*" While Thidwick escapes, the hunters get his antlers and the pesky guests staying in them. However, the most memorable use of this device may be: "Every *Who* / down in *Who*-ville / Liked Christmas a lot . . ." Turn the page: "But the Grinch, / Who lived just north of *Who*-ville, / Did NOT!"

Seuss may have learned the narrative power of meter and rhyme from his earliest experiences reading. When asked in 1980 "what books [he] read as a child," Seuss recalled reading Peter Newell's *The Hole Book* (1908) when he was "six or seven years old," and went on to quote some of its lines: "Tom Potts was fooling with a gun / (Such follies should not be), / When—bang! the pesky thing went off / Most unexpectedly!" (Cott 19).[5] That Seuss—some sixty years after first reading *The Hole Book* —could call up a precise quotation from Newell's poetry suggests his early affinity for narrative verse. As Seuss said, "You [. . .] establish a rhythm, and that tends to make kids want to go on. If you break the rhythm, a child feels unfulfilled" ("Somebody's Got to Win" 126).

More so than in Newell's, the rhythm in many of Seuss's works enhances the accretion of ridiculousness. As do Seuss's anapests, Newell's iambs lead the reader to the next episode; but, unlike Seuss, Newell does not build each event on the previous one. On one two-page spread of *The Hole Book*, a mouse, cornered by a cat, seeks escape: "Just then the bullet made a hole—/ A fair sized hole at that—/ And in it dashed the frightened mouse, / And thus escaped the cat." Turn the page and "A thief was stealing in the door—/ A clever chap was he / For he had waited till the gong had summoned all to tea." The bullet frightens him away, of course. The connection between these events—as with events in Newell's *The Slant Book* (1910) and *The Rocket Book* (1912)—is the item itself (in this case, the bullet) and Newell's iambic meter. Dr.

Seuss's *Mulberry Street*, *If I Ran the Zoo*, *If I Ran the Circus* (1956), *Scrambled Eggs Super!*, *Green Eggs and Ham*, *Ten Apples Up on Top!* (1961, written as Theo. LeSieg), *Hooper Humperdink . . . Not Him!* (1976, as LeSieg), and *Because a Little Bug Went Ka-Choo!* (1975, as Rosetta Stone) are similarly episodic, but the rhythm of the verse does more than merely connect the episodes. It aids in building up suspense, amplifying the outrageousness of the tall tale as it grows taller and taller.

As Sam-I-am and his nameless companion barrel down the train tracks in *Green Eggs and Ham*, so Seuss's verse bounces and jostles forward, varying the meter just enough to keep it interesting. In *If I Ran the Circus*, Morris McGurk imagines being proprietor of a circus in a vacant lot owned by Sneelock, who will (Morris believes) be participating in a series of stunts that become increasingly dangerous as the story unfolds. When Sneelock deftly races down a narrow red concourse full of prickly Stickle-Bush Trees, Morris says the verse scanned in figure 1.2. The first three lines and fifth line of Morris's hyperbole are mostly

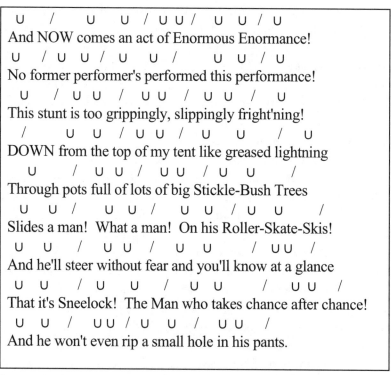

Figure 1.2. Scanning a passage from *If I Ran the Circus* (1956) by Dr. Seuss.

anapestic, but each begins with an iamb and ends with an additional light syllable known as a feminine ending. In four of the first five lines, the metrical effect moves us forward, but bumpily, as each line's anapestic pattern receives a nudge from its opening iamb and concluding feminine ending. The fourth line abruptly reverses rhythmic direction by switching to dactyls—each stressed syllable followed by two light syllables—which calls attention to Sneelock's journey "DOWN [. . .] like greased lightning." The bumps and irruptions of the first five lines vanish during the final triplet. The last three lines, all perfect anapestic tetrameter, increase the pace. No longer introduced by iambs or ending on light syllables, each line is regular and relentless, propelling Sneelock, the man "who takes chance after chance," along his perilous descent.

The meter may encourage forward movement, but the poetic devices and linguistic games invite us to linger. "No former performer's performed this performance" exploits the fact that one root (form) can make many different words: an adjective (former), a noun (performance), a possessive noun (performer's) and a verb (performed). [6] Morris's verbal games extend to a delight in the sounds of words. Beyond their end rhymes, these three couplets and one tercet contain many internal rhymes: "grippingly, slippingly," "pots full of lots," "steer without fear." Alliterative words like "top of my tent," "Skate-Skis," and the three variations on "perform" highlight the fun to be had with words. The playful language delights the ear and the imagination, while the rollicking rhythms drive the narrative onwards.

Paradoxically, the anapest—often found in the limerick—may also be why Seuss is rarely studied as a poet. The limerick is the punch line of poetic forms. For example, in *Harry Potter and the Chamber of Secrets*, Ron advises Harry not to read a mysterious book, suspecting that it may be enchanted: "everyone who read *Sonnets of a Sorcerer* spoke in limericks for the rest of their lives," he warns (231). That joke would not work so well if the readers were forced to speak in sonnets or villanelles. Seuss's metrical kinship with the limerick has led even his sympathetic critics to dismiss his verse as non-literary. Even though Selma G. Lanes admires Seuss and praises his "inventiveness of language" (88), she also consistently refers to his verse as "doggerel" (81, 87).[7] Ruth K. MacDonald, whose book argues that Seuss's works "deserve consideration as literature" (preface), nonetheless says that "Seuss's verse is particularly unpoetic" (16).[8] And, after all, Horton's "I meant what I said and I said what I meant" has but one anapest more than "There was a young man of Nantucket." Perhaps this explains why—with the notable exception of Donald Hall's *Oxford Book of Children's Verse in America* (1985)—Seuss appears in very few anthologies of children's poetry, and why he is not (for example) included on the Academy of American Poets' website, though other twentieth-century "children's poets" such as Jack Prelutsky and Shel Silverstein are listed there. However, as the most popular nonsense poet America has produced, Seuss deserves recognition as one of the great purveyors of literary nonsense, alongside of Silverstein, Carroll, and Lear.

The Rise of Nonsense: Playing Games with Language

Seuss's literary career coincides with the twentieth century's growing interest in nonsense. According to the *Oxford English Dictionary*, the first recorded use of the word "limerick" occurs in a letter from Aubrey Beardsley, written in 1896—some eight years before Seuss was born. Edward Lear's first limericks were published half a century before then, and the form we know as the limerick dates back centuries.[9] But the limerick and nonsense verse gained popularity when young Theodor Seuss Geisel was growing up: newspapers and manufacturers often sponsored limerick contests, an activity which became popular enough to inspire books like Kenneth R. Close's *How to Write Prize-Winning Limericks* (1930) (Baring-Gould 64–67). In the artistic avant-garde of the teens, twenties, and thirties, Dadaists and Surrealists drew inspiration from nonsense; in academe, the first book-length critical study of nonsense, Emile Cammaerts's *The Poetry of Nonsense*, was published in 1925. As Mark I. West has noted, "The twentieth century has seen a proliferation of nonsense poetry for children" (155).

Seuss is a central figure in the history of nonsense poetry, though his absence from even nonsense anthologies suggests that—despite the advocacy of critics like MacDonald, Celia Catlett Anderson, and Marilyn Fain Apseloff—his contributions are not widely recognized. So little are they recognized that a review of a recent reprint of Mervyn Peake's *Captain Slaughterboard Drops Anchor* compared the book to Seuss's work, and went on to note that Peake preceded Seuss (Heller 21). But *Captain Slaughterboard* was first published the same year as *Mulberry Street*, and the two authors are contemporaries, born only seven years apart. Though Noel Malcolm has traced literary nonsense's origins back to the twelfth

21

century (53), Seuss's literary predecessors date to the renaissance of nonsense led by Edward Lear (1812–1888), Lewis Carroll (1832–1898), L. Frank Baum (1856–1919), Peter Newell (1862–1924), Gelett Burgess (1866–1951), and others. Born in 1904, Seuss is of a newer generation of nonsense-writers who popularized and developed the form for twentieth-century readers. I'm thinking here of James Thurber (1894–1961), Ogden Nash (1902–1974), Walt Kelly (1913–1973), Mervyn Peake (1911–1968), Spike Milligan (1918–2002), and P. L. Travers (1899–1996).

Until the publication of *McElligot's Pool* in 1947, Seuss's children's books showed few signs that Dr. Seuss would gain a place among the great nonsense-writers. His magazine cartoons displayed a knack for creating fantastic creatures, but such creatures rarely entered his work for children.[10] Looking back on *Mulberry Street* many years later, Seuss said, "I think I was a little too aloof there. [. . .] It was written from the point of view of my mind, not the mind of a child" (Nichols). Inspired by childhood fishing trips with his father (Wilder 63), *McElligot's Pool* led Seuss back to the mind of a child and marked the beginning of a richly inventive phase in his career as a children's author. Marco, who led us along Mulberry Street, here introduces the variety of fish he might catch in McElligot's Pool. Though Seuss stops short of providing them with the creative names that his later creatures will receive, he invents over two dozen kinds of fish and several other kinds of water-dwelling animals. *McElligot's Pool* initiates what we might call Seuss's bestiary books, a group which includes *If I Ran the Zoo* (1950), *Scrambled Eggs Super!* (1953), *On Beyond Zebra!* (1955), *If I Ran the Circus* (1956), *Happy Birthday to You!* (1959), *One fish two fish red fish blue fish* (1960), *Dr. Seuss's Sleep Book* (1962), *There's a Wocket in My Pocket!* (1974), and *Oh, the Thinks You Can Think!* (1975). Each book offers anywhere from a dozen to several dozen imaginary animals, and, starting with *If I Ran the Zoo*, each unusual creature has a name to match. In *Scrambled Eggs Super!* alone, Peter T. Hooper meets the Ruffle-Necked Sala-ma-goox, the Tizzle-Topped Grouse, the Shade-Roosting Quail, the Lass-a-lack, the Spritz, the Flannel-Wing Jay, the Twiddler Owl, the Kweet, the Stroodel, the Kwigger, the Long-Legger Kwong, the Grice, the Pelf, the Single-File Zummzian Zuks, the Mt. Strookoo Cuckoo, the three-eyelashed Tizzy, the Grickily Gractus, the Ziff, the Zuff, the Moth-Watching Sneth, the Dawf, the Bombastic Aghast, the Mop-Noodled Finch, the Beagle-Beaked-Bald-

Headed-Grinch (apparently unrelated to the famous Grinch), Wogs ("the world's sweetest frogs"), the Ham-ikka-Schnim-ikka-Schnam-ikka Schnopp, and a Jill-ikka-Jast.

The quantity and variety of new creatures demonstrates that, in terms of inventiveness, Dr. Seuss is heir to Edward Lear. All nonsense writers invent fantastic animals: to name but one creation each, Carroll has given us the Jabberwock; Peake, the Guggaflop; Shel Silverstein, the Flying Festoon; Edward Gorey, the Wuggly Ump; and Jack Prelutsky, the Snopp on the Sidewalk. However, Lear invented more than most, including the Jumblies, the Quangle-Wangle, the Dong with a luminous Nose, the Pobble who has no toes, the Yonghy-Bonghy-Bo, and an extraordinary range of fantastical flora. Seuss has dreamed up Dike Trees, Beezlenut Trees, Truffula Trees and Stickle-Bush Trees, but Lear takes the prize in nonsense botany, having catalogued the Bong-tree, Bottlephorkia Spoonifolia, Smalltoothcombia Domestica, Phattfacia Stupenda, Manypeeplia Upsidedownia, Shoebootia Utilis, Barkia Howlaloudia, and many others. As Jonathan Cott observes, "more than any other children's book artist—except perhaps for Edward Lear [. . .]—Dr. Seuss has created the most extraordinary variety of ingeniously named, fantastical looking animals" (11).[11] In so doing, Seuss the poet begins to explore what language can do.

To borrow what Elizabeth Sewell says of Lewis Carroll, Seuss's "works are not merely in words, they are very frequently about words" (18). Like great nonsense literature, Seuss's poetry reveals language as a complex game, with rules made to be bent, and meanings that shift as quickly as their context changes. In *Through the Looking-Glass and What Alice Found There* (1871), Alice explains that, to make bread, one must "*ground*" flour. The White Queen asks, "How many acres of ground?" playing on the fact that *ground* can be either verb or noun (254). Seuss, too, reminds readers that a word's meaning shifts depending on its function in a sentence. In *Oh Say Can You Say?* (1979), Seuss's narrator uses *spot* as noun and verb: "the spots on a Glotz / are about the same size / as the dots on a Klotz. / So you first have to spot / who the one with the dots is. / Then it's easy to tell / who the Klotz or the Glotz is." In the phrase "spots on a Glotz," *spots* are nouns designating the rounded mark on the Glotz, but in "you have to spot," *to spot* is a verb meaning *to detect* or *to locate*. Underscoring the fact that *bed* can refer to both *flower-bed* and *bed-that-people-sleep-in*, the Tiger-lily in *Through the Looking-*

Glass tells Alice that, in "most gardens, [. . .] they make the beds too soft—so that the flowers are always asleep" (159). Highlighting that spreading a bedspread and spreading butter are quite different kinds of spreading, *Oh Say Can You Say?* observes that "Bed Spreaders spread spreads on beds / Bread Spreaders spread butters on breads." While illuminating the variant connotations of *beds* and *spread*, Seuss and Carroll demonstrate that language can be used for one's amusement *as well as* for communicating with others.

In one of the more famous exchanges in *Through the Looking-Glass*, Humpty Dumpty emphasizes precisely this point:

> "When *I* use a word," Humpty Dumpty said, in a rather scornful tone, "it means just what I choose it to mean—neither more nor less."
>
> "The question is," said Alice, "whether you *can* make words mean so many different things."
>
> "The question is," said Humpty Dumpty, "which is to be master—that's all." (213)

Humpty Dumpty asserts that his words mean just what he chooses them to mean, but the skeptical Alice has already learned that words can have a life of their own, beyond what the speaker intends. As Wendy Steiner writes in *The Colors of Rhetoric* (1982), "Humpty Dumpty presides over *Finnegans Wake* and countless other fictions of our day as the genius of the paradox that language can be both arbitrary and motivated, a self-sufficient system and one affected by extra-linguistic meaning, a social and an individual tool" (93). In other words, language is both practical and impractical, both a means of communication and a game played for the sheer fun of it. Seuss discovered this fundamental paradox of language through compulsory Latin, which he both hated and found very useful. As he said, "any writer my age who studied Latin is a better writer because it allows you to adore words—take them apart and find out where they came from" (qtd. in Wilder 64).[12]

In his works' ever-present neologisms, Seuss expresses his adoration of taking words apart and reassembling them. As Ruth MacDonald points out, the High Gargel-orum—a pair of creatures from *On Beyond Zebra!* (1953)—have "height like Angelorum, the Latin word for angels" and wear fuzzy collars around their necks, where presumably they would gargle (MacDonald 92). Seuss's High Gargel-orum is a portmanteau word, having "two meanings packed up into one word," as Humpty Dumpty would say (Carroll 215). Carroll's best-known examples, both of which appear in "Jabberwocky," are *galumphing*, a combination of *galloping* and *triumphant*; and *chortle*, a blend of *chuckle* and *snort*. These words have entered the English language, as have Lear's *runcible spoon* (from "The Owl and the Pussycat"), Seuss's *nerd* (from *If I Ran the Zoo*) and *Grinch* (from *How the Grinch Stole Christmas!*). Technically, Seuss did not invent the word *grinch*. The *Oxford English Dictionary* finds exactly two earlier examples: a 1635 instance of *grinched*, meaning "tightly closed, clenched" in reference to the teeth, and an 1892 instance of *grinch*, meaning "to make a harsh grating noise." However, Seuss did create the sense in which we now use the word *Grinch* (for more on this subject, see Chapter Six). Though gauging literary merit is a contentious issue, to have written poetry that actually changed the language itself suggests that Seuss is as inventive and as deserving of critical recognition as Carroll or Lear.[13] As Anderson and Apseloff write in their *Nonsense Literature for Children: Aesop to Seuss*, Dr. Seuss is the "twentieth-century creator of nonsense who undoubtedly holds the prize for new nonce words" (56).

Carroll's penchant for portmanteau words and Seuss's delight in creating new ones illuminate the pleasures of language, encouraging readers to be creative—an ideal suggestion for the child newly acquainted with the written word. As Anna Quindlen wrote, Seuss turned words "into balloon animals, [. . .] took words and juggled them, bounced them off the page. No matter what the story in his books, the message was clear and unwavering: words are fun." In its playfulness, nonsense encourages children to learn how language works by experimenting with language's rules. In *Dr. Seuss's ABC*, the entry under "X" pokes fun at spelling and teaches how to spell: "X is very useful / if your name is / Nixie Knox / It also / comes in handy / spelling ax / and extra fox." The initial sounds of "Nixie" and "Knox" are identical, but spelled differently, emphasizing the inconsistencies between letter and sound. Throughout, *Dr. Seuss's ABC* highlights the arbitrary nature of the sign—an idea that interested Seuss at least since his early cartoon "Ough! Ough! Or Why I Believe in Simplified Spelling" (1929), which uses the phrase "The Tough Coughs as He Ploughs the Dough" to illustrate "the evils of the '*ough words.*'" The cartoon's narrator, "a young Roumanian student of divinity," recalls seeing "a tough, coughing as he ploughed a field which (being quite nearsighted) I mistook for pie dough. Assuming that all *ough words* were pronounced the same, I casually remarked, 'The tuff cuffs as he pluffs the duff!'" His companions suspect him of "cursing in Roumanian" and he is expelled from school. Wryly admitting the inconsistent rules of spelling, Seuss is a sympathetic teacher.

If "Nixie Knox" and "The Tough Coughs as He Ploughs the Dough" dramatize the disconnect between sound and spelling, onomatopoetic words explore the occasional connections between sound and sense. One of the themes of the *Through the Looking-Glass* is whether words should sound like what they mean, as when Alice asks, *"Must a name mean something?"* and Humpty Dumpty replies, "Of course it must [. . .] *my* name means the shape I am—and a good handsome shape it is, too. With a name like yours, you might be any shape, almost" (208). Embodying Humpty Dumpty's theory of onomatopœia, *One fish two fish red fish blue fish* gives us the "Wump," a creature with a "hump" who is bumpy to ride: the Wump sounds like its name. *On Beyond Zebra!* introduces the "Sneedle" whose "hum-dinger stinger is as sharp as a needle." *Mr. Brown Can Moo! Can You?* (1970) presents the gifted Mr. Brown, who can imitate the rain ("DIBBLE DIBBLE / DIBBLE DOPP"), a horn ("BLURP / BLURP / BLURP / BLURP"), "a big cat drinking" ("SLURP / SLURP / SLURP") and even "a hippopotamus / chewing gum" ("GRUM / GRUM / GRUM GRUM / GRUM / GRUM / GRUM"). *Grum* combines *gum* with the *gr* of *grinding teeth*, and *dibble dopp* makes a softer-sounding rain by removing the *r*'s from *dribble drop*. *One fish two fish . . .*, *Mr. Brown Can Moo!*, and *On Beyond Zebra!* are all specifically about language, but Seuss's political books are equally poetical. In *The Lorax*, the Once-ler's machinery goes "Gulppity-Glupp" and "Schloppity-Schlopp," which has the effect of "glumping the pond where the Humming-Fish hummed!" The Lorax himself, choking on the "smogulous smoke," speaks with a "cruffulous croak." The verb "glumping" sounds like dumping clumps of goo, "smogulous" turns "smog" into an adjective, and "cruffulous" sounds like a crusty, huffing, wheezing old man. These words not only sound like what they mean—they're fun to say. As Evelyn Schroth observes, "Dr. Seuss is writing to be read aloud" (749).

Onomatopoetic words demonstrate the ways in which sound contributes to sense, but much of language's joy and humor derives from sounds that lead the reader away from sense. In *Through the Looking-Glass*, a Daisy says that the tree says "Bough-wough!" and "That's why its branches are called boughs!" (158), punning on the idea that the word for a dog's bark sounds the same as the word for a branch. Seuss's demonstrations of sound subverting sense depend less on puns and more on tongue twisters. *Dr. Seuss's Sleep Book* informs us that "Moose juice, not goose juice, is juice for a moose / And goose juice, not moose juice, is juice for a goose." In *Scrambled Eggs Super!*, Peter T. Hooper rides "on the top / Of a Ham-ikka-Schnim-ikka-Schnam-ikka Schnopp." The books full of tongue twisters—*Fox in Socks* and *Oh Say Can You Say?*—take Seuss's joy in sounds to its most extreme. In the former, "Luke Luck likes lakes. / Luke's duck likes lakes. / Luke Luck licks lakes. / Luke's duck licks lakes. // Duck takes licks / in lakes Luke Luck likes / Luke Luck takes licks / in lakes duck likes." Spend any time reading these words aloud and you may arrive at the same conclusion as Knox, who, in *Fox in Socks*, remarks, "I can't blab / such blibber blubber! / My tongue isn't / made of rubber!" Taking rhyme, alliteration, consonance, and assonance to their illogical extremes, Seuss reduces words to sounds, amusing to say, but distracting from sense.[14]

On Beyond Zebra! is Seuss's most radical in its linguistic experiments. The book starts where most alphabet books end, inventing an entirely new twenty-letter alphabet for words that cannot be spelled with the usual twenty-six. In the "tall tale" style of Marco, Gerald McGrew, Morris McGurk, and Peter T. Hooper, the narrator of *On Beyond Zebra!* explains, "In the places I go there are things that I see / That I *never* could spell if I stopped with the Z. / I'm telling you this 'cause you're one of my friends. / *My* alphabet starts where *your* alphabet ends." True to the narrator's grandiose claims, *On Beyond Zebra!* goes beyond disassembling words: it deconstructs the alphabet, creating not just portmanteau words but portmanteau *letters*. The character for the letter "HUMPF" has the letters *H*, *m*, *P*, *u*, and *f* embedded in it. Without such a letter, our guide tells us, one "just can't spell Humpf-Humpf-a-Dumpfer," a furry-headed creature who lives in a "swampf." In its willingness to blend letters and words to create new ones, *On Beyond Zebra!* is Seuss's *Finnegans Wake*. In fact, what Garrett Stewart has said of Joyce could as easily be said of *On Beyond Zebra!*: "Word *by* word, Joyce's writing at its most extreme aspires to continuous neologism" (241).

As Seuss's writing at its most extreme, *On Beyond Zebra!* best embodies Wim Tigges's definition of literary nonsense as presenting "an unresolved tension [. . .] between presence and absence of meaning" (51). Seuss creates this tension by underscoring the constructedness of the alphabet itself. We take the alphabet for granted, a "natural" system that allows us to form the words we use to make sense of the world. *On Beyond Zebra!* challenges this basic assumption by suggesting that the building blocks of language are but an arbitrary pattern of symbols. So, while the letter pronounced "FLOOB" does convey meaning, it also questions the reliability of the standard twenty-six-letter alphabet: "FLOOB" makes possible the spelling of Floob-Boober-Bab-Boober-Bubs, but the need for such a letter exposes the inadequacies of the accepted letters. In going after the most fundamental units of language, *On Beyond Zebra!* reveals language as an ideological construct that may limit what we can see. It shows that words convey many meanings while simultaneously concealing others, and it invites readers to confront this quandary—or "Quandary," the creature spelled with "QUAN" who wonders "Is his top-side his bottom? Or bottom-side top?"—by inventing a new language. The book concludes with its most elaborate portmanteau letter yet, and asks, "what do you think we should call this one, anyhow?"

Although it does not encourage readers to create a new alphabet, Seuss's next book—*If I Ran the Circus*—shares its predecessor's interest in taking the language apart. Nearly halfway into the book, Morris McGurk introduces "A Juggling Jott / Who can juggle some stuff / You might think he could not . . . / Such as twenty-two question marks, / Which is a lot. / Also forty-four commas / And, *also*, one dot!" Instead of playing with letters, the Jott plays with punctuation—literally. Seuss has drawn his little Jott juggling exactly forty-four commas, twenty-two question marks, and one dot. The Jott does to punctuation what the narrator of *On Beyond Zebra!* does to letters. By removing these symbols (letters, punctuation) from their usual contexts, they call attention to the wayward nature of printed signs. If we change their location, then punctuation marks cease providing order to a sentence and instead become playthings. *If I Ran the Circus* and *On Beyond Zebra!* both suggest that if we free letters and punctuation from practical obligations, then they can help us dream of new worlds.

I Can Rhyme It All By Myself

While some have seen Seuss's Beginner Books as marking a diminished interest in linguistic inventiveness, these works in fact mark a new phase in Seuss's poetic career. With the exceptions of *The Cat in the Hat* and *The Sneetches*, John P. Bailey derides all other work after 1956 as "crass," maintaining that in the Beginner Books Seuss's "writing has lost the natural flow, and from rhythm we have moved to cadence" (11). It's true that Seuss has written some less-inspired works (*Hunches in Bunches* comes to mind), but the Beginner Books are not among them. These books have a different "flow" and rhythm than Seuss's larger-sized books because the Beginner Books and the Bright-and-Early Books (for even younger readers) deliberately use a limited vocabulary. Seuss worked under restrictions which required him to be *more* inventive, not less. What Seuss does in these books is comparable to what Georges Perec does when he writes an entire novel without using the letter *e*. *The Cat in the Hat* is not *La Disparition* (1969; translated as *The Void*, 1994), but the limitations of the form compel each author to be more resourceful than he would otherwise need to be. Seuss may have the advantage of writing a shorter work, but verse adds an extra layer of limitations to his already difficult task—as a poet, he must be constantly aware of meter, rhyme, and the rhythms of language.

As Seuss fans and scholars may know, an article by John Hersey was the catalyst behind Seuss's Cat in the Hat, the character who launched the Beginner Books series. In "Why Do Students Bog Down on First R?", published in a 1954 issue of *Life* magazine, Hersey accused the "bland, idealized" and "pallid primers" of contributing to illiteracy in America. Why, he asked, should children "not have pictures that widen rather than narrow the associative richness the children give to the words they illustrate—drawings like those of the wonderfully imaginative geniuses among children's illustrators, Tenniel, Howard Pyle, 'Dr. Seuss,' Walt Disney?" (148). As the Morgans report in their biography, William Spaulding, the director of Houghton Mifflin's education division, posed the challenge directly to Seuss. "Write me a story that first-graders can't put down!" he said, stipulating that Seuss limit the book's vocabulary to no more than 225 different words, choosing those words from a prescribed list of 348 (Morgan and Morgan 154; Cahn 42). Though Seuss tells several versions of how he invented the Cat,[15] one theme recurs in all: the challenge of working within the word limits. Depending on the version, *The Cat in the Hat* took anywhere between nine months and a year and a half to write because, as he said, "it's painful to write when you can't use any adjectives and few nouns" (Beyette 5). He kept getting stuck because "you got an idea and then found out you had no way to express yourself" (Clark D4).

He did find a way to express himself and, as a result, Seuss's Beginner Books not only teach us to read but also teach us to enjoy poetry. Too often, students view poetry as rarefied, difficult, elitist; bringing in a book by Dr. Seuss reminds them that they have been enjoying poetry since their earliest years.[16] His success at exploiting the limitations of poetic form demonstrates the fun of taking poetry seriously. *The Cat in the Hat* not only uses rhythms to maintain the pace of the story but varies its meter to reflect the differences in character and mood. For the first several pages of the book, the narrator tends to speak in anapests, albeit sometimes punctuated by iambs: "The sun did not shine. / It was too wet to play. / So we sat in the house / All that cold, cold, wet day." The first two words comprise an iamb, but the rest of the lines follow the pattern of two lightly stressed syllables followed by an emphasized one. This is significant because, in his first few lines, the Cat speaks in dactyls. The narrator introduces the Cat's first words as follows: "And he said to us / 'Why do you sit there like that?'" In my reading, *said*, *Why*, *sit*, and *that* receive the emphasis. While the Cat's words could be read as a continuation of the anapestic meter used by the narrator (every third word is heavily stressed), that the stressed "Why" begins the Cat's speech allows that line to be read as a dactyl. A dactyl is the opposite of an anapest: a dactyl's stressed syllable followed by two light syllables exactly mirrors the anapest's two light syllables followed by a stressed syllable. While neither character speaks exclusively in one meter or the other, the rhythmic difference here subtly introduces their oppositional relationship. As the Cat hits his stride, he does speak in anapests; however, when he gets carried away with himself, then his meter shifts away from anapests, following no apparent pattern. On the page prior to his fall from the ball, the Cat begins:

/   U   /
"Look at me!

/ U / / U U /
Look at me now!" said the cat.
 U U / U U /
"With a cup and a cake
 U U / U U /
On the top of my hat!
 U U / U / /
I can hold up TWO books!

In "Look at me!" and "Look at me now!" either all syllables receive the stress or all but "at" do. The line "I can hold up TWO books!" also disrupts the pattern because "TWO" has been printed in small caps for emphasis. Coming after many lines of anapestic dimeter, these lines signal the imminent collapse of the Cat's stunt. At the very least, the instability of the meter echoes the precariousness of the Cat's position. In other words, to examine the poetics of *The Cat in the Hat* is to understand that meter matters.

It certainly mattered to Seuss, who frequently relied on shifts in meter to underscore his themes. At a crucial moment in *Yertle the Turtle*, the narrative switches meter to emphasize Mack's revolutionary burp: "And that plain little lad got a little bit mad. / And that plain little Mack did a plain little thing. / *He burped!* / And his burp shook the throne of the king!" Two lines of anapestic tetrameter jump to iambic monometer (for the burp) and then turn to anapestic trimeter, illustrating the role meter plays in dramatizing Yertle's fall. Visually, too, the change in meter creates the appearance of one very short line holding up seven much longer lines; the text looks as precarious as the stack of turtles. While talking about meter is unlikely to spark a class's enthusiasm, a lively demonstration of Seuss's uses of meter can engender a greater appreciation for the music and techniques of poetry.

Seuss's drafts make visible the challenge of deploying the poetic skills he had honed in larger books (like *Yertle*) when writing the smaller Beginner Books. As Seuss's biographers note, *The Cat in the Hat*'s line "He came down with a bump / From up there on the ball" began as "He fell off of the ball," which Seuss first revised to "He came down from the ball," before changing it to the published version (Morgan and Morgan 155). The diction and meter of the final version convey more effectively the image of the Cat falling to the floor. "He came down" brings the Cat to earth; "with a bump" conveys the sound of the fall. In the next line, "from up there" directs us back up to the heights from which the Cat fell, creating a contrast between where he is now and where he was a moment ago. The alliteration of the *b*'s in *bump* and *ball* are more fun to say, and the rhythms of the anapestic dimeter propel the reader forward. If one were teaching poetry, then examining the difference between Seuss's original and final versions might teach students the art of revision, and why the revised version works better. As Seuss once said, "To produce a 60-page book, I may easily write more than 1,000 pages before I'm satisfied. The most important thing about me, I feel, is that I work like hell—write, rewrite, reject, re-reject, and polish incessantly" (Hopkins, "Dr. Seuss" 257).

Green Eggs and Ham, a masterpiece of minimalism and of nonsense poetry, would push Seuss's skills in invention and revision to their limits. Bennett Cerf, his publisher at Random House, bet Seuss fifty dollars that he could not write a book using only fifty different words (Morgan and Morgan 167). Seuss's response garnered praise from the critics and would go on to become his most popular book. As the *New Yorker* said in its review of *Green Eggs and Ham*, Seuss "can play so many tunes on his simplified keyboard that, reading him, one is hardly aware that there *are* more than fifty words" (Maxwell 226). Though its poetry seems effortless, the drafts of *Green Eggs and Ham* reveal the considerable effort behind this absurdist classic. Take the scene where mouse, fox, and Sam-I-am sit in the car, perched at the top of the tree: the black-hatted character faces them, his arm raised in protest. In the published version, the black-hatted character says,

> I would not, could not in a tree.
> Not in a car! You let me be.
> I do not like them in a box.
> I do not like them with a fox.
> I do not like them in a house.
> I do not like them with a mouse.
> I do not like them here or there.
> I do not like them anywhere.
> I do not like green eggs and ham.
> I do not like them, Sam-I-am. (30–31).

If you look at Seuss's rough sketches for *Green Eggs and Ham*, you will see a similar illustration, but the first three lines differ: "I do not like them in a tree. / ~~Sam I am. You let me be~~. Not in a car. You let me be! / I do not like them in a ~~house~~ box" (figure 1.3). In this earlier version, Seuss had not yet worked out the rhyme of the "would not, could not" that he uses throughout the book. The tone is a little more hostile, too. Not only does "You let me be!" have the exclamation point (instead of "Not in a car!" as in the published book), but Seuss is also considering using "Sam I am. You let me be," which he crosses out before settling on "Not in a car. You let me be!" By removing the proper name and changing "Sam I am" to "Not in a car," Seuss makes the "You let me be" a bit less personal in his final version.

Seuss typed the draft verse on rice paper, which he then pasted to the illustrated page. If you hold the paper up to the light, you can see, beneath, an even earlier version written in pencil:

> I do not like them
> On a tree.
> Green ham and eggs
> On a green green tree.
> I do not like you
> Sam I am
> your tree, your eggs
> your car, your ham.

The black-hatted character is still more hostile here ("I do not like you / Sam I am"), and the verse does not yet have its verve. The rhymes are less inventive—instead of rhyming "tree" with "be," Seuss rhymes "tree" with "tree"—and the meter lacks forward momentum. Most significantly of all, Seuss has not written "Green eggs and ham" but the more bland "Green ham and eggs." As Chuck Jones observed of the final version, Seuss took "the common phrase, *ham and eggs*, and commanded attention by reversing it" (Morgan and Morgan 170–71). "If you say, 'Would you like some eggs and ham?' somebody would say, 'Yeah, I've never heard of that,'" Jones says ("An Awfully Big Adventure"). Changing the order of the words makes the mundane *ham and eggs* sound intriguing. Seuss's work, Jones explains, "has that quality of puzzlement. He uses Sam-I-am, not just Sam, and Sam-I-am not only rhymes with green-eggs-and-ham, but has the same metric emphasis" (Morgan and Morgan 171). In addition to being poetically wanting, the earliest draft

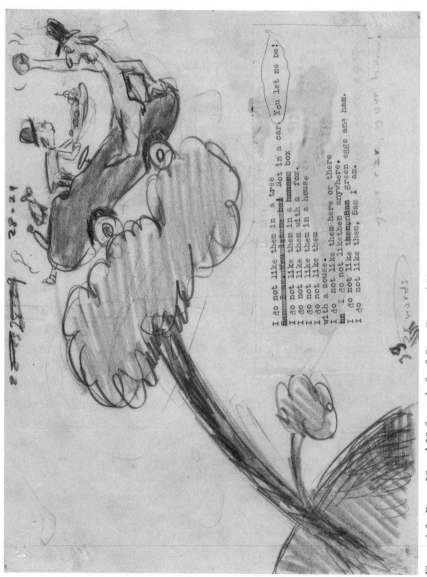

Figure 1.3. Pages 28 and 29 from draft of *Green Eggs and Ham*

lacks the puzzlement created by the reversal: "Green ham and eggs" is odd, but it is not nonsense.

Green Eggs and Ham is not only nonsense but meticulously crafted verse. At the bottom of each page of the draft, you can see Seuss keeping track of how many different words he has used, being careful not to go over 50. For example, at the bottom of the rough sketches discussed above, Seuss has written "33," and then "34" over that number, before revising his estimate one last time—"28 words"—and circling this final count. He worked so intensely on this project that he could recall its exact statistics even late in life: the words he used most frequently were *not* (82 times) and *I* (81 times), as the Morgans relate in their biography (170).[17] Reading *Green Eggs and Ham* or *The Cat in the Hat* teaches children to read, to appreciate poetry, and—given a glimpse of the drafts—to understand that all good writing is 99 percent revision. As Seuss said in response to Bennett Cerf's frequent claim that he was a genius, "If I'm a genius, why do I have to work so hard? I know my stuff looks like it was all rattled off in 28 seconds, but every word is a struggle and every sentence is like the pangs of birth" (Freeman, "Dr. Seuss from Then to Now").

The Beat Goes On:
The Seussian Turn in Contemporary Children's Books

Though he is rarely studied as a poet, the nonsense poetry of Dr. Seuss has established verse at the center of the children's book genre. Reviewing Sylvia Plath's *The It-Doesn't-Matter Suit* (a posthumous work, adapted for children) in 1996, Adam Gopnik wrote, "Dubious readers who expect from the gloomy poet a sort of 'Ariel' set to the rhythms of Dr. Seuss ('It's back on black / The Grinch insists! / Let's all go home / and slash our wrists') may find the Plath book [. . .] disappointing" (101). In R.E.M.'s "The Sidewinder Sleeps Tonite" (1992), during a passage that evokes childhood, lyricist Michael Stipe sings of "A candy bar, a falling star, reading from Dr. Seuss." Stipe, who has described his lyrics as "beautiful nonsense," sings in a later verse, "The Cat in the Hat came back, but wreaked a lot of havoc on the way / Always had a smile and a reason to tell" (Zahn). In 2002, an advertisement for Eden Ross Lipson's *New York Times Parent's Guide to the Best Books for Children* asked,

"Would you, could you, find that book? / Yes, you can—with just a look." Neither Seuss nor *Green Eggs and Ham* were mentioned in the ad: it needed only to adopt Seuss's poetic style to invoke children's books in general.

Perhaps because people perceive Seussian verse as a defining characteristic of the Children's Book, Dr. Seuss's style has inspired many imitators, some whose work is admirable and others less so. Celebrities who venture into children's books frequently attempt Seussian rhythms. Katie Couric's *The Brand New Kid* (2000), describing the trials of Lazlo S. Gasky, explains, "So these first weeks were lonely for this brand new kid. / They made fun of him, all that he said and he did. / So he kept his head bowed and stopped trying to please / and simply prepared for the next taunt and tease." If her verse is not quite of Seuss's quality, Couric does adopt those characteristic anapests and rhythmic, Irish-sounding names. The brand-new kid's classmates—Ellie McSnelly, Carrie O'Toole, and Susie McGraw (who ultimately befriends Lazlo)—recall Seuss's Gerald McGrew (*If I Ran the Zoo*), Morris McGurk (*If I Ran the Circus*), and Peter T. Hooper (*Scrambled Eggs Super!*). John Lithgow, whose *Remarkable Farkle McBride* (2000) also evokes Seuss's character names, favors anapestic verse as well. In *Micawber* (2002), the best of Lithgow's three children's books, the eponymous, artistic squirrel borrows a human artist's paints: "He returned thirty times by the following fall, / And the paintings poured fourth like a geyser. / He fastened them all to the living-room wall, / And the woman was never the wiser." Although Lithgow is not as linguistically inventive as Seuss, he does have a better sense of poetic rhythm than Couric, and writes verse that seems equally influenced by Seuss and Lear. If the works of Lithgow and Couric demonstrate how difficult it is to imitate Seuss's style, they nonetheless show excellent taste in choosing Seuss as a model.

Seuss's influence emerges in the work of more accomplished children's book writers as well. Sandra Boynton, whose work shares with Seuss's a sense of exuberant goofiness, appears to have spent a lot of time with his Beginner Books. Describing fish, the Beginner Book *One fish two fish red fish blue fish* tells us, "Yes. Some are red. And some are blue. / Some are old. And some are new." Describing pajamas, Boynton's *Pajama Time!* (2000) observes, "Now, some are old and some are new. / Some are red and some are blue." *Oh My Oh My Oh Dinosaurs!* (1993) also seems to have been written under the influence of *One fish two fish red fish blue fish*. Boynton's couplet "Dinosaurs HAPPY and dino-saurs SAD. / Dinosaurs GOOD and dinosaurs BAD" echoes Seuss's lines "Some are sad. / And some are glad. / And some are very, very bad." However, what makes Boynton, more than Lithgow or Couric, a true literary heir of Seuss is that her work has progressed beyond imitation to develop a unique voice. Also, where their didacticism tends to tread on the poetry, her messages—such as they are—never overwhelm the verse, and her books always retain a sense of humor. *Hey! Wake Up!* (2000), a whimsical ode to the joys of mornings, ends with, "Morning snack is here for you. / Milk and cookies. And broccoli stew." The hippo remarks, "Ew," and then the narrator corrects, "For the bunny, not for you." The bunny smiles, and the hippo replies, "Oh. Phew." The hu-morous tone of Boynton's *Snoozers: 7 Short Short Bedtime Stories for Lively Little Kids* (1997) also undercuts the book's ostensible goal, which, in this case, is encouraging children to sleep. The "Silly Lullaby," Boyn-ton's final "snoozer," is as likely to provoke laughter as it is snoozing. In waltz time, a parent bear sings to a child, "Go to sleep, my zoodle, / My fibblety-fitsy foo. / Go to sleep, sweet noodle. / It's time to say, 'Ah-choo.' // The chickens in the bathtub, / The closet full of sheep, / The sneakers in the freezer / Are all drifting off to sleep." Though its legions of odd creatures and tongue-twisting "moose juice/goose juice" section incites the imagination, even *Dr. Seuss's Sleep Book* ends on a quieter note than Boynton's *Snoozers*, encouraging readers to go to sleep and conclud-ing with the words "Good night." Just as They Might Be Giants' noisy "Bed Bed Bed" (2002) challenges the lullaby, so Boynton's *Snoozers* seems more intent on subverting the genre of the bedtime story.

Books like *Snoozers*, Calef Brown's *Polka Bats and Octopus Slacks* (1998), Toby Speed's *Brave Potatoes* (2000, illus. Barry Root), and Johnny Valentine's *One Dad Two Dads Brown Dad Blue Dads* (1994, discussed in Chapter Six) are Seuss's literary heirs not because they adopt Seussian rhythms (although they sometimes do) but because they develop the subversive power of nonsense. As Susan Stewart points out in *Nonsense: Aspects of Intertextuality in Folklore and Literature* (1979), "Nonsense bares the ideological nature of common sense, showing common sense's pre-carious situation—rooted in culture and not in nature" (49). Like Seuss's Sam-I-am, Speed's brave potatoes challenge the conventional wisdom about food, inviting readers to question their assumptions. Why not try ham of a different color? Why wouldn't potatoes like to ride the

Ferris wheel? In *Brave Potatoes*, after Hackemup the chef has brought the potatoes from the fairground's amusements into his kitchen, he tells them, "Better follow orders! Prepare to meet your fate! / It's too late / to be anything / but dinner on a plate!" The spuds, however, ignore him: "potatoes never listen. / Potatoes have no ears." Suggesting the power to be gained by organizing and agitating for one's rights, the potatoes then rise up as one against the chef, knock him into the soup, and free the other vegetables. As Speed's narrator puts it, "Brave potatoes in formation! / Brave potatoes in a troupe! / Now they've got the chef surrounded. / See the chef go alley-oop! / (It's a puzzle where he's landed. / Would you care to taste the soup?)" Unionized potatoes may seem as ridiculous as green eggs, but that's part of the point. Their absurdity underscores the fact that reality is culturally defined and therefore open to challenge. Speed's potatoes and Seuss's characters encourage children to ask questions of their world and to investigate the ways in which it often defies common sense.

As Seuss said, "Nonsense wakes up the brain cells. And it helps develop a sense of humor, which is awfully important in this day and age. Humor has a tremendous place in this sordid world. It's more than just a matter of laughing. If you can see things out of whack, then you can see how things can be in whack" (Corwin 3). In other words, by awakening the brain cells, nonsense can be subversive. As we will see in the next chapter, Seuss's interest in humorous nonsense extends well beyond laughter, literacy, and inspiring children's imaginations. Seuss makes reading fun, but he also wants to make his readers into better thinkers and even better citizens. In using nonsense rhymes not only to teach reading but to develop reasoning, Seuss returns to one of the earliest uses of nonsense. Although, as Noel Malcolm writes in his *The Origins of English Nonsense* (1997), nonsense poetry "was a literary phenomenon long before it became an ostensibly political one" (25), its use as a means of topical satire dates back to the seventeenth century, when, criticizing the political uses of nonsense, Royalist John Taylor wrote, "Nonsense is Rebellion, and thy writing, / Is nothing but Rebellious Warres inciting" (repr. in Malcolm 184).[18] Well before Seuss became the U.S. laureate of nonsense, he used this poetic form not to incite rebellious wars but to prompt his fellow Americans to be prepared for an inevitable entry into the Second World War. As he said, by showing us "things out of whack," nonsense can show us "how things can be in whack."

Chapter 2

Dr. Seuss vs. Adolf Hitler

A POLITICAL EDUCATION

L ong before Theodor Seuss Geisel became the Dr. Seuss famous for *The Cat in the Hat* and over forty other children's books, he was a successful advertising artist and a political cartoonist. During the late 1930s, he published a handful of political cartoons under the name "Tedd." However, in 1940, Dr. Seuss was best known for his "Quick Henry, the Flit!" advertising campaign (figure I.2) and was just starting to build a reputation as an author of children's books. At the time, he had published only four: *And to Think That I Saw It on Mulberry Street* (1937), *The 500 Hats of Bartholomew Cubbins* (1938), *The King's Stilts* (1939), and *Horton Hatches the Egg* (1940). He began his next, *McElligot's Pool*, in 1941, but did not return to it until 1947, because his concerns about the rapidly expanding World War had begun to simmer (Clark D4).[1] Convinced that America would be drawn into the wars in Europe and the Pacific, he feared that American isolationism left the country vulnerable. In late January of 1941, he expressed his frustration by sending a sketch of Mussolini's chief propagandist, Virginio Gayda, to the independent New York newspaper *PM*, where both cartoon and his letter were printed on January 30. Less than three months later, Seuss began his twenty-one-month career as a political cartoonist for *PM*, publishing over 400 cartoons between April 1941 and January 1943. As Seuss remembers, "while Paris was being occupied by the klanking tanks of the Nazis and I was listening on my radio, I found I could no longer keep my mind on drawing pictures of Horton the Elephant. I found myself drawing pictures of Lindbergh the Ostrich" (Seuss, letter to Americus Vesputius Fepp, 2–3).

According to a Gallup Poll from April 1941, 80 percent of Americans opposed going to war with Germany, but 73 percent were in favor of the U.S. Navy escorting aid to Britain and, if attacked by the Germans, returning their fire. Probably referring to this 80 percent, Seuss's cartoon of May 29, 1941, depicts Hamilton Fish, representative from New York, talking on the phone with Adolf Hitler. Fish says, "Now, Adolf, Just Forget What Franklin Said. 80 Per Cent of Us Here Want to Let You Have Your Fling." Strongly disagreeing with Fish and the 80 percent, Seuss was not only in favor of aiding Britain but saw that war with Nazi Germany would be inevitable. As Seuss wrote in his never-published "Non-Autobiography," "we were going to have no choice in the matter" (Morgan and Morgan 103). He added, "N.B. To the younger generation: I'm not talking about Korea, Vietnam, Cambodia. I'm talking about a war that had to be fought. If my philosophy irritates yours, please write me in care of Justin Hoogfliet, the boy who stuck his finger in the dike, Foedersvlied, Holland 09037" (311). A cartoon from June 1941 expresses his views quite directly and in verse: a bird representing Uncle Sam relaxes in an easy chair while bombs explode all around him (figure 2.1). The caption reads:

Said a bird in the midst of a Blitz,
"Up to now, they've scored very few hitz,

Figure 2.1. "Said a bird in the midst of a blitz" by Dr. Seuss.

So I'll sit on my canny,
Old Star Spangled fanny . . ."
And on it he sitz and he sitz.

These rollicking anapests lack the sparkle of the poetry in his children's
books, but this cartoon does introduce the primary effect that World
War II had on Dr. Seuss's postwar works. During the war, and especially
during his stint as a cartoonist for the left-leaning *PM*, Seuss not only
grew more interested in social issues but wanted to make his readers
care about these issues, too. Richard H. Minear's *Dr. Seuss Goes to War*—
which omits this cartoon—does an excellent job situating Seuss's cartoons historically, but it might do more in situating them in the context
of Seuss's children's books. Since Minear is a professor of history, he
should not be faulted for his emphasis. However, we would do well to
consider how the war shaped the artist who became Dr. Seuss. His
career as cartoon propagandist made Seuss more willing to confront his
readers—even at the risk of offending them. Furthermore, Seuss's work
in the fight against Fascism both galvanized his commitment to various
social issues and motivated him to write books that encourage readers
to challenge certain structures of power.

Seuss Confronts His Readers

PM often reprinted its credo that "*PM* is against people who push other
people around," a message which resonated with Dr. Seuss. As he has
said, "*PM* was against people who pushed other people around. I liked
that" (qtd. in Morgan and Morgan 101). Taking no advertising for its
first six years and billing itself as the "one newspaper that can and dares
to tell the truth," *PM* did not pause to spare anyone's feelings—and
neither did Seuss. Following Charles Lindbergh's first openly anti-Semitic speech, delivered September 1941 in Des Moines, *PM*'s headline
called him "Jew-Baiter Lindbergh" and implied that he was colluding
with the Nazis. Seuss drew Lindbergh, shovel in hand, standing atop a
"Nazi Anti-Semite Stink Wagon," busily "Spreading the Lovely Goebbels
Stuff." In November 1942, when Southern senators filibustered to preserve poll taxes, *PM* accused them of being childish and undemocratic,
asking "Who Is the No. 1 Lollipop of the U.S. Senate?" and encouraging its readers to mail lollipops to the filibusterers. Seuss contributed

"Buck Bilbo Rides Again," a cartoon showing Mississippi Senator Theodore Bilbo riding a galumphing beast named "Filibuster." In his unpublished "Non-Autobiography," Seuss speaks of *PM*'s staff as "a bunch of honest but slightly cockeyed crusaders," and, if his description seems to mix admiration with irony, it's because he was one of those crusaders (Morgan and Morgan 103). The paper's idealism appealed to him but, often self-deprecating when speaking of his own work, Seuss would not say so directly. As he remarked when looking back on his *PM* cartoons later in life, "I was intemperate, un-humorous in my attacks . . . and I'd do it again" (311). Intemperate but actually quite humorous, Seuss's work at *PM* develops the confrontational style later used to great effect in his children's books—especially in the overtly political ones.

While there is a political component to the satirical illustrations, cartoons, stories, and even children's books that Seuss wrote in the 1930s, none were quite as blunt or acerbic as his *PM* cartoons. One difference was a lack of time to revise—as he says, the *PM* cartoons are "full of snap judgments that every political cartoonist has to make between the time he hears the news at 9 a.m. and sends his drawing to press at 5 p.m." (Minear, "The Political Dr. Seuss"). When creating children's books, Dr. Seuss was a consummate perfectionist, revising and revising again. But making such "snap judgments" and writing, on average, four to five cartoons every week left little time to polish his work. In his "Non-Autobiography," he speaks of these cartoons as "rather shoddy" art, but likes "their honesty and their frantic fervor" (Morgan and Morgan 103). While the art is hardly "shoddy," the "short-order business" (Seuss's words) of drawing political cartoons inspired work more raw and provocative than anything he had published before (103), manifesting a desire to grab readers by the lapels—something he does not seem to have considered before then. Seuss set about disillusioning his countrymen, drawing Isolationists as ostriches, the America First organization as the Siamese twin of the Nazi Party, and one Isolationist senator as a horse's ass. In April 1942, four months after America entered the war, Senator Gerald P. Nye of North Dakota was still arguing that Americans should stay out of it. Nye's letter endorsing Gerald L. K. Smith's pro-Fascist *The Cross and the Flag* appeared in that magazine's edition of April 23. In *Dr. Seuss and Mr. Geisel*, Judith and Neil Morgan describe a breakfast-time conversation between Seuss and his wife, just after they had heard one of Nye's pro-isolation speeches on the radio:

> "That horse's ass!" Ted blurted.
> "Ted, don't use language like that!" Helen said.
> "But he *is* a horse's ass! I'll draw a picture of him as a horse's ass and put it in *PM*!"
> "You can't," she said. "It's a vulgar idea." (Morgan and Morgan 101)

He did draw the cartoon, and despite publisher Ralph Ingersoll's warning that it would get the newspaper in "a million-dollar lawsuit" (102), *PM* printed it on April 26 (figure 2.2). Seuss received a letter from the Senator, *not* threatening to sue but politely requesting the original cartoon. Laughing as he read the letter aloud to his wife, Seuss asked if she

Figure 2.2. "GOD MADE ME A RABBLE-ROUSER!" by Dr. Seuss.

thought that they should send the cartoon to Senator Nye. As Seuss remembers it, "Helen, who never used any bad language, said, 'No, he's a horse's ass!'" (102).

If Dr. Seuss calling a senator a "horse's ass" surprises fans of his children's books, it shouldn't. The blunt, agitational style of many of these cartoons—"WHAT HAVE YOU DONE TODAY TO HELP SAVE YOUR COUNTRY FROM THEM?" asks one from March 1942— enters his children's books, too. Many of his books end by posing a question. On the last two pages of *The Cat in the Hat*, the narrator asks, "What would you do / If your mother asked you?" Should the children describe an actual experience which their mother will think they imagined, or an imagined experience which she will accept as actual? If you were a child who had just spent the day with a 6-foot-tall cat, would you tell your mother? Pitting the desire to be honest against the desire not to get in trouble is a genuine dilemma for a child (and, one hopes, for some adults). Most of Seuss's books do not end with such a direct question, but they often conclude by inviting the reader to contemplate further the book's message. His cartoons do the same, addressing YOU directly, asking YOU to intervene. The cartoon depicting Nye as a horse's ass, for example, portrays Robert Reynolds, the isolationist Senator from North Carolina, as the horse's front and shows Gerald L. K. Smith himself riding on their backs, brandishing a sword labeled "DE-FEATISM." As if trying to ensure that this bold attack directly hits the reader, Seuss draws the "defeatist" sword breaking through the cartoon's frame, rising up from its flat surface to point at the person holding the newspaper.

When Seuss tries to cross the boundary between the page and his reader, he often does so by putting the matter in his reader's hands. As I argue in *The Avant-Garde and American Postmodernity: Small Incisive Shocks*, this proclivity for confrontation aligns Seuss's work with that of the historical avant-garde (Nel 41–42 and passim); however, it seems significant that Seuss's deliberately contentious style emerges first in his work against the totalitarian governments of Germany and Japan in the 1940s. In one of the *PM* cartoons, he draws Hitler and Japanese Prime Minister Hideki Tojo standing on either side of a larger-than-life "WORLD ATLAS," both pushing to slam the book shut. Caught with his head inside the atlas is a figure labeled "YOU" (figure 2.3). The cartoon, titled, "Awkward Predicament . . . For YOU to Solve," clearly

Figure 2.3. "Awkward Predicament . . . For YOU to Solve" by Dr. Seuss.

states Seuss's goals not only in these cartoons but in later works like *The Lorax* and *The Butter Battle Book*: he wants to push the reader to get involved. What the "Awkward Predicament" cartoon does with its "WORLD ATLAS," *The Butter Battle Book* achieves in its tale of an escalating arms race between Yooks, who butter their bread butter-side up, and Zooks, who butter theirs butter-side down. A Yook grandfather tells his grandson about a Cold War that, near the book's conclusion, culminates in the "Bitsy Big Boy Boomeroo," a "bomb" that "can blow all of those Zooks clear to Sala-ma-goo." However, when the grandfather arrives at the wall dividing these two countries, his longtime enemy (a Zook named Van Itch) is there, also holding a version of the "Big Boy Boomeroo." After everyone else has entered fallout shelters, the two stand poised on the wall, each holding the Seussian nuclear bomb over his opponent's side of the wall, threatening to drop it. The book's last words are:

"Grandpa!" I shouted. "Be careful! Oh, gee!
Who's going to drop it?
Will *you* . . . ? Or will *he* . . . ?"
"Be patient," said Grandpa. "We'll see.
We will see . . ."

When asked how he hoped people would react to this ending, Seuss replied, "I want people to think" (Sheff 55). Or, in the words of the *PM* cartoon, an awkward predicament . . . for YOU to solve.

The Butter Battle Book, which Seuss once described as "an echo of my days as a political cartoonist" (Freedman A12), offers the most striking example of his ability to drop a problem in the reader's lap, but it is not the only work to do so. *The Lorax* and *Yertle the Turtle* each achieve a similar result with the words "Unless" and "maybe." In the concluding couplet of *Yertle*, we learn that "turtles, of course . . . all the turtles are free / As turtles and, maybe, all creatures should be." When asked "Why 'maybe' and not 'surely'?" Seuss responded, "I wanted other persons to say 'surely' in their minds instead of my having to say it" (Cott 28). In a more subtle manner than the *Butter Battle Book*, *Yertle the Turtle* solicits the reader's involvement by ending on a "maybe" that (Seuss hoped) would prompt a "surely." *The Lorax* strives for a similar response with "UNLESS," the last word left by the Lorax, the creature "who speaks for the trees," birds and other wildlife. This story, too, finishes by placing responsibility in the hands of the reader. The Once-ler, now a repentant ex-industrialist, tosses the last Truffula seed to the narrator (identified only as "you"), and the last image is of the seed in transit, about to land in "your" hands. As the Once-ler says, "UNLESS some one like you / cares a whole awful lot, / nothing is going to get better. / It's not." Instead of asking you to help save the country from Fascism, Seuss asks you save the environment from pollution. The message has changed, but the method of delivery has not.

From Hats to Oobleck: The Post-War Shift in Seuss's "Message" Books

The blunt political fables of *The Lorax* and *The Butter Battle Book* develop from Seuss's experience writing cartoons for *PM*, a task which sharpened his ideological commitment. As he told his biographers, "I had no great causes or interest in social issues until Hitler" (Morgan and Morgan 98). It's true: the works he wrote after the war are quite different from those written prior to it. What we might call Seuss's "message books" are a distinctly postwar phenomenon, beginning in 1949 with the publication of *Bartholomew and the Oobleck.* We have met Bartholomew before the war, in *The 500 Hats of Bartholomew Cubbins.* This earlier book focuses on one boy, unjustly sentenced to death for a failure to remove his hat: Bartholomew's plight is real (it's not his fault that new hats keep appearing on his head), but the king's actions primarily affect Bartholomew alone. By contrast, in *Bartholomew and the Oobleck*, King Derwin's misrule affects the entire kingdom. The King's wish for unusual weather creates an ecological catastrophe, prefiguring *The Lorax*'s more deftly dramatized fable of environmental destruction. Bright green, gluey goop covers animals, people, farm equipment, and everything in sight. In this postwar work, dictatorial blundering affects not just Bartholomew but the entire nation.

The careful reader might argue that the influence of world events enters Seuss's work prior to September 1939; however, such influences are but echoes when compared to *Oobleck* and later "message" books. For example, Mary Galbraith contends that *And to Think That I Saw It on Mulberry Street* (1937), conceived of during Seuss's return from a European trip coincident with the 1936 Berlin Olympics, registers fears about the Nazis' ambitions. Though Seuss did not actually attend these Olympic Games, *Mulberry Street*'s parade recalls the "parade of nations" presented in Leni Riefenstahl's *Olympia* (1938): in *Mulberry Street*, the "Mayor's small moustache and raised arm evoke Hitler, while the brass band and international cast of characters evoke the parade of nations at the opening of the games" (128). Galbraith's most compelling point may be the idea that *Mulberry Street*'s "simple horse and wagon—which evokes the peaceful Germans of Geisel's home town and thus the everyday, non-threatening behavior of Germany—will transform itself gradually into a military monolith [. . .] marching down the main street as an airplane drops confetti" (128). If *Mulberry Street* does bear the marks of Hitler's military aspirations, they remain coded: there is little reason to suspect that a contemporary reader would glean anxieties about the Nazis from reading this book. Furthermore, Marco's failure to tell his father what he saw does not appear to have any negative consequences for himself or others. By contrast, Jo-Jo, the smallest of the Whos in *Horton Hears a Who!* (1954), needs to speak out in order to save *all* Whos from imminent destruction.

A better candidate for a pre-war book manifesting signs of European dangers is *The King's Stilts*, published in September 1939. In the book, King Birtram, depressed by the theft of his stilts, abandons his kingdom to the Nizzards, who eat at the roots of the Dike Trees protecting his island nation. Reviewing *The King's Stilts* for the *Dartmouth Alumni Magazine*, Seuss's classmate Alexander Laing remarks, "the Dr. may not have meant it, but to me those contemptible Nizzards are bombing planes." Whether or not other contemporary readers noticed parallels between the book and the war in Europe, *The King's Stilts* is the sole pre-war Seuss work in which a king's behavior affects his entire country. Written on the eve of the Second World War, the book might register Seuss's anxieties about the growing global crisis. As a leader who has grown lazy about the potential dangers to his country, King Birtram could represent Isolationists' influence in both America and Great Britain. The phonetic bond between "Birtram" and "Britain" links Seuss's King to England's Prime Minister, another appeaser who fails to act against the powerful threats to the island he governs.

While *The King's Stilts* may dramatize the dangers of appeasement, one main feature marks it as a pre-war work. In contrast to the un-elected leaders in Seuss's postwar work, this king is not a childish despot. Seuss often depicted Hitler as a tyrannical baby, as in the series titled "Mein Early Kampf," where Hitler appears as an infant "giv[ing] the hotfoot to" a stork delivering him (20 Jan. 1942), "reject[ing] milk from Holstein cows as Non-Aryan" (21 Jan. 1942), and taking a bite out of a bust of Bismarck (29 Jan. 1942) (figures 2.4 and 2.5). This view of Hitler very much informed his portrayal of rulers in later books like *Yertle the Turtle* and *Bartholomew and the Oobleck*. However, King Birtram, like the pre-war King Derwin of *The 500 Hats of Bartholomew Cubbins*, is less a dictatorial menace and more a misguided human being. After Lord Droon steals the stilts and blames the robbery on "the townsfolk," the king grows "sadder and sadder," neglecting his Patrol Cats and his kingdom. The real villain of the story is not the king—who is basically a benevolent, if fallible, monarch—but Lord Droon, who dislikes laughing ("spoils the shape of the face," he says) and thinks bounding about on stilts is insufficiently kingly. Likewise, in *The 500 Hats of Bartholomew Cubbins*, the villain is Grand Duke Wilfred, a capricious child of Bartholomew's age. Though the King is at first quite angry that Bartholomew's head keeps producing more hats, his general mood throughout the book is puzzlement. It is Wilfred who suggests that the King

Figure 2.4. "Mein Early Kampf: I reject milk from Holstein cows . . ." by Dr. Seuss.

chop off Bartholomew's head—something the King clearly does not want to do. "A dreadful thought," says the King while "biting his lip"; emphasizing King Derwin's misgivings, Seuss accompanies these words with the first picture in which Derwin does not look either angry or haughty. No longer the commanding figure of earlier illustrations, the King sits in his throne, his eyes wide open, eyebrows raised, as he bends over to listen to his nephew (who does look haughty). The Kings of *500 Hats* and *The King's Stilts* offer a marked contrast to the King in *Oobleck* who, though ostensibly the same character as *500 Hats'* King, is much more like the tantrum-throwing Hitler than these earlier Kings. Influenced by their author's portrayal of Hitler, postwar Seuss books tend to portray un-elected leaders as irrational tyrants.

Emphasizing the higher degree of danger in *Oobleck*, Seuss's art grows more dynamic and energetic. Though the haste with which Seuss drew his *PM* cartoons may be the immediate reason behind this stylistic shift (all of Seuss's postwar books evince a more boisterous, more expressive use of line), the effect is to underscore this later Derwin's status as a

Figure 2.5. "Mein Early Kampf: I cut my first tooth on a Bust of Bismark"

more harmful leader and Bartholomew's mission as much more serious than it was in *500 Hats*. There, he had to prove his own innocence, which should not be too difficult since, as Bartholomew reminds himself, he *is* innocent: "the King can do nothing dreadful to punish me, because I really haven't done anything wrong." In *Bartholomew and the Oobleck*, however, he has both to save an entire kingdom from environmental catastrophe and to convince a tyrant to change his mind. Accentuating the earlier book's relative lack of danger, each of the stops on Bartholomew's journey in *500 Hats* occurs at a leisurely pace: the Yeoman of the Bowmen fails to remove his hat, the magicians fail to charm away his hat, and the executioner cannot chop off Bartholomew's head because he "can't execute anyone with his hat on." The drawings accompanying each of these scenes convey stasis more than movement: the Yeoman stands still, his bow drawn; the musicians stand in a circle, singing; the executioner flicks hats of Bartholomew's head before shaking the boy's hand. Appropriately, the art complements the relatively unhurried narrative—after all, a hat-wearer does not threaten national security. By contrast, in *Oobleck*, Bartholomew dashes from royal bell ringer, to royal trumpeter, to Captain of the Guards, all with an increasing sense of urgency. As oobleck rains down, he races to warn the people and to stop this toxic, green substance before everyone is "hopelessly caught in the goo." Seuss emphasizes Bartholomew's haste in bristly lines that show the boy always in motion, running up stairs, running to open a door, running to warn people. The deliberately rougher style of these pictures recalls the vitality of his *PM* cartoons and heightens the crisis of *Oobleck*.

Amplifying the danger in *Oobleck*, the more turbulent lines of Seuss's cartoons contribute to the sense that this King is more erratic, infantile, and dictatorial than he was in *500 Hats*. Unlike the prior version of Derwin, Seuss depicts this one striding around the castle, beating his chest, closely resembling a child throwing a tantrum. Though the King Derwin of *500 Hats* does display a temper, his emotional state is more grumpy indignity than childish impatience. When Bartholomew stands at the threshold of *500 Hats'* Throne Room, the King stares down at him, eyebrows furrowed, as the sharp features of his face congeal into a scowl. However, even when covered in oobleck, the later King Derwin waves his arms while the narrator compares him to an infant: "There he sat . . . Old King Derwin, proud and mighty ruler of the Kingdom of Didd, trembling, shaking, helpless as a baby." His eyes squinting, dripping juicy tears above his oval-shaped mouth, the King appears too immature to handle the responsibility of governing. It is with a sense of relief that we see Bartholomew, unable to "hold his tongue [any] longer," rebuking the King and telling him to apologize; when King Derwin does, the oobleck "simply, quietly melted away." The success of Bartholomew's quest and the perils that Didd faces emphasize the need to stand up to an unjust leader, especially one who poses a danger to the lives and welfare of his citizens.

The King Derwin of *Oobleck* is an early version of Yertle the Turtle, whose career Seuss has said "was modeled on the rise of Hitler" (Cott 29). Yertle, tyrannical king of the turtles, literally builds his throne on the backs of his subjects, because the higher he sits, the more territory he rules. As Derwin wishes to "rule the sky" and exults "that beautiful oobleck! [. . .] it's mine! All mine!" so Yertle proclaims himself "King of the air!" and "the ruler of all that I see!" Just as these rulers' attempts to control the sky results in their undoing, Seuss frequently depicts Hitler as overextending himself, seen most vividly in a cartoon first printed in January 1942: Hitler stands in a doctor's office, where icicles labeled "RUSSIA" hang from his head and his trousers have been singed off, revealing a thigh labeled "LIBYA" (figure 2.6). Coupling the slapstick humor of a bare-assed Hitler with stereotyped Hollywood-German syntax ("Doktor! I got frozen up here"), Seuss's drawing transforms the German ruler's ambitions into broad farce. But the comedy has a serious point. At left, a skull looks impassively on, a reminder of Hitler's murderous armies and, perhaps, suggesting that this "disease" of a war on many fronts may bring about the Nazi leader's demise. One can see the wartime cartoons recurring in the behaviors of dictators from *Oobleck* to *Yertle:* their grandiose designs lead to the regime's collapse.

Seuss's interest in the deleterious effects of such governments also stems from his war work. The *PM* cartoon of 7 October 1942 argues that Hitler maintains his empire by starving his people: in it, an emaciated father explains to his hungry son, "Food? We Germans don't eat *food!* We Germans eat countries!" Likewise, Mack, spokesturtle for those at the bottom of Yertle's pile, complains, "I know, up on top you are

Figure 2.6. "Doktor! I got frozen up here, and sunburned down here . . ."

seeing great sights, / But down at the bottom we, too, should have rights. / We turtles can't stand it. Our shells will all crack! / Besides, we need food. We are starving!" Like *Yertle*, *Bartholomew and the Oobleck* displays the suffering inflicted by a cruel ruler. Indeed, if we see oobleck as a physical manifestation of an ideological condition, this book may go even further than *Yertle* in its depiction of the effects of living under a tyrant: not only is the King a megalomaniac but his ambitions mire his country in chaos and pain—a view which perfectly coincides with Seuss's view of Hitler.

Horton Hears a Heil: Racism and Anti-Racism

Bartholomew's King Derwin is not the only character to undergo a postwar transformation. In the pre-war *Horton Hatches the Egg* (1940), Horton nurtures a single egg, carefully protecting it from harm.[2] However, in *Horton Hears a Who!* (1954), Horton must protect an entire civilization from annihilation. If he cannot save the speck-sized planet from its sneering adversaries, a nation of Whos will be destroyed. Significantly, Seuss wrote the book directly after his return from Japan: he visited that nation in 1953 to see how the American occupation had changed the ideas of young people, learning that they were less interested in militarism and more interested in the West, as reported in "Japan's Young Dreams," a *Life* magazine article about his trip. Seuss dedicated *Horton Hears a Who!*—a book which the *Des Moines Register* called "a rhymed lesson in protection of minorities and their rights"—to "My Great Friend, Mitsugi Nakamura," a Kyoto University professor he met on his tour of Japan (Morgan and Morgan 151).[3] While the Whos could represent children or any minority populations, given that the book was written upon Seuss's return from Japan and influenced by his visits to Japanese schools (Morgan and Morgan 144), it is reasonable to assume that Seuss was thinking of the Japanese people when he created these Whos. While the Whos in *How the Grinch Stole Christmas!* do not appear to be specifically connected with the Japanese, the fact that Horton's Whos are threatened by total annihilation suggests a parallel with the atomic bomb, two of which the United States dropped on Japan in August of 1945. Richard Minear rightly points out this parallel in his *Dr.*

Seuss Goes to War, noting that "[i]f Who-ville is Japan, Horton must stand for the United States" (263).

However, Minear—perhaps influenced by Ruth K. MacDonald's claim that "*Horton Hears a Who!* is Dr. Seuss's statement about the Japanese people" (75)—may press this parallel a bit too much when he begins to *equate* Horton with the United States and to accuse Seuss of a wishful rewriting of history. Noting that even before the use of atomic bombs, the U.S. bombing of Japan was "unprecedented in its thoroughness and in the devastation it caused" (263–64), Minear finds Horton's rescue of Who-ville a "willful amnesia" on the part of Seuss. Horton may be praised by Whos for saving "our houses, our ceilings and floors / [. . .] our churches and grocery stores," but the United States fire-bombed much of Japan, destroying over half of its sixty largest cities, Minear explains (264). Yet, if we consider *Horton Hears a Who!* not as a literal rewriting of American actions against Japan during the Second World War but instead within the context of Seuss's children's books *and* racist cartoons caricaturing the Japanese, we might arrive at a different conclusion. Taken in light of his burgeoning awareness of world affairs, the book's refrain "A person's a person, no matter how small" might be seen as a postwar parable favoring the protection of all people, not only the Japanese. True, "no matter how small" could be seen as an ethnic slight or as patronizing, but, in the story, size functions as an arbitrary mark of difference for which the Whos are mistreated, and thus can be seen as analogous to race, creed, sex, or nationality. So, if we look at Seuss's political development as an artist, we could see the book not as "willful amnesia" but as an allegory advocating equal treatment of all people.

Even if one were to equate the Whos with the Japanese, then *Horton Hears a Who!* is especially significant in light of Seuss's tendency to stereotype the Japanese in his *PM* cartoons. He often represented the German people sympathetically (though not their leaders), spoke out against the poll tax, and criticized anti-Semitism at home and abroad. But the Japanese did not receive a similar treatment. Whether inadvertently or intentionally, a cartoon from February 1942 provides justification for Japanese Internment Camps (figure 2.7). In it, a line of Japanese men stretches all along the West Coast (from Washington to California). They are lining up to pick up packages of "TNT" from another Japanese man working at a kiosk labeled "Honorable 5th Column." On the roof of

Figure 2.7. "Waiting for the Signal from Home . . ." by Dr. Seuss.

the building, a Japanese man looks through a telescope: he is "Waiting for the Signal From Home," according to the caption. Then dividing his time between an apartment in New York and a summer home in La Jolla, California, Seuss clearly absorbed some of the West Coast's anti-Japanese hysteria.

While the racism of these anti-Japanese drawings is striking in contrast to his cartoons critical of both anti-Semitism and unjust treatment of black Americans, Seuss's caricatures of the Japanese are no more derogatory than those of his contemporary cartoonists.[4] For example, consider two cartoons from late June of 1941, one by Seuss and the other by David Low, the New Zealand-born cartoonist who drew for London's *Evening Standard*. After Germany attacked the Soviet Union, some wondered whether Japan would begin attacking the Russians as well: though Japan (like Germany) had signed a neutrality pact with the Soviets, a similar agreement had not prevented Japan from attacking China and, furthermore, Japan was allied with Germany. In Seuss's cartoon of 30 June, a male figure wearing a "JAP" hat has unbuttoned his shirt and is looking at two tattoos on his chest, "NAZI PACT" (with Swastika insignia) and "RUSS[IA] PACT" (with the Hammer and Sickle) (figure 2.8). He thinks, "Gosh, I wonder how easy this Tattoo Stuff comes off . . . !" The man's slanty eyes, glasses, and pointy mustache clearly uphold Western caricatures of the Japanese. But David Low's response to the same event goes even further in its pursuit of cultural stereotypes: hanging by his tail from a palm tree is a monkey with slanty eyes, glasses, and wide grin. On his behind is the word "JAP," and in his hand a sharp knife. The tree is in the middle of the Pacific; to his left and right are men with their backs to the monkey: a man identified as "U.S.S.R." (left) and two men labeled "U.S.A." and "BRIT" (right). The "JAP" monkey is counting, "Eeny, meeny, miney mo . . . ," as he decides which one to stab in the back first. In depicting this particular event, Low's cartoon appears more xenophobic than Seuss's; by portray-

Figure 2.8. "Gosh, I wonder how easy this Tattoo Stuff comes off . . . !" by Dr. Seuss.

ing the Japanese person as a monkey, Low suggests that the "JAP" is not even human. Though other of Seuss's *PM* cartoons exhibit greater degrees of anti-Japanese racism, Seuss uses animals much less frequently than Low and only once portrays the Japanese as a monkey. While Low's more common use of the Japanese-as-monkey trope does not excuse Seuss, it does place his xenophobia in context. As Minear judiciously observes, "Depicting the Japanese as monkeys or apes was a common practice of American and British political cartoons of the war era" (118).

However, Seuss's later work, both during and after the war, manifests greater sympathy toward people of Japanese origin, as Seuss's initial racism gives way to a deeper understanding. Seuss scripted a military training film, *Your Job in Japan* (1945), which General MacArthur considered too sympathetic toward the Japanese people and prevented from being shown. Seuss and his wife Helen co-wrote *Design for Death* (1947), a film that "portrayed the Japanese people as victims of seven centuries of class dictatorship" (Morgan and Morgan 119). In a letter to a friend, Seuss described it as "an attempt to show the means used on one particular nation to whip its people into war. But the point we try to make is that this particular nation is no different, actually, than any other." He continued, "it is the same old universal story of power-racketeers who manoeuvre people into war, and make them like it. Story of Germany, Italy and every other country that's ever waged aggressive war" (Geisel, letter to Bill). In 1948, this film won the Academy Award for Best Documentary. As in these films, in *Horton Hears a Who!* one might see Seuss's treatment of the Japanese growing more sympathetic and, perhaps, an implicit criticism of America's use of the atomic bomb on Japan. Horton's determination to protect the Whos' small island nation from certain and total destruction suggests that, after his visit to Japan, Seuss may have sensed the possibility that race played a role in the United States' decision to use the bomb.

If read as parable in defense of the Japanese, Horton's paternalistic "I've *got* to protect them. I'm bigger than they" smacks of U.S. imperialism and the oft-repeated "A person's a person, no matter how small" may sound condescending. But, as argued above, if we see the Whos as a metaphor for not only the Japanese but all minority groups, then size, too, is a metaphor. After all, the Whos' smallness is not important; the fact that Whos are people is very important. That Jo-Jo, the smallest

Who of all, shouts the "Yopp!" that saves his country suggests that even those who seem insignificant in the larger social order are significant and even powerful. As Henry Jenkins puts it, "Jo-Jo endangers his community by withholding his small voice from their noisemaking efforts. [. . .] *Horton* is not only a plea for the rights of the 'small,' but also an acknowledgement that even the 'small' have an obligation to contribute to the general welfare" (188).[5] Inasmuch as Whos *may* be analogous to minority populations, *Horton Hears a Who!* indicates that Seuss's understanding of racism and xenophobia had progressed considerably during the decade since his *PM* cartoons.[6] Suggesting that his burgeoning cultural sensitivity eventually included people of Chinese origin, Seuss later revised *And to Think That I Saw It on Mulberry Street* (1937). As he explained, "I had a gentleman with a pigtail. I colored him yellow and called him a Chinaman. That's the way things were fifty years ago. In later editions I refer to him as a Chinese man. I have taken the color out of the gentleman and removed the pigtail and now he looks like an Irishman" (Morgan and Morgan 276). Where he once perceived Asians in terms of cultural stereotypes, Seuss ultimately includes them among those groups who deserve protection from race-based bigotry.

In many senses, *Horton Hears a Who!* looks ahead to the *Sneetches*, which Seuss has said "was inspired by my opposition to anti-Semitism" (Cott 29–30), a political stance first expressed in his *PM* cartoons. On the front page of the *PM* of September 22, 1941, sits an American bird, wings and feet locked in the stocks, a sign hanging from his beak: "I AM PART JEWISH," it says. Leaning against the stocks, a placard states, "PUBLIK NOTICE: THIS BIRD IS POSSESSED OF AN EVIL DEMON!" and has been signed by "Sheriffs" Lindbergh and Nye. Directing the viewer to oppose the anti-Semitic jailers, the drawing creates sympathy for the imprisoned, "PART JEWISH," and—given his star-spangled hat—clearly American bird. In contrast, the misspelling of "PUBLIK," the phrase "EVIL DEMON," and the stocks themselves make the "Sheriffs" look both uneducated and cruel, if not positively medieval. Visually, the persecuted bird of this cartoon looks ahead to the Plain-Belly Sneetches who, years after this criticism of American anti-Semitism, will be treated as second-class citizens by Star-Belly Sneetches: by the end of the book, both groups learn that "Sneetches are Sneetches / And no kind of Sneetch is the best on the beaches." Indeed, in his article "Horton Hears a Heil" Art Spiegelman suggests that "those stars on thar bellies" are "Stars of David" (63). Although Seuss's inspiration for *The Sneetches* was opposition to anti-Semitism, the book also works as an anti-racism fable, another concern introduced in the *PM* cartoons. Several cartoons attack discrimination: many question Jim Crow labor practices; one criticizes Eugene Talmadge, the white supremacist Governor of Georgia; another shows a line of people waiting to be inoculated by a "Mental Insecticide" that gets rid of the "racial prejudice bug."

Fighting prejudices is one of the legacies that Seuss's cartoons and children's books attempt to leave in the postwar world. A later version of the "mental insecticide" cartoon shows Uncle Sam working a bellows labeled "'PSYCHOLOGICAL DISARMAMENT' OF AXIS YOUTH." The bellows goes in one ear of a German child, blowing bugs (presumably versions of the "prejudice bug" depicted in the earlier cartoon) out of the other ear; meanwhile, a Japanese child awaits the same treatment. Appropriately, Seuss titled the cartoon "We'll Have to Clean a Lot of Stuff Out Before We Put Peace Thoughts In." As his wartime caricatures of the Japanese indicate, this remark applies equally well to Seuss himself, signaling the transformation his own attitudes would undergo. Examining the impact of Seuss's World War II cartoons on his later career reveals not only the way he changed but the extent to which he hoped his work would shape a better world.

After the war, Seuss returned to political cartooning only a handful of times. In the 1980s, he created an anti-drug poster, "Dope! You Need It Like You Need a Hole in the Head!" In 1972, he drew a cover for *San Diego Magazine*: the illustration, titled "Leave Something Green," was used (with his permission) by Citizens to Save Open Space, a group trying to curb overdevelopment.[7] In 1956, he wrote "Signs of Civilization," a pamphlet opposing billboards in La Jolla; writing it lost him his account with Holly Sugar, for whom he was then writing advertisements (Morgan and Morgan 147). And in a 1947 issue of the *New Republic*, he published a cartoon critical of anti-Communist hysteria.[8] Apart from occasional projects such as these, his politics emerge after 1945 only in his children's books and not in political cartoons. Having drawn cartoons that encouraged the United States to join the war, Seuss felt an obligation to join the fight himself. As he later recalled, "When the United States got into the war I started receiving a lot of letters saying I was a dirty old man who had helped get us into the war, and I was too old to fight. So I enlisted" (Webb A21). During 1942, he contributed cartoons to *Victory* and designed posters for the Treasury Department and the War Production Board. His last *PM* cartoon appeared on January 6, 1943. On January 7, the 39-year-old Theodor Seuss Geisel became a captain in the Army's "Information and Education Division." He worked in California under Major Frank Capra at what was known as "Fort Fox," making animated and documentary films in support of the Allied war effort.

Dr. Seuss Goes to War

Captain Geisel's one venture into the war itself happened in November and December of 1944 when he visited Europe to premiere one of his educational films before military personnel. In a pocket-sized notebook, he kept a diary of his trip. Confirming his belief that dictators starve their people ("'we need food! We are starving!' groaned Mack"), while visiting Germany Geisel found "Poverty more apparent here. People digging in garbage cans" (61). He visited concentration camps at Strudhof and Shirmek, took notes, and found "enough horror" to "condemn the Nazi system forever" ("Atrocities"). In a memo written after his visit, he stressed that the United States should not make any claims about the camps unless the claims could be verified because "If we overplay one detail, and have to retract, our audience will be apt to disbelieve everything" ("Atrocities").[9] What he says about accurate reporting underscores his philosophy of writing for children: if you want them to trust you, then you have to level with them. "Children welcome good writers who talk, not down to them as juveniles, but clearly and honestly as equals," he often said ("Pied Piper of Bookland").

Geisel already had faith in the persuasive power of straight talk, and his trip to Europe confirmed his belief that children need ideological education—especially the children of former Axis nations. In his notebook, he wrote a list of four "Problems" that the postwar German citizenry would face: "digging out streets," "Police force," "Children. Education," "Coal—but how to get it in" (62o). As the notebook indicates, for Geisel the education of children was as important as transportation, law, and fuel. Similarly, in *Your Job in Germany*, his screenplay advises soldiers that German youth "are the most dangerous" because they "were brought up on straight propaganda—products of the worst educational crime in the entire history of the world." As the voice-over tells us, "Practically everything you believe they were brought up to hate." In lectures he gave at the University of Utah in July 1949, Seuss returns to the subject again, noting that "Dictators [. . .] indoctrinated kid's [*sic*] minds politically. (A Job the US Army is trying to undo now)." As Henry Jenkins puts it, "What horrified Seuss about fascism was what he saw as its exploitation of children's minds and bodies, its transformation of education into indoctrination" (194–95). In his children's books, Seuss hoped to guide children to become thoughtful citizens who would, in turn, build a better and more just society. As Seuss writes in an essay published in 1960, "children's reading and children's thinking are the rock bottom base upon which the future of this country will rise. Or not rise." He continues, "In these days of tension and confusion, writers are beginning to realize that books for children have a greater potential for good or evil than any other form of literature on earth" ("Writing for Children: A Mission"). In his post-war message books, Seuss seeks to develop that potential for good, to help children imagine a better future.

In addition to recording his thoughts on how the hopes of a country depend upon the education of its children, his wartime notebook also bears witness to how war shatters people's lives: "We go through a typical destroyed house. Broken toy in the plaster. In a cupboard with the rain soaking through—somebody's hope chest of linens. A doctor's lab. Broken bottles + test tubes. An inch of water on the floor. Take-apart models of a cow + a horse. Chaos." In the margins, he adds, "House shakes with explosions" (59o). Before his European tour ended, he would have firsthand experience of such destruction. One day, he bumped into Ralph Ingersoll, former editor of *PM* and then a lieutenant colonel in army intelligence. Ingersoll offered to show him some fighting in "a quiet sector" that turned out to be anything but quiet. As a result, he ended up behind enemy lines for three days during the Battle of the Bulge. "Nobody came along and put up a sign saying 'This is the Battle of the Bulge,'" Seuss later remembered. "How was I supposed to know?" (Kahn 68). Fortunately, he was later rescued by British troops.

The *PM* cartoons may not have the polish of his books, but they do show us the degree to which World War II influenced not only his later work but all of us who grew up reading that work—books that encouraged us to ask questions instead of accepting answers, and taught us that

even smallish Whos and little turtles can speak out and make a difference. Look at the cartoon from October 1, 1941, and you can see Seuss
already thinking about how books for children shape their beliefs (figure
2.9). In it, a mother named "America First" reads a fable called "Adolf
the Wolf" to her two children: "and the Wolf chewed up the children
and spit out their bones . . . but those were *Foreign Children* and it really
didn't matter," she tells them. As in many of his *PM* cartoons (such as
the "Mein Early Kampf" strips, pictured in figures 2.4 and 2.5), a cat
bears witness to the event, its wide-eyed expression suggesting that we,
too, should keep our eyes open. The cat and two children appear a bit
surprised to hear that Adolf the Wolf's murder of these "Foreign Children" doesn't matter, simply because the children happen to be "Foreign." Like this cartoon, Seuss's children's stories state that it *did* matter
and it *does* matter. For older readers raised on these stories and younger
readers encountering them for the first time, Seuss offers preparation
for the often dangerous world beyond his books, where flawed individuals need to remain mindful of the rights of others, and strive to make
choices that cause the least harm and the most good.

Figure 2.9. ". . . and the Wolf chewed up the
children and spit out their bones . . ." by Dr. Seuss.

Chapter 3

The Doc in the Smock

In addition to offering a moral education, Dr. Seuss's books also provide an artistic one. Seuss himself ventured into art instruction on the afternoon of January 31, 1954, when he, Burgess Meredith, Hans Conried, Dorothy Donahue, and a horse appeared on a live, half-hour television program, broadcast from NBC studios in New York. Written by Seuss, the program—titled "Modern Art on Horseback"— sought to help viewers make sense of modern art. Meredith, portraying an "average American man," meets up with Donahue, playing his wife: they're going to the pictures. When it dawns on him that by "the pictures," she means "an art gallery" and not "the movies," he exclaims, "Modern art! Not that! Not that!" and backs away in terror. They enter the gallery, become confused by what they see, and meet a phony intellectual (played by Conried) who intimidates them further. Then, stepping out of character, Conried admits that modern art baffles him, too: "Why *don't* they draw things that look like what they're supposed to look like?" he asks. Meredith agrees, and suggests that they might undertake an experiment conducted by Dr. Seuss, whom he describes as a "famous artist" and author of "the most widely read humorous children's books in America today." Enter Seuss, who confesses that he knows "very little about Modern Art" but hopes "to learn something" from this experiment: "The thing I want to find out most is . . . when a modern artist paints a picture of a horse . . . why doesn't the horse LOOK like a horse?" To find out, Seuss tells us, "I started the experiment by bringing my horse."

Enter the horse. As Seuss explains, he took a photograph of the horse, and then asked six modern art students from Cooper Union to come and paint pictures of the horse. In the discussion that follows, we learn that they represent the horse in different and often abstract ways in order to present that aspect of the animal that most inspires them— such as rhythm, tiredness, movement, or the idea of capturing multiple

63

perspectives simultaneously. Though the Seuss on TV claims not to know much about modern art, the Seuss who wrote the script clearly did. While he lacked formal artistic training, Seuss had a profound understanding of how art works.

Drawing Upside Down: Seuss's Narrative Art

Though often self-deprecating when speaking of his artistic ability, Seuss was fond of telling at least one story that implied he had an intuitive artistic sense. Asked whether he had any formal education as an artist, Seuss would describe an art class he took at Springfield's Central High School. At "one point during the class," he says, "I turned the painting I was working on upside down—I didn't exactly know what I was doing, but actually I was checking the balance: If something is wrong with the composition upside down, then something's wrong with it the other way." His teacher saw what he was doing and told him, "Theodor, real artists don't turn their paintings upside down" (Cott 18). Feeling that he "wouldn't learn much from that teacher," Seuss "walked out of the class and never took another lesson" (Jordan 25; Steinberg 88).[1] Whether we look at his books upside down or right side up, Seuss does have a keen sense of contrast, perspective, and color. However, to appreciate Seuss's artistic talents, one must first examine the relationship between his art and the story. It is the balance of words and pictures that makes the books work. As John Cech observed after seeing the exhibition *Dr. Seuss from Then to Now*, "when pictures from Seuss's books are displayed on museum walls, one sees how utterly tied most of them are to the printed page and thus to Seuss's texts. For Seuss is a true artist of the picture book, a brilliant master of that bimedial form, more than he is an artist whose visual works can (or are designed to) stand alone" ("Pictures and Picture Books on the Wall" 185). Though Seuss has created art that stands alone (more on that later in the chapter), the picture-book art is always interdependent with his text.

In his books, the art complements the narrative movement of the story, as when Seuss introduces the back-and-forth tension of *Green Eggs and Ham* right in its opening pages. On the first page of the story (page three), Sam-I-am stands atop a dog who bounds to the right. Turning the page, Sam and dog have swept past the seated black-hatted figure on page four and have nearly disappeared from page five: we see only the back halves of Sam and dog as they move ahead, presumably to page six. However, turn the page, and they are not on page six. Nor is Sam moving from left to right: on page seven, he rides a cat leftward, back toward the beginning of the book. The following two pages find Sam vanishing off to the left of page eight, while his foil in the black hat complains that he "do[es] not like / that Sam-I-am!" (9). Just as Sam-I-am and the black-hatted figure will debate the pros and cons of green food, the first pages of Green Eggs and Ham send the reader in opposite directions—first right, and then left. And then right again. On the next two pages (ten and eleven), Sam reverses direction once more, entering from page left and moving toward page right. Turn the page again and the scene is static: Sam stands at left, offering a platter of green food; the figure in the black hat stands at right, proclaiming, "I do not like them, / Sam-I-am. / I do not like / green eggs and ham" (12). Soon Sam will be in pursuit of the fussy eater, and the movement will be consistently toward the right, but Seuss offers one more page where Sam points—using large, red, artificial hands—both to the left and to the right. Constantly sending us to and fro, the art amplifies the central conflict of the story: Sam-I-am promotes the pleasures of eating green eggs and ham, while the taller character resists them.

Even in books without the kind of narrative tension of Green Eggs and Ham, Seuss provides a sense of visual continuity that both under-scores the plot and suggests possibilities beyond it. During three succes-sive two-page spreads of Dr. Seuss's Sleep Book, we first see the round, fuzzy heads of the Foona-Lagoona Baboona; then, the fluffy pom-poms of the Jedd; and finally the spherical, floating Offts. The recurring motif of soft, mostly yellow circular shapes are a subtle thread, visually tying the pictures to one another, as we drift from one bedtime scene to the next. The language enhances the cushiness of the illustrations and veri-fies that "the bed of a Jedd / Is the softest / Of beds in the world / It is said." The Jedd, eyes closed and a smile on his face, sleeps nestled in a U-shaped curve, at the top of a heap of fluffy pom-poms. The word "softest," which recurs when we learn that "he's sleeping right now / On the softest of fluff," makes that pile of pom-poms look very comfy. However, Seussian pictures tend to exceed the boundaries of the poetry, which, in this instance, does not explain why the Jedd's bed would be perched on a cliff, or what prevents a pile of pom-poms from rolling off the cliff, bringing the Jedd down with them. Those questions are left to our imagination, as are the precarious positions of the Offts (who float, unanchored, near another cliff) and the Foona-Lagoona Baboona (who sleep while hanging, one-handed, from a tree). The illustrations mingle comfort with discomfort, lulling us to sleep while hinting at darker possibilities for some of Seuss's sleepers.

That Seuss's art always goes beyond (and sometimes against) his text may explain why the words reviewers most frequently use are "fantastic" and "imaginative." The art conveys the endlessly inventive quality of a Dr. Seuss book: not only do you meet new creatures on each page, but you see much more than the text prepares you to expect. Even in the more restrained illustrative style of *And to Think That I Saw It on Mulberry Street*, the pictures provide ideas not suggested by the verse. Seuss's poetry neither discloses the types of instruments in the brass band nor explains how the elephants came to be blue. The tension between words and pictures sustains readers' interest by inviting them to think about the relationship between the two (Why is the elephant that color? And, later, where did the plane come from?). Seuss explores the practical possibilities of this creative tension in the Beginner Books when he uses illustrations to represent items not on the word lists, such as the umbrella in *The Cat in the Hat*, the telephone in *One fish two fish red fish blue fish*, and the cactus in *Hop on Pop* ("NO PAT NO / Don't sit on that"). As Maria Nikolajeva and Carole Scott write in *How Picturebooks Work*, when there is tension between words and images, this tension "alerts the reader to the interplay inherent in picturebooks" and "argues for a reevaluation of" the interaction between text and pictures (10). By compelling the reader to continue thinking and imagining, the gaps between what we read and what we see give good picture books—like Seuss's—their appeal.

A frequent extratextual element in Seuss's work is the bystander, the (usually) silent witness who signals how we should think or feel. When this character speaks—as the fish does in *The Cat in the Hat*—we suddenly notice.[2] However, even when we don't notice, the character is there, looking on, and he or she is often a bird. In *Horton Hatches the Egg*, a fish looks on as Horton, seasick and sitting on the nest, passes by on a ship: the fish looks surprised. On the opening page of *The Lorax*, a frowning, scraggly bird flies over The Street of the Lifted Lorax. The dark scene and the sad bird establish a tone of loss and despair, as the "you" of the book walks through a polluted landscape. As the Grinch is about to dump the sleigh from the "tiptop" of Mt. Crumpit, a bird looks up, its eye wide open as if it cannot believe what it is seeing. In *Did I Ever Tell You How Lucky You Are?* (1973), "poor Ali Sard" mows his uncle's vast backyard, and a lavender bird looks down on him with sympathy. Different-colored relatives of the bird appear throughout the book, and, on the final page, an orange bird has joined the boy who serves at the tale's audience: both boy and bird smile, recognizing how lucky they are not to be someone or something else. Seuss always uses realistic animals to play the "witness" role, perhaps inviting us to identify with a familiar creature so that we may better understand the fantastic ones. Choose your favorite Seuss book and, with few exceptions,[3] you'll find an animal observer, offering emotional cues.

The presence of these witnesses underscores the multiple and contradictory uses of the narrative frame, a device which Seuss deploys in many of his books. *McElligot's Pool*, *If I Ran the Zoo*, *Scrambled Eggs Super!*, *On Beyond Zebra!*, *If I Ran the Circus*, *I Had Trouble in Getting to Solla Sollew*, *Did I Ever Tell You How Lucky You Are?*, *The Lorax*, and *The Butter Battle Book* are all stories-within-stories. They begin and end in the world or moment of the storyteller, but their action occurs in a separate place or places—either imagined or in the past. In these books, the "observer" characters affirm our status as audience members, reminding us that this is just a story—and that we are watching it unfold from the safe vantage point of the frame. Yet, in the very act of calling attention to the frame these onlookers *break* the frame; as they extend a sympathetic wing (or paw, or fin) to us, they demonstrate that the boundary between "story" and "world" is permeable. In *Did I Ever Tell You How Lucky You Are?*, the five birds, two cats, one dog, one fish, and one rat join with the reader in looking *at* the unfortunate characters, but their facial expressions encourage us to feel *for* these characters, too. Watching the construction of the aptly named Bunglebung Bridge, the fish looks concerned and so prompts our concern: the workers on this project dangle from a pile of planks, lean dangerously from a ladder, balance on a moving pulley, and look as if they and the bridge will come crashing down if we watch for a moment longer. However, that the fish watches accentuates the fact that we, too, are merely looking at this spectacle—we don't need to be involved. In other words, Seuss's witnesses make the story feel both more real and less so. They foster a kind of creative tension, as they draw the reader in and push her away.

Just as that tension may create a more emotionally engaged reader, so may the ways in which Seuss's colors create contrast. By "contrast," I do not only mean the way that (for instance) the difference between the reds and whites on the Cat's hat makes each color more visible, although this meaning of the word is important, too—"contrast enables us to see," as Molly Bang observes (80). Seuss's sense of contrast develops not only from the notion of adjacent colors making each other visible but also from how the fantastic and the realistic throw each other into relief. Perry Nodelman nicely illustrates both senses of contrast when he observes, "The egg that Horton hatches [. . .] is often the only red object on a page otherwise black and white; the only other color in the book, a bluish green, is usually used for the background." In other words, red makes the egg stand out—a conventional sense of contrast. However, as Nodelman suggests, the unconventional sense of contrast really makes the picture work: "In these circumstances, a small amount of red is so attractive that Dr. Seuss uses it to give weight to objects that could not possibly be red—for instance to highlight lightning flashes in a storm" (142). So, then, Seuss often uses unrealistic colors to make an object feel more "real."

This particular stylistic trait of Seuss's emerges most vividly in *The Lorax*. The institutional gray, smudgy browns, and dark blues of the post-industrial wasteland make the subsequent Technicolor brilliance of un-polluted nature that much more striking. At the edge of the opening narrative frame, as the Once-ler "slupps" down the orange Whisper-ma-Phone, the orange—the first bright color of the book—highlights how drab the brown and gray-blue surroundings are. As the Once-ler begins to tell the story of the Lorax, he says, "It all started way back . . . / such a long, long time back . . ." We turn the page to a shock of color. The pinks, oranges, and yellows of the Truffula Trees, the deep blue sky, the aqua-blue pond, and the green grass appear dazzling after the dark pages preceding them. In its intensity, the turn of the page parallels the moment when Dorothy leaves the black-and-white world of Kansas and steps out into Oz, in the 1939 film *The Wizard of Oz*. We experience these scenes as real precisely because they are not: the con-trast between the too-gray world and the too-bright world creates intensity. How real something feels has little to do with its actual reality; intensity makes it feel real, as Seuss's contrast does here.[4]

Rather like turning your picture upside down to ensure that it works when rightside up, Seuss's art embodies the idea that everything depends on its opposite. Reality depends on fantasy, and fantasy on reality—the tension between these notions invigorates the visual experience. So, in his art as in his verse, Seuss brings these two sides into close proximity. The Once-ler drives a covered wagon we recognize into a landscape we do not; ordinary children meet an extraordinary cat. Or these opposing qualities may combine in individual characters, like Gerald McBoing Boing and Mr. Brown (of *Mr. Brown Can Moo!*), who both look like average people but speak only in sound effects. It is in the contact zones between real and fantasy worlds where Seuss's books become exciting. Presenting a world both fantastical and real, Seuss gives us both sides of the looking glass at once. His worlds are recognizable, and utterly foreign—this combination gives his books their appeal.

Cartoons: An Invisible Art

However, Seuss's popularity may work against him when it comes to being recognized for his artistic contributions. As John Cech has speculated, "The common, knee-jerk reaction among many of the taste-setters in academic and library circles is that Seuss is 'too commercial' to be taken seriously, and so he is left to the popular press, where these same critics feel his work more properly belongs in the first place" ("Pictures and Picture Books on the Wall" 185). In other words, there are always academics and librarians for whom popularity incites suspicion. This tendency has manifested itself most recently in dismissal of the *Harry Potter* novels as aesthetically inferior, as a fad, or as successful only due to their marketing: the books' literary merits, and the fact that they caught on prior to the aggressive marketing campaigns, escape Harry's detractors. The popularity problem for Seuss is compounded by the fact that his artistic medium is that of the cartoon—"the invisible art," to borrow the subtitle of Scott McCloud's *Understanding Comics* (1993).

Cartoon artists do not, as a rule, receive the respect and acclaim accorded children's book illustrators who work in other mediums. Of the sixty-six picture books awarded the Caldecott Medal since its inception in 1938, only a very few might be classified as "cartoon art": *Sylvester and the Magic Pebble* (won in 1970), by William Steig, then best known for his *New Yorker* cartoons; David Wiesner's *Tuesday* (1992), which, despite a densely "realistic" visual style, uses successive comic book panels to convey narrative; Wiesner's *The Three Pigs* (2002), which rearranges panels to de- and re-construct narrative; Judith St. George's *So You Want to Be President?* (2001), illustrated by David Small; and Eric Rohmann's *My Friend Rabbit* (2003).[5] Though he never won the top prize, Seuss was not ignored by the Caldecott committee, which gave him Honor Books for *McElligot's Pool* (in 1948), *Bartholomew and the Oobleck* (1950), and *If I Ran the Zoo* (1951). That said, the winning books for those years lack illustrations as memorable as Seuss's: Alvin Tresselt's *White Snow, Bright Snow*, illustrated by Roger Duvoisin (won in 1948); Leo Politi's *Song of the Swallows* (1950); and Katherine Milhous's *The Egg Tree* (1951). I do not mean to suggest that these works are inferior.[6] I do mean to suggest that award committees tend to pass over children's books that use cartoon-style art, as indicated by the critical neglect of books like Jon Agee's *Milo's Hat Trick* (2001) and Crockett Johnson's *Harold and the Purple Crayon* (1955). So, Seuss gets the second prize (the Caldecott Honor), and works that have proven less influential get the first prize (the Caldecott Award).

Although Seuss drew only one bona fide comic strip—the short-lived "Hejji" (April–June 1935)—he was enthusiastic in his support for the medium. "At its best," he said, "the comic strip is an art form of such terrific wumpf! that I'd much rather spend any evening of any week re-reading the beautifully insane sanities of George Herriman's Krazy Kat than to sit myself down in some opera house to hear some smiling Irish tenor murdering Pagliacci" (Seuss, letter to Andy Gump Fepp). Though Seuss may have always preferred comic strips to grand opera, it was not until the 1970s and 1980s that comic art gained the respect accorded "high art" mediums. In 1978, Will Eisner published *A Contract with God* (1978), the graphic novel that coined the term "graphic novel"; in 1985, he wrote *Comics and Sequential Art* (1985), a pioneering critical study of how comics work. In 1986 came what most people consider the definitive graphic novel—the first volume of Art Spiegelman's *Maus*, a memoir of the author's father and the Holocaust.[7] The two volumes of *Maus* won a Pulitzer Prize in 1992, the year after Theodor Seuss

Geisel died. Seuss did ultimately gain critical recognition, winning a Pulitzer Prize in 1984 for "his contribution [. . .] to the education and enjoyment of America's children and their parents" (Morgan and Morgan 255). His artwork, however, has never received comparable respect, in part because he was a cartoonist working in a field (children's books) that did not value cartoon art, and in part because cartoons gained critical acclaim too late for the art of Dr. Seuss to be appreciated during his own lifetime.

Polished Spontaneity: The Development of Seuss's Style

In fairness, though, we must note that Seuss may have compounded this problem. Some artists will tell you how to read their work, but Seuss was more likely to tell you what was wrong with his work.[8] Maurice Sendak speaks of his affection for George Cruikshank, Walter Crane, and Edward Ardizzone; he tells us how he was influenced by Randolph Caldecott, Beatrix Potter, and Winsor McCay. Chris Van Allsburg explains why he feels drawn to the surrealism of René Magritte. Seuss, on the other hand, often confessed that he could not draw. "I still can't draw," he would say. "I always get the knees in wrong, and the tails. I'm always putting in too many tails. I just can't draw, I guess. Take people like the Grinch. I started out to draw a kangaroo and it turns out to be a Grinch. I don't know, all my creatures seem to turn out catlike" (Hammond). He could draw, but his perfectionism led him to be self-critical, a trait which in turn helped to undermine his critical reception.

To establish Seuss's place in art history, we might begin by considering his influences and his evolution as an artist. There are three phases of Seuss's style. The early Seussian style, exemplified by the early magazine cartoons and by *And to Think That I Saw It on Mulberry Street*, has a controlled, restrained sense of line. His stylistic influences—notably Gluyas Williams and Rube Goldberg—are evident but have not yet been synthesized. The classic Seussian style develops gradually in the works after *Mulberry Street*, starting with *Horton Hatches the Egg*, continuing through the wartime cartoons, *McElligot's Pool* and *Bartholomew and the Oobleck*. This style, which we most associate with Dr. Seuss, reaches fruition in *If I Ran the Zoo*, and flourishes up through the books of the early 1970s.

In this classic period, Seuss's work has synthesized and transformed its many influences, including not only the aforementioned cartoonists but also George Herriman, M. C. Escher, Antonio Gaudí, and the Surrealists. Most importantly, Seuss's exuberant, loopy sense of line now roams unhindered across the page, giving his drawings their particular sense of energy: As Seuss's hand moves more freely, his sense of line grows playfully looser, and he permits himself increasingly elaborate architecture. Finally, the later Seussian style is best characterized as uneven, in the senses both of irregular quality and of a bumpier line. In some works, like *The Butter Battle Book*, Seuss matches or exceeds the best work of his classic period; in others, like *The Cat's Quizzer* (1976) or *Hunches in Bunches* (1982), the artwork can be cluttered or sketchy, suggesting an early draft instead of a finished one. One characteristic of all works from the mid-1970s until 1990 is a shakier, even jumpier line—largely attributable to the health problems that accompany aging. In 1976, following surgery to correct glaucoma, Seuss noticed "more distortion" in vision and reported, "Lines seem to move as I draw them" (Morgan and Morgan 228).

While the lines of his earliest drawings lack the verve of his middle period or the shakiness of his late one, the cartoons from the 1920s and 1930s have the virtue of displaying their influences openly. During this period of his artistic apprenticeship, Dr. Seuss published hundreds of these cartoons, most of them appearing in humor magazines like *Judge* and the old *Life* (not the *Life* founded by Henry Luce in 1936). Aware of his affinity for the inventions of Rube Goldberg, Seuss spoofs him in a cartoon from the 19 May 1928 issue of *Judge* (figure 3.1). Attributed to "Rube Goldbrick" though (in fine print) "Really drawn by Dr. Seuss," the cartoon shows "UTTER STRANGER," who "FIRES RIFLE (B) STRIKING TARGET," a bull's-eye on the posterior of a Moravian Chickadee, which stands atop a perch while holding a sashweight. In steps C through F, the Moravian Chickadee awakens and drops the weight onto one side of a see-saw. The resulting action lights the fuse of a "CANNON CRACKER" attached to Officer Kelley's back. When it explodes, he "SMELLS RAT (L)"—Seuss has drawn a picture of a rat here—"AND RINGS IN ALARM." Such inventions recur in the early cartoons: the "Little Midget Shaving Machine" (*Judge*, 17 Dec. 1927), the "Xylophone made entirely out of cats" (*Judge*, 21 July 1928), the "Suitor-Evicting Model" of cuckoo clock (*Judge*, 30 Aug. 1930), and a

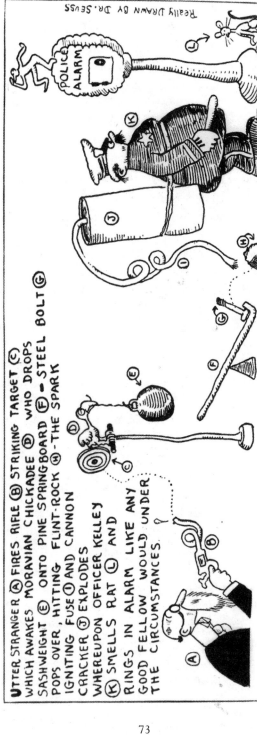

Figure 3.1. "LAUGH IS LIKE THAT!" by Rube Goldbrick (Dr. Seuss)

machine designed to make "soap-bubble blowing [. . .] a truly fascinating pastime" (*Life*, 13 Sept. 1929). As many have observed,[9] unusual gadgets turn up in one form or another in many of Seuss's books: the Bad-Animal-Catching-Machine in *If I Ran the Zoo*, the Star-On and Star-Off Machines in *The Sneetches*, the Wuff-Whiffer ("our Diet-Devising Computerized Sniffer") in *You're Only Old Once!* (figure 3.2), and the Triple-Sling Jigger, the Utterly Sputter, and the Eight-Nozzled Elephant-Toted Boom-Blitz in *The Butter Battle Book*.

Though without the allegorical purpose of *The Butter Battle Book*'s weaponry, the gadgetry of the early cartoons shares a skepticism toward the promise that scientific progress will improve our standard of living. A common theme in Seuss's cartoons for *Judge*, *Life*, and *Liberty* is that the inventions designed for better living will either fail or will require new inventions (and, often, pets) to fix the flaws of the old ones and are likely, in the process, to introduce new problems. To compensate for the short leg on the card table, the Tapered-Tailed Dingo will sit with his head in your lap and his "schwanz" under the table leg (*Liberty*, 11 June 1932). To calm worried investors, Seuss—in a cartoon published one month after the stock market crash—presented an oilcloth ticker tape "which speculators may read under a cold shower thus avoiding high blood pressure" (*Life*, 29 Nov. 1929). Like Gluyas Williams's work (which appeared in many of the same publications), Seuss's magazine cartoons poke fun at the foibles of bourgeois life—the upwardly mobile's penchant for useless gadgets, their drive to attain social status through expensive inventions or animals. In terms of their style, Seuss's pen-and-ink drawings are as detailed as those by Williams, but never quite approach his understated quality. Indeed, during this period, Seuss's lines are thick, even leaden, making the characters look waxy, embalmed, or perhaps possessed. Of the early Seuss, Richard Marschall has aptly observed, "his people wore dazed, almost crazed expressions; drawn with bugged eyes and carefully rendered eyelashes, they seemed like dippy mannequins floating through bizarre tableaux" (*Tough Coughs* . . . 12). Perhaps, in their quest for consumer fulfillment through conspicuous consumption, these people have become products themselves—they have become the mannequins in the store window. Or perhaps Seuss is still learning how to draw.

Through many years of practice, Seuss becomes a more confident draftsman, a fact already in evidence by the time of *Mulberry Street*. From

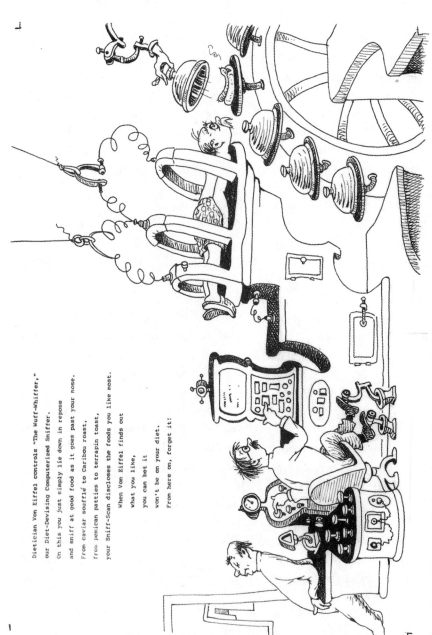

Dietician Von Eiffel controls "The Wuff-Whiffer,"
our Diet-Devising Computerized Sniffer.
On this you just simply lie down in repose
and sniff at good food as it goes past your nose.
From caviar soufflé to Caribou roast,
from pemican patties to terrapin toast,
your Sniff-Scan discloses the foods you like most.
    When Von Eiffel finds out
    what you like,
    you can bet it
    won't be on your diet.
        From here on, forget it!

Figure 3.2. Original finished ink drawing of the Wuff-Whiffer, from *You're Only Old Once!*

that book up to *If I Ran the Zoo*—which, I believe, marks the beginning of his second phase—Seuss's style undergoes a gradual change. It loosens up from the overly controlled style of *Mulberry Street*, growing more free and fluid. Surely, the squiggly trees on mountainsides in *Horton Hatches the Egg*, and the Gaudí-esque architecture behind the flower-loving fish in *McElligot's Pool* begin to chart Seuss's evolution to this second phase. But it is not until the 1950s that Seuss has synthesized his many influences, arriving at this new phase that we would recognize as The Seussian Style. *If I Ran the Zoo*, *Horton Hears a Who!*, *On Beyond Zebra!*, *If I Ran the Circus*, *Happy Birthday to You!*, and other works from the '50s, '60s, and early '70s exemplify the style that is classic Seuss.

Looking at the books from this period, one can see the influence of George Herriman's "Krazy Kat." In *Scrambled Eggs Super!*, the "Great happy gay families with uncles and cousins / All laying fine strictly fresh eggs by the dozens" do their egg-laying amidst zig-zagging pillars of rock similar to those in the "Krazy Kat" landscapes. Except for the fact that Herriman's wildlife generally appears in flower pots, the opening pages and closing page of *Did I Ever Tell You How Lucky You Are?* so resemble Coconino County that one almost expects to see Ignatz's brick flying towards Krazy's noggin. A key difference is that while Herriman's scenery tends to remain in the background, Seuss's is frequently in the foreground, too. It is as if Seuss headed for those chunky, curvy rock formations sprouting along the horizon of a Herriman cartoon, and, upon arriving, so liked what he saw that he decided to set up shop there. When the narrator of *I Had Trouble in Getting to Solla Sollew* (1965) pulls the One-Wheeler Wubble (including its driver and camel), he looks as if he is walking atop the tall and weather-carved natural rock sculptures of the American Southwest, scenery which Herriman favored for his backgrounds. Gilbert Seldes described Herriman's backdrops as "in a continual state of agitation" (17), a phrase which highlights another difference between Seuss and Herriman. Though their landscapes look similar, Herriman plays jokes on the reader, so that from scene to scene small elements of the background will change—a rock will change its shape, a hut will become a church. If these visual switcheroos give Herriman's backgrounds their vitality, the energy in Seuss's come from his keen sense of line.

In his classic works, the verve of Seuss's line beckons the eye to follow it along. Never static, this line is going somewhere, inviting the reader to find out where. On a planet the size of a dust speck, Who-ville in *Horton Hears a Who!* (1954) has freewheeling landscapes with careening curves and a sense of endless, unstoppable movement. As the Mayor rushes "from the east to the west," encouraging citizens to speak up, he does so along a zig-zagging red path that turns up, down, then up stairs, before squiggling off behind a building at the right. In *Happy Birthday to You!*, as "you" and the Birthday Bird ride "two Hooded Klopfers named Alice," the road curves back, forth, down, up, and finally arrives at the "Birthday Pal-alace." A horizontal line, implying stability, may allow the eye to rest, but the swerving yellow line that traveled here seems wild and unpredictable. Given that his line embodies the idea of going places, it is apt that Seuss's final book was *Oh, the Places You'll Go!*

The deliberate sketchiness of Seuss's line helps create this feeling of movement because it allows the illustrations to look as if they are still *being* sketched—almost as if Seuss got up from the drafting table, and invited us to sit in his chair, and look at his latest work-in-progress, its ink still drying. Speculating on why "clumsy drawings" were more appropriate illustrations for nonsense literature than "the more finished productions of the professional artist," Emile Cammaerts claimed that "[t]here must necessarily be a certain unfinished quality in all the works [nonsense] inspires. It cannot be elaborate or well thought out; it must be, or at least seem to be, improvised on the spur of the moment" (70). While I would not be willing to endorse the general principle that non-sense illustrations must appear unfinished—such a claim would disqual-ify (for example) Fred Marcellino's beautiful illustrations for Edward Lear's *The Pelican Chorus*—Cammaerts's idea does describe the feel of the paintings and children's-book artwork from Seuss's classic period. The effect of Seuss's loopy, flowing, energetic line is to make the draw-ing appear to be improvised. We seem to have come upon the drawing as it is being drawn, watching it take shape before our eyes. It is not, of course, improvised. What we see, instead, are the results of a perfection-ist improvising, transforming his influences into something new.

Palmer Cox's *The Brownies: Their Book* (1887) may have inspired Seuss's images of figures in constant motion, drawing the reader's atten-tion in different directions at once. As Seuss says, "I loved the Brown-ies—they were wonderful little creatures; in fact, they probably awakened my desire to draw" (Cott 19). Visually, these little creatures appear to be antecedents of the Whos. In Palmer Cox's drawings, the Brownies are often engaged in so many and different activities that your eye cannot decide where to look first because there's so much going on (figure 3.3). In "The Brownies at the Gymnasium," some swing from "the high trapeze," others hang by their knees from rings, and still others walk on their hands on the parallel bars (39). Similarly, in *How the Grinch Stole Christmas!*, when the Grinch imagines the Whos playing with their toys, there are an array of activities going on, with little Whos skiing downstairs, banging on a big bass drum, stilt-walking, and playing at an unnamed sport while roller-skating (figure 3.4). Whether to depict Whos making noise in *Horton Hears a Who!* or friends arriving from all over Katroo in *Happy Birthday to You!*, Seuss creates drawings with action in many corners of the page. As Cox does with his Brownies, Seuss holds our attention by giving it much to look at.

As M. C. Escher understood, drawings that convey instability or unresolved motion may appeal to a viewer's curiosity. Well before Chris Van Allsburg's *The Mysteries of Harris Burdick* (1984) paid homage to Escher in its "THE THIRD-FLOOR BEDROOM" or David Wiesner used Escher's *Metamorphose III* as the basis of *Free Fall* (1988), Seuss was

Figure 3.3. "The Brownies at the Gymnasium" by Palmer Cox

78

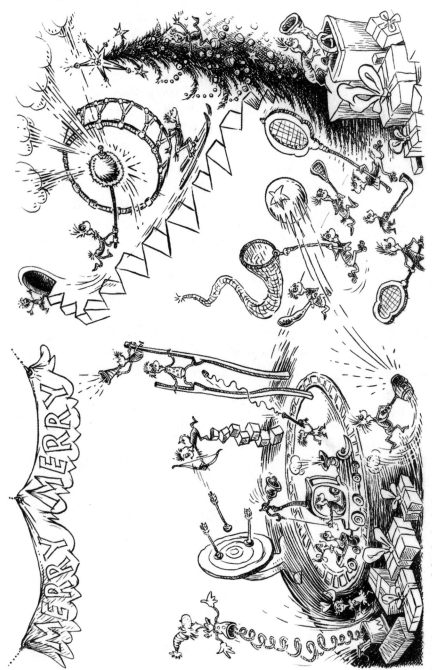

Figure 3.4. Original finished ink drawing from *How the Grinch Stole Christmas!* by Dr. Seuss

incorporating motifs from the great Dutch graphic artist. Echoing Escher's drawings of the *Symmetry Work* series and *Regular Division of the Plane* series, Seuss draws lines of figures going in opposite directions. Though these are not interlocking figures as in Escher's birds in *Symmetry Work 18* or *Day and Night* (both 1938), the To-an-Fro Marchers of *If I Ran the Circus* move are similarly interdependent. The foot of each marcher marching "to" rests on the head of every one marching "fro," and vice versa apparently ad infinitum—they march off the page in each direction, implying that there is no limit as to how many marchers there are. This motif so intrigued Seuss that he returned to it on two separate occasions, first in "The economic situation clarified: A prognostic re-evaluation" (1975), where smiling Sneetch-like creatures achieve upward mobility by stepping on the heads of the downwardly mobile, frowning Sneetch-like creatures (figure 3.5). Underscoring the precariousness of these marchers, Seuss has them marching up (or down) a forty-five degree incline. The accompanying verse explains, "As of now, the Uppers are upping / and the Downers are droobling down / excepting on alternate Thursdays / when it works the other way round." Dramatizing economic instability, some of the birds are out of step, and if the action were to continue, they would fall, possibly bringing the entire structure down with them. The verse minimizes the possibility of total collapse, instead focusing on the hazards for the individual: "And there occasionally are occasions / when some Upper comes a cropper / and bottoms out at the bottom. / *Then* . . . / some Bottomer is the Topper." The motif appears once again in the "Life's a Great Balancing Act" illustration of *Oh, the Places You'll Go!*: in fact, Seuss has used a photocopy of "The economic situation," and simply pasted in his main character (the boy identified only as "you").[10] Hinting at the danger, the "you" who leads us through the book is walking downward, his right foot pushing off from the head of one of the bird marchers, and his left foot about to land in thin air—the marcher coming in the opposite direction is not yet close enough for him to land safely.

If I Ran the Circus was published just after a dramatic rise of interest in M. C. Escher in the early 1950s,[11] suggesting that Escher's popularity caught Seuss's attention. On the other hand, given the Escher-like staircases and architecture in some of the early paintings reproduced in *The Secret Art of Dr. Seuss* (1995), it's possible that Escher's work had caught Seuss's attention before the 1950s. It difficult to say exactly when Seuss

**The economic situation clarified:
A prognostic re-evaluation**

By The Dr. Seuss Surveys

As our graph shows, Trends are trending.
This is good. Yet, nevertheless,
the destination of the trendlings
is not simple to assess.

As of now, the Uppers are upping
and the Downers are droobling down
excepting on alternate Thursdays
when it works the other way round.

And there occasionally are occasions
when some Upper comes a cropper
and bottoms out at the bottom.
Then . . .
some Bottomer is the Topper.

Consequently, on the other hand,
I believe this can be said:
you'll be wise if you step gently
whilst you tread on your neighbor's head.

Dr. Seuss—whose grown-up name is Theodor
Seuss Geisel—says it has been 17 years since he
last addressed himself to adults, and does so now
because he is "plain worried about the economy."

Figure 3.5. "The economic situation clarified" by Dr. Seuss

first met Escher's art, just as we cannot know when he may have come into contact with the work of Antonio Gaudí.[12] Nonetheless, Seuss's buildings share features in common with those of Gaudí. Antonio Gaudí once answered critics of his work by claiming that "there are no straight lines in nature" (Duncan 52). This phrase aptly describes Dr. Seuss's architecture: the curvy buildings both echo and amplify the landscape surrounding them. In *If I Ran the Zoo*, the arch bearing the words "City Zoo, G. McGrew, Manager" recalls arches of Art Nouveau in general and Gaudí in particular. It both complements the trees on either side of the zoo entrance and anticipates the more elaborate "McGrew's Zoo" archway and gates we will see when Morris returns "from the wilds of Nantasket" later in the book. Beyond incorporating the twists and turns of the natural world, Seuss's curvy architecture frequently makes his imaginary worlds more exotic. Even more brightly colored than Gaudí's ceramic-tiled Park Güell and Casa Batlló, the cities of Solla Sollew and Katroo promise pleasures new and foreign.[13] The many and curved windows and doors of these deliberately unconventional buildings invite the eye to peer in and to ponder the mysteries of their construction. As a side note, upon first reading these books, I also thought that these structures would be great places to play. When I was a child, I liked to climb things (trees, rocks, furniture), and I can remember finding Katroo's multiple stairways and archways inviting—I wanted to explore them all, with or without the Birthday Bird. Looking at them as an adult, I am content to do all the exploring with my eyes; the thought of entering those gravity-defying structures gives me vertigo.

If the prolific curves, archways, and staircases of Seuss's architecture display the influences of Gaudí and Escher, his buildings and objects also draw upon memories from home. That is, his works frequently find inspiration in the places Seuss lived, and especially the two places where he lived for the longest periods of time—Springfield, Massachusetts and La Jolla, California. He grew up in Springfield, lived in New York City from 1927 to 1943, and lived in La Jolla (which he first visited in 1928) from 1948 until his death in 1991. Seuss's first book most obviously incorporates places familiar to him: Mulberry Street, which runs into Bliss Street in Springfield, just as it does in *And to Think That I Saw It on Mulberry Street*. Its police officers ride red motorcycles, the traditional color of Springfield's Indian Motorcycles.[14] However, the works in Seuss's middle (or classic) period do the most interesting job of synthesizing and transforming these influences. Though *The Lorax* was written during a trip to Kenya, its rolling hills (and arches, for that matter) could also have been inspired by La Jolla. Seuss's studio window in his home atop La Jolla's Mount Soledad provided beautiful views of the surrounding hills. While *The Lorax*'s hills may resemble La Jolla's, its factories recall Springfield's. The Once-ler's Thneeds factory recalls the Springfield Gas Company, as it would have looked in the early 1920s, at about the time Seuss was to leave Springfield for Dartmouth College (figures 3.6 and 3.7). As a former Massachusetts boy living in California, Dr.

Figure 3.6. Springfield Gas Company, c. 1920s

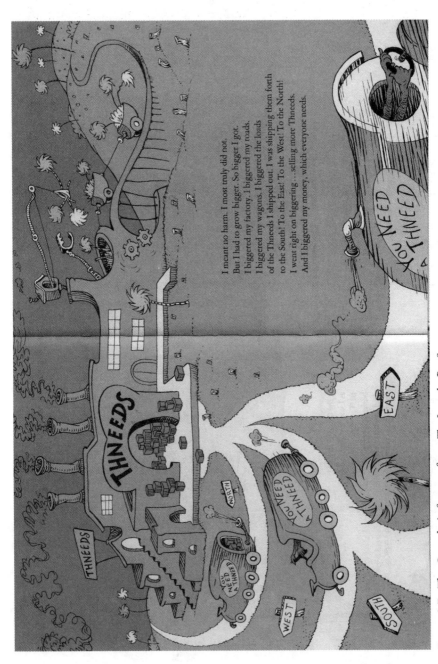

I meant no harm. I most truly did not.
But I had to grow bigger. So bigger I got.
I biggered my factory. I biggered my roads.
I biggered my wagons. I biggered the loads
of the Thneeds I shipped out. I was shipping them forth
to the South! To the East! To the West! To the North!
I went right on biggering...selling more Thneeds.
And I biggered my money, which everyone needs.

Figure 3.7. The Once-ler's factory, from *The Lorax* by *Dr. Seuss*.

Seuss combined the influences of either side of the United States, commingling Springfield's architecture with La Jolla's architecture and landscape.

Whether due to failing health or faltering inspiration (or both), the books from the mid-1970s on are a mixed bag. Since dwelling on the artistic shortcomings of *The Cat's Quizzer, I Can Read with My Eyes Shut!* (1978) or other less visually compelling works would be neither challenging for me to write nor interesting for you to read, we will instead focus on two masterpieces from Seuss's late period, starting with *The Butter Battle Book*. When examining the book closely, the wobbliness in his line grows apparent, and some of his distinctive waviness seems to have diminished. However, if we step back and look at two-page spreads, his drawings—of the wall, the hills, most trees—retain the fluid, undulating movement characteristic of Dr. Seuss. In any case, even if his line lacks some of the effortless feel of earlier work, the book's art gains strength in its willingness to pare down. Just as the culmination of the book's weaponry is destructive power at its most condensed, so the emotional power of the book's art derives from its conciseness. While there is still more activity in these illustrations than in, say, the spare drawings of Crockett Johnson's picture books, *The Butter Battle Book* is much more visually succinct than *Horton Hears a Who!* or almost any of the larger Seuss books. Without the typical level of detail, *Butter Battle* relies on a few repeated visual tropes: the arched doorway to the Boys in the Back Room, the gadgets, the wall, the hills, the houses, and the trees. As the trees do on the road to Solla Sollew, the trees here reflect the main character's emotional state. When the Yook solider and Daniel the Kick-a-Poo Spaniel (likely descended from Max, the Grinch's dog) stride into battle, the leaves on the treetops look springy, full of energy. After being "bested and beat" by Van Itch, the Yook warrior "dragged" and "sagged," as do the leaves above him. As the physical embodiment of the division between the countries, the thick, chunky wall—remarkably realistic, for a Seuss drawing—grows taller as the enmity between Yooks and Zooks escalates. As our Yook narrator explains, initially "the Wall wasn't so high / and I could look any Zook / square in the eye." The wall grows from about waist height for the first few confrontations, to shoulder height by the time that Van Itch unveils the Zooks' Jigger-Rock Snatchem. When Van Itch rides in on the Zooks' Eight-Nozzled, Elephant-Toted Boom-Blitz, the wall is higher than either character's head. Finally, the wall approaches the height (if not the width) of the Great Wall of China. The expanding wall dramatizes the growing conflict, while the identical houses and trees on either side remind us of how much Yooks and Zooks have in common, and consequently how little reason they have to go to war. Much as he has simplified the nuclear arms race into one Yook versus one Zook, Seuss has pared down his illustrations, sharpening our perspective by guiding us to the basic symbols of the story.

Where the art of *The Butter Battle Book* condenses one book's worth of themes into a few tropes, the illustrations of *Oh, the Places You'll Go!* distill an entire career's worth. Seuss has always recycled, of course. *On Beyond Zebra!*'s Umbus—a "sort of a Cow," but with "ninety-eight faucets"—shows up in "Americanizing the Milk Industry" (*Judge*, 22 Sept. 1928), "The head eats . . . . . . the rest get milked" (*PM*, 19 May 1941), and "The Great McGrew Milk Farm" (*Children's Activities*, Apr. 1955).[15] However, in *Oh, the Places You'll Go!*, Seuss offers his greatest hits, both visually and morally. In this summation of Seuss's art and ideas, a two-page illustration of striped pillars that balloon outward as they extend upward recalls a two-page spread in *Oh, the Thinks You Can Think!*, where a fluffy-eared horse trots between red-and-white striped pillars that rise up from a field of pink. The stripes convey a sense of motion, and the columns extend beyond the edges of the page, suggesting heights beyond what we can see. This brightly colored, dynamic picture emphasizes the possibility suggested by the accompanying verse: "You can think about red. / You can think about pink. / You can think up a horse. / Oh the THINKS you can think!" The analogous illustration in *Oh, the Places You'll Go!* enhances this effect by including "perspective" lines of black and yellow that stretch back to a similarly striped vertical plane that rises up behind the pillars and their billowing stripes of red, white, pink, and blue. Adding more colors and angles for the striped patterns further enhances the optimism of the verse, which here exclaims "*OH! THE PLACES YOU'LL GO!*"

As Seuss's recycling of *If I Ran the Circus*'s To-an-Fro Marchers reminds us, some of the places you'll go may elicit anxiety, sadness, or dread. As "you" of *Oh, the Places You'll Go!* rows his small boat up the "frightening creek" where "the Hakken-Kraks howl," the darkness and fear recalls the scene on Roover River when the "I" of "What Was I Scared Of?" rows away from the pair of pale green pants with nobody inside them. In both instances, the main character is alone in a rowboat, in the dark: in the earlier tale, empty pants in active pursuit of our hero creates a feeling of suspense; in *Oh, the Places You'll Go!*, the size of the Hakken-Kraks and the apparently limitless expanse of water dramatize the danger of the situation. As Seuss's narrator warns on the previous two-page spread of *Oh, the Places You'll Go!*, "All Alone! / Whether you like it or not, / Alone will be something / you'll be quite a lot."[16] Despair can come in groups, too. Though lines of people recur with some regularity in Dr. Seuss's work, *Oh, the Places You'll Go!* uses them to symbolize hopelessness. Just as the line of Hawtchers "watching on Watch-Watcher-Watchering-Watch" do in *Did I Ever Tell You How Lucky You Are?*, the lines of people at the Waiting Place in *Oh, the Places You Go!* stretch out into the distance beyond the page's edges. Time has grown stagnant here, and these people will be standing around indefinitely.

Ultimately, though, *Oh, the Places You'll Go!* suggests that by not standing around, we can succeed. Reviving an image from *Scrambled Eggs Super!*, *Oh, the Places You'll Go!* has "you" move a mountain propped up on supports attached to wheels: the hyperbole of this picture conveys a sense of determined optimism. Similarly upbeat in the earlier book, Peter T. Hooper moved the massive Zinzibar-Zanzibar tree, propped up on supports strapped to elephants. These pictures convey their faith through overstatement. It is preposterous for these elephants to be transporting such a massive tree or for "you" to be pulling an entire mountain on wheels. Much in the way that a tall tale does, these illustrations use exaggeration to create belief. Emphasizing this message of exaggerated optimism, the verse to the illustration in *Oh, the Places You'll Go!* asks, "And will you succeed? / Yes! You will, indeed! / (98 and 3/4 percent guaranteed) / KID, YOU'LL MOVE MOUNTAINS!" Though Dr. Seuss's books are not always optimistic, *Oh, the Places You'll Go!* does suggest that those who struggle against adversity are more likely to prevail than those who do not. As the narrator of *Solla Sollew* explains when he returns home to the Valley of Vung, "I've bought a big bat. / I'm all ready, you see. / Now my troubles are going / To have troubles with me!" *Oh, the Places You'll Go!* offers a similar verse: "I know you'll hike far / and face up to your problems / whatever they are." Their accompanying pictures are different, but their messages are similar, telling readers that if they keep trying, they may go places.

Seussism

Though his status as cartoonist-illustrator may have denied Seuss entry into the museums of respectability, this same status might have helped his imagination to go places. That is, the freedom of being a cartoonist-illustrator may have liberated Seuss from adhering to the "respectable" styles of the day, giving him license to borrow widely and eclectically from other arts. In *The Great Comic Book Heroes* (1965, repr. 2003), Jules Feiffer eloquently describes such creative permissiveness as one of the virtues and pitfalls of working in comics or cartoons, media considered to be "junk" (72). As he puts it,

> Junk is a second-class citizen of the arts; a status of which we and it are constantly aware. There are certain inherent privileges in second-class citizenship. Irresponsibility is one. Not being taken seriously is another. Junk, like the drunk at the wedding, can get away with doing or saying anything because, by its very appearance, it is already in disgrace. It has no one's respect to lose; no image to endanger. Its values are the least middle-class of all the mass media. That's why it is needed so. (73)

In other words, perhaps working in a "junk" medium made Seuss feel he was allowed to ignore the critical consensus. Perhaps the medium granted him the creative space he needed to experiment, allowing him to develop a style that one reviewer described as "a blend of Dali and Goldberg" (Hines, "The Cat and the Hat"). Certainly, the paintings Seuss did for his own amusement represented just such a free space.

These paintings, collected in *The Secret Art of Dr. Seuss* (1995), have inspired the most insightful analyses to date of Seuss the artist. In his review of the book, Jon Agee offers what may be the first fully fledged definition of Seussism:

> Seussism (*Soos-izm*), n. Fine Arts. A style of art characterized chiefly by a grandubulous sense of ornamentation and color, where exotic, snergelly architecture twists, turns and schloops into countless grickelly filigrees and flourishes, and rippulous shapes loom about in space as if they were some kind of new-fangled noodles let loose in zero gravity.

Playfully adopting Seussian language, Agee identifies some key traits: a strong sense of color, architecture that "twists and turns," and a rangy, unfurling looseness—"noodles let loose in zero gravity." In his introduction to the book, Maurice Sendak touches on similar motifs, notably the squiggly, kinetic movement; the vibrant color; and an otherworldliness suggestive of dreams. Sendak describes the "slippery, sloppery, curvy, altogether delicious Art Deco palazzos [that] invited you to slide and bump along, in and out of flaming colored mazes [. . .], and past grand, even apocalyptic, oceans and skies." Adding to these "slippery" qualities, Sendak characterizes "the private Seussian dreamscape" as a place "where loops and hoops and squares and limp bagel shapes, all charged with exotic color, have the demented nightmare effects provoked by a dinner of green eggs and ham." Where Agee invokes outer space as a metaphor for the unusual, Sendak speaks of "exotic color" and the "nightmare effects" of Sam-I-am's favorite food. But both pick up on the Surrealism within Seussism.

Surrealism, Cubism, Art Nouveau, Art Deco, and cartoons—some of the many styles Seuss synthesizes in his work—all emphasize the subjectivity of perception. In this sense, Seussism develops along an artistic trajectory that stretches from Impressionism to Post-Impressionism to Modernism. On those few occasions when he does not mock his artistic abilities, Seuss ventures to classify his work within specific artistic genres but seems unable (or unwilling) to settle on one specific style or movement. Indicating that he might classify his artwork among the modernists, Seuss describes his paintings as "fragmented modern" (Lyon 10). Seuss, who had a Picasso hanging on his wall (Burchell 91), certainly had an affinity for modernist art, and several of the paintings in The Secret Art of Dr. Seuss bear the influence of Cubism.[17] For instance, in Cat Detective in the Wrong Part of Town (1969), Seuss has painted angular apartment buildings from several perspectives at once. As his eyesight began to falter, Seuss even described his vision in terms of Cubism. In the early 1980s, explaining the effects of his eye surgery, Seuss invoked both Picasso and Whistler to characterize his particular Cubist perspective. "I've slowed down because of my second cataract operation," he said. "It was impossible for me to mix a palette—I didn't know which colors were which. With my cataract I had two color schemes—red became orange, blue became slightly greenish: my left eye was like Whistler and the right one was like Picasso—seeing things straight and clear in primitive colors" (Cott 15). Two eyes juxtaposing two different scenes *could* be called Cubism. Or, given that one eye sees like Picasso and the other like Whistler, perhaps such a way of seeing should be called a blend of Cubism and Impressionism? Seuss does not provide further clarification, but he never suggests that his aesthetic inclinations extend further back than Impressionism. In 1968, preparing for an exhibition of his paintings, Seuss offered the following characterization of his artwork: "You could call it impressionism or expressionism. At any rate it's not realistic. There are reminiscences of Dr. Seuss in each of them" (Shepard).

His willingness to locate his work within modernist and pre-modernist art shows that Seuss knew more about art history than he usually admitted. The "Dr. Seuss" persona who granted interviews or narrated a television program about modern art may pretend to be naïve, but Theodor Seuss Geisel, author of that program's script, knew what he was talking about. In the program, "Modern Art on Horseback," after one of the Cooper Union students explained that they had to learn how to draw realistically before they graduated into a more abstract style, Seuss says, "I'm glad you explained that. [. . .] I think it's important for everyone out there to know that you young modern artists *can* draw things just exactly like they look . . . if you want to. But you don't want to . . . that's OK with me." This can be said of Seuss himself. Despite his tendency to protest that his style was a way of compensating for his limited talents, he did in fact know how to draw realistically but chose to draw abstractly. And that's the true "secret at the heart of *The Secret Art of Dr. Seuss*," as Art Spiegelman says in "The Doc in the Smock," his review of the book. Seuss would

really like to have been considered a capital-A Artist. The joke, of course, is that he was. A Real Original. He imposed a unique sensibility onto the world; redefined what children's literature could be [. . .]; operated throughout his career with an exemplary integrity and shaped more psyches than most artists working in the traditional heroic molds. Like many culture workers in the Low Art ditches, even an artist as overwhelmingly successful as Dr. Seuss—in aesthetic as well as economic terms—learned to develop a slouching inferiority complex.

However, as Spiegelman concludes, "Theodore Geisel was some kind of capital-A Artist, and he rarely stumbled."

Spiegelman is correct, and to fully understand why, we need to recognize that, whether we classify Seuss's work as low art or high art, Theodor Seuss Geisel was a talented artist. In his *Comics and Sequential Art*, Will Eisner suggests that the "cartoon is a form of impressionism" because the "cartoon is the result of exaggeration and simplification" (151). Seuss's cartoons *are* impressionist, exaggerated and simplified both. Eisner's comment nicely hints at a link between high art and low art: if cartoons are a form of Impressionism, then we can see the common ground shared by an "invisible" art form (cartoons) and an acclaimed one (Impressionist painting). This high-art-low-art connection is vital to make here because, artistically, Seuss is a cultural sponge. He absorbs the styles of twentieth-century artistic movements and transforms them into his own unique style, an energetic cartoon surrealism. I use these three words—*energetic cartoon surrealism*—to define Seussism because (as I have shown) two defining features of his style are the energy of his line and his roots in cartooning.

As for Surrealism, though Seuss might balk at being called a surrealist, his style and his goals—to use nonsense to awaken the brain cells (as he liked to put it)—are more closely aligned with the Surrealists than with any other artistic movement. Stylistically, there's something in the twists, turns, and slipperiness that brings to mind melting clocks, work boots sprouting human toes, and other incongruous juxtapositions. As one review of *You're Only Old Once!* put it, Seuss's cartoons are "[r]ound and billowing, in pink, blue, green and yellow, as if sculptured in ice cream" (Smith). The loopy-ness of Seuss's style, nicely captured here in the image of sculptured ice cream, brings to mind the drippy and leaking objects in the works of Salvador Dalí and Yves Tanguy. One reason is that Seuss knew the works of the Surrealists, whose influence is on display in *The Secret Art of Dr. Seuss*. As Jon Agee wrote in his review of *The Secret Art*,

A couple of strange, hallucinogenic landscapes recall the paintings of Max Ernst or Yves Tanguy—except that in each case, somewhere in the scene, there's a cat. Surrealism, even Cubism, is apparent, as in the fractured perspective of a city where a feline detective pursues its quarry. The titles of the paintings

("The Rather Odd Myopic Woman Riding Piggyback on One of
Helen's Many Cats") are comparable to those of the Dadaists.

Echoing Agee's remarks in his review, Art Spiegelman noted that Seuss's
art "owes much to Paul Klee, Max Ernst, Yves Tanguy and the rest of
the European Surrealist guys." Some of the paintings seem to refer directly to the historical avant-garde. The oppressively angular, geometric
shapes of Seuss's *Minor Cat in a High-Yield Emerald Mine* (undated) bear
a stylistic similarity to those in Oscar Domínguez's *Nostalgia for Space*
(1939).

Usually, however, Seuss seems to adopt a Surrealist technique without any particular Surrealist work in mind. In an untitled painting that
might be characterized as "Rube Goldberg Surrealism," mechanized industry and men in military uniforms appear to be inflicting pain on a
naked woman. Like many surrealist works, the painting creates an analogy but neglects to indicate precisely *what* the analogy means: does the
image condemn *or* take pleasure in sadism against women? It's difficult
to say. The tendency of Seuss's creatures to metamorphose into other
objects—often into machines, as they do in this painting—recalls Kurt
Seligmann's *Life Goes on* (1942) as well as some of the *Exquisite Corpse*
experiments by Breton, Yves Tanguy, and others. In the Surrealists' *Exquisite Corpse* game, Jacques Hérold might draw a neckless violin in the
top fourth of the paper, extending two parallel vertical lines down from
his image, and then fold down his contribution to prevent his colleagues
from seeing it. He would then pass the paper on to Breton, who draws
a naked, six-breasted female torso, folding down what he had drawn
before giving Tanguy a turn. And so on. When unfolded, four disparate
images make a single figure (in this case, having the head of a violin).
Similarly, Seuss's paintings of incongruous images convey the impression
that various sections of the drawing had never met until the drawing was
finished.

Stylistically, some of Seuss's work bears the hallmarks of surrealist
art, but, ideologically, much more of his work might be classified as
surrealist. As I argue in *The Avant-Garde and American Postmodernity*, the
strongest link between Seuss and the twentieth-century avant-garde is
that both want their art to stimulate thought. Whether raising specific
political questions or simply encouraging creative thinking, Dr. Seuss
strives to engage the audience of his work—whether that work be paint-

ings, picture books, or even a museum. Just as Dadaists and Surrealists strove to break down the boundary between art and audience, so Seuss conceived of a museum that would break down the boundary between exhibit and visitor. As E. J. Kahn tells us, in 1956 Seuss "wrote and acted in an 'Omnibus' television show devoted to an imaginary Seuss Museum. It differed from the general run of museums in that children going through it were not forbidden to touch the displays; on the contrary, the exhibits were all marked 'Do Touch.'" Seuss explained, "I want a museum that will have a real, operable printing press alongside a shelf of books, and blocks of wood and chisels alongside woodcuts, so that children can watch and work at the same time" (Kahn 80). While this may have started out as a purely imaginary exercise, he soon set about drawing up plans to make exactly such a museum. In these plans, under the heading "Purposes," Seuss writes, "To help a child's imagination get off the ground before it's pinned down to the ground forever." In order to inspire children to keep thinking, Seuss conceived of the museum as never being finished, but always being in flux so that children could perpetually be involved in creating it. As he put it, "I would keep the museum forever in an uncompleted state . . . not a state of confusion, but a state of challenge. Pitting the fresh (but usually impractical) excitement of youth against the mature (but usually stuffy and stodgy) wisdom of us elders." For example, he envisioned an "ever-changing pathway" between two wings of the museum. One year, children would work "under the supervision of a Mexican brick maestro" to make a brick pathway. Three years later, perhaps they would remake the walkway as a glass-and-tile mosaic. Later still, the children might "dig it up and replace it with a red wood boardwalk." In this way, he hoped to provoke children to think, to be creative, and to challenge the grownups. As he put it, "I want to see a bunch of scrappy kids talking back to us. And I want to sit back among the elders and tell that kid, 'O.K., Bud, I think, according to my experience, you're wrong. But if you're so sure of yourself that you think the back steps should be painted magenta—get your gang together and paint them magenta. We'll buy you the paint'" (Seuss, "Kids' Participation in Building the Museum"). Although that project never materialized, with Seuss's help one wing of La Jolla's Museum of Art has been devoted to an interactive museum, embodying the philosophy that children be allowed to experiment. As a *Newsweek* article reported in 1967, "grade-school kids excitedly picked through piles of Barbie-doll heads, eyeballs, limbs, and torsos for parts to build an abstract model of a city. Elsewhere, they lugged $2,100 movie cameras about to film the summertime activity at the museum" ("The Logical Insanity of Dr. Seuss" 58).

For any style of art to gain a permanent place in a museum, it needs to be instantly recognizable, and it needs to inspire followers. Seussism has met the first requirement: his style is uniquely recognizable, and his art is distinctive enough to merit its own adjective, "Seussian," a term also applied to his verse. In Douglas Carter Beane's play As Bees in Honey Drown (1997), con artist Alexa Vere de Vere says of the Hotel Paramount's lobby, "It's not so much a lobby as a lobby as told to Theodor Geisel" (7–8). The "sensuous, loony physicality" (to borrow Sendak's description) of Theodor Seuss Geisel's architecture is sufficiently famous for Beane to know that his audience will get the reference.

As for the second requirement, the Seussian aesthetic (Seussism) has shaped the imaginations of visual artists, albeit not as many as one might expect. As both a style and an outlook, Seussism has influenced filmmaker Tim Burton and illustrator Lane Smith. Burton says that, when he was growing up, Rudolph the Red-Nosed Reindeer and How the Grinch Stole Christmas! were his favorite holiday specials. In The Nightmare Before Christmas (1993), he paid tribute to these influences by "design[ing] something that's sort of like the reverse of that—it's like the Grinch in reverse" ("The Making of Tim Burton's The Nightmare Before Christmas"). He calls the film "the Grinch in reverse" because Nightmare protagonist Jack Skellington so likes Christmas that he takes it over, whereas the Grinch so hates Christmas that he tries to stop it. The film's visuals are a kind of reverse Seuss, too. That is, Christmastown has the feel of Seuss's illustrations, but Halloweentown (Skellington's domain) looks more like a Dr. Seuss book as drawn by Edward Gorey. As the film's director Henry Selick says, Halloweentown is "German Expressionism combined with Dr. Seuss" ("The Making of . . .").[18] In contrast, when Jack arrives in Christmastown, Selick explains that "there's an overall more 'Dr. Seuss' feel to these hills [. . .] Things [in Christmastown] are softer, more toylike, and far more colorful" (DVD audio commentary).

Though the filmmakers do not mention it, the closest cinematic antecedent for Nightmare may not be Chuck Jones's animated Grinch but Seuss's own The 5,000 Fingers of Dr. T (1953), a live-action musical closer in mood to Gorey or Burton than to most of Seuss's works. A nightmare dreamed by reluctant piano player Bart Collins, *5,000 Fingers* has an air of menace usually absent from Seuss's picture books. Much as the architecture of Burton's Halloweentown does, the Dr. Terwilliker Institute's tall, curvy towers and their Seussian gargoyles seem to leer at the characters below (figure 3.8). Burton, who says that "Dr Seuss's books were perfect" and offered "great subversive stories" (Salisbury 19), provides ample subversion in his film, too. *Nightmare*, like *5,000 Fingers*, challenges the wisdom of adults through its trickster characters. Jack Skellington, a "good" trickster, kidnaps Santa and turns Christmas into a nightmare. At least Skellington's motives are not all bad: loving Christmas but unable to understand it, he gets the idea to run it himself. On the other hand, Oogie Boogie, the parent figure for three children (Lock, Shock, and Barrel), is a purely malevolent creature, interested only in his own sadistic pleasures. More like Oogie Boogie than Jack Skellington, Seuss's Dr. Terwilliker (played by Hans Conried) is a mean trickster. He plots to enslave five hundred boys to play his massive piano, and when Bart Collins tells this to another adult—the otherwise likeable Mr. Zablodowski—that adult does not believe him. In both films, the surreal, intimidating architecture dramatizes the dangers facing the characters, making Seuss's Bart and Burton's Sally look small and powerless. Not only are they without reliable adult figures, but they are imprisoned by the buildings they inhabit.

Though a bit less dark than Tim Burton, Lane Smith also has a feel for the subversive. Though Smith does not claim Dr. Seuss as an influence, he does mention reading Seuss's books as a child[19] and, with Jack Prelutsky, helped create *Hooray for Diffendoofer Day!* based on an unfinished manuscript by Dr. Seuss. In *Diffendoofer Day*, and as the illustrator of *The True Story of the Three Little Pigs by A. Wolf* (1989) and *The Stinky Cheese Man* (1992) by Jon Scieszka (who frequently cites Seuss's influence[20]), Lane Smith has had the opportunity to create illustrations that develop the rebellious side of children's picture books. As Seuss and Burton do, Smith uses caricature to enhance the disruptive elements of the tale. When Thidwick's big-mouthed guests yell their refusal to leave his horns, Seuss has exaggerated the size of their mouths so that some of the birds have mouths that seem larger than their heads. Taking this approach a step further, Lane Smith's hen in *The Stinky Cheese Man* has a mouth that is much larger than her head. Adding to the boisterous effects of such caricature, both authors favor characters that stare di-

Figure 3.8. "The Terwilliger Institute." Sketch by Dr. Seuss.

rectly at the reader, as A. Wolf of *The True Story*, Jack of *The Stinky Cheese Man*, Thidwick, and Yertle all do. Frequently, these illustrations accompany text that addresses the reader: Jack, looking sideways at us as he explains the upside-down dedication page, says, "If you really want to read it—you can always stand on your head." Thidwick looks at us, as the text asks the reader an earlier version of the questions that conclude *The Cat in the Hat*: "NOW what was the big-hearted moose going to do? / Well, what would YOU do / If it happened to YOU?" These similarities notwithstanding, Lane Smith is not as visually Seussian as Burton is: if Burton's visuals are a combination of Seuss and Gorey, Smith's combine Seuss with Chuck Jones and Pop Art. In *The Stinky Cheese Man*, the cow dropping its jaw in surprise seems closer to Jones than Seuss, and although Seuss also uses juxtaposition in his art, Smith tends to achieve this effect through mixed media, where Seuss does not. Whatever other influences they have, Lane Smith and Tim Burton create unruly artwork that seems inspired at least in part by Seuss.

The dynamic, even insurgent, quality of Seussism may be its most profound legacy. As the Surrealists did, Seuss estranges the familiar, creating pictures that encourage readers to look twice and to think twice. Perhaps, as suggested by the art class where his teacher reprimanded him for looking at his artwork upside down, Seuss simply could not help looking at the world from this slightly "upside down" perspective. As he was fond of saying, "I have a Seuss astigmatism in both eyes so that I see things as if they've been put through a Mixmaster or viewed through the wrong end of a telescope. It's not intentional. That's just the way I see things" (Crichton 23).

Chapter 4

The 5,000 Fingers of Dr. S

THE OTHER SIDES OF DR. SEUSS

W hy Dr. Seuss sees things through the "wrong end of the telescope" may be related to the source of his creativity, which comes not from childhood but from adolescence and adulthood. Seuss addressed this subject in 1982, when he and Maurice Sendak sat on a stage in San Diego, answering questions from the audience and talking with one another. Glenn Edward Sadler, the moderator, asked both men to comment on how much their early childhood influenced their work.

Seuss replied, "Not to a very great extent. I think my aberrations started when I got out of early childhood. [. . .] Generally speaking, I don't think my childhood influenced my work. But I know Maurice's did."

Sendak agreed. "I have profited mightily from my early childhood," he said.

Seuss: "I think I skipped my childhood."

Sendak: "I skipped my adolescence. Total amnesia."

Seuss: "Well, I used my adolescence."

Sendak: "Isn't that interesting, because you get your inspiration from young manhood, and I go all the way back to the crib days for mine" (Sadler 248–49).

This conversation captures the essential difference between the two artists and identifies a source of Seuss's satirical world view. Sendak's work develops from the primal fears and joys of childhood, but Seuss's comes from the subversiveness of adolescence. Seuss likes to keep grown-ups on their toes, puncturing holes in their adult logic. Of course, Seuss *is* an adult: that he writes from "young manhood" highlights the obvious fact that he is a grown-up writing for children. As U. C. Knoepflmacher and Mitzi Myers have pointed out, "Authors who write for children inevitably create a colloquy between past and present selves" (vii).

Since studies of Dr. Seuss frequently ignore the "adult" self of Theodor Seuss Geisel, this chapter focuses particularly on the adult sensibilities behind the popular children's author. It does so by looking at Seuss's creations for an adult audience, and by rereading the children's books from the perspective of "adult" and other lesser-known works. In other words, I read for those facets of Dr. Seuss that are not part of his public persona, examining the biographical undercurrents of his better-known books.

From D.T. Beasts to Fantastic Creatures

To glimpse the adult psyche behind the children's books, we begin at the bar. In a 1979 profile, poet Karla Kuskin observed that Seuss's characters "have two family characteristics: slightly batty, oval eyes and a smile you might find on the Mona Lisa after her first martini" (42). Many others have linked Seuss's creatures to altered states of mind. Asked why his novel *Bunny Modern* (1998)—a dystopian comedy of gun-toting nannies and dwindling fertility rates—is dedicated to "Dr. Spock, Dr. Seuss, and Jonathan Lethem, M.D.," David Bowman replied, "I do not know anything about children, so I was referring to baby books— including Dr. Spock. Lethem and I took drugs one night and decided that everything we saw was going to be from Dr. Seuss. Later on, I just thought about the 'Dr.' bit—Dr. Spock and Dr. Seuss. Then I decided to dedicate the book to Dr. Spock, Dr. Seuss and Jonathan Lethem MD" ("Re: Seuss and Bunny Modern and . . ."). Entrepeneurs have sold T-shirts featuring the Cat in the Hat with, as Audrey Geisel puts it, "a marijuana cigarette drooling out of his mouth" (Grimsley)—one of many counterfeit products that prompted her to allow Seuss's characters to be merchandised (Smith B1), a subject explored fully in Chapter Five.

Of course, some people want to attribute creativity to drug use: my students often ask me what Lewis Carroll was *on* when he wrote *Alice in Wonderland*, as if drugs could be the only explanation for such a fantastic imagination. So, in some senses, attempts to link Seuss's characters and substance abuse might prove only that the public imagination remains fixated on the artist as Decadent. However, while Theodor Seuss Geisel was not a heavy drinker, his pseudonym and his characters have many connections to altered states of mind. He told many an interviewer that he adopted the pseudonym "Seuss" following a drinking incident in his college days. During the spring of 1925, Geisel, then a senior at Dartmouth College, was an editor of and contributor to *Jack-o-lantern*, the college's humor magazine. The night before Easter, he and nine friends were caught drinking gin in his room. They were summoned before Dean Craven Laycock who put them all "on probation for violating the laws of Prohibition, and especially on Easter Evening," as Geisel told Edward Connery Lathem (17). The Dean also stripped Geisel of his editorship of *Jack-o-lantern*. Evading the Dean's punishment, Geisel continued to publish cartoons, but did so under other names—L. Pasteur, L. Burbank, D. G. Rossetti '25, Thos. Mott Osborne '27, T. Seuss, and Seuss. This was the first time he signed his work with the name "Seuss."

Given that Geisel first signed himself as "Seuss" to avoid punishment for drinking gin, it should not surprise us that some of his earliest imaginary creatures are hallucinations brought on by too much drink.[1] Mind you, it is not Geisel but his *characters* who are overdoing it, as in "Christmas Sprits and Their Effects," a December 1927 *Judge* cartoon in which Geisel (signing himself "Seuss") has drawn the variety of creatures you might see when intoxicated. Too much champagne brings on a leaping creature with a dizzy grin on its face, and trailing four tails that look like balloons on strings. Too much Bacardi rum, and you will be carried off by a clover-spotted creature and his grinning, polka-dotted companion. And so on. In the early cartoons, Seuss spins many variations on this motif. In "Quaffling with the Pachyderms OR Why I Prefer the West Side Speak-easies" (*Judge*, March 1928), Seuss's narrator goes drinking with elephants, and shows what creatures a drunken elephant may see— such as "a slightly different make of serpent," which looks like a cross between a snake and an elephant. "The Waiting Room at Dang-Dang" (*Judge*, Sept. 1928) invites us "Where the D.T. Animals Stay When They're Not Out on Jobs." And in "FORGOTTEN EVENTS OF HISTORY," "Noah's dissolute brother, Goah, preserves the D.T. beasts of his day for posterity" (*Life*, July 1930). Among the animals boarding Goah's "Gark" are ancestors of characters in Seuss's children's books: the two elephant-birds resemble Horton's, in *Horton Hatches the Egg*; the two birds walking up the ramp might be prehistoric relatives of the Mt. Strookoo Cuckoos from *Scrambled Eggs Super!*

That the children's-book creatures may come from the same family tree as the D.T. beasts does not suggest that *Oh, the Thinks You Can Think!*

really should have been called *Oh, the Drinks You Can Drink!* During this period, much of the humor in *Judge* and *Life* centered around Prohibition: a cartoon by R. B. Fuller from the *Judge* of 23 April 1927 features a top-hatted man swinging from a tree, surrounded by a variety of fantastic creatures. Instead, the alcohol-inspired animals of Seuss's cartoons highlight his rebellious imagination and a dispositional distaste for rules and regulations. Just as the Volstead Act did not prevent Geisel from drinking during Prohibition, so no book of etiquette will prevent Sam-I-am from insisting that you eat green food. As many of Seuss's books do, *Green Eggs and Ham* celebrates a creativity that breaks the rules.[2] After reading one of the rhymes in *Oh Say Can You Say!*, one of his two tongue-twister books, Seuss says that it "can't be done after three martinis. It's a two-martini tongue twister" (Beyette 5). Indeed, reading *any* of Seuss's books requires so nimble a tongue that, if used as a sobriety test, it would be too difficult—the teetotaler and the soused alike will stumble over the language. In suggesting the use of martinis to measure reading levels, Seuss recognizes the lifelong thrill of misbehaving: the Cat may pick up all his toys at the end, but the fun of the book is the chaotic roller-coaster ride that leads there. When the sun does not shine and it is too wet to play, we welcome the joyous anarchy of the Cat in the Hat.

"Someday, kiddies, you will learn about SEX": Gender, Humor, and Naked Women

Perhaps a desire to surprise people inspired Seuss's mischievous—and definitely adult—sense of humor. Although Seuss was fond of saying, "Adults are obsolete children, and the hell with them," he also admitted, "The first draft of all my stuff is written completely for adults. To keep the story going, to keep in the swing, I'll write swear words and dirty words and everything else—ending up with an adult piece of writing that a child could comprehend. Then I go back and clean up, have a little fun with it" (Pace D23; Dangaard 5). To make sure that his editors were paying attention, he liked to slip dirty jokes into his manuscripts. In the documentary, "An Awfully Big Adventure: The Making of Modern Children's Literature" (BBC, 1998), Michael Frith shows a draft page from *Dr. Seuss's ABC*, in which Seuss has drawn a large-breasted woman and the following verse: "Big X, little x. X, X, X. / Someday, kiddies, you will learn about SEX." The joke here is its inappropriateness: bringing sexuality into an alphabet book, Seuss introduces a concern of grown-ups (and teens) into a genre intended for very young children. In 1970, he sent his publishers "two and a half chapters of Philip Roth-inspired dirty book," and, for fun, demanded that it be published. Seuss describes this work as "the dirtiest thing ever written. The supreme one of all times." He never intended that the book be published (and it wasn't); instead, he wanted to "scare the blazes out" of his editors at Random House.[3] Even beyond his manuscripts, Seuss enjoyed upsetting people's expectations about how a children's author should behave. Lark Grey Dimond-Cates, his stepdaughter, remembers him as "a shy, digni-fied man" with a ribald sense of humor. As she recalls, "One time a very well-endowed woman approached us in a restaurant, and Ted said, 'Here comes someone with full frontal friendliness'" (Schuman 15).

The Seven Lady Godivas was Seuss's sole attempt to represent "full frontal friendliness." A commercial failure when published in 1939 and a curiosity when republished in 1987, The Seven Lady Godivas was Dr. Seuss's first "adult book." Apparently, Seuss created The Seven Lady Godi-vas as a reaction against the children's books he had been writing: as he told the Wilson Library Bulletin that year, he wrote the book "to escape the monotony of writing about nothing but 'men folks and children, dragons or fish'" ("Dr. Seuss"). The inside front flap of the first edition identifies Seuss as "the author of two tremendously successful juveniles: To Think That I Saw It on Mulberry Street and The 500 Hats of Bartholomew Cubbins." It then adds, "We hope that it is unnecessary to point out to you that The Seven Lady Godivas belongs in a very different category" (Younger et al. 166). It does belong to a different category than chil-dren's books, but it is not exactly "softcore Seuss," as some have de-scribed it (Sullivan, "Oh, the Places He Went!" 29). The premise of the book is that there are seven Lady Godivas (or Ladies Godiva?), each of whom is engaged to a different Peeping brother. As Seuss explains in the Foreword, "So far as Peeping Tom is concerned, he never really peeped. 'Peeping' was merely the old family name, and Tom and his six brothers bore it with pride." When Lord Godiva is thrown from his horse and killed, the Godiva "girls were left with a grim obligation. Horses must be studied and charted, made safe for posterity." So, Clem-entina "Teenie" Godiva, Dorcas J. Godiva, Arabella Godiva, Mitzi God-iva, Lulu Godiva, Gussie Godiva, and Hedwig Godiva each swears that she shall not wed until bringing "to the light of this world some new and worthy Horse Truth, of benefit to man." Peeping Tom, Peeping

Dick, Peeping Harry, Peeping Jack, Peeping Drexel, Peeping Sylvester and Peeping Frelinghuysen will just have to wait.

Despite this risqué setup, the humor that follows is not particularly bawdy, but more closely resembles the humor of his magazine cartoons and children's books.[4] For example, looking into the mouth of a mare that had been a gift of her Uncle Ethelbert, Teenie gets her nose bitten off. She learns "*Don't ever look a gift horse in the mouth*" and then marries Peeping Tom. There are lots of puns like these, but none of them racy. Mitzi creates a horse-propelled rowboat that runs on "sea-horsepower." Running on a treadmill connected to oars gives one horse "Hoof Burn," so Teenie develops a new version of the boat using two horses—when one gets Hoof Burn, the other can take his place. However, switching horses during the voyage does not work: thus Mitzi learns, "*Never change horses in the middle of the stream*" and then goes off to marry Peeping Jack. This sort of humor is also the kind of humor we find in Seuss's books for children. These "Horse Truths" have both literal and figurative meanings, just as, in *The 500 Hats of Bartholomew Cubbins,* the name of Sir Snipps refers both to his job as "maker of hats" (a scissors hangs from a loop by his waist) and to his personality (which is rather snippy). In its pun-ny wordplay, *The Seven Lady Godivas* is quite in the same category as the children's books.

Well, except for the fact that the Godiva women are completely naked (figure 4.1). The only explanation for their lack of clothes is Lord Godiva's observation that "Nowhere [. . .] could there be a group of young ladies that wasted less time upon frivol and froth. No fluffy-duff primping, no feather, no fuss. They were simply themselves and chose not to disguise it." On one level, the comment that they "were simply themselves" seems correct because Seuss's naked ladies are not particularly erotic. As Alexander Laing observes, in what may be the sole contemporary review of the book, *The Seven Lady Godivas* "is crawling with nudes but has not a single prurient scene or moment." Seuss, blaming himself for the book's commercial failure, says, "I attempted to draw the sexiest babes I could, but they came out looking absurd" (Jennings 108). "I don't think I drew proper naked ladies," he explains. "I think their ankles came out wrong, and things like that" (Gorney B3). Looking at a copy of the book, he points to his Ladies Godiva and adds, "look at them—they're neuter and sexless and have no shape at all" (Freeman, "Who Thunk You Up, Dr. Seuss?" 169). Seuss's self-deprecating re-

Figure 4.1. Finished pencil-and-gouache drawing from *The Seven Lady Godivas* by Dr. Seuss

marks about his artistic ability aside, he is absolutely correct: the Godivas are not erotic. "Tijuana Bibles," eight-page pornographic comics with a wide and illegal distribution in the 1930s, provide an instructive comparison here.[5] The women and men in these mostly anonymously authored works are rendered in explicit anatomical detail, the humor is generally lewd, and the characters exist solely to participate in sexual duos (or trios, foursomes, etc.). In contrast, Seuss's Ladies Godiva do *not* find their "Horse Truths" by copulating with their horses—as they surely would in Tijuana Bibles. Seuss's women lack realistic detail (no nipples, for example), his humor avoids bawdiness, and sex is completely absent: he never shows what happens when the Godivas at last marry their Peepings. That said, while the Godivas' nakedness does not make them erotic, it does make them figures of fun.

Though I expect that Seuss enjoyed surprising interviewers by telling them about his book of naked ladies, the truly shocking thing about *The*

Seven Lady Godivas is that it is one of the only Dr. Seuss book published during his lifetime that features semi-sympathetic female main characters. (*Daisy-Head Mayzie* and *Hooray for Diffendoofer Day!*, both published posthumously and discussed in the next chapter, do have admirable female central characters.) As Alison Lurie pointed out in a 1990 essay, Seuss's work has an "almost total lack of female protagonists": "little girls play silent, secondary roles" (51) and adult females, like Mayzie of *Horton Hatches the Egg* or Gertrude McFuzz (one of the "other stories" in *Yertle the Turtle and Other Stories*), appear as vain or selfish. One little girl who does not play a secondary role soon learns that she should. In "The Glunk that Got Thunk" (from *I Can Lick 30 Tigers Today! and Other Stories*) she thinks up a dangerous Glunk, which her brother then must un-think. Lurie concludes, "Moral: women have weak minds; they must not be ambitious even in imagination" (52). Seuss responded to her criticism by noting that most of his characters were animals, adding, "if she can identify their sex, I'll remember her in my will" (Morgan and Morgan 286). Whether or not we agree with Seuss's reply, we can identify the sex of the Ladies Godiva and, while they are more admirable than Gertrude McFuzz or the little girl who thinks up the Glunk, they are also there for us to laugh at.

As "young ladies" who do not waste "time upon frivol," "froth," or "fluffy-duff primping," the seven Godiva sisters might be read as parodies of liberated women—in other words, they have taken their liberation to such an extreme that they have even dispensed with clothes. In *The Seven Lady Godivas*, as in his magazine cartoons, Seuss also mocks reform-minded women for their role in the temperance movement. For the cover of *Judge* (9 Jan. 1932), Seuss drew an urbane gent leaning out of a window to chip the end of a neighboring building's icicle into his cocktail shaker. The icicle in question hangs from a sign reading "W.C.T.U." and the members of the Women's Christian Temperance Union look quite scandalized as they watch. As Richard Minear points out, "even though there was never a serious possibility that Prohibition would return during the war," Seuss also returns to this theme in a *PM* cartoon from 22 Oct. 1942, caricaturing Carrie Nation (1846–1911), a temperance advocate famous for attacking saloons with hatchets ("The Political Dr. Seuss" 4; figure 4.2). In *The Seven Lady Godivas*, Arabella, determined to find her Horse Truth, works her horse Brutus so hard that she literally drives him to drink. After he has "degenerated into a

Your Nutty Aunt Carrie Is Loose Again!

Figure 4.2. "Your Nutty Aunt Carrie Is Loose Again!" by Dr Seuss

drunken bum," she asks her sisters for a new horse, but they refuse, pointing out that her severe treatment of Brutus has led him to find refuge in alcohol. When Brutus is "suffering the most extravagant hangover ever experienced by man or beast," Arabella decides then and there that he "would have to be reformed." Thinking that fresh water will help, she drags him to the pump, and he responds, "Pump stuff! [. . .] I'll die before I drink it." He does die, leading her to the moral "*You can lead a horse to water, but you can't make him drink.*"

Seuss does mock male reformers in (to name one example) "The Scale Reform Movement," a cartoon from *Life* of March 1930: a reformer proposes that SOL and TI be removed from the scale because "both mean something awful in ancient Persian" ("Life's LITTLE EDUCATIONAL CHARTS: The Latest Developments in Vocal Education"). However, the zealous reformers in his works tend to be female and, given his biography, this trait is understandable. His father, Theodor Robert Geisel, worked in the family business, Kalmbach and Geisel—a brewery co-founded by Seuss's grandfather—which later merged with another company to become Springfield Breweries. Just after Seuss's father had just been elected president of the Springfield Breweries, the Volstead Act passed and Prohibition went into effect. Given that the temperance movement put his father out of work, it is not surprising that Seuss mocks crusading women like Arabella Godiva and the kangaroo in *Horton Hears a Who!* An advocate who resorts to extreme measures, the kangaroo (with her child in her pouch) leads the movement against Horton, telling him that his "silly nonsensical game is all through" and that the dust-speck planet of Whos will be boiled in "a hot steaming kettle of Beezle-Nut oil!" As a woman reformer, this kangaroo is singularly cruel, but she and her followers *do* relent at the end of the book, offering to protect the Whos. Inasmuch as the kangaroo may be a descendent of Carrie Nation, her conversion to Horton's cause may indicate that Seuss no longer considered female activists to be as intransigent as he once did. Perhaps his position was softening.

Many of his stereotypes soften or disappear over time, as exemplified by the changing representation of the Japanese in his work (discussed in Chapter Two). Like the wartime stereotypes of the Japanese, caricatures of Africans and African-Americans in the early cartoons would be equally appalling to modern readers. These, too, vanished from Seuss's work as times changed and Seuss changed with them. At the time he drew them, these stereotypes were acceptable, common in humor and in cartoons. In *Boners* (1931), a collection of "school boy howlers," Seuss draws thick-lipped Africans telling dirty jokes as an illustration for "General Smuts are what all the different black races are called in the north-western quarter of Africa." Perhaps in recognition of the inappropriate-ness of such a drawing, neither it nor the "boner" that inspired it appear in later versions of the *Boners* books, such as *The Pocket Book of Boners* (1941) or *Herrings Go About the Sea in Shawls and Other Classic Howlers from Classrooms and Examination Papers* (1997). "Cross-section of the World's Most Prosperous Department Store," a cartoon from a June 1929 issue of *Judge*, shows a white salesman inviting a white customer to consider purchasing one of two dozen thick-lipped black men. The sign over their heads reads, "TAKE HOME A HIGH-GRADE NIGGER For Your WOODPILE! SATISFACTION GUARANTEED."[6] During the war, Seuss returns to this image, but without the racist caricature. Looking at an upper-class white man affixing a sign to a log in a massive woodpile, one dark-skinned man says to another, "There seems to be a white man in the woodpile!" (*PM*, 8 July 1942). The woodpile is labeled "WAR WORK TO BE DONE," and the sign reads, "NO COLORED LABOR NEEDED." In contrast to the earlier cartoon, this one criticizes racism. While *If I Ran the Zoo*'s "African island of Yerka" does revert to racial caricature, it is an exception. In general, as his career progresses, Seuss not only removes racially insensitive stereotypes, but even responds sympathetically to other sensitive subjects. In the original version of *The Lorax*, the title character tells us that he is sending the Humming-Fish off: "Oh, their future is dreary. / They'll walk on their fins and get woefully weary / in search of some water that isn't so smeary. / I hear things are just as bad up in Lake Erie." When researchers from the Ohio Sea Grant Program wrote to say that Lake Erie had since been cleaned up, Seuss agreed to remove the final line from future editions (Morgan and Morgan 276).

Though Seuss did agree to make changes to passages that might have been offensive to blacks, Asians, or even people living near Lake Erie, he would not budge when charged with being offensive to women and girls. Seuss's flippant, funny response to Alison Lurie ("If she can identify their sex, I'll remember her in my will") has its roots in complaints about a verse from *And to Think That I Saw It on Mulberry Street*. Near the beginning of the book, when Marco decides that his imagined parade needs to be more exciting, he tells us, "Say—*any*one could think of *that*, / Jack or Fred or Joe or Nat—/ Say, even Jane could think of *that*." In the 1970s, some women asked Seuss to change the line "Say, even Jane could think of *that*" because it was "blatantly sexist." Though he said he was "in favor of women's lib," Seuss objected to requests that he "clean up" the line about Jane, calling the suggestion "beyond contempt" (Diehl 38; Beyette). In 1971, upon first receiving complaints about the "Jane" line, Seuss said, "my immediate reaction was to write some kind of blistering answer in rhyme." However, he said, writing back to these critics would simply provoke them: "These gals obviously have a lot of time on their hands to write letters, and I think answering them would just be stirring up a female hornets' nest (There I go again! I guess I *am* discriminatory.)" (Geisel, Vanguard correspondence). In 1975, after receiving similar complaints, Seuss not only held his ground, but took aim at his critics who, he said, "were violently determined to think of Dr. Seuss as a Latter Day Adolf Hitler and *Mulberry Street* as a Latter Day *Mein Kamp* [*sic.*]." He added, "If the letters were coming in by the hundreds, I would believe that the 'Jane' line in the book should perhaps be expunged. But a total of only five letters of this sort in 38 years convinces me that they were written by Extreme-Fringe-Woman-Libbers" (Vanguard). Finally, in a 1978 letter agreeing to change *Mulberry Street*'s "Chinaman" into a less stereotypical "Chinese man," Seuss added a parenthetical note: " 'Even Jane could think of that,' however, should never be changed, for I am a male chauvinist peeg" (Vanguard).

Perhaps removing one line from *The Lorax* or changing "Chinaman" to "Chinese man" seemed easier than tampering with the verse in *Mulberry Street*: in the former case, one line is omitted, and the rhyme remains; in the latter, "Chinese man" not only rhymes but has the same number of syllables as "Chinaman." Given Seuss's legendary attention to poetic form, his resistance may be at least partially on aesthetic grounds. On the other hand, replacing "Jane" with another one-syllable name does not seem any more or less challenging than these other alterations. The source of Seuss's resistance here can be found not in his perfectionism but in his tendency to characterize these women in the same language he otherwise reserves for temperance activists. He classifies them as an "Extreme-Fringe" group, and underscores what he views as their extremism, first, by suggesting that they are equating *Mulberry Street* with *Mein Kampf*, and, second, by caricaturing them as what Rush Limbaugh would later term "feminazis." That is, in spelling "pig" as "peeg," Seuss seems to give his critics a Hollywood-German accent, echoing anti-Nazi films of the 1940s.

Part of Seuss's willingness to caricature his critics derives from his resistance to being told what to do. Significantly, many of his editors were female. As Phyllis Cerf said of the conflicts that developed between Seuss and his editors, "It wasn't really Ted. It was his maleness of not wanting to be bossed by all women. He had an agent (Phyllis [Jackson]), he had a partner (Phyllis [Cerf]), he had a wife (Helen)—you know, he was surrounded by women telling him what to do" ("An Awfully Big Adventure"). His many female editors may explain his resistance to taking orders from women, such as those who wanted him to remove the line about Jane. Unfortunately, there were other consequences: having Helen as his editor may have led to problems in their marriage.

Probing biographical connections between an author's life and work will always be a speculative undertaking. That said, no thorough discussion of gender in Seuss's books would be complete without reference to his first marriage. As the Morgans detail in their thorough biography, Theodor Seuss Geisel's relationship with Helen Palmer Geisel had many layers to it. They fell in love at first sight, married in November 1927, and had a very close relationship. Helen first encouraged Ted to pursue his cartooning instead of graduate studies—they met at Oxford in 1925 and, from the doodles in his notebook, she could see that his interests were not in the lectures. She stuck by him during the leaner periods of his career, and served as his at-home editor. A profile published in the *Saturday Evening Post* of 6 July 1957 provides a glimpse of their close working relationship. At the time, he was writing *How the Grinch Stole Christmas!*, and had some questions about one of the pages:

> "Helen, Helen, where are you?" Geisel shouted, emerging from his den into the living room. "How do you like this?" he said, dropping a sketch and a verse in her lap.
>
> Helen shook her head. Geisel's face dropped. "No," she said, "this isn't it. And besides, you've got the papa Who too big. Now he looks like a bug."
>
> "Well, they are bugs," said Geisel defensively.
>
> "They are not bugs," replied Helen. "Those Whos are just small people."
>
> Geisel retreated to his den again to fix the picture and try again with the verses. (Cahn 46)

That Helen was actively involved in shaping Ted's books may have introduced some tension into their relationship. Yet Ted clearly depended upon her judgment, and so perhaps he needed precisely such tension. Similarly, while it is certainly tempting to read "Wife Up a Tree" (1953) as foreshadowing marital troubles, there is scant evidence that the poem about the overly neat Mrs. Phoebe McPhee refers to Mrs. Helen Geisel. In the poem, Mrs. McPhee, a bird, would "twitter and chirp at her poor husband, Gus" as she cleans and dusts their tree's leaves, twigs, knothole, shoots, and even roots. Unhappy with Phoebe, Gus spies Ruth, who "was awfully mussed up, and she wasn't brushed neatly / And just for that reason, Gus went nuts completely!" He leaves Phoebe to nest "with Ruth . . . / Happy, untidy, unkempt and uncouth." If this story of a male bird who leaves a controlling wife seems to depict Ted Geisel's discomfort with Helen's editorial input on his work, the biographical circumstances surrounding its publication provide no confirmation. While Helen was then offering her editorial assistance, the two remained close, and he relied upon her to run the business side of "Dr. Seuss," granting him privacy from visitors and keeping track of finances. In May of 1954, when Helen fell ill with the potentially fatal Guillain-Barré syndrome, he stayed by her side, and worked hard to help nurse her back to health (Morgan and Morgan 149–50). She recovered, had a small stroke in April 1957, and recovered again, prior to the *Saturday Evening Post* story in which she helps Ted with his Whos. However, as the Morgans report, she "never recovered completely from her traumatic paralysis" brought on by Guillain-Barré (182).

Whatever the catalyst may have been, Ted fell in love with Audrey Dimond, eighteen years his junior and then married with two children. He dedicated *Fox in Socks* (1965) to "Mitzi Long and Audrey Dimond of the Mt. Soledad Lingual Laboratories," and he dedicated *The Cat in the Hat Songbook* (1967) to Audrey's daughters, "Lark and Lea of Ludding-ton Lane." Though the Morgans' biography allows the reader to infer the nature of Audrey and Ted's relationship, *Dr. Seuss and Mr. Geisel* never in so many words calls it an affair (Morgan and Morgan 194–95). However, in November of 2000, Audrey Geisel addressed the subject quite openly, telling the *New York Times*' Joyce Wadler that she and Ted did have an affair. On October 23, 1967, and in "the wake of their affair, Mr. Geisel's wife, Helen, committed suicide, causing, as Mrs. [Audrey] Geisel puts it, 'a rather large ripple in the community of La Jolla'" (Wadler). In early 1968, Audrey divorced Grey Dimond, and on June 21, 1968, Theodor Seuss Geisel married Audrey Dimond (Morgan and Morgan 200–01).

For those who wish to convict Dr. Seuss and his books of sexism, these facts of his biography may confirm their suspicions. However, while the affair and Helen's suicide do not speak in his favor, a full analysis of gender in Dr. Seuss's works is necessarily more complex. First, there are *some* sympathetically represented female characters in Dr. Seuss's works. A boy narrates the first half and a girl narrates the second half of *The Shape of Me and Other Stuff* (1973), a book originally intended to be published under the pseudonym Theo. LeSieg.[7] Contrary to the message of "The Glunk That Got Thunk," the girl in this book has the more active imagination and she is *not* reprimanded for it. While the boy thinks of the shapes of "a bug," "a balloon," "a bed," and "a bike," the girl's imagination tends toward the abstract, such as the "MANY shapes of chewing gum," "the shape of smoke," and the shapes of several fantastic creatures, including "a BLOGG." Suggesting that she is the more unconventional thinker (a trait admired by Seuss), the girl also poses the book's central philosophical question, asking readers to imagine *themselves* with a different shape: "Suppose YOU were shaped like these . . . / . . . or those / . . . or shaped like a BLOGG! / Or a garden hose!" Credited to Geisel's less-famous pen name of Theo. LeSieg, *Maybe You Should Fly a Jet! Maybe You Should Be a Vet!* (1980) offers a greater variety of roles for women. Michael J. Smollin's illustrations show a female dentist, chemist, construction worker, and a woman piloting a jet. Just before the page featuring the female airline pilot, the book admits, "Some girls make good lion tamers," hinting at the possibility of an *If I Ran the Circus* with a female ringmaster. Smollin should take some credit for the gender parity in the illustrations, but Seuss deserves credit, too. While Seuss's original illustrations do not always clearly specify the gender of the person, his drawings of the dentist and lion tamer clearly show them to be women. As John Gough observes in his essay "The Unsung Dr. Seuss: Theo LeSieg" (1987), "Feminists could not quibble about the balance between male and female jobs that are offered. [. . .] Equal Opportunity is alive and well in LeSieg's world" (185). Finally, as Tim Wolf suggests, given that "Sam" is a common nickname for "Samantha," *Green Eggs and Ham*'s Sam-I-am could be androgynous: "Sam has no physical characteristics that mark him or her as either male of female, and Seuss never uses a gender-specific pronoun when referring to Sam" (153). If Sam-I-am is not clearly gendered, then perhaps s/he could be included with the girl from *The Shape of Me and Other Stuff* and the professional women from *Maybe You Should Fly a Jet!* as characters who defy gender stereotypes. In any case, given these books and the posthumous appearance of Miss Bonkers (in *Hooray for Diffendoofer Day!*) and Daisy-Head Mayzie, Seuss may have been moving toward writing books featuring likeable female protagonists.

Though Seuss did not provide central or sympathetic female characters until late in his career, his work has always offered a variety of masculinities, some very stereotypical and others much less so. These characters, along with the non-traditional roles for women provided by some of the books mentioned above, suggest that he saw gender as a social construct—that is, as a set of learned behaviors. Seuss's "message" books are much more likely to present characters who offer alternate masculinities or highlight flaws in culturally sanctioned masculine behaviors. In their insightful article, "Getting to Solla Sollew: The Existential Politics of Dr. Seuss" (1987), Betty Mensch and Alan Freeman argue that the title character of *Thidwick the Big-Hearted Moose* (1948) embodies "a traditionally feminine virtue—hospitality" (116). After all, the recurring refrain sounds more "Ms. Manners" than "Dr. Seuss": three times, the book repeats the line "a host, above all, must be nice to his guest." Granted, Thidwick does ditch those freeloaders in the end, an action that may undermine this moral. But the "soft-hearted moose" is the hero of the tale, and he is considerate even when the increasing number (and weight) of guests on his antlers makes his life difficult. As he tells the Bingle Bug who first asks if he might ride in his horns, "There's room there to spare, and I'm happy to share! / Be my guest and I hope that you're comfortable there!"

In *Horton Hatches the Egg*, Horton is a gentle, maternal male elephant who so nurtures the egg that its occupant takes on some of his characteristics. When hatched, the bird has become "an elephant-bird," as it "*should* be, it SHOULD be like that! / Because Horton was faithful! He sat and he sat! / He meant what he said / And he said what he meant." Though, as Jill Deans has pointed out, *Horton Hatches the Egg* vilifies Mayzie, the "lazy" mother, the book nonetheless offers a positive representation of an adoptive father. Rewarded for being "faithful, one hundred percent," Horton returns in *Horton Hears a Who!* to teach us that "A person's a person, no matter how small." In both books, Horton's tender concern for the small—in this case, a dust-speck-sized universe—is presented heroically.

Complicating these interpretations, the Horton of *Horton Hatches the Egg* is likely a revised version of Matilda, the main character in "Matilda, the Elephant with a Mother Complex," published in the April 1938 issue of *Judge*. Although Seuss liked to tell people that he got the idea for *Horton Hatches the Egg* when the wind blew his drawing of an elephant (done on transparent paper) onto his drawing of a tree,[8] the tale of an elephant hatching an egg probably began with Matilda's story, published two years before *Horton Hatches the Egg*. In this earlier version, "an Old Maid Elephant named Matilda" sees a tiny chickadee egg that is "deserted and motherless." She tells the rest of the herd, "Go on without me. My maternal instinct dictates that here I remain." Thinking her "insane," the herd moves on, leaving the "Old Maid Elephant [. . .] alone with her egg." Much as in *Horton Hatches the Egg*, "Small sarcastic animals came out of the jungle and twitted her unmercifully." As Horton does, "Matilda ignored them and stuck to her vigil." However, quite unlike *Horton Hatches the Egg*, "Matilda, the Elephant with a Mother Complex" appears to agree with the sarcastic animals. After enduring twenty-six days on the egg, Matilda hears a peep and trumpets, "Eureka! My foster child is hatched!" As Matilda bends over to "caress her new baby chickadee," the chickadee does not respond as Horton's elephant-bird does. Instead,

> the chickadee, confronted by an elephant, cried out in terror. Shaking the eggshells out of his feathers, he spread his little wings and flapped off frantically over the tree tops.
>
> Matilda never laid eyes on him again. Nor was she ever able to locate her herd. Today she roams the jungle, alone and friend-less . . . a woebegone creature, with nothing at all to show for her pains except a very bad case of lumbago.
>
> *Moral:* Don't go around hatching other folks' eggs.

The ending to this story punishes the adoptive mother (Matilda) for her efforts, whereas *Horton Hatches the Egg* rewards an adoptive father (Horton) for his. By implying that Matilda is meddling in areas that should not concern her, the moral also chastises her for being so independent. As the "president of the herd" tells her when she announces her decision to hatch the egg, "Why, girl, you're insane! Elephants don't hatch chickadee eggs!" In response, " 'Well here's one that does,' retorted Matilda hotly. 'Now bustle along.' " The fable's conclusion proves him right, and leaves the rebellious "Old Maid" alone.

However, before concluding that Seuss is criticizing another free-thinking female, it is worth considering the following passage in light of his own childless state: "Like most individuals who own no children, Matilda was very, very envious. She would not walk with the others . . . but a little behind them, always watching the happy family groups through an eye that was dim and misty with tears." In this passage, the fable does not call Matilda an "Old Maid," but instead presents her with sympathy: she is "Like most individuals who own no children." Given that Ted and Helen Geisel had no children of their own (Helen could not have children), Matilda could represent *either* one of them. Perhaps Matilda is not just a female elephant, but also a version of Ted Geisel. Consider his Infantograph and the Geisels' imaginary child. To silence friends who bragged about their own children, he liked to boast of the achievements of his daughter, Chrysanthemum-Pearl (Morgan and Morgan 90). He even dedicated *The 500 Hats of Bartholomew Cubbins* to "Chrysanthemum-Pearl (aged 89 months, going on 90)" and included her on Christmas cards, along with Norval, Wally, Wickersham, Miggles, Boo-Boo, Thnud, and other purely fictional children (figure 4.3). For a photograph used on one year's Christmas card, Geisel even invited in half a dozen neighborhood kids to pose as his and Helen's children. The card reads, "All of us over at Our House / Wish all of you over at / Your House / A very Merry Christmas," and is signed "Helen and Ted Geisel and the kiddies."[9] Suggesting that he wanted to know what his own kiddies might have been like, in 1939 he and business partner Ralph Warren tried to invent an Infantograph, which promised to show what a couple's children would look like. Although they never quite got it to work, Geisel did write advertising copy for the camera's expected debut at the World's Fair: "IF YOU MARRIED THAT GAL YOU'RE WALKING WITH, WHAT WOULD YOUR CHILDREN LOOK LIKE? COME IN AND HAVE YOUR INFANTOGRAPH TAKEN!" (Morgan and Morgan 92). Given the frequency with which he returns to children during this period of his life, the humor in his prank Christmas cards and in stories of elephants who adopt children may conceal some sadness.[10] Both Matilda and Horton are adoptive parents: for one, the adoption fails; for the other, it succeeds. We might take both elephants together as manifestations of Seuss's mixed feelings towards parenthood and his own lack of children.

Biographical interpretations of Dr. Seuss's books can suggest the ways in which Ted Geisel's views on sex, gender, or parenthood may enter into his books, but they can do little more than suggest—indeed, I doubt if Geisel himself was conscious of how such beliefs manifested themselves in his work.[11] Nonetheless, examining several possible intersections between the artist's life and his work has, I hope, depicted the subject with suitable complexity. That is, the point of raising these questions about sex and gender is neither to accuse Seuss of sexism nor to praise him for writing gender-inclusive books for children. Women won the right to vote in 1920, the year Ted Geisel turned sixteen: one might expect a man of his generation to create more male protagonists than female ones. On the other hand, given his sensitivity to stereotyping of blacks and Asians, it is surprising that he moved much more slowly in

Figure 4.3. Christmas card from Dr. Seuss

admitting admirable female characters into his stories. And yet, however long it took him to include strong and likeable females, his prominent atypically gendered males—Horton and Thidwick—suggest that his understanding of masculinity was not confined by stereotypes. This hypothesis, too, cannot be offered without some qualification. Although Seuss does offer some male characters with more traditionally feminine characteristics, the majority of his male characters have one thing in common: they are con men. Indeed, perhaps one reason that Seuss has few female characters is that his main characters tend to be confidence *men*, and, often, confidence boys.

You're a Mean One, Mr. Guido: Confidence Men, Confidence Boys, and Other Storytellers

The Grinch makes his first appearance in "The Hoobub and the Grinch," a thirty-two-line poem published in the May 1955 issue of *Redbook*. In the accompanying illustration, a Hoobub lies stretched out on the ground, his back propped up against a tree; this Grinch, a smaller character than in the book, stands on a rock, looking down at the Hoobub. Suggesting that there may be more Grinches, this Grinch is "a Grinch," and so perhaps not "the Grinch" of *How the Grinch Stole Christmas!* (1957). However, we can tell that this Grinch is at the very least related to that famous Grinch because both are con artists. In the book, when two-year-old Cindy-Lou Who asks the Grinch, "Santy Claus, why, / *Why* are you taking our Christmas tree? WHY?" he cons her into thinking he's doing a good deed: " 'Why, my sweet little tot,' the fake Santy Claus lied, / 'There's a light on this tree that won't light on one side. / So I'm taking it home to my workshop, my dear. / I'll fix it up *there*. Then I'll bring it back *here*.' " Similarly, in the "Hoobub and the Grinch," a Grinch meets a Hoobub relaxing in the "wonderful, warm summer sun" and convinces him that a piece of green string is "worth a lot more than that old-fashioned sun":

> "That sun, let me tell you, is dangerous stuff!
> It can freckle your face. It can make your skin rough.
> When the sun gets too hot, it can broil you like fat!
> *But this piece of green string, sir, will NEVER do that!*

THIS PIECE OF GREEN STRING IS COLOSSAL! IMMENSE!
AND, TO YOU . . . WELL, I'LL SELL IT FOR 98 CENTS!"
And the Hoobub . . . *he bought!*
(And I'm sorry to say
That Grinches sell Hoobubs such things every day.)

While this logic might appeal to the recently sunburned, Seuss clearly intends his readers to scoff at the notion that a piece of green string could be more valuable than the sun. The concluding couplet reinforces the moral of this cautionary tale. He is "sorry to say / That Grinches sell Hoobubs such things every day" because Hoobubs are easily conned and Grinches are fast-talking swindlers. Tellingly, in the draft version of "The Hoobub and the Grinch," the Grinch was originally called "Guido," a name with connotations shadier than the merely grouchy "Grinch."

As Dr. Seuss's most frequently recurring character type, the con artist locates Seuss's work in a rich American tradition that includes Herman Melville's *The Confidence Man*, Meredith Willson's *The Music Man*, L. Frank Baum's *The Wonderful Wizard of Oz*, William Faulkner's Flem Snopes, and *Seinfeld*'s Kramer. As Gary Lindberg writes in his *The Confidence Man in American Literature* (1982), "the confidence man is a covert cultural hero for many Americans" (3). The confidence man's prominence in Seuss's books indicates that Seuss is one of those Americans, as does the fact that Seuss based two of his most famous con men on himself: the Grinch and the Cat in the Hat. In December 1957, when *How the Grinch Stole Christmas!* appeared simultaneously in *Redbook* and in book form, Seuss explained the origins of the story:

> I was brushing my teeth on the morning of the 26th of last December when I noted a very Grinchish countenance in the mirror. It was Seuss! Something had gone wrong with Christmas, I realized, or more likely with me. So I wrote the story about my sour friend, the Grinch to see if I could rediscover something about Christmas that obviously I'd lost. (Hart 3)

He accompanies this story with a self-portrait of himself looking into his bathroom mirror and the Grinch looking back. Seuss told many variations on this story, but always mentions his identification with the

Grinch, once describing him as a "nasty anti-Christmas character that was really myself" (Clark D1). Although his license plate read "GRINCH," Seuss also identified with the Cat in the Hat. A self-portrait of himself as the Cat accompanied the profile in the *Saturday Evening Post* of 6 July 1957, and appears on the cover of this book. As his editor Michael Frith observed, "The Cat in the Hat and Ted Geisel were inseparable and the same. I think there's no question about it. This is someone who delighted in the chaos of life, who delighted in the seeming insanity of the world around him" ("An Awfully Big Adventure").

Seuss delighted in contributing to that "seeming insanity" by inventing stories, some obviously fictional and others that mingled fact and fiction. In the first substantial profile of Seuss, which appeared in *The Dartmouth* in May 1934, Seuss begins by saying, "Let's see, you want an interview, a sort of life story as it were." The interviewer nods. Seuss asks, "Truth or fiction?" The interviewer replies, "A little bit of both ought to do quite well," and Seuss goes on to conduct that and all subsequent interviews in the same spirit, embellishing his answers in order to fashion a narrative that he thinks will most entertain his listener (Warren 3). As mentioned in Chapter One, Seuss often said that he had the idea for *And to Think That I Saw It on Mulberry Street* while crossing the Atlantic aboard the SS *Kungsholm*: to pass the time, he put words to the rhythm of the ship's engine. However, while the ship always figures prominently into Seuss's tales about the origin of *Mulberry Street*, he changes, adds, or omits certain details in the story. While he often says that children's books were one of the few items his Flit contract did not prohibit, he does not always indicate what prompted him to begin composing verse to the engines' beat. Often he says, "The chug of the engine was relentless, so all of a sudden I found myself writing a book for children and myself to its rhythm" (Gelber). On occasion, he will say that Helen suggested he make up the rhymes: "Finally Helen suggested I think up nonsense rhymes to be said to the rhythm of the damned engines—just to get rid of it" (Jennings 108). Another version has him and Helen "playing a game of making up rhymes to the rhythm of the ship's motors," and this activity then leads him to invent the couplet, "And that is a story that no one can beat / And to think that I saw it on Mulberry Street!" (Lindsay 34). Where and how long it took him to write *Mulberry Street* also varies. In one of the fullest accounts of the book's creation, he says:

> I was on a long, stormy crossing of the Atlantic, and it was too rough to go out on deck. Everybody in the ship just sat in the bar for a week, listening to the engines turn over: da-da-ta-ta, da-da-ta-ta, da-da-ta-ta . . . .
>
> To keep from going nuts, I began reciting silly words to the rhythm of the engines. Out of nowhere I found myself saying, "And that is a story that no one can beat; and to think that I saw it on Mulberry Street."
>
> When I finally got off the ship, this refrain kept going through my head. I couldn't shake it. To therapeutize myself, I added more words in the same rhythm.
>
> Six months later, I found I had a book on my hands, called *And to Think That I Saw It on Mulberry Street*. (Lathem 21)

In contrast to this version, Seuss has also said that the idea for the book preceded the ocean voyage and took more than six months to create. After getting stuck composing his first children's book, he travels to Sweden, and has a breakthrough on the trip home (Osterman 16). Apparently confirming this account, he told one interviewer, "I had been working on *And to Think That I Saw It on Mulberry Street*, my first book, for about three years" (Berman). If these particular interviews support the idea that he composed all but the first two lines after disembarking in the United States, at times he will instead say that he actually began writing the book on board the ship, telling the interviewer, "I had it about half written when we landed" (Associated Press) or "I got ashore and found I had about a third of a kids' book finished" (Salzhauer 6).

While some of the variation here may be attributable to what the reporter chose to include in the story or simply to the murkiness of long-term memory, Seuss's tales about his first book nonetheless contradict one another. That said, to ask (as one may be inclined to do), "Which version is true?" is to miss the point. Dr. Seuss is not interested in how long the book took to write, just as he does not keep track of how many publishers rejected it before Vanguard accepted it. The facts are not important; Seuss just wants to tell a good story. Whether 20,

26, 27, 28, or 29 publishers turned down the manuscript,[12] the number dramatizes his persistence: as he told *Parents* magazine in 1960, "Anyone who writes and needs a little encouragement should know that I went to twenty-eight publishers before I sold it" (Silverman 44). Whether he got the idea during his return voyage or before he left, the ship's engines remind us of Seuss's poetry, creativity, and most of all, his luck. "I began writing kids' books by accident," he liked to say. "I was in a trans-Atlantic crossing and it was too damn stormy to go on the deck, so I sat inside at the bar for eight days listening to the engines turn over. They were turning over in a rhythm . . ." and you know the rest (Salzhauer 6). Seuss often concludes the story by emphasizing his good luck. If he had not been walking down Madison Avenue and run into former class-mate Mike McClintock, who had just been appointed juvenile editor of Vanguard Press, then Seuss would have burned the book. Of course, he did meet McClintock, who promptly took him up to his office (Van-guard's offices were on Madison Avenue), where they signed a contract for *Mulberry Street*. As Seuss puts it, "That's one of the reasons I believe in luck. If I'd been going down the other side of Madison Avenue, I would be in the dry cleaning business today!" (Lathem 21). It is doubtful that Seuss *really* would have been in the dry cleaning business, but the "dry-cleaning" line makes it a better story.[13]

Seuss's penchant for self-invention reminds us that the storyteller is a kind of kind of con artist, persuading you to believe in his or her creations. The very first narrators of Seuss's tales are exactly such figures: boys who fib with such conviction that their lies seem true. Marco of *Mulberry Street* and *McElligot's Pool*, Gerald McGrew of *If I Ran the Zoo*, Peter T. Hooper of *Scrambled Eggs Super!* Morris McGurk of *If I Ran the Circus*, and the narrator of *On Beyond Zebra!* all ask us to believe in their tall tales. In *Mulberry Street*, Marco backs down at the end, unwilling to share his fantastic tale with his father. However, as Seuss gains confidence as a writer, his narrators gain confidence in their storytelling abilities. A decade after *Mulberry Street*, when Marco finishes explaining the wonders of McElligot's Pool, he appears to have convinced the skeptical farmer that there may indeed be a vast underground river connecting the apparently shallow pool to the sea. No longer laughing at Marco, the farmer has his hand on his chin, looking as if he is ready to accept this story. The bird, initially lacking expression, now smiles with interest while looking into the pool.[14] Although the current zookeeper seems unmoved by Gerald McGrew's plans for the "New Zoo, McGrew Zoo," the audience for Seuss's other storytellers listen with greater conviction. By the end of *Scrambled Eggs Super!*, Peter T. Hooper's sister and cat continue to listen with intense interest; on the last page of *If I Ran the Circus*, Sneelock now eyes Morris McGurk with wide-eyed concern; and at the conclusion of *On Beyond Zebra!* Conrad Cornelius o'Donald o'Dell is now ready to explore on beyond zebra. The audience knows that the storyteller not only believes in these stories but will try to make them come true. These narrators have gained the confidence of their listeners. As Lindberg says, "a confidence man *makes belief*" (7).

In lectures Dr. Seuss gave at the University of Utah in July 1949, he offered advice on how to make belief—specifically, on how to write believable fantasy. He said, "A child analyzes fantasy. They know you're kidding them. But there's got to be logic in the way you kid them." Children like "making believe they believe" your story, he says, but only "if you obey certain Rules of Logic." To elaborate on this point, Seuss explains, "They'll gladly accept your basic fantastic situation. You can tell them a story about a man with two heads. But when those heads start speaking, they've got to speak logically. They've got to react like a two-headed man *would* react." In other words, Seuss, says, "These two heads have got to be concerned about *real* problems that a child understands." By way of examples, Seuss suggests the "Problem of getting two hair cuts, two hats, two neckties, two toothbrushes." His analysis of how to make a story believable suggests some connections between a storyteller and a con artist: to make the lie believable, inventiveness needs to be grounded in reality. However, his analysis also reminds us how a con man and a storyteller are different: we resent being swindled by the former and ask to be persuaded by the latter. Children "like making believe they believe," and they know "the difference between fact and fantasy," as Seuss says, but neither they nor anyone else likes being cheated. In other words, it's crucial to consider to how these fantastic stories are being used.

In his books, Dr. Seuss considers the uses of fictions by giving his confidence-characters different roles to play. Sometimes, the confidence man is the hero, but just as often he is as the villain. When the story lacks a larger moral purpose, the con artist tends to be an appealing fellow; when the story intends to advance a moral, the con is more likely to be a shadier, less likeable sort. Like Professor Harold Hill in *The Music Man* or the Wizard in *The Wonderful Wizard of Oz*, the Cat in the Hat, Sam-I-am, and the narrator of *On Beyond Zebra!* are all characters who use the imagination to create possibility. As Seuss was fond of saying, "If you don't get imagination as a child, you probably never will [. . .] because it gets knocked out of you by the time you grow up" ("Logical Insanity of Dr. Seuss" 58). So, instead of remaining secure behind social or linguistic norms, these characters encourage us to explore what happens when we break the rules. In so doing, Harold Hill brings joy into River City, the Cat brings excitement into a dull suburban home, and Sam-I-am invites us to taste the unexpected. They may wheedle or exaggerate in order to get what they want, but the results of their fictions are ultimately liberating.

In those Seuss books where the confidence artist does not offer freedom, he tends to be connected with advertising. Like Melville's Confidence Man and several members of Faulkner's Snopes clan, Seuss's Grinch, Once-ler, Sylvester McMonkey McBean, and Dr. Terwilliker all swindle their victims using the slippery locutions of advertising. In *The Sneetches*, Sylvester McMonkey McBean tells the Plain-Belly Sneetches, "I've come here to help you. I have what you need. / And my prices are low. And I work at great speed. / And my work is one hundred percent guaranteed!" After giving them stars on their bellies with his Star-On Machine, McBean turns around and sells the original Star-Belly Sneetches the services of his Star-Off Machine. At the end, each Sneetch has been through each machine so many times that neither group knew "which one was what one . . . or what one was who." They do know that they've lost all their money to McBean, just as those who buy Thneeds squander their earnings on a useless product. Like the host of an infomercial, the Once-ler trumpets the virtues of his product without regard for the plausibility of his claims: "A Thneed's a Fine-Something-That-All-People-Need! / It's a shirt. It's a sock. It's a glove. It's a hat. / But it has *other* uses. Yes, far beyond that. You can use it for carpets! For pillows! For sheets! / Or curtains! Or covers for bicycle seats!" As Francelia Butler observes, "the Once-ler sounds like a slick salesman, and Seuss parodies such a man" (176). In parodying salesmen, Seuss

may be parodying his earlier advertising work or, at the very least, parodying the genre in which he once made his living.

"You have no right to push and shove us little kids around": Children and Power

Dr. Seuss frequently turns to satire and parody because his creativity
comes from adolescence. Although it was not until World War II that
Seuss became a fully committed political artist, three events in the second decade of his life shaped his critical perspective—a way of seeing
that frequently led him to express himself through humor. In 1915, just
before he entered adolescence, Americans' responses to World War I
fueled anti-German sentiments, and he was teased for being a German-
American. As the Morgans put it, "Feeling the first sting of the outsider,
Ted tried to appear jovial and outgoing to prove that the gibes didn't
hurt" (16). In 1919, when he was a junior in high school, the Volstead
Act passed, effectively ending the Geisel family business. As discussed
earlier in the chapter, for the rest of his life he remained skeptical of
anyone who reminded him of temperance advocates. In 1921, beginning
his freshman year at Dartmouth, not a single fraternity invited him to
pledge. As he told the Morgans, "With my black hair and long nose, I
was supposed to be Jewish. It took a year and a half before word got
around that I wasn't. I think my interest in editing the Dartmouth
humor magazine [Jack-o-lantern] began . . . that Pledge Week" (27). So,
the boy picked on for his ethnicity and (presumed) religion develops a
sharp sense of humor, and grows up to attack prejudice in books like
The Sneetches and Horton Hears a Who! The adolescent whose family was
disenfranchised by zealous reformers becomes an adult who parodies the
self-righteous in characters like the kangaroo (who threatens Horton's
Whos) and Lord Droon (who steals the King's stilts). Facing "adult"
problems as both an adolescent and a child, Theodor Seuss Geisel knew
that childhood can be a difficult time. As Maurice Sendak said when
accepting the Caldecott Medal for Where the Wild Things Are, "from their
earliest years children live on familiar terms with disrupting emotions, [
. . .] fear and anxiety are an intrinsic part of their everyday lives, [. . .
and] they continually cope with frustration as best they can" (Caldecott &
Co. 151). Sendak argues that books which evade such realities deny the

often frightening experiences of childhood. Seuss also knew that children could not be insulated from things that may frighten or disturb them. His adolescent and pre-adolescent experiences, in part, explain the adult presence in his works, and shows us why his children's fictions address adult concerns.

The 5,000 Fingers of Dr. T. is a case in point. In the film, young Bart Collins, played by Tommy Rettig (who would later play Timmy in TV's "Lassie"), fights a lonely crusade against the nasty Dr. Terwilliker, who is equal parts con artist and megalomaniacal dictator.[15] Bart is required to take on a role of an adult, opposing a totalitarian regime that, as Seuss has imagined it, resembles a Fascist state. Terwilliker, dressed in a costume that mingles Busby-Berkeley band leader with military general (figure 4.4), is preparing to run a piano prison camp for boys—complete with electric fence to prevent anyone escaping. Early on and standing atop a gigantic, two-tiered piano that has seats for 500 boys, Terwilliker outlines his grandiose plans: "Tomorrow, we will celebrate the official grand opening. Tomorrow, down below me, I will have five hundred little boys. Five thousand little fingers. And they'll be mine, all mine—practicing 24 hours a day . . . 365 days a year!" Seated down below, Bart interjects, "I don't believe it! This is crazy!" Terwilliker responds, "Who are you to tell me what is crazy? Away! Go back to your cell. And put on your official Terwilliker beanie!" Each Terwilliker beanie has the words "HAPPY FINGERS" on its front and a hand sticking out of its top: near the end of the film, when 500 beanie-wearing children sit at the massive piano, their hats viewed from above suggest a crowd with hands raised in a Fascist salute. The camera shots from the perspective of Terwilliker, who conducts the boys from atop the piano, amplify this echo of a Nazi rally. Whether or not that is the intended echo, Seuss clearly points out that all of these children have been coerced into their role. When they arrive at what is supposed to be a summer camp, the scene instead in some respects resembles entry into a concentration camp. Dr. Terwilliker's uniformed personnel line up all the boys, open the suitcase of each one, and search it for any item not related to playing the piano. They then confiscate all such toys—comic books, tennis rackets, baseballs, slingshots—assign each child a number, and place a "HAPPY FINGERS" beanie on top of each child's head. The long lines of children being stripped of their belongings and identities recall images of people being forcibly relocated.

Figure 4.4. "Dr. Terwilliger, Costume for the Great Concert." Sketch by Dr. Seuss.

Fortunately, Bart arrived before the other children did and has had time to develop a plan to foil Dr. T. With the help of an initially reluctant Mr. Zabladowski—the plumber working at the Terwilliker Institute—Bart has invented a "Music Fix," a bottle that when opened sucks all the sound out of the air. So, when Dr. Terwilliker raises his baton to conduct the 500 boys assembled at the piano, Bart opens his bottle and disrupts the proceedings. Dr. Terwilliker's men advance on Bart, who stands up, brandishing the "Music Fix" bottle, and announces, "You come any closer, I'll blow you to smithereens!" Dr. Terwilliker asks, "Is it—is it atomic?" Bart replies, "Yes sir—very atomic!" The soldiers shout, "Atomic?!" and run away. Under the threat of Bart's atomic weapon, Dr. Terwilliker agrees to free Bart's mother, Mr. Zabladowski, and all the boys. The boys tear up their sheet music, throw it in the air, and then take Dr. T. to the dungeon to lock him up, while Bart conducts the remaining group in a raucous, off-key version of "Chopsticks." As he conducts, atomic steam rises up from the bottle, making the shape of a mushroom cloud. The boys flee, and then the bottle explodes into what the screenplay describes as "a multi-colored Bikini-like cloud" (91). Bart wakes from his dream.

His fantasy, however, has had effects in the world beyond his imagination: Bart, whose father is dead, had hoped that his mother and Mr. Zabladowski would get married. They now appear romantically interested in one another. Tellingly, the "blood oath" that Bart insisted Mr. Zabladowski take in his dream also appears to have occurred beyond the dream world. To his surprise, Mr. Zabladowski sees that he has a Band-Aid on his thumb—just as Bart has on his—indicating that they did take the oath. Bart's dream is the fantasy through which he accomplishes mastery over what, in his real life, he has no control. As Sendak says of the heroes of his own books, "They all have the sane need to master the uncontrollable and frightening aspects of their lives, and they all turn to fantasy to accomplish this" (*Caldecott & Co.* 152). The nice twist Seuss adds is that, unlike most fantasies, Bart's fantasy actually achieves results in the real world.

Tellingly, the most difficult part of Bart's job is convincing adults that children should be taken seriously. During "The Kids' Song," which he sings about halfway through the film, Bart protests adults' unwillingness to treat him with the respect he feels he deserves:

> Now just because we're kids, because we're sort of small,
> Because we're closer to the ground,
> And you are bigger pound by pound,
> You have no right, you have no right
> To push and shove us little kids around.

> Now just because your throat has got a deeper voice
> And lots of wind to blow it out
> At little kids who don't dare shout,
> You have no right, you have no right
> To boss and beat us little kids about.

The context in which he performs this number demonstrates that he is *not* just another kid complaining about having to follow rules. Bart has a genuine grievance here. His mother is unreliable, his father is dead, and Mr. Zabladowski is reluctant to intervene. It's all up to Bart to expose Dr. T's nefarious scheme. Bart's struggle shows us what an uphill job the children in *The Cat in the Hat* would have were they to try to convince their mother of what they had seen. Despite Bart's attempts to convince his mother and Mr. Zabladowski, they remain hypnotized by Dr. Terwilliker. As Bart is the sole character who has seen through Dr. T's hypocrisy, his defense of children's rights here seems all the more apt. Though children may lack the power to fight back, these adults "have no right / To push and shove us little kids around."

Just as he creates children who protest the powerlessness of childhood, Seuss encourages adults to remember the difficulties of their own childhoods, so that when they grow up, they treat children with respect. As Bart sings in the final verse of his song,

> But we'll grow up someday, and when we do, I pray
> We won't just grow in size and sound.
> And just be bigger pound by pound
> I'd hate to grow, like some I know,
> Who push and shove us little kids around.

Seuss clearly did remember the frustrations of his own childhood, and created child characters who tackle the problems—often big problems—that children may face. Given that Bart is a child alone in a world of adults for much of the film, Seuss suggests one reason that children have to cope with adult problems: they are alone. And yet, however alone they may be, children can be capable, intelligent, and resilient. As Seuss said in his lectures at the University of Utah, "Children are just as smart as you are. The main difference is they don't know so many words, and you'll lose them if your story gets complicated. But," he added, "if your story is simple, you can tell it just as if you're telling it to adults."

After glimpsing the adult and the adolescent behind his children's books, we might then deduce that Seuss doesn't distinguish between adults and children. Asked, "Are there any hidden adult meanings in your books?" Seuss replied, "Well, I don't think there's any difference between adult meanings and children's meanings" (Salzhauer 6). Of course, this claim is not literally true, and Seuss knew it was not literally true—as he says, children don't know as many words as adults do, and for this reason, his books use a vocabulary that children can understand. He also knew that while it was fine to use swearwords as he composed a book, he needed to take them out for the final version. Instead, the claim that there is no difference between children's meanings and adult meanings reminds us that Seuss saw children as being as smart as grown-ups, and knew that they understand more than grown-ups give them credit for. As Maurice Sendak has said, "I remember my own childhood vividly . . . I knew terrible things, but I knew I mustn't let adults *know* I knew . . . It would scare them" (Spiegelman and Sendak 81). Though their inspiration comes from different places, Sendak and Seuss agree that you should not talk down to children, and their willingness to speak without condescension earns the respect of their readers. All great children's writers—Virginia Hamilton, Ruth Krauss, Beatrix Potter, Philip Pullman, Maurice Sendak, Chris Van Allsburg—honor the intelligence of their readers, which is one reason their books appeal to adults, too. As Ludwig Bemelmans observed, "Dr. Seuss treats the child as an adult, and I think a children's book, to be good, must not be made for an inferior creature, for the diaper brigade. Because children are very, very, very alert, you know?" ("Sneetches, Sugar, and Success" 74). Alert enough to read about con men? we might ask. Whatever our own answers may be, Dr. Seuss's answer is "yes, they are." Given the popularity of characters like Sam-I-am and the Grinch, Dr. Seuss appears to be right.

Chapter 5

The Disneyfication of Dr. Seuss

FAITHFUL TO PROFIT,
ONE HUNDRED PERCENT?

I n the now-classic holiday picture book, *How the Grinch Stole Christmas!*, the Grinch is shocked when—despite his having stolen everything from the Christmas trees to the last can of *Who*-hash—"Every *Who* down in *Who*-ville, the tall and the small, / Was singing! Without any presents at all!" Against all his efforts to prevent it, Christmas arrives "just the same!" Like Scrooge on Christmas morning, the Grinch on Christmas morning is a changed man—or, at least, a changed Grinch. In his memorable epiphany,

> "Maybe Christmas," he thought, "*doesn't* come from a store."
> "Maybe Christmas . . . perhaps . . . means a little bit more!"

Like Charles Schulz's *A Charlie Brown Christmas* (1965), which made its television debut the year before Chuck Jones's animated *Grinch* (for which Seuss himself wrote the screenplay), the book *How the Grinch Stole Christmas!* criticizes the commercialization of the holiday. Now, as Schulz's TV special did and as popular holiday records—such as Stan Freberg's "Green Chri\$tma\$" (1958)—have done, Seuss's *Grinch* profited from satirizing those who exploit Christmas for profit. CBS-TV paid MGM \$315,000 for the rights to air the animated *Grinch* before Christmas in 1966 and 1967; the TV special has gone on to become a holiday tradition (Morgan and Morgan 191). And, noting this irony, one might be inclined to point to the book's complicity in that which it criticizes: after all, doesn't Seuss's *Grinch* sell well every holiday season precisely because it *is* a Christmas book—a Christmas book promoted by its own TV special?

Such a charge suggests that Seuss could launch a critique from out-side the economic system of which he was a part and that he would want to oppose a system in which he had succeeded. By the time of his death in 1991, "Dr. Seuss" was a multimillion-dollar industry; in 1998, Herb Cheyette of Dr. Seuss Enterprises estimated that over 400 million Dr. Seuss books had been sold ("An Awfully Big Adventure"). As a former advertising man, Seuss may well have viewed the financial success of the *Grinch* as a moral success: the more people who see Jones's *Grinch* or read Seuss's *Grinch*, the more who receive Seuss's message. As his World War II cartoons and political books demonstrate, when writing as a propagandist, Seuss wished to persuade as many people as he could. He might have enjoyed the irony of having written a successful commer-cial against commercialism.[1]

But would Seuss approve of the past decade's hyper-commercializa-tion of his work? During his life, Dr. Seuss did license spin-off products other than animated TV specials. There were "World of Dr. Seuss" lunch boxes, Cat in the Hat plush toys, and the "Sam-I-Am" See-'n-Say Storymaker, to name but a few. For the most part, the products permit-ted by Seuss tend to encourage creative play. The Seuss Multi-Beasts introduced by Revell in 1959 and 1960 had interchangeable parts: you could make Tingo, "the noodle topped stroodle," you could combine Tingo's parts with those of Gowdy, "the dowdy grackle," or Busby, "the tasselated afghan spaniel yak." As their boxes proclaimed, "SNAPS TOGETHER—PULLS APART in THOUSANDS of ways"—the first four Multi-Beasts could be combined in 14,000 ways, by Revell's esti-mate ("Revell, Inc." 53). And, of course, a child could playact with a Cat in the Hat plush toy or create new stories from the See-'n-Say Storymaker. Seuss did not allow characters from his books to be used in advertising for unrelated products, and often turned down requests to license his work, once remarking, "I'd rather go into *The Guinness Book of Records* as the writer who refused the most money per word" (Morgan and Morgan xviii). However, since his death, Seuss's name has been attached to a wider range of items, including a Seuss theme park in Orlando, Florida, and commercials featuring Seuss's characters. Con-tradicting the notion that Christmas "*doesn't* come from a store," the Grinch himself has sold Kellogg's Frosted Mini-Wheats, Nabisco's Ritz crackers, VISA credit cards, and York Peppermint Patties.[2] It is time we look at the Disneyfication of Dr. Seuss, examining how a man whose books encourage critical thinking became a brand name.

Disneyfication

In *Inside the Mouse: Work and Play at Disney World* (1995), Karen Klugman defines "Disneyfication" as "the application of simplified aesthetic, intellectual, or moral standards to a thing that has the potential for more complex and thought-provoking expression" (Klugman 103). The film of the *Grinch* (2000) is the cinematic embodiment of this definition and the most vivid example of the Disneyfication of Dr. Seuss. To be fair to the filmmakers, they do get the central message of Seuss's book: indeed, the film has Cindy-Lou Who and the Grinch each undergo spiritual crises about the meaning of Christmas so that each may separately conclude that the holiday is more about community than capitalism. The Grinch (played by Jim Carrey) retains Seuss's lines about Christmas not coming from a store but meaning a little bit more. To emphasize this moral, prior to the Grinch's pronouncement the film provides a scene in Who-ville's town square on Christmas morning. Cindy-Lou Who's father Lou-Lou Who (Bill Irwin) tells us, "I'm glad he took our presents. I'm glad." In the tone of a villainous sitcom boss, the mayor replies, "He's glad. You're glad. You're glad everything is gone. You're glad that the Grinch virtually wrecked—no, no, no, not wrecked—*pulverized* Christmas! Is that what I'm hearing from you, Lou?" Cindy-Lou Who gazes adoringly at her father, as he responds, "You can't hurt Christmas, Mr. Mayor, because it isn't about the gifts or the contests or the fancy lights. That's what Cindy's been trying to tell everyone. And me. She's been trying to tell me." Finally, to make absolutely sure we get the point:

> MR. MAYOR: What is wrong with you? This is a child!
> LOU-LOU WHO: She's my child, and she happens to be right, by the way. I don't need anything more for Christmas than this right here: my family. Merry Christmas everybody!

The scene is overdone, the dialogue is cloying, but it does spell out how Christmas means "a little bit more." Although it simplifies aesthetically and intellectually, the screenplay does emphasize Seuss's moral, even if—as the *New York Times*' A. O. Scott points out—the moral "is learned not so much by the Grinch but by the Whos themselves, who must overcome their corrupting materialism before they get their mountains of presents, a perfect Hollywood moral" (Scott 105).

Regrettably, the excesses of the production undercut even the Hollywood-ized moral message. The film imagines not only Who-ville but even the Grinch's cave as elaborate, gadget-filled amusement parks. While Seuss's books display a fondness for Rube-Goldberg-esque inventions, the special-effects-encumbered *Grinch* film seems designed to encourage viewers to buy these inventions, to purchase the action figures, to come to the theme park. Who-ville's remarkably clean garbage chute, which empties into the Grinch's mountaintop cave, is like a waterslide that works both ways: The Grinch and Cindy-Lou Who delight in riding it down and up the mountain. As the camera follows them around turns, catching the mirthful expressions on their faces, the Grinch whoops and Cindy-Lou screams in delight, suggesting a commercial for a Wet 'n Wild theme park or Orlando's "Seuss Landing" theme park. Even the Grinch's sled behaves like an amusement-park ride—appropriate, given that Seuss Landing offers a sled-ride with the Grinch down Mt. Crumpit (Palmer 8). On the way down the mountain the first time, it's a sled-spaceship hybrid, complete with rocket boosters; on the way down the second time, it's a sled-motorboat, with Cindy-Lou driving and the Grinch skiing behind it, hanging on to a rope in a manner that suggests waterskiing. The film feels like a commercial because it dwells on spectacle at the expense of character and narrative. As director Ron Howard has said, "What we tried to do with *The Grinch* is use the latest state-of-the-art technology to be able to really create an atmosphere, scope, and scale that's really pretty seamless" ("We All Dream of Oz"). His film may be seamless, but it emphasizes "state-of-the-art" production values more than the story itself.

The narrative of the film, unlike that of the book or of Jones's animated version, stresses the values of self-improvement, emphasizing a quintessentially American narrative: if you work hard, anything is possible! Young, blonde, and spunky, Cindy-Lou Who is equal parts social worker, therapist, and investigative reporter. Perceiving the Grinch's essential virtue, she interviews the Grinch's guardians and childhood acquaintances, discovering the truth about his sad childhood: after being mocked by his peers and suffering an unrequited love for Martha-Mae Who, the eight-year-old Grinch exiled himself to the mountaintop cave. Before Cindy-Lou intervenes, the Grinch is given to announcing, "Now to take care of those pesky memories" and then smacking himself in the head with a mallet. But that adorable Cindy's message of love and community involvement helps the Grinch reform. In Seuss's book, he changes from Grumpy Grinch to Good Citizen, too, but there's no emphasis on self-improvement: he hears the Whos singing, has an epiphany, and he's a new Grinch. In contrast, the film emphasizes the recovery process: Cindy-Lou suggests that his dislike of Christmas may be "just a misunderstanding" and counsels the Grinch to "reunite with the Whos and be a part of Christmas." It is a misunderstanding, and his joining with the Whos is the final step in his 12-step program. As Interbrand consultancy president Martyn Straw has observed, "American brands are about anything being possible—the core value of all of them is optimism. America is not a country, it's an idea. [. . .] [T]he Disney brand is almost exclusively dependent upon that" (qtd. in Weber 78–79). The Seuss brand is becoming dependent upon that, too.

Even an original Seuss book like *Oh, the Places You'll Go!* is not as optimistic as its status as perennial graduation gift would suggest. Its central character lands in "the Lurch," "a Slump," and "the Waiting Place," all of which make the possibility of failure very real. However, recent ersatz Seuss books bring the Seuss brand much closer to the Disney brand, promoting the idea that anything is possible as long as one keeps a positive outlook. Tish Rabe's *Oh, the Things You Can Do That Are Good for You!* (2001) and Bonnie Worth's *Oh Say Can You Seed?* (2001), both marketed as volumes in "The Cat in the Hat's Learning Library," are saccharine, moralistic guides to self-improvement. Seuss did write more overtly "educational" books, like *I Can Read with My Eyes Shut!* and *The Cat's Quizzer*, but in these books the Cat in the Hat retains some of his subversive appeal. The Cat may not be the anarchist that he is in *The Cat in the Hat* (1957) or *The Cat in the Hat Comes Back* (1958), but his narration of both *I Can Read with My Eyes Shut!* and *The Cat's Quizzer* happily mocks the "educational" genre of which both books partake. In the former, the Cat advises a young cat about reading, which (if done with eyes open) can teach you about "fishbones . . . and wishbones. You'll learn about trombones, too. You'll learn about Jack the Pillow Snake and all about Foo-Foo the Snoo." The latter includes such absurd questions as "What would you do if you jumped in the air and didn't come down?" (41) and provides appropriately whimsical answers, like "If you get stuck in the air, fly to the nearest telephone. Dial '0' and ask for a ladder" (60).

In contrast, the Cat of *Oh, the Things You Can Do That Are Good for You!* and *Oh Say Can You Seed?* takes himself quite seriously. He's still smiling, but now he works out. The former book's cover shows him clad in running shorts and a tank top, going jogging with Thing One and Thing Two, all carrying water bottles in their hands. He introduces the Tac-Toe-Tapping Tweets who "are strong and they're wise, / for they know to stay healthy / they need exercise!" (9). Thing One and Thing Two, formerly pure id, are now all superego: they lift weights, stay clean, and do their homework. The now well-behaved Cat shows us the Zanz who sings a "song / about washing your hands" (14): "Wash your hands carefully. / It's up to you. / Use soap and warm water. / It's easy to do. / Rinse them and while / we all sing this refrain, / germs from your hands / will slide right down the drain!" (16–17). *Oh Say Can You Seed?* trots out the Cat to explain botany to young readers: "Just what is a seed, / you are wondering, maybe? / Well, you might say a seed / is a tiny plant baby!" (12). The book concludes with verses such as "But whether they stick / or they blow or they fly, / seeds bring us life, / and now you know why" (38). These books turn the Cat in the Hat into precisely what the original Cat in the Hat rebelled against: preachy, didactic, obviously "educational" primers. Of course, books like *The Cat in the Hat*, *The Butter Battle Book* and *The Lorax* do have morals, but they deliver these morals by provoking their readers, not by preaching to them.[3]

To be fair to the authors of these books, we should note it is difficult to imitate Dr. Seuss—a challenge that may have been compounded by the tangled origins of "The Cat in the Hat's Learning Library." As Herb Cheyette explains, NASA in 1993 asked if its new robotic space probes could be named DRSEUSS, "an acronym for Data Relay Solar Electric Upper Stage Spacecraft." An image of the Cat in the Hat would be featured on the probes, and NASA also wanted the Cat to serve as narrator for a series of "children's beginning science books" that were to be "based on NASA supplied materials." After five years of negotiation, contracts had been signed by Dr. Seuss Enterprises and Random House, and, just as NASA was about to sign, "everyone involved in the project on NASA's side was either fired or reassigned, and the project was peremptorily aborted by the agency." Having invested a great deal of time and money into the project, Dr. Seuss Enterprises and Random House decided to go ahead with the idea of "using the Cat as a narrator to teach simple science" (Cheyette, letter, 22 May 2003). Despite the project's difficult beginnings, *Oh Say Can You Seed* won the 2003 Ohio Farm Bureau Children's Literature Award for books with an agricultural theme. The books also feature an endorsement from Barbara Kiefer, Associate Professor of Columbia University's Teachers College: "The Cat in the Hat's Learning Library™ shows young readers that books can be entertaining and educational at the same time. This is a wonderful series!" While I do not concur with these assessments, we must note that "The Cat in the Hat's Learning Library" does have some admirers: in this respect, the series has overcome both its troubled start and its aesthetic deficiencies.

Fortunately, if you know the original Seuss books, the "new" ones are obviously not Seuss books. As Herb Cheyette says, "To suggest that anyone would buy one of these books thinking it was by Dr. Seuss is absurd; almost as absurd as thinking that comparing their literary quality to that of an inimitable genius provides a demonstration of critical acumen" (letter, 22 May 2003). But the unwary may take the iconic image of the Cat in the Hat (or, in some cases, the name "Dr. Seuss") as a sign of the book's authorship. For example, though Ron Howard's *Dr. Seuss's How the Grinch Stole Christmas!* (2000) differs from Dr. Seuss's version, it uses Seuss's name in the title and its phenomenal success (it grossed $55 million in its first weekend alone) may make it the best-known version of Seuss's story.[4] The film, the pseudo-Seuss books, and the television show *The Wubbulous World of Dr. Seuss* (its title an obvious play on *The Wonderful World of Disney*) sanitize Dr. Seuss. Contrary to these projects' heavy-handed moralism, Seuss was a contrarian who enjoyed challenging people to reconsider their assumptions. He was a mainstream publishing phenomenon who used his celebrity to promote an activist agenda. As discussed in Chapter Two, he wrote *The Sneetches* to criticize anti-Semitism, modeled *Yertle the Turtle* (1958) on the rise of Hitler, created *The Lorax* to call attention to corporate abuse of the environment, and penned *The Butter Battle Book* as a critique of Reagan's enthusiasm for the nuclear arms race. Turning Seuss into another Disney threatens to make "Seuss" synonymous with the ambiguous power of global capitalism.

Just What the Doctor Ordered?

Before we too quickly attribute the Disneyfication of Dr. Seuss to the machinations of the marketplace, we must consult Dr. Seuss Enterprises, the corporation which oversees the licensing of all Seuss merchandise— everything from the original books and TV specials to the action figures and the theme park. All major decisions by Dr. Seuss Enterprises are arrived at by consensus of the Board of Directors (Audrey Geisel, Karl ZoBell, and Herb Cheyette), of which Mrs. Geisel is *prima inter pares*. Seuss saying that he'd "rather go into *The Guinness Book of Records* as the writer who refused the most money per word" may indicate that Cheyette and Geisel are not upholding Seuss's wishes. However, the source of the *Guinness* anecdote is none other than Herb Cheyette. Recalling that Theodor Seuss Geisel "was reluctant to merchandise Seuss characters," Cheyette tells the story of "a major television advertiser who offered a vast sum of money for the right to use a Dr. Seuss character in a holiday message" (Lathem, *Theodor Seuss Geisel* 24). Jed Mattes, then Geisel's book agent, sent some unpublished Seuss verses to the delighted sponsor, who in turn created storyboards based on the verses. When Ted saw the storyboards, he "indicated that he really didn't want Dr. Seuss to be connected to a particular religious holiday or with a product large doses of which might have uncertain effects on children" (25). In response, the sponsor offered even more money. Ted still wouldn't allow the commercial.

In a final attempt to persuade him, Cheyette said, "Let me put on my agent's hat for a minute. These verses consist of less than a hundred words. If you accept this deal you will go into *The Guinness Book of Records* as the writer who was paid the most money per word." Ted thought for a moment, and then answered, "I'd rather go into *The Guinness Book of Records* as the writer who refused the most money per word" (26).

Though Dr. Seuss objected to this particular project, Cheyette says that he was not philosophically opposed to marketing schemes.[5] He reports that Seuss responded "to more than one marketing proposal" by asking, "Why should I spend my time correcting the works of others when I can spend the same amount of time creating new works? There will be plenty of time after my death" (Cheyette, letter, 3 Oct. 2001). In other words, Seuss's resistance to marketing proposals may have arisen not out of any desire to prevent what I have been calling Disney-fication, but out of perfectionism. As Cheyette explains, Seuss was a "still-creative perfectionist" in the "final quarter of his life": were he to involve himself with marketing proposals, his creative output would suffer.

Seuss's biographers agree that his perfectionism led him away from "commercial decisions in his final years," but doubt that Seuss would approve of "the swift flood of after-death marketing" (Morgan, email). In 1997, Judith Morgan, who was also a neighbor of Ted and Audrey Geisel, told the *New York Times'* Dinitia Smith, "You look back: there weren't even t-shirts." Of the recent flurry of marketing, she said, "I do not think he would have allowed it. It's become an empire since his death. It used to be one man and one desk" (qtd. in Smith B12). Christopher Cerf, the son of Bennett Cerf (Seuss's publisher at Random House), appears to agree with Ms. Morgan. Interviewed for the same article, Cerf observed, "If he were around, he would be absolutely resist-ing this, or riding herd like the perfectionist he was. I hope things remain true to his vision" (qtd. in Smith B12). Though Cerf, like Chey-ette, identifies perfectionism as the cause of Seuss's resistance, he does not express any enthusiasm for the recent hypercommercialization of Seuss. Seuss's opposition may, indeed, have stemmed from perfection-ism. In 1959, he was critical of the Revell Corporation's versions of Seuss creatures; in the 1980s, he didn't like Coleco's versions either— and in 1987, Cheyette arranged for a buyout of the rest of Seuss's contact with Coleco (Morgan and Morgan 164, 259–60).

"The Morgans' portrayal of Ted Geisel as a monetarily indifferent idealist is only partially true," Cheyette says (letter, 3 Oct. 2001). After all, Seuss's roots were in advertising: before writing children's books, Seuss sold mail-order sculptures and made his name with campaigns for Flit bug spray and Essolube motor oil. Seuss has even credited his adver-tising experience with being "helpful to me as a writer of children's books," because it "taught me conciseness and how to marry pictures with words" (Wintle and Fisher 115). Professing indifference to wealth (Seuss often called money "a necessary evil" [123]), Seuss gave away much of his. Through the Dr. Seuss Foundation (established in 1958), Seuss gave to the Scripps Clinic and Research Foundation in La Jolla; Tougaloo, a small Mississippi college; and SOFA (Strongly Organized for Action), "a non-profit group that operated a child care center for La

Jolla's ethnic community" (Morgan and Morgan 258). He and his first wife established an endowed chair at Dartmouth College—the Ted and Helen Geisel Third Century Professor in the Humanities. Through legal arrangements made before he died, Theodor Seuss Geisel (class of 1925) is a major continuing benefactor of Dartmouth. In 1998, when San Diego's Old Globe Theatre wanted to give poorer children free tickets to its stage production of *How the Grinch Stole Christmas!*, Audrey Geisel "waived all royalty payments and donated more than $100,000 from the Dr. Seuss Foundation to help cover costs" ("Giving a Grinch for the Holidays"). In addition, Mrs. Geisel gives to most of the charitable organizations in San Diego and La Jolla, including the San Diego Museum of Art and the Museum of Photographic Art. She also provided a $20 million endowment for the University of California at San Diego, and was the principal donor for the Dr. Seuss National Memorial. Today, the Dr. Seuss Foundation provides primary support for over one hundred medical, cultural and socially active institutions. As Cheyette puts it, "A literary and artistic genius not indifferent to the relationship of art and commerce, [Seuss] spent a great deal of thought making certain that his estate would continue to generate income to benefit society" (letter, 3 Oct. 2001).

Some may be inclined to ask, surely Seuss's many books and several TV-specials generate enough income to keep the Dr. Seuss Foundation in robust fiscal health? That is, the continued popularity of the Seuss oeuvre may prompt speculation about whether or not the more recent projects are desirable.

Trademark vs. Copyright

Herb Cheyette, Audrey Geisel, and Karl ZoBell (who is also Mrs. Geisel's lawyer) all say that the best way to protect an author's rights is through trademark, not copyright. As Cheyette points out, "A peculiarity of the American legal system is that commerce is valued more than art. As a consequence, copyrights are protected for a limited period of time, trademarks are enjoyed in perpetuity. Trademarks can only be acquired by utilizing works for commercial purposes" (letter, 3 Oct. 2001). Zo-Bell notes, "Under the rules governing trademarks, if you don't defend them or use them you lose them and they fall into the public domain.

In order to protect the characters, we had to go into the marketplace" (qtd. in Smith B12). Or as Audrey Geisel says, "I wish the Cat to go on indefinitely as a literary cat, not a cartoon cat. The alternative was to kill it" (qtd. in Smith B1).

If the alternative to pursuing trademark protection was to "kill" the Cat in the Hat by allowing him to remain under the protection of copyright alone, then we might wonder how and why trademark would be more advantageous than copyright. According to U.S. Copyright Law (title 17, passed 1976), copyright applies to "original works of authorship fixed in any tangible medium of expression, now known or later developed, from which they can be perceived, reproduced, or otherwise communicated, either directly or with the aid of a machine or device" (*Copyright Law of the United States*). Copyright does *not* protect titles, names, short phrases, or slogans (U.S. Copyright Office, "Circular 1: Copyright Basics"). In contrast, trademark is "a word, name symbol or device which is used in trade with goods to indicate the source of the goods and to distinguish it from the goods of others," according to the U.S. Patent and Trademark Office ("What Are Patents, Trademarks . . ."). In plain English, copyright protects authors (and artists), but trademark protects products and the marks attached to those products. So, copyright protects the TV special or book of *The Cat in the Hat*, but trademark protects the image of the Cat himself, as the logo of Random House's "Beginner Books" series or as attached to any product.

Another strength of trademark is its duration. Trademarks last as long as they remain in use, although they need to be renewed every ten years (if granted on or after November 16, 1989) or twenty years (if granted prior to November 16, 1989). In contrast, copyright lasts for a fixed period of time. As per the Sonny Bono Copyright Term Extension Act, signed into law on October 27, 1998, copyright on works published after 1978 now lasts for the author's life plus seventy years. For "pre-1978 works still in their original or renewal term of copyright," copyright lasts ninety-five years from "the date that copyright was originally secured" (U.S. Copyright Office, "Questions Frequently Asked in the Copyright Office . . ."). So, *The Cat in the Hat* and *How the Grinch Stole Christmas!* both published in 1957, will remain under copyright until 2052. In contrast, a Grinch action figure could be protected by trademark indefinitely—as long as it's being made, the trademark would be enforced. In other words, Mr. Cheyette, Mr. ZoBell, and Mrs. Geisel have a point. If trademark is more powerful (and therefore more desirable) than copyright, then why not bring the Cat and the Grinch into the marketplace? Since trademark protects products, take a literary character and turn him into a commodity. Under American law, "commerce is valued more than art," as Mr. Cheyette says.

Theodor Seuss Geisel may have arrived at the same conclusion in 1968 when he encountered "Dr. Seuss's Merry Menagerie," a series of six different vinyl dolls based on cartoons he had drawn for *Liberty Magazine* in 1932. The resulting lawsuit—*Geisel v. Poynter Products Inc., Alabe Crafts Inc., Linder, Nathan & Heide Inc., and Liberty Library Corporation*—offers a glimpse into how and why Dr. Seuss and his heirs would seek protection under trademark instead of copyright. Dr. Seuss's cartoons ran in *Liberty* from June through December of 1932, for which Geisel was paid $300 apiece. Regarding ownership of these cartoons, Geisel understood that "while Liberty had the complete rights to publish these works in one issue of *Liberty Magazine*, Liberty held all other rights to this work (including the right to renew the copyright and the right to make other uses of the work) in trust" for him. However, there was no written agreement. Fulton Oursler, *Liberty*'s editor-in-chief, thought that Dr. Seuss cartoons would be "very suitable" for the magazine. Geisel agreed, and Oursler said, "Glad to have you on board." That conversation was the contract.

Liberty Magazine ceased publication in 1950, and Lorraine Lester—herself an author of stories that appeared in the magazine—bought its copyright library. In 1964, at the suggestion of Robert Whiteman, she founded the Liberty Library Corporation in order to "make money by exploiting the literary properties" contained in the magazine. In December of 1964 Whiteman invited Geisel to join with Liberty Library in developing products based on this material or to repurchase the rights to these works. Geisel declined, and his attorney, Frank Kockritz, sent a telegram indicating that he did not recognize Liberty's rights to these cartoons and that he "reserv[ed] the right to institute a lawsuit." Without his or Geisel's consent, Liberty Library signed an agreement with Universal Publishing, which in 1967 published *Dr. Seuss's Lost World Revisited: A Forward-Looking Backward Glance*, marketing it as "A book for grown-ups by the celebrated author-illustrator of the most popular children's books of our time." That same year, Liberty sold to Poynter Products the rights to produce dolls based on the cartoons. When they hit the marketplace in March of 1968, the dolls were advertised as "Dr. Seuss's Merry Menagerie" and "From the Wonderful World of Dr. Seuss." In April, Geisel filed an injunction against Poynter, Liberty, Alabe Crafts (distributor of Poynter's products), and Linder, Nathan & Heide Inc. (manufacturer's representative for Alabe), claiming that they had violated trademark laws by "falsely representing these dolls as the product of Dr. Seuss, which they are not, or as having been approved by Dr. Seuss, when they were not." In a New York federal court on April 9, Judge William Herlands declared that there was a "reasonable probability" of Geisel's success in proving this claim, and ordered the defendants to stop:

A. Representing that defendants' doll, toy or other similar product has been created, designed, produced, approved or authorized by plaintiff [Geisel];
B. Describing defendants' doll, toy or other similar product as having been created, designed, produced, approved or authorized by plaintiff; or
C. Representing, describing or designating plaintiff as the originator, creator, designer or producer of defendants' doll, toy, or other similar products.

So, Geisel won that round and was poised to win the case.

However, the defendants paid close attention to the language of this preliminary injunction, and realized that all they needed to do was to change *their* language. Which they did. After the injunction, they changed the tags from "Dr. Seuss's Merry Menagerie" to "Merry Menagerie. Toys Created, Designed & Produced Exclusively By Don Poynter. Based on Liberty Magazine Illustrations By Dr. Seuss." And they not only continued to sell the toys but stripped away the strongest element of Geisel's legal case: protection under the Lanham Act (also known as the Trademark Act of 1946), which prohibits "false or misleading description" likely to deceive the public into thinking (in this case) that Dr. Seuss had authorized production of the dolls. As Judge Herlands concluded on December 10, 1968, the new tag's use of the phrase "based on" now "accurately clarifies the genetic link between the cartoons and the dolls."

Geisel had also objected that the dolls were "tasteless, unattractive and of an inferior quality." If you compare the Poynter dolls with the Seuss Multi-Beasts produced by Revell (and authorized by Geisel), then you will see that this objection is absolutely right. Poynter's dolls are not nearly as attractive products, and their ugliness entitled Geisel to protection against defamation: poor-quality dolls bearing the name "Dr. Seuss," Geisel's lawyers argued, "hold him up to ridicule and contempt in his profession as a distinguished artist and author." While conceding that Dr. Seuss was a "distinguished artist and author," the judge lacked the aesthetic sensibilities to perceive the dolls' mediocre quality, concluding instead that the dolls had been "made with great care skill and judgment by a qualified designer and manufacturer." Since the judge had not deemed the products inferior, Geisel's case was all but hopeless in U.S. courts. The Berne Convention recognized Geisel's right "to object to any distortion, mutilation or alteration of his work" even *after* the copyright had been transferred to another party, but the United States did not (and does not) uphold the Berne Convention. More damaging to Geisel's lawsuit was the judge's conclusion that Liberty Library (as owners of *Liberty Magazine*) owned the copyright to Seuss's cartoons and that *because* they owned this copyright, Dr. Seuss had "no absolute monopoly in the name 'Dr. Seuss.'" In other words, though Ted Geisel had been using the pseudonym "Dr. Seuss" since 1927, the court ruled that he did not own exclusive rights to his name: Liberty Library owned at least the portion of his name connected to these cartoons. In a ruling that was at times sarcastic and condescending—it called two of Geisel's expert witnesses "incredible and facetious" and their testimony "simplistic and unconvincing"—Judge Herlands decided in favor of the defendants. Dr. Seuss lost. He was unable to prevent production of these products, and he received no financial compensation from their sale.

This experience may well have led Seuss and his agents to conclude that, in America, copyright can best be protected in the marketplace, via trademark law. As Charles Cohen writes, "On the heels of the Poynter case, Ted approved the largest single production of Seussiana as the new decade began." In 1970, characters from Seuss's children's books appeared on lunch boxes and bedroom sets (including beds, bedspreads, sheets, curtains, wallpaper, tables, towels, and bath mitts), and in the form of puppets, talking dolls, and educational toys (figure 5.1). So, what I have been calling the Disneyfication of Dr. Seuss is *not* strictly

Figure 5.1. Two pages from brochure advertising Sears' "Dr. Seuss Combolation" of furnishings and "aSeussories"

a posthumous phenomenon. It begins in 1970, as Seuss accepts his lawyers'—and the court's—conclusion that trademark is more powerful than copyright. As Jane M. Gaines points out in her *Contested Culture: The Image, the Voice, and the Law* (1991), since the landmark Sam Spade case (1954) entertainment law has come to favor trademark over copyright. The Sam Spade case—officially known as *Warner Brothers, Inc. v. Columbia Broadcasting Co.*—"turned on whether Warner Brothers' motion picture rights to the novel *The Maltese Falcon* included the right to enjoin author Dashiell Hammett from using the character in sequels." The court allowed Hammett "to continue to use his literary creation," but it also decided that characters were "mobile pieces in relation to the *work*, the wholeness and totality of which is crucial to copyright law" (Gaines 211). The result was that the "Characters—the 'mere chessmen,' devices, or vehicles for telling the story—were now seen as less protectable as authorial creations than the work itself" (211–12). Where copyright law failed to protect the characters or title of a work, trademark, "with its emphasis on source, origin, and sponsorship, not authorship, protected both title and character if one or the other 'indicated' programs or stories emanating from the same source" (212). Seuss had been operating under an older version of copyright law, and his loss in *Geisel v. Poynter Products* taught him that the law had changed since 1932. Since copyright law no longer protected him as it once had, Seuss did what many in the entertainment industry did. He sought protection under trademark law.

Regarding the use of trademark law, James Wadley, Professor of Law at Washburn University, suggests that Dr. Seuss Enterprises' motives may differ from Dr. Seuss's motives. Wadley, who specializes in intellectual property, notes that "[u]sing a Seuss character as a trademark will not undo" the copyright law: barring another copyright term extension act, *The Cat in the Hat* and *The Grinch* will go into the public domain in 2052 whether or not action figures bearing their likenesses are being sold. The real motive of going for trademark protection, Wadley suspects, is to scare others away from using it. As he says, "What the Seuss people are telling you is that given the inevitability of things moving into the public domain, the best they can hang onto is some of that as trademark."

Wadley's remarks bring to mind an earlier—and perhaps the earliest—definition of Disneyfication. Ariel Dorfman and Armand Mattelart's *How to Read Donald Duck: Imperialist Ideology in the Disney Comic* (1975) says that Disneyfication "is Dollarfication: all objects (and, as we shall see, actions [. . .]) are transformed into gold" (62). While Seuss himself was not averse to marketing his own work, his books have a literary, artistic and (often) moral value in addition to their capacity to generate profit. In contrast, many "new" Seuss items add little to his creative legacy, and some detract from that legacy. This is the key difference between spin-off products produced prior to Seuss's death and similar products produced after it.

The Posthumous Seuss: A Reader's Guide

These spin-off products are symptoms of a legal system that has, in effect, reversed trademark law. As Gaines explains, trademark law is supposed to protect the public, guaranteeing that "the buyer could expect, from the source behind the goods, the same values and qualities received with the last purchase." However, "the inversion of this principle in American common law" means that "the trademark comes to ensure *not* that the public is protected against fraud but that the merchant-owner of the mark is protected against infringers" (211). This "inversion" of trademark law leaves the public vulnerable: legal experts and businesspeople can readily tell you that a Seuss spin-off is just that, but average consumers may not be as adept at doing so. For example, of the *Grinch* film and related posthumous "Seuss" creations, Cheyette says that "there was no pretence that any of them were created by Dr. Seuss. I cannot believe that even the most fanatical Janeite would claim that a book derived from the movie *Clueless* diminished the literary reputation of Jane Austen" (letter, 15 Oct. 2001). Yet, given that the title of Amy Heckerling's 1995 film is not *Jane Austen's Clueless* or even *Jane Austen's Emma* but simply *Clueless*, its title does not suggest that the film will accurately represent Austen's novel (though it captures the spirit of *Emma* quite well). In contrast, a film titled *Dr. Seuss's How the Grinch Stole Christmas* does at least imply an authorized version of the source text.

That said, Dr. Seuss Enterprises has made an effort to distinguish Seuss's Grinch from Howard's. As Cheyette notes,

the commercials for Frosted Mini-Wheats, Nabisco, Visa, and Peppermint Patties all relate to the promotion by Universal of the *How the Grinch Stole Christmas* motion picture and do not use illustrations from what Dr. Seuss Enterprises commonly refers to as classic Dr. Seuss (i.e. the books). (As a matter of fact, in order to reinforce this distinction, Dr. Seuss Enterprises required Universal to depict the Grinch as he appears in the motion picture rather than in the book illustrations. For similar reasons, the Cat in the Hat puppet in the Wubbulous World of Dr. Seuss was required to differ from the classic Cat in the Hat.) (letter, 22 May 2003)

While Dr. Seuss Enterprises has worked to clarify the differences between the Grinches, the marketing of some posthumous "Seuss" products makes these differences less clear. The name "Dr. Seuss" appears on all covers and related packaging, and, when a book has been altered for a new format, its cover does not announce this fact. For the sake of Seuss's literary reputation, it is important that readers do not confuse (for example) the "Fabulous Flaps" version of *Green Eggs and Ham* with Dr. Seuss's original *Green Eggs and Ham*; for the same reason, it is equally important that people recognize that some books published since 1991 are valuable additions to the Seuss canon. Not all recent Seuss products are examples of Disneyfication. Here's how to tell the difference.

Exhuming Seuss: The Recommended, the Unfinished, and the Mediocre

The Secret Art of Dr. Seuss (1995) and Richard H. Minear's *Dr. Seuss Goes to War* (1999) are two outstanding posthumous Dr. Seuss books because they contain his original work, unaltered. The former offers a generous selection of Seuss's paintings which, as Maurice Sendak says in his introduction to the volume, convey a "milky, thirties movieland dippiness" suggesting "the private Seussian dreamscape." As I discuss at length in Chapter Three, *The Secret Art of Dr. Seuss* also reminds us that even though Seuss never would have called himself a "serious artist," he was indeed a serious artist. *Dr. Seuss Goes to War* introduces us to Seuss the political agitator, and Minear provides valuable historical context. Notably, both it and the University of California at San Diego's website *Dr. Seuss Went to War* take the warts-and-all approach: we meet the heroic Seuss, championing the rights of Jewish and black Americans, and the not-so-heroic, stereotyping Japanese Americans.

These cartoons remind us that even without Disneyfication, there are Seuss books that are not politically progressive in their thinking. One expects that Dorfman and Mattelart might describe *If I Ran the Zoo* (1950) and *Scrambled Eggs Super!* (1953) as imperialist narratives that create "a parody of the underdeveloped peoples" and that use adventure "to mask the origin of wealth" (Dorfman and Mattelart 98, 73). Arguably, both books encourage the child to imagine himself (both protagonists are male) into the role of American capitalist, exploiting underdeveloped nations for his own gain. In *If I Ran the Zoo*, Gerald McGrew envisions a grand "New Zoo, McGrew Zoo" full of creatures from exotic parts of the world. In order to catch the Bustard and the Flustard, he'll "hunt in the mountains of Zomba-ma-Tant / With helpers who all wear their eyes at a slant." After that adventure, he decides to "capture a scraggle-foot Mulligatawny," the "beast that the brave chieftains ride," concluding: "A Mulligatawny is fine for my zoo / And so is a chieftain. I'll bring one back, too." Though these books were written at a time when ethnic jokes were not seen as insensitive, helpers who "wear their eyes at a slant," the importation of a "chieftain" as if he were a raw material, and the illustration of the natives from "the African island of Yerka" will to modern readers seem at odds with the pro-equality message of *The Sneetches* and with Seuss's *PM* cartoons attacking racism.[6] In *Scrambled Eggs Super!*, Peter T. Hooper, similarly disappointing by contemporary standards, instructs "brave Ali" to take eggs from the Mt. Strookoo Cuckoos. Though Ali is viciously attacked by the birds, Seuss presents his suffering comically, focusing instead on the fact that Hooper gets his eggs. And, contrary to the pro-conservationist message of *The Lorax* (published twenty-five years later), Hooper orders a massive tree to be cut down because it's good for the egg acquisition business: "I ordered a tree full. The job was immense, / But I needed those eggs, and said hang the expense!" In each book, the peoples of fictional third-world nations appear as objects of fun, ready to help the American businessboys (Gerald McGrew, Peter T. Hooper) carry their country's riches back home. To borrow Dorfman and Mattelart's language, the "treasure is attained by a process of adventuring, not producing. Yet another name [. . .] to mask the origin of wealth" (73).

The Dr. Seuss of *If I Ran the Zoo* and *Scrambled Eggs Super!* is not the Dr. Seuss of *The Sneetches, The Lorax, Yertle the Turtle, How the Grinch Stole Christmas!,* or *Horton Hears a Who!* One reason for the discrepancy, as

Judith Morgan suggests, may be that *If I Ran the Zoo* and *Scrambled Eggs Super!* were published before *The Cat in the Hat*. After *The Cat in the Hat*, Seuss grew much more popular, and, using the clout conferred upon him by this popularity, "his messages grew stronger" (Morgan, email). A related reason for the discrepancy, I think, is that Seuss did not see the earlier two books as political, and he did see these other, later books as political. Of course, all books have political dimensions, and one should not overlook these ideological blind spots. At the same time, most of Seuss's other original works present much more progressive messages about wealth, power and people of different racial and ethnic backgrounds. He was very worried, for example, when someone told him that the stars on his Sneetches might be seen as anti-Semitic. As his publisher Robert L. Bernstein remembers, Seuss "despised even the slightest hint of any kind of racism, and had to be convinced that his book would not be misinterpreted" (Lathem, *Theodor Seuss Geisel* 42).

Though Seuss created many books that were progressive in their racial politics, virtually no book published during his life presents an admirable female protagonist. However, *Daisy-Head Mayzie* (1994), published after his death, offers a strong female in the character of Mayzie McGrew, who inadvertently grows a flower out of the top of her head. As in David Small's *Imogene's Antlers* (1985), the problem is not the unusual item sprouting from the girl's head, but grown-ups' reactions to it. If flower or antlers are metaphors for each child's imagination, then both books appear to praise girls' minds while satirizing those who are offended by such "abnormal" cranial activity. Though the flower disappears near the end of *Daisy-Head Mayzie*, we learn on the final pages that it "occasionally" pops up "now and then" and that Mayzie is "getting used to it."

Valuable for its central female character, *Daisy-Head Mayzie* succeeds less well in its story and in its art. The book derives from a draft of a script by Seuss, which was then finished and animated by Hanna-Barbera Cartoons. While its verse is never as leaden as that in *Oh Say Can You Seed?* or other ersatz "Seuss" books, *Daisy-Head Mayzie*'s poetry does feel more like an early draft than a finished product. Its illustrations are not Seuss's but, according to the dust jacket, "were inspired by Dr. Seuss's sketches found in his original manuscript." When reading the verse or looking at the pictures, it is not clear how much comes from Seuss's original, and how much was adapted or revised by Hanna-Barbera.

Though Seuss's verse is not with his papers at the University of California at San Diego, photographs of his drawings are. In addition to changing Seuss's unique artistic style (and, curiously, each character's hairstyle), Hanna-Barbera makes a number of other changes, most of which center on what appear to be efforts to make the illustrations more "exciting." Seuss uses an ordinary man as his narrator, where Hanna-Barbera uses the Cat in the Hat. Daisy's teacher follows Daisy out of the classroom in Seuss's original, but carries her out in Hanna-Barbera's. Although Seuss's shows many books in the principal's office, Hanna-Barbera goes a step further, using these books as building blocks for arches and towers. Finally, in Seuss's illustrations, the teacher waters the flower with an ordinary glass of water, but in Hanna-Barbera's, she uses a large urn of water.

The other differences between Seuss and Hanna-Barbera concern the tale's political implications. Though both Mr. McGrews are shoe salesmen, Seuss's Mrs. McGrew carries a tray of dishes, where Hanna-Barbera's Mrs. McGrew is a welder. Changing her occupation makes the book more "feminist" than Seuss's original: in giving Mayzie's mother an occupation traditionally held by men, the published version of *Daisy-Head Mayzie* offers an empowering portrayal of even a secondary female character. Though I do not know whether an agent character appears in Seuss's text, the greasy-haired Finagle the Agent does not appear in his pictures. If this character is Hanna-Barbera's invention, his presence introduces a subtext critical of commercial exploitation. In the book, Finagle's licensing and merchandising agreements bring "Daisy-Head burgers, / Daisy-Head drinks. / Daisy-Head stockings, / And Daisy-Head sinks. / Daisy-Head buttons, / And Daisy-Head bows. / Mayzie was famous, / The star of her shows." Though these earn Mayzie "Piles of money stacked in tens," her wealth does not make her happy. As Hanna-Barbera's Cat in the Hat asks, "But what is money without friends? / A dream had led her far astray. / That was the price she had to pay." Whether or not Hannah-Barbera has introduced this lesson into Seuss's story, its presence and the occupation of Mayzie's mother both provide moral emphases absent from Seuss's original drawings. The book ought to acknowledge how and why Seuss's original was altered, especially given the significant differences between Seuss's version and Hanna-Barbera's, and the fact that Seuss's illustrations are sufficiently finished to merit their use in the book.

Hooray for Diffendoofer Day! (1998) solves the problems of *Mayzie* by including a facsimile of the original draft at the end of a book, in a section titled "How This Book Came to Be." Offering readers a glimpse at the creative processes of Dr. Seuss, the section also distinguishes Seuss's contributions from those of his collaborators, each of whom is quite distinguished in his own right. Poet Jack Prelutsky and illustrator Lane Smith do not merely try to imitate Dr. Seuss: each brings his own distinctive style to the project, and in so doing enters into a genuine artistic collaboration that succeeds magnificently. The result is not a Dr. Seuss book; it is a Seuss-Prelutsky-Smith book, and a good one at that. Smith, a Caldecott honoree for Jon Scieszka's *The Stinky Cheese Man and Other Fairly Stupid Tales* (1992), and Prelutsky, known for his irreverent verse in books like *The Snopp on the Sidewalk* (1977), share Seuss's ability to view the world from the wrong end of the telescope. Like Seuss's, theirs is a wacky creativity, a nonsense that ignites the imagination. In Diffendoofer School, Seuss, Prelutsky, and Smith create a delightfully off-beat classroom. Unlike the test-driven world of today's public schools, Diffendoofer School's "teachers are remarkable, / They make up their own rules." From a faculty full of unconventional teachers, Miss Bonkers is the students' favorite: "She even teaches frogs to dance, / And pigs to put on underpants. / One day she taught a duck to sing—/ Miss Bonkers teaches EVERYTHING!" More than just an admirable adult female character, Miss Bonkers answers the question, "If the Cat in the Hat had a (human) cousin who became a teacher, what would she be like?" Through its surprising teachers, the book suggests that unconventional methods work best: when forced to take a standardized test, the students of Diffendoofer receive "the highest score!" and their principal declares it "Diffendoofer Day!" and gives everyone the rest of the day off. *Diffendoofer Day!* is a not-Seuss book that is very much in the spirit of Seuss. Along with *The Secret Art of Dr. Seuss* and *Dr. Seuss Goes to War*, *Hooray for Diffendoofer Day!* is one of the three best "Seuss" books to be published since his death.

If *Diffendoofer Day!* deserves three cheers, then *My Many-Colored Days* (1996) deserves about two. Accompanied by illustrations done in the style of color-field painting, Seuss's verses affirm the varieties of emotional experience: "Some days are yellow. Some are blue. / On different days I'm different too. You'd be surprised how many ways / I change on Different Colored Days," Seuss advises. Its co-illustrator Steve Johnson has, like Lane Smith, worked with Jon Scieszka, but Johnson adopts a style here that's less zany (and less Seussian) than his work in Scieszka's *The Frog Prince Continued.* According to Mrs. Geisel, the illustrations of Johnson and Lou Fancher are intentionally different: "Though his inspiration for this book was personal, he [Seuss] felt that someone else should bring his or her own vision to it. He wanted the illustrations to be very different from his," she observes on the back inside flap of the dust jacket. The front inside flap of the dust jacket quotes a letter from Seuss, in which he hopes "a great color artist who will not be dominated by me" would illustrate the book. In the portion of the letter not quoted on the dust jacket, Seuss adds, "Of course I would love to paint this book myself, but I have so many major Dr. Seuss books that I have got to do, I just won't have time." Earlier in the letter, Seuss identifies *My Many-Colored Days* as "one of three I am working on for next year's [1974's] Beginner Book Bright and Early line, under different bylines. One will probably be a Seuss, one a LeSieg, and this color book probably under another nom de plume" (Geisel, letter to Phyllis Jackson). While the published version of *My Many-Colored Days* was illustrated by "great color artists," it was not done as a Bright and Early Book under a different pseudonym—Seuss used different names (most frequently Theo. LeSieg) on books he felt were not quite up to the "Dr. Seuss" standard. So, if *My Many Colored-Days* does not rank with the greatest Dr. Seuss books, we should know that Seuss did not want his famous pseudonym associated with it. While the book does not appear to have been produced entirely in accord with his wishes, it does offer readers another side of Seuss, and it is not Disneyfication.

Even among the worthy posthumous Seuss projects, we have something of a mixed bag: *Hooray for Diffendoofer Day!*, *The Secret Art of Dr. Seuss*, and *Dr. Seuss Goes to War* are welcome additions to the Seuss oeuvre and to children's literature. Though lesser works, *Daisy-Head Mayzie* and *My Many-Colored Days* are nonetheless of interest, showing other facets of Dr. Seuss. In any case, in the realm of posthumous Dr. Seuss books, these are the best of the bunch.

The Aphoristic Seuss

Seuss-isms (1997), *Seuss-isms for Success* (1999), and *Oh, Baby, the Places You'll Go!* (1997) all bear the "Dr. Seuss" name, but they are not really

"Dr. Seuss" books. At twenty-seven pages in length and less than six inches tall, the books seem designed to be sold at the checkout counter as an "impulse" purchase. Each capitalizes on Seuss's penchant for aphorism by providing "Seuss-isms" selected or adapted from Seuss's works. Given Seuss's gift for providing pithy morals, one can see the appeal of such a project. Many Americans could quote "A person's a person, no matter how small" (*Horton Hears a Who!*) and "I meant what I said, / and I said what I meant . . . / An elephant's faithful / One hundred percent" (*Horton Hatches the Egg*). The latter appears in *Bartlett's Familiar Quotations* (16th ed., 1992), next to a quotation from *The Cat in the Hat*. Of these three small "Dr. Seuss" books, *Seuss-isms: Wise and Witty Prescriptions for Living from the Good Doctor* most nearly lives up to its premise. The quotations are both well chosen and well captioned. For example, though *One fish two fish red fish blue fish* may not be explicitly about diversity, the caption "On diversity" works well when accompanying verses like "We see them come. / We see them go. / Some are fast. / And some are slow. Some are high. / And some are low. / Not one of them / is like another. / Don't ask us why. / Go ask your mother." Placing this quotation under this heading suggests that in *One fish two fish red fish blue fish* (1960) Seuss was still thinking about the anti-discrimination message of "The Sneetches," first published in the July 1953 issue of *Redbook* and then as the title story of *The Sneetches and Other Stories* in 1961. "On equality and justice" is the perfect heading for "I know, up on top you are seeing great sights / But down at the bottom we, too, should have rights," a couplet from *Yertle the Turtle*, a book that advocates standing up for one's rights. In her introduction to the volume, Audrey Geisel wisely suggests that Seuss's "books contain more sane, sensible, and just plain hilarious advice for living than most of the self-help books crowding bookstores today." While it is not known whether Seuss himself aspired to publish self-help books, *My Many-Colored Days* and some pieces for *Redbook* could certainly be placed in the self-help genre. As Mrs. Geisel concludes, "I think Ted would have approved of *Seuss-isms*."

While he may well have approved of *Seuss-isms*, it is doubtful whether Dr. Seuss would have endorsed *Seuss-isms for Success: Insider Tips on Economic Health from the Good Doctor*, and perhaps the absence of any introductory remarks from Mrs. Geisel signals a tacit acknowledgment of this fact. Under the heading "On Growth" is the following quotation from *The Lorax:* "I laughed at the Lorax, 'You poor stupid guy! / You never can tell what some people will buy.' // Business is business! And business must grow / regardless of crummies in tummies, you know." Though the excerpt provides no indication, the "I" is the Once-ler, Seuss's repentant ex-industrialist, explaining how his business practices destroyed the environment. Seuss's book criticizes the Once-ler for giving the Brown Bar-ba-loots "crummies in tummies," but *Seuss-isms for Success* conveys the impression that "crummies in tummies" are a natural part of "growth": for business to expand, people will suffer—don't worry about it. Seuss's *The Lorax* disagrees with this message and with the Once-ler's proud claim "You never can tell what some people will buy." *The Lorax* quite clearly condemns the Once-ler's Thneed corporation for exploiting the environment, but *Seuss-isms for Success* praises the Once-ler's business acumen. Unlike *Seuss-isms*, which does not twist Seuss's verse to promote values that Seuss opposed, *Seuss-isms for Success* snips quotes from context, sometimes bending them against their author's intentions.

Like the *Seuss-isms* books, *Oh, Baby, the Places You'll Go!: A Book to Be Read In Utero* bears the name "Dr. Seuss" on the spine. Unlike these other books, the front cover includes the words "adapted by Tish Rabe from the works of" (in a small font) prior to the name "Dr. Seuss" (in a font nearly three times that size). If it does at least acknowledge its "adapted" status on the cover, *Oh, Baby, the Places You'll Go!* takes a step beyond the aphoristic Seuss, creating a bland pastiche of *Oh, the Places You'll Go!*, *Happy Birthday to You!*, *Yertle the Turtle and Other Stories*, *The Sneetches and Other Stories*, *Thidwick the Big-Hearted Moose*, *The Cat in the Hat*, *Horton Hears a Who!*, *Green Eggs and Ham*, *Scrambled Eggs Super! How the Grinch Stole Christmas!*, *McElligot's Pool*, *Hop on Pop*, *On Beyond Zebra!*, *And to Think that I Saw It on Mulberry Street*, *I Had Trouble in Getting to Solla Sollew*, *If I Ran the Circus*, *If I Ran the Zoo*, and including references to *Daisy-Head Mayzie*, *Hunches in Bunches*, and *The 500 Hats of Bartholomew Cubbins*, thrown in for good measure. All of that in twenty-seven small pages. As might be expected, blending pieces of twenty books creates an incoherent mess. However, the book's inspiration, according to its introduction, is Dr. Seuss's interest in research on babies whose "mothers and fathers read aloud to [them] in utero." The parents read *The Cat in the Hat*, and researchers found "increased uterine activity during the reading." The book does not cite any research indicating why parents would want or need to switch from a first-rate Seuss book (like the *Cat in the Hat*) to a third-rate amalgamation (like *Oh, Baby, the Places You'll Go!*), but let us suppose that this research may be still ongoing. Whatever the intentions of Ms. Rabe may have been, *Oh, Baby, the Places You'll Go!* reads rather like a commercial for Dr. Seuss. It ought to be called *Dr. Seuss's Greatest Hits*, since its narrative consists of introducing a baby (who in at least one drawing resembles R. F. Outcault's "Yellow Kid") to Dr. Seuss's characters: "There's Daisy-Head Mayzie / and Cindy-Lou *Who*, / Hunches in bunches / and Lolla-Lee-Lou." And "Bartholomew Cubbins, / Marco, and Max, / and also the North- / and the South-Going Zax." And on and on.

Wubbulous

If Rabe's "adaptation" of Seuss creates a bland pastiche, then the "Wubbulous" books embrace pastiche in a truly Jamesonian sense. They are (in Fredric Jameson's terms), "blank parody," a "neutral practice of [. . .] mimicry, without any of parody's ulterior motives, amputated of the satiric impulse" (*Postmodernism* 17). Books labeled "The Wubbulous World of Dr. Seuss" are not of Dr. Seuss's world. Derived from Jim Henson Productions' television series of the same name, the "Wubbulous" books star Muppets dressed up as Seuss's characters, with a supporting cast of other Muppets portraying what are supposed to be Seuss character types. Suffering from fundamentally flawed scripts, these particular Muppets put on saccharine productions that deliver morals in a heavy-handed way. As "The Cat in the Hat's Learning Library" series does, *The Song of the Zubble-wump* (1996) transforms the wily Cat in the Hat into a paternalistic moralist. Upon rescuing a Zubble-wump's egg from the Grinch (who, in the illustration, looks like the love child of Grover and Oscar the Grouch), the Cat announces, "That egg is a miracle!" and then delivers a homily on sharing. Megan Mullaly, the Muppet-child to whom the sermon is addressed, demonstrates that she's learned her lesson by reciting a speech that ends with "amen." However, in his own writing, Seuss resisted such preachy clichés: he avoided ending *How the Grinch Stole Christmas!* with "Amen" precisely because he did not want to "sound like a second-rate preacher or some biblical truism" (qtd. in Morgan and Morgan 158). Wubbulous books seem quite comfortable with such clichés, however.

As David Hiltbrand writes in a review for *TV Guide*, the scripts "leave much to be desired." "The Wubbulous World of Dr. Seuss," he concludes, "doesn't live up to its pedigree. If you're going to put Dr. Seuss's name in the title, you had better be wubbulous and then some." *The King's Beard* (1997) resurrects Yertle, casting him as advisor to King Lindy, a Muppet with a long beard. "Good King Lindy," though "no one thought he was clever," remains on the throne because he has the longest beard. Where *Yertle the Turtle* encourages political protest, *The King's Beard* does not. In Seuss's original, Mack's "burp" topples the despotic King Yertle; in *The King's Beard*, Yertle is cast in the role of "Great Crowd Unrester." Suggesting that activists have purely selfish motives, Yertle pits Kings Lindy and Noodle against one another. As Yertle explains, "when these kings go to war, / the result will be chaos like never before. / And when the smoke clears, *I'll* be king—for all time! / King Yertle the Turtle of Nug *and* of Lime!" In the end, one king's daughter marries the other's advisor, and both kings rule benevolently over their kingdoms. While it is accurate to cast Yertle in the role of the villain, the book is at variance with Seuss books in suggesting that activists are sneaky and monarchs benevolent. As Henry A. Giroux says of Disney's films, "The seemingly benign presentation of [. . .] dramas in which [. . .] leadership is a function of one's social status suggests a yearning for a return to a more rigidly stratified society, one modeled after the British monarchy of the eighteenth and nineteenth centuries" (63). In this sense, *The King's Beard* is much more like Disney than like Seuss, whose postwar books tend to be skeptical of leaders whose primary qualification is their social status. If there is good news here, it is that the Wubbulous books—which, incidentally, have produced spin-offs of their own, such as *The Zubble-wump!* (a "Chunky Shape Book"), *What's a Zubble-Wump?* (a "Lift-And-Peek-A-Board Book")—may soon be unavailable. The television show, which remains available on videocassette, was canceled and the books are now out of print.[7]

Whatever the aesthetic failings of the *Wubbulous* series or the *Grinch* film, it is vital to understand that Dr. Seuss Enterprises does *not* have complete control over the final product. The company chooses people with a good track record, such as Jim Henson Productions, which has given us the delightful series *Bear in the Big Blue House* (1997–); Ron Howard, the director of some successful films, including *Splash* (1984), *Apollo 13* (1995), and the Academy-Award-winning *A Beautiful Mind*

(2001); and Brian Grazer, who, in addition to producing *The Grinch*, has been nominated for twenty Academy Awards and seventeen Emmys. After making these choices, Dr. Seuss Enterprises has to trust the creative and commercial instincts of the people it has chosen. As Herb Cheyette explains,

> Movie and television productions cultivate a mass audience. Because it costs far more to produce a movie than a book, studio and networks are unlikely to violate the norms of popular culture to avoid deterring possible ticket buyers and viewers. A rights holder such as Dr. Seuss Enterprises can either abstain from mass media exploitation or agree to such exploitation under the most favorable auspices. Because of its financial responsibilities and objectives, and knowing that Ted had entered into two motion picture agreements himself, Dr. Seuss Enterprises chose the latter course. The wisdom of this decision is attested by the fact that the commercial success of the motion picture dramatically stimulated book sales and prompted many foreign publishers to seek translation rights. (Cheyette, letter, 22 May 2003)

So, then, as Cheyette points out, Jim Henson Productions, Ron Howard, and Brian Grazer sought to conform to "the norms of popular culture" in order to cultivate the widest possible audience—and, given their "commercial success," they succeeded. Or, as Karl ZoBell wrote after reading an earlier version of this chapter, "Mr. Nel's opinions concerning the artistic merit of *The Grinch* motion picture, or of the television series, are of little interest. Neither was made for him; Universal and Henson had other audiences in mind" (letter to Herb Cheyette, 22 May 2003). And, as Cheyette says, Dr. Seuss Enterprises' choices regarding both the film and the series can be justified by the projects' financial rewards.

I also find it interesting that gifted people stumble when adapting Dr. Seuss. Just as Jim Henson Productions and Ron Howard have done some excellent projects, so the authors of the book and lyrics of *Seussical the Musical* have some great work to their credit. Eric Idle, credited with the concept, was a member of Monty Python and of the Beatles-parody group the Ruttles; Lynn Ahrens wrote "A Noun Is a Person, Place, or

Thing" and "Interjections!" for ABC-TV's *Schoolhouse Rock* (1973–1985); Ahrens and composer Stephen Flaherty wrote the musical *Ragtime*. Though *Seussical* may have its problems, Idle, Flaherty, and Ahrens do much better than Jim Henson Productions or Ron Howard. As Ben Brantley wrote in his review of the musical, "The show isn't dreadful in the manner of" that "conspicuous eyesore of a movie, *Dr. Seuss's How the Grinch Stole Christmas!*" Unlike Tish Rabe's *Oh, Baby, the Places You'll Go!*, *Seussical*'s pastiche has been assembled with much greater care. And, to be fair, we should note that Ahrens and Flaherty may have been hampered by copyright restrictions, limiting which Seuss books they could use. As Ahrens recalls, "We didn't have the rights to use the actual Cat in the Hat books, although we did have the right to use the character" ("You Will Love It on a Page, or on CD, or on a Stage"). Featuring the Cat in the Hat as emcee, the main plot mixes *Horton Hears a Who!* with *Horton Hatches the Egg*, weaving in subplots borrowed from *McElligot's Pool*, *The Butter Battle Book*, *Oh, the Thinks You Can Think!*, *I Had Trouble in Getting to Solla Sollew*, *Yertle the Turtle and Other Stories*, *Did I Ever Tell You How Lucky You Are?*, *Hunches in Bunches*, *Oh, the Places You'll Go!* and references to *If I Ran the Circus*, *The Lorax*, and *Green Eggs and Ham*. If the romance between Horton and Gertrude McFuzz (who here is Horton's "next-door neighbor") feels a bit forced, casting the Cat in the Hat and Horton as defenders of the imagination is very much in the spirit of Dr. Seuss. Unlike the "Wubbulous" Cat, *Seussical*'s Cat in the Hat is much more like Seuss's anarchistic original. To its credit, the musical also retains some of the darkness absent from Howard's *Grinch* and from the Wubbulous books. Not only is there every indication that Horton may fail, but the Cat in the Hat's performances of "How Lucky You Are" are both undercut by the dangerous contexts in which he performs them. When he first sings the song, the planet of Whos is plummeting to earth; the second time, we see bandaged Whos and the Cat himself getting caught in a rope. To judge by the show's mixed reviews, the problems of *Seussical* may have resided more in the staging and direction than in the script. On the Original Cast recording, a relentless cheerfulness can overwhelm the irony and dull the edginess of the book and lyrics. As Brantley writes, "The heightened brightness of the ingredients—the eye-searing design palette, the dizzying lighting effects, the bouncy orchestrations, those mega-watt smiles—perversely meld into a general gray dimness." He concludes, "The Whos may survive the predations of a larger, destructive universe; *Seussical*, sadly, does not."

Repackaging Seuss: Board Books and Other Products

While *Seussical* might have fared better in a different production (or a different reviewer), the Dr. Seuss "board books" and "flap books" would not. Although it may seem that they were produced in an attempt to secure new copyright dates and to obtain legal protection under trademark law, Herb Cheyette says that this is not the case. "Far from being part of a nefarious plot to deceive the unwary or to extend the life of the original copyright," he says, "they are designed for fans of the original who have now become parents or grandparents and want to introduce toddlers to the joys of the books at the earliest possible age" (letter, 22 May 2003). Although I am willing to take Mr. Cheyette at his word, I think it worth noting that the covers of Seuss's board books might state more clearly that they are abridged versions of the original. The cover of the board-book version of *The Carrot Seed* identifies it as being written by Ruth Krauss and illustrated by Crockett Johnson, and it does in fact contain the same text and illustrations as the original edition, published in 1945. However, the board books of Seuss's *Mr. Brown Can Moo! Can You?*, *The Foot Book*, *Dr. Seuss's ABC*, and *There's a Wocket in My Pocket!* have all been truncated for the new format while retaining the original cover design. Small print on the copyright pages does disclose that each book is "adapted from" the original, and the covers provide a subtitle: *The Foot Book* is *Dr. Seuss's Wacky Book of Opposites*, and *Dr. Seuss's ABC* is *An Amazing Alphabet Book*. While perhaps these items should be sufficient notice of the changes, not everyone is paying attention to the subtitles and the announcements on the copyright page. My own informal interviews with students, booksellers, and parents lead me to believe that, despite Dr. Seuss Enterprises' good intentions, some consumers are confusing the originals with the shortened versions.

If this phenomenon is more widespread, it would be unfortunate. For instance, the board book of *Dr. Seuss's ABC* diminishes Seuss's poetry and may confuse a reader unfamiliar with the original version. The original *Dr. Seuss's ABC* introduces us to "L" with "Little Lola Lopp / Left leg. / Lazy lion / licks a lollipop." The board book offers "lion with a lollipop." For "M," the original describes "Many mumbling mice / are making / midnight music / in the moonlight . . . Mighty nice." But the board book provides only "Mice in the moonlight." As David Handelman wrote of the board-book versions of P. D. Eastman's *Go, Dog, Go!* and *Dr. Seuss's ABC*, "both use the art from the original books but muffle the voices of their authors." Supporting Handelman's claim, the letter "S" in the original *Dr. Seuss's ABC* observes, "Silly Sammy Slick / sipped six sodas / and got / sick sick sick." The board-book *ABC* says only "Sammy's sipping soda pop." Since Seuss accompanies this description with an illustration of a green-faced Sammy and six nearly empty soda glasses, board-book readers may wonder: why is he green? Why does he look sick? Board books can be wonderful for infants and toddlers more interested in chewing than reading. That said, it bears noting that these board books have a different flavor than the original versions.

The same is true of the "Flap Book" versions of Seuss classics, which have also been "adapted," a fact again made clear in the fine print. The "Flap Book" of *Green Eggs and Ham*, an orange-covered book very slightly shorter and about two centimeters wider than its original, may appear to be the *Green Eggs and Ham*. However, a few clues highlight its differences from the classic version: the words *With Fabulous Flaps and Peel-Off Stickers* are on the cover, albeit in smaller print than the title. The cover art includes Sam-I-Am, though the original's cover art does not. And, while the original book bears the words "By Dr. Seuss" at the bottom, the flap book says only "Dr. Seuss" at the bottom. Placed side-by-side, these differences easily mark the "Flap Book" as a new product. But a reader not familiar with the original or who does not read the small words "Adapted by Aristides Ruiz" (located at the bottom of the back cover) might think that Dr. Seuss actually wrote this book. Yet, as Herb Cheyette explains, any confusion is unintentional. The advantage of "Flap Books" is that they "possess the quality of interactivity," a feature which may appeal more to younger readers than the original version does (letter, 22 May 2003).

While Cheyette may be right, the alterations give these "Flap Books" few other appeals. In addition to moving the verse around, "Flap Books" take characters out of their original context, squash some artwork into smaller spaces, redraw other artwork, and rearrange the layout. Near the end of the original *Green Eggs and Ham*, Sam-I-Am, the (unnamed) black-hatted character, a goat, a mouse, a fox, a car, and a train all tumble down on to a boat. Emphasizing the playful nature of this higgledy-piggledy collision, each character is far enough apart from the next one, suspended in mid-fall. The "Flap Book," however, tries to merge that illustration with an earlier illustration *and* to include a flap to be lifted. As a result, the lightness and playfulness of the original drawing gets crowded out. Instead of being spread across the page, Sam-I-Am, the black-hatted character, goat, mouse, fox, et al. are all crammed into a tiny flap. Perhaps Mr. Ruiz, the book's adapter, thought that doing so would leave ample room to bring in the train tracks from the original book's previous two-page spread *and* to type the verse above the tracks. But it doesn't leave enough room. What was spread over four pages is now wedged into a single page.

Why? These books have new copyright dates, which led me to suppose that extending the copyright was the reason for creating the books. According to the U.S. Copyright Office's "Circular 14: Copyright Registration for Derivative Works," a derivative work eligible for a new copyright "must be different enough from the original to be regarded as a 'new work' or must contain a substantial amount of new material." Both "Flap Books" and board books are different enough to warrant a new copyright date and to claim protection under Trademark law: the "Flap Book" of *Green Eggs and Ham* is "TM & © 2001 Dr. Seuss Enterprises, L. P." and the board book of *Dr. Seuss's ABC* is "TM & © 1963, 1996, renewed 1991 Dr. Seuss Enterprises, L. P." However, when I made this claim in an earlier version of the chapter, Mr. Cheyette said that extending copyright was *not* the reason for creating the books. As he told me,

> As [for] your contention that the books are part of a secret conspiracy to extend the copyright of the originals, be advised that the derivative copyright only protects the new content. Since the derivative books contain nothing but material from the originals, the new copyright only protects the derivative format. The contents will become public domain when the original copyrights expire. (Cheyette, letter, 22 May 2003)

So, while it may appear that the later, lesser *Green Eggs and Ham* will remain under copyright after the original is not, the contents of the board books and "Flap Books" will also become public domain when the original copyrights are up—in this case, that would be 2061, seventy years after Seuss's death.

Fortunately for Dr. Seuss Enterprises, copyright law is likely to be extended again before Seuss's books run into any danger of wandering into the public domain. As Lawrence Lessig notes in his *The Future of Ideas* (2001),

> In the first hundred years [of copyright law], Congress retrospectively extended the term of copyright once. In the next fifty years, it extended the term once again. But in the last forty years, Congress has extended the term of copyright retrospectively eleven times. Each time, it is said, with only a bit of exaggeration, that Mickey Mouse is about to fall into the public domain, the term of copyright for Mickey Mouse is extended. (107)

If Lessig's prediction holds true, then creating "new" Seuss items to which a trademark might be applied may well prove redundant. Mickey first appeared on screen in 1928; *And to Think That I Saw It on Mulberry Street* was published nine years later. As long as the Disney Corporation continues to lobby on behalf of Mickey's copyright, Dr. Seuss's works will continue to enjoy protection under copyright law. Since Mickey is nine years older than the first Dr. Seuss book, copyright term extensions on behalf of Disney's mouse should grant legal protection to Dr. Seuss's characters well in advance of their copyright's expiration.

Dr. Seuss from Then to Now

The legal system does value commerce more than art, and so we can certainly understand why Dr. Seuss and his heirs would seek protection under trademark laws. Copyrights on the original *Green Eggs and Ham*, *Dr. Seuss's ABC*, and *The Cat in the Hat* will expire in 2055, 2058, and 2053 (under current copyright law). Protecting the original work by means of spin-off products is a legally sound solution. As Cheyette observes, there is "no pretence that any of" these spin-off products "were created by Dr. Seuss," and careful readers familiar with the originals should see the imitations for what they are. However, some may confuse the imitations with the originals because spin-off products bear the Dr. Seuss name or characters: a reader encountering a "Flap Book" of *Green*

Eggs and Ham for the first time may have no knowledge of the original, may not be aware that there are two versions, or may think that both versions are essentially "the same." According to *Publishers Weekly*, the board book of *Mr. Brown Can Moo, Can You?* now outsells the original version (Turvey 25–26). Either these sales figures suggest that many people think they are the same or, as Cheyette says, the "success of *Mr. Brown Can Moo* as a board book attests to its appeal to toddlers and the correctness of Random House's market analysis" (letter, 22 May 2003).

Irrespective of why the board book has succeeded, the increasing presence of repackaged versions of classic children's books will likely inspire more critics to claim, as David Handelman has, that "In today's marketplace, it seems as though authors can be regarded almost as nuisances who, while they are alive, needlessly limit their own earning potential." Seuss's characters have always been commodities, but if Handelman is correct, they risk becoming *only* commodities, existing to inspire consumption but not to inspire imagination or critical thinking. The lesser quality of most spin-offs, the presence of Dr. Seuss characters in advertising, and the proliferation of products bearing the "Dr. Seuss" imprimatur all create the impression that these items intend to promote consumption for its own sake. As Dorfman and Mattelart write, "Surely it is not good for children to be surreptitiously injected with a permanent compulsion to buy objects they don't need. This is Disney's sole ethical code: consumption for consumption's sake" (66).[8] Seuss was a businessman, but his ethical code was never consumption for its own sake. As a 1958 *Publishers Weekly* article describing Seuss's "autographing tour" notes,

> Dr. Seuss feels very strongly that children shouldn't be forced to buy, and he objects to it when stores attempt to remove youngsters from the waiting lines if they have not actually spent any money. [. . .] He has autographed countless cards and slips of paper as well as books. The publishers also supplied huge cut-outs of Dr. Seuss characters to be used as wall decorations in the book departments he visited. Neither these cut-outs nor the buttons carry any promotion copy. ("The One and Only Dr. Seuss . . ." 13)

If it seems hard to reconcile the Dr. Seuss portrayed in this *Publishers Weekly* article with the "new" Dr. Seuss, whose characters sell crackers, credit cards, and candy, then we should remember that the article was published forty-five years ago.

The business of publishing children's books has changed since 1958, and Dr. Seuss knew that it had changed. As Cheyette points out, in 1990, "Ted licensed film rights to Columbia for *Oh, the Places You'll Go!* [. . .] The license included a grant to the producers of all movie related merchandising. The deal was unattainable otherwise. Ted knew this and accepted it" (letter, 22 May 2003).[9] In other words, just as the *Poynter* lawsuit did, the investment required to make a film prompted Seuss to enter into a variety of licensing agreements. Not only did Seuss agree to this merchandising, but he endorsed the idea of a theme park. As Cheyette recalls,

> In 1989 or 90, Marvin Josephson [founder of International Creative Management] and I visited Ted to convey a proposal for a theme park. Ted responded by asking, "What would you call this thing?" Someone responded, "Seussville." "Well," he said, "it's too late in my life for this." Then he turned to me and asked, "Do you want to be mayor of Seussville? That's something for you to look forward to."[10]

In other words, as the culture industry changed, so did Dr. Seuss.

Whatever one may think of it, Seuss is part of a trend: Curious George appears in advertisements for Altoids (in the ad, the phrase "The Curiously Strong Mints" puns on George's name), Warner Brothers has licensed a variety of schlock bearing Harry Potter's name, and Winnie-the-Pooh sells his own brand of cereal, "Hunny B's." As Gary Cross's *Kids' Stuff: Toys and the Changing World of American Childhood* (1997) and Stephen Kline's *Out of the Garden: Toys, TV, and Children's Culture in the Age of Marketing* (1993) point out, characters from children's books are routinely transformed into corporate pitchmen. In his *Creating Ever-Cool: A Marketer's Guide to a Kid's Heart* (1998), marketer Gene Del Vecchio reports that American children "spend about $11 billion in such categories as snacks, sweets, toys/games, and clothing [. . .]. And beyond their own income, children also influence the purchase of more than $160 billion in *family* goods and services. And there is no abatement in sight as some estimate that kid wealth has been growing at a rate of 20 percent a year" (20). Children are a huge market; so, from a businessperson's perspective, it could make sense to use Dr. Seuss to reach that market, generating profits for companies and the estate. Children's books are big business, and it is impossible to pretend otherwise. As Jack Zipes explains in his *Sticks and Stones: The Troublesome Success of Children's Literature from Slovenly Peter to Harry Potter*, the children's-book publishing business has grown more interested in creating marketable products than in nurturing good-quality books (51–52, 59). If, as he contends, the industry itself now caters more toward blockbuster books, then we can hardly be surprised at the increasing use of characters to sell products.

According to the U.S. Trademark and Patent Office, Dr. Seuss Enterprises has filed trademarks for "Seuss Wear," "Hop on Pop Ice Cream Shop," "Gertrude McFuzz' Fine Feathered Finery," "Circus Mcgurkus Cafe Stoo-Pendous," "Sylvester McMonkey McBean's Very Unusual Driving Machines," and even the "Once-Ler's House." Dr. Seuss Enterprises has also sought trademarks on many characters for use in merchandise. For example, it applied for a trademark (serial number 75613066) to use the Lorax in connection with over one hundred goods and services, including: trading cards, iron-on transfers, paper place mats, envelopes, gloves, sweaters, plush toys, bowling balls, bath toys, toy wagons, "decorative pencil top ornaments," "stand alone video output game machines," and "tutorials and seminars in the field of literacy." This range of products may seem ironic, given that Seuss's Lorax specifically argues against consumption for its own sake. However, it would not be fair to say that Dr. Seuss Enterprises is merely heeding the counsel of a marketing expert, trying to sell spin-offs to as many children as possible. As Herb Cheyette explains,

> Under the rules of the trademark office, trademark applications can be narrowed, but not expanded. Therefore, it is customary practice for trademark lawyers to originally file for the widest possible scope with the understanding that the application will be reductively amended when the client finalizes plans. Most of these trademark applications were filed at the behest of Universal while it determined its merchandising plans for the *How the Grinch Stole Christmas* motion picture. (Cheyette, letter, 22 May 2003)

In addition to it being standard practice for trademark lawyers to file for "the widest possible scope" and then to amend that scope later, a second but equally important consideration is that trademark law must constantly be used to remain enforceable. As Gaines tells us, "American trademark law gives an emphasis to 'use' that it doesn't have in other countries, where, for instance, it is not necessary to demonstrate 'use' [. . .] *before* registering a mark. Whereas in other countries, first registration guarantees the monopoly [. . .], in the U.S. 'use' stakes out the owner's claim" (223). In other words, Dr. Seuss Enterprises not only need apply for licenses that cover a much broader range of products than it plans to license, but also must license *some* merchandise in order to protect the legal rights of Dr. Seuss.

Tellingly, many of the trademarks for which Dr. Seuss Enterprises have applied appear to be motivated primarily by legal concerns. For example, that it has applied for a trademark on the word "Nerd" (which first appears in *If I Ran the Zoo*) suggests that these trademark applications may be more of a preemptive strike than a marketing plan. That is, would many people wear "clothing articles and apparel, namely T-shirts, tops, made of all processes including knits and wovens, in all infant, children's and adult sizes" if these items bore the trademarked "Nerd"? Given the negative connotations of the word "nerd," one suspects that Nerd T-shirts might be a hard sell. In addition to following the standard procedure of applying for the widest possible range of products, this trademark application can prevent others from capitalizing on "Nerd." Considering Seuss's willingness to seek legal protections in the marketplace (as evidenced by the post-1968 marketing bonanza), Dr. Seuss Enterprises is not intentionally contradicting Ted Geisel's wishes. In light of trademark law's strength, the Disneyfication of Dr. Seuss must be seen as a symptom of a legal system designed to benefit capitalism more than moral or artistic values. If the close relationship between commerce and law begat Dr. Seuss's Disneyfication, then the United States might consider adopting the Berne Convention, thereby strengthening copyright law and removing the need for artists or their heirs to seek protection under trademark law. The United States signed the Berne Convention in 1988, but did so in a way that exempts itself from upholding it: as the chair of the Republican Policy Committee wrote at the time, "Its provisions are not directly enforceable in U.S. Courts; instead, the private rights granted by the Convention exist only to the extent provided by U.S. Law" (Updike). If Dr. Seuss Enterprises has to sell lesser versions of Dr. Seuss's work in order to strengthen that work's legal standing, then there's something wrong with the system—and perhaps enforcing the Berne Convention would help fix that system. Although I understand the legal reasons for pursuing so many trademarks, it is truly staggering to see such range of items. On the day I used the Trademark and Patent Office's Trademark Electronic Search System (T.E.S.S.) to search for "Seuss" trademarks, I found 162, of which 71 were "live" (i.e., currently active). On that same day (26 March 2002), I found only 17 for "Harry Potter," 16 of which were active.

While American trademark law requires licensing agreements in order to be enforceable, one nonetheless wonders what H. A. and Margret Rey would think of the Altoid advertisements, or what A. A. Milne would think of "Hunny B's" cereal. "Mickey Mouse" is a synonym for mediocrity and, to prevent "Dr. Seuss" from becoming a synonym for mediocrity, we need to grow wary of what we are being sold. If a consumer knows the difference between the original and the spin-off, then she will know which one to buy. If a reader learns to examine closely any "Dr. Seuss" book with a copyright date after 1991, then he won't mistake the "Wubbulous" for the real thing. And, if U.S. copyright law were to enforce the provisions of the Berne Convention, then Dr. Seuss Enterprises wouldn't have to license Seuss spin-offs in order to gain the stronger protections provided only under trademark law. Otherwise, under these marketing plans, the iconoclastic Seuss risks being overpowered by the marketing-icon Seuss—faithful to profit, one hundred percent.

Chapter 6

The Cat in the Hat for President

DR. SEUSS AND THE PUBLIC IMAGINATION

S o far, Dr. Seuss has continued to mean more to Americans than just a marketing icon. As poet, artist, and political fabulist, Seuss's imagination has become part of the public imagination. Seussian characters, verse, and ideas frequently recur in popular culture: examining these manifestations of Seuss shows us how his work continues resonates in many ways beyond its capacity to generate profit. "Dr. Seuss" as we think of him today begins in 1957, the year he became an icon of children's literature. Prior to that point, he had written twelve books for children and was known as a children's author, but he was equally famous for his advertising work. In 1957, that perception would change forever.

In that year, two decades into his career as a children's writer, Dr. Seuss published two books, each of which would come to typify the different ways he is perceived in the public mind: *The Cat in the Hat* and *How the Grinch Stole Christmas!* The Dr. Seuss of *The Cat in the Hat* is that Seuss who teaches children how to read, the Seuss who promotes literacy by making reading exciting. The Dr. Seuss of *How the Grinch Stole Christmas!* is Seuss the political fabulist who uses rhymes to teach moral lessons. You might object, correctly, that my tale of two Seusses—one a reading teacher, the other a propagandist—doesn't recognize that the Seuss of *The Cat in the Hat* and the Seuss of *The Grinch* are both propagandists of a sort. The Grinch criticized those who exploit Christmas solely for profit, and the Cat in the Hat challenged not only the then-prevalent *Dick and Jane* readers but authority figures in general. Both the Grinch and the Cat refuse to act as responsible adults should. However, while they are both rebellious and while their original meanings have long since given way to a wide variety of new meanings, Dr. Seuss himself continues to be the two different Seusses suggested by each book. In the public mind, "Dr. Seuss" represents both "venerable educator" and "sly satirist."

In this chapter, I focus on how Seuss's creatures and ideas have moved from his books into the American popular imagination. From Robert Coover's "The Cat in the Hat for President" (1968), which envisions the Cat disrupting the electoral process, to Rob Suggs's "The Binch" (2001), which imagines Osama Bin Laden as a Grinch-like character, Americans have used Seuss's work as a way to re-see themselves and their place in the world.

Dr. Seuss, the Original Rapper?

All of Seuss's memorable phrases—whether political or apolitical—are in verse, and Seuss's influence as popular poet is part of his iconic status. 1980s rapper Kool Moe Dee learned to rhyme from Muhammad Ali's self-promotional poems ("Float like a butterfly / sting like a bee . . .") and from Dr. Seuss's *How the Grinch Stole Christmas* (Romanowski and Warren 555). Toronto-based quartet Moxy Früvous discovered affinities between rap and Seuss in their over-the-top version of "Green Eggs and Ham" (1990), which has since become a concert favorite: Jian Ghomeshi, playing the role of Sam-I-Am, sings, "You say you don't like this and you don't like that / Well you're starting to sound like a finicky cat / Just try them, try them / And you may find / You like nothing better than / Two greenish eggs over easy in the fry-pan." Deee-Lite's top-ten hit "Groove is in the Heart" (1990) includes a nonsensical rap that plays on one of Seuss's books: "the depth / of hula groove / move us to the nth loop / we're goin' thru to / horton hears a who." Though his rhymes have inspired raps, these rhythms alone do not establish Seuss as an early rapper.[1]

In popularizing verse as a medium for political protest, Dr. Seuss lays a stronger claim to the title of the original rapper. In *Horton Hears a Who!*, the title character protects a dust-speck-sized universe of people: " 'Should I put this speck down? . . .' Horton thought with alarm. / 'If I do, these small persons may come to great harm. / I *can't* put it down. And I *won't*! After all. / A person's a person. No matter how small.' " When his enemies are about to boil the speck in "a hot steaming kettle of Beezle-Nut oil," Horton exhorts the people of the speck to speak up for their rights: "Don't give up! I believe in you all! / A person's a person, no matter how small! / And you very small persons will *not* have to die / If you make yourselves heard! *So come on, now and TRY!*" This book, *The Sneetches*, *The Lorax*, and *The Butter Battle Book*, all deliver their political messages in rhyme.

So, in the public imagination, Seussian rhyme has become a popular mode for social commentary. Appropriately, then, reviewers compared the raps of Senator Jay Bulworth—Warren Beatty's character in the film *Bulworth* (1998)—to the poetry of Dr. Seuss. Bulworth's raps offer the movie's most blunt analysis of the political establishment: "One man, one vote / Now is that really real? / The name of our game / Is let's make a deal / Now the people got the problems / the haves and the have-nots / But the ones that make me listen / Pay for 30-second spots." Though the name "Dr. Seuss" is never mentioned in the film, the *Baltimore Sun*'s Ann Hornaday called Beatty's "white-boy rap" a "tortured hybrid of Snoop Doggy Dogg and Dr. Seuss"; writing in the *New Yorker*, Henry Louis Gates Jr. described the raps as "closer to Dr. Seuss than Dr. Dre" (Hornaday 1E; Gates 62). The tone of the reviewers' comparisons suggests that likening Seuss's rhymes to rappers' rhymes may be insulting to rappers. But it isn't an insult—it's a compliment. Both Seuss and rappers have used poetry as a medium of dissent.

Significantly, the rhythms of rap and of Seuss have been adapted for wildly divergent political purposes. In their hit "Pop Goes the Weasel," early '90s rappers 3rd Bass lament that "Hip-hop got turned into hit pop" and proclaim, "we gotta make sure / that real rap has got to endure." Although their distinction between "real rap" and "hit pop" creates a false dichotomy between "art" and "commerce," they are correct to notice that popular rap tends to be apolitical: the "Weasel" in the song's lyrics is one-hit-wonder Vanilla Ice, whose "Ice Ice Baby" topped the charts in 1990. Not incidentally, 3rd Bass's line "won't eat the green eggs and swine" riffs on Seuss's *Green Eggs and Ham* to emphasize its case against pop rap.[2] In contrast to political hip-hop, Seuss's political books have been as popular as his less political ones; or, to put it in 3rd Bass's terms, his raps have always been pop. However, where he used his status as popular children's writer to advance a liberal Democratic agenda, his rhyming style has been adopted by groups of an array of political opinions.

While Seuss himself did not comment on gay rights, several books have deployed Seussian verse in support of same-sex parenting, notably Johnny Valentine's *One Dad Two Dads Brown Dads Blue Dads* (1994) (figure 6.1) and *Two Moms, the Zark, and Me* (1993). Inspired by Seuss's *One fish two fish red fish blue fish* (1960), *One Dad Two Dads Brown Dads Blue Dads* begins by illustrating the dads of its title. Then, a young white girl asks, "Blue dads? / BLUE dads!? / I don't know who / has dads that are blue!" Enter Lou, a black child of the same age, who replies, "I do! / My name is Lou. / I have two dads / who both are blue." Blueness becomes a metaphor for the dads' sexual orientation, and Lou explains how his dads do the same sorts of things that other dads do. Our female narrator asks, "Do they work? / Do they play? / Do they cook? / Do

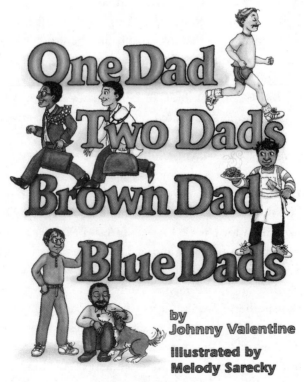

Figure 6.1. *One Dad Two Dads Brown Dads Blue Dads* by Johnny Valentine

they cough? / If they hug you too hard, / does the color rub off?" The reply: " 'Of course blue dads work! / And they play and they laugh. / They do all of these things,' said Lou. / 'Did you think that they simply / would stop being dads, / just because they are blue?' " *Two Moms, the Zark, and Me* is even more direct in advocating the rights of gay parents. A male child visits the zoo with his two moms. While the moms chat with a female friend, he meets the Zark, plays with the Zark, and then gets lost. He then meets the McFinks, a husband and wife who offer to help him find his "mother and father." When the child says that he has two mothers, the McFinks are not pleased: " 'Two moms? And no dads? I'm shocked!' said McFink. / 'It's wrong! It's a sin! Not at all how I think! / The only true family's a family like ours: / With a mom, and a dad, and two kids, and two cars." The child replies, "Though I know this will not seem polite, / From the books I have read, I do not think you're right." The McFinks will have none of this: " 'There is no need to read. There is no need to think. / We have done all that FOR you!' roared Mr. McFink." The McFinks try to find heterosexual parents for the boy, but the boy runs off to the Zark, who helps him thwart the McFinks and find his two moms. *Two Moms, the Zark, and Me* is more didactic than *One Dad Two Dads Brown Dads Blue Dads*, explicitly support-ing same-sex parenting and criticizing religious conservatives who op-pose it.

Appropriating Seuss's rhymes in the name of tolerance is congruent with *The Sneetches*' anti-prejudice message and with Horton's world view. Indeed, even though *One fish two fish red fish blue fish* is not one of Seuss's "message" books, it could be read as embracing diversity and therefore as an apt inspiration for *One Dad Two Dads Brown Dads Blue Dads*. Accom-panying an illustration of a boy and girl smiling at a variety of different "things," Seuss describes the creatures like this: "Some are fast. / And some are slow. / Some are high. / And some are low. / Not one of them / is like another. / Don't ask us why. / Go ask your mother." The matter-of-fact tone in which he enumerates these differences and the line "Don't ask us why" suggests that variety ought to be accepted. Why are some fast and others slow, some high and others low? They simply are that way. As Lou explains near the end of *One Dad Two Dads Brown Dads Blue Dads*, "They are blue because—well—/ because they are blue. / And I think they're / remarkable wonders—don't you?"

Political Mythologies: A Mayor, a Turtle, the Lorax, and the Loggers

Seuss's rhymes have been adopted as political slogans, and Seuss's characters have entered the American vernacular, providing a shorthand for political conversation. They have achieved the status of myth, but not always in Barthes's sense of myth as a cultural formation that naturalizes history and stifles the impulse to challenge the powerful (*Mythologies* 142, 151, 155). While Seuss's myths have been deployed for an array of ideological purposes, *one* such purpose has been to challenge the powerful. After his re-election to a second term in 1981, New York Mayor Ed Koch began to "consolidate power," extending his control of the city government (Haberman A1). In the process, Koch did not hesitate to disparage those who disagreed with his plans. In an interview in the *New York Post*, Koch publicly called New York's City Council President Carol Bellamy "a horror show" who "likes to torture other people" (Arzt 4). In response, Bellamy presented Mayor Koch with a copy of *Yertle the Turtle* and remarked, "Some days Ed Koch wakes up and decides he wants to be Yertle for the day." Alluding to Mack's burp, she continued, "Whenever that happens I find myself with a terrible case of indigestion" ("Carol: Ed's just playing a shell game!"). Koch apologized, admitting that it was "stupid, self-indulgent and wrong" for him to have disparaged Bellamy (Arzt 4). The *New York Times* summarized the incident in a verse editorial, rewriting Bellamy's words as: " 'Like Yertle the Turtle,' she said with sweet glee, / 'You yearned to be ruler of all you could see. / His story, dear sir, is one you should read / For lessons in kingship; it's all that you need.' " The editorial concluded that Bellamy "had offset his offensive diction / By branding His Honor a juvenile fiction. / Like Mack, whose dyspepsia dethroned a turtle / We had one reaction—like his to poor Yertle / We burped!" ("At the Court of King Edward"). While Koch was not literally a dictator (as Yertle is), Bellamy made the comparison between the Mayor and the Turtle King in a satirical spirit, using Seuss to make His Honor look ridiculous.

As Yertle symbolizes tyrannical behavior, so the Lorax represents environmental conservation. *The Lorax*—named for its central character who "speak[s] for the trees"—was published in 1971, followed by an animated version shown on television in 1972. The story immediately resonated with both children and adults, who not only took the book's message to heart but began to take action. As the Once-ler realizes at the book's conclusion, "the word of the Lorax seems perfectly clear. / UNLESS someone like you / cares a whole awful lot, / nothing is going to get better / It's not." In 1972, ten-year-old Carol Holland wrote to Dr. Seuss to tell him that *The Lorax* "really made me think hard. I felt like crying in some parts." She resolved to do her part by picking up "the pollution by the roadside" (Holland). In 1973, students and teachers at Elliot Elementary School in Lansing, Michigan cared enough to form a conservation group that they called "The Loraxes." They protested against developers who were cutting down trees, they transplanted some of the trees, and they circulated petitions to try to prevent the destruction of more trees. As fifth-grader Martha Mantikoski said, "We speak for the trees and the flowers and the animals. We are REALLY MAD. We don't want apartment buildings. We want our forest" (Morello). Appropriately, when Keep America Beautiful gave Dr. Seuss an award in November 1971, the anti-litter organization's chairman predicted that *The Lorax* would "undoubtedly charm many children—and adults as well—into becoming pollution fighters" ("Anti-Litter Organization Gives Award to Dr. Seuss"). This prediction has proven so accurate that it now seems something of an understatement. *The Lorax* has done more than inspire others: the book's title character is now an icon for environmental conservation.

In the years since the book's publication, the Lorax has become the symbol of American Forests, "the nation's oldest non-profit citizen conservation organization" ("Be a Lorax Helper"). In 1997, American Forests launched a campaign inviting us to "Be a Lorax Helper—Help Build the Dr. Seuss Lorax Forest." The organization solicited contributions that would pay for trees to be planted in "the Dr. Seuss Lorax Forest"—actually the Francis Marion National Forest, located just north of Charleston, South Carolina. When Bush the Younger nominated Gale Norton as his Secretary of the Interior in January 2001, a cartoon captioned "Gale Norton, Keeper of All Things Wild" featured a display case of dead animals pinned and neatly labeled: the spotted owl, the monarch butterfly, and the Lorax were all included. The cartoon implied that Norton would kill not only wild animals but their legendary protector, the Lorax—a reasonable inference, given Norton's support for drilling in the Arctic National Wildlife Refuge, and her belief that the Endangered Species Act and the Clean Air Act are both unconstitutional.

Suggesting the political power of Seuss's myths, the Lorax is a fictional character with real enemies. He has so come to symbolize environmental conservation that he has become a target of the logging industry. In 1989, Sammy Bailey, an eight-year-old from Laytonville, California, read *The Lorax*, arrived home from school and asked his mother, "Papa doesn't love trees anymore, does he?" (Glionna). His father—Bill Bailey, who sold logging equipment—was so upset that he and his wife launched a campaign to have *The Lorax* removed from the second-grade reading list. They took out an ad in the local paper, which read: "Teachers [. . .] mock the timber industry, and some of our kids are being brainwashed. [. . .] We've got to stop this crap right now!" (Arias and McNeil 68). The campaign failed, but loggers' opposition to the Lorax has not diminished, and attempts to remove the book from libraries has earned it a place on the American Library Association's poster for "Banned Books Week," which encourages us to "Celebrate the Freedom to Read." In 1997, the National Oak Flooring Manufacturers' Association (NOFMA) published Terri Birkett's *Truax*, a pro-logging rebuttal to *The Lorax*. The book caricatures environmentalists as "Guardbark" (a militant, brown character) who rails against Truax (a kind, white logger). As Guardbark jumps up and down with his fists in the air, he "snarl[s]," "I'm Guardbark, I tell you, keeper of trees. / Our future, you know is dependent on these. / You must stop this hacking and whacking and stacking / You should NOT be here. I MUST send you packing" (figure 6.2). Truax patiently explains to Guardbark that loggers plant new trees for the ones they cut down, that dense woods are in greater danger of forest fires, and that logging doesn't threaten biodiversity. "Cutting the trees sends SOME critters running, / But others move in, some cute, and some cunning / They munch on the leaves. The grow on the bark / And none loves it more than the Pink-spotted Lark," says Truax, possibly referring to the spotted owl, an endangered species whose habitat has been threatened by logging. Near the end of the book, Guardbark is surprised to discover, "We want the SAME things?—Treewhacker and I?" On the book's final pages, Guardbark endorses Truax's plans for forest management and flies away. In the illustration, woodland creatures watch his departure with smiles on their faces, presumably glad that the cranky conservationist has at last gone (figure 6.3). As

Figure 6.2. Pages 3 and 4 from *Truax* by Terri Birkett, illustrated by Orrin Lundgren

"You know, Mr. Guardbark, I've thought and I've dreamed.
I've fumed and I've steamed. I've figured and schemed.
I want the best future for my little boy.
I want trees to be here, for him to enjoy."

With that, he looked at me straight in the eye.
Then he shook my left hand and took to the sky.

He said, "I am Guardbark, ward of the trees—
And I like the way that you're managing these.
"I'm glad that we chatted, conversed, and confided.
I now think our views aren't quite so one-sided.

"And perhaps best of all," the Guardbark beamed,
"I think things ARE NOT quite as bad as they seemed!"

Figure 6.3. Concluding pages from *Truax* by Terri Birkett, illustrated by Orrin Lundgren

NOFMA says on its website, the book was written "specifically to counter the book *The Lorax* by Dr. Seuss"; *Truax* "more closely represents todays [*sic*] forest management than the scenario described by Dr. Seuss."

Responding to criticism of his book, Seuss said, "*The Lorax* doesn't say lumbering is immoral. I live in a house made of wood and write books printed on paper. It's a book about going easy on what we've got. It's antipollution and antigreed" (qtd. in Morgan and Morgan 278).[3] As Seuss sees it, the Once-ler represents not all loggers but greedy people who plunder natural resources; however, as Birkett, Bailey, and many loggers see it, the Once-ler represents loggers in general.[4] If the logging industry does what Birkett describes in *Truax*, then loggers and Seuss are both "antipollution and antigreed." The conflict may arise from a problem inherent to any moral fable: the allegory required to teach the lesson can be interpreted in ways other than intended. In representing environmentalists as a short-tempered brown hippie and loggers as a patient white man, Birkett inadvertently invokes racist ideologies in support of her point—that is, when a good white person corrects a misinformed, ill-mannered brown person, we cannot escape the racial overtones, even though those overtones may not have been intentional. Where Birkett's white logger leads her book into racially insensitive caricature, Seuss avoids such problems by wisely keeping his symbols abstract: the Lorax is a furry anthropomorphic creature, and the Once-ler is a pair of hands (we never see the rest of his body)—an appropriate symbol of greed. That said, one can certainly understand how the logging industry might focus on the fact that Seuss's irresponsible industrialist is a destroyer of trees, even though the Once-ler's fouling of the air and the water is as much at issue in *The Lorax*. However, Seuss's tale does point out that the problem with the Once-ler is *not* just that he cuts down trees or pollutes the environment, but that he is motivated solely by greed. After selling his first Thneed (made from the tufts of the Truffula trees), the Once-Ler "laughed at the Lorax, 'You poor stupid guy! / You never can tell what some people will buy.'" That he treats his customers as suckers tells us that the Once-ler is driven only by profit, a lesson Seuss emphasizes when the Once-ler's Thneed company decimates the Brown Bar-ba-loots' food supply. "[B]usiness is business! / And business must grow / regardless of crummies in tummies, you know," the Once-ler explains. As an icon of environmental conservation, *The Lorax*'s activist message endures: Unless people act upon their concerns, nothing will get better. As if to underscore this point, the Lorax sculpture at the Dr. Seuss National Memorial features the verse, "UNLESS someone like you / cares a whole awful lot, / nothing is going to get better / It's not."

Misappropriating Seuss:
How the Grinch Stole _____.
(fill in the blank)

At the dedication of the Dr. Seuss National Memorial, one protester carried a sign reading,

> Dr. Seuss knew!
> A PERSON'S A
> PERSON, NO
> MATTER HOW
> SMALL

She explained that she was carrying the sign to send a message to abortion supporters Senator Ted Kennedy and Congressman Richard Neal, both of whom were there to give short speeches on Seuss and the memorial. Contrary to the pro-life supporter's beliefs, Seuss did not intend Horton as a mascot opposing a woman's right to choose. Decades earlier, when an anti-abortion group began printing "A person's a person, no matter how small" on its stationery, Seuss threatened legal action and the group stopped doing so (Morgan and Morgan 277).[5] If Horton offers one instance of the misappropriation of Seuss's characters, the Grinch—more than any other Seuss creation—exemplifies how his characters have come to signify well beyond their original symbolism.

As Thomas A. Burns wrote in 1976, the original *Grinch* story entered the American popular Christmas tradition because it "successfully addresses materialism" and "suggests that the Christmas celebration *may* involve Christian religious belief but it need not do so to be meaningful" (200). Equal parts Scrooge, Santa Claus, and anti-materialist, the Grinch is the villain and (by the story's end) the hero of a secular Christmas celebration. Some popular re-appropriations of the Grinch retain most of these principal meanings. A holiday episode of NBC's "Just Shoot

Me" has Finch (played by David Spade) as the Grinch, stealing Christmas presents and later relenting. An episode of "Ed" from 2001 had a story line in which an eccentric millionaire enlists the help of Ed (Thomas Cavanaugh) to give people anything they want for Christmas. When it turns out that the millionaire has no money and the checks he's written will bankrupt the foundation named for him, Ed goes around asking people to give their presents back: "I feel like such a Grinch," he says.

More often, though, the Grinch has lost his primary meaning as anti-materialist grouch, and has instead become a generic villain—albeit one who often steals something. In the mid-1990s, the Capitol Steps (a satirical troupe) began performing "How the Gingrinch Stole Congress," which began: "Every Who / Down in Whoville / Liked Elections a lot . . . // But Newt Gingrinch, / Who lived on Mount Gridlock, / Did NOT!" In this narrative, the DemoWhos (Democrats) are defeated by Republican House Speaker Newt Gingrinch and his allies, who "slithered and slunk, with smiles most unpleasant, / Obnoxiously trashing the left, past and present" (Strauss and Newport). Gingrich's name and (depending on one's perspective) duplicitous behavior appear to have prompted the comparison to Grinch.[6] Yet, while Gingrich took many liberties with the facts, he is far from the cynical critic of consumerist morality invented by Dr. Seuss.

The Grinch-as-thief motif was very popular in late 2000 and early 2001, when both Al Gore and George W. Bush appeared as Grinch-like characters in the aftermath of the American election, the outcome of which depended upon an accurate count of the Florida vote. As the recounts got underway, Nancy Renko's "How Al Sore Stole the Election" was making the rounds on email. It began, "Every voter / Down in Florida / Liked elections a lot // But Al Sore, / Who lived North of Florida / Did NOT!" Renko's poem cast Al Gore as Al Sore, a losing candidate determined to win by fixing the vote. On "Politically Incorrect," host Bill Maher read "How the Grinch Stole the Election," which instead cast Bush as the Grinch and made much of the many elderly Jewish voters who, confused by Florida's "butterfly ballots," accidentally voted not for Gore but for Pat Buchanan, an outspoken anti-Semite. Maher's parody began in a typically "politically incorrect" manner: "Every Jew down in Jewville liked elections a lot / But the Grinch, who lived over in Austin, did not." When Maher's narrative reaches the election confusion, he tells us, "All eyes turned to Jewville to sort out the mess / but Hymen and Herschel and dear old Aunt Bess, / were too senile to vote for the one they liked. / They poked the wrong hole and joined the Third Reich." A month later, after the Supreme Court appointed Bush the victor in a 5–4 decision, novelist Salman Rushdie wrote his own version of Bush-as-Grinch, titled "How the Grinch stole America." In this version, "Every Vote down in Voteville liked Voting a Lot, / But the GRINCH, who lived West of Voteville, did not." Because he thinks "the Veep" is "a creep," the Grinch works to prevent the votes from being counted. He calls on fellow Grinches to help him, and "they Grinched the election. / They Grinched, day by day, / Until all the options were whittled away. / They Grinched it with lawyers, / they Grinched it with writs, / They split all the hairs, / and they picked all the nits. / And when it came up to the Ultimate Bench, / They Grinched it away with one final Wrench." At the conclusion, Rushdie writes, " 'For whole years of Grinchdom!' / the Grinch cries with glee / 'There's Only One Person who Counts now / . . . That's / ME.' " That the Grinch can be appropriated by supporters of opposing Presidential candidates testifies to his status as stock scoundrel, erasing his original significance as opponent of commercialized Christmas.

Exemplifying the Grinch's status as universal "bad guy," even Osama Bin Laden has been compared to the Grinch. A couple of days after September 11, 2001, Rob Suggs, a Christian humorist and educator (best known for co-writing *The Prayer of Jabez for Young Hearts*), sent "The Binch" to a few friends. Within a very short time, "The Binch" was being forwarded across the internet, read on radio stations, and featured in newspapers across the United States. In this narrative, the Grinch has been re-named "the Binch," a character based on Bin Laden: "Every U down in Uville liked U.S. a lot, / But the Binch, who lived Far East of Uville, did not. / The Binch hated the U.S! the whole U.S. way! / Now don't ask me why, for nobody can say! / It could be his turban was screwed on too tight. / Or the sun from the desert had beaten too bright." Many of the "Grinch" parodies discussed here offer some version of the "shoes were too tight" line, but only this one invoked ethnic differences. According to Suggs, he "was attacked by some for bigotry" for using the word "turban," and was "told that turbans have religious significance within Islam" (email to Bill Ellis). Though it is certainly understandable how lines like "Whatever the reason, his heart or his turban, / He stood facing Uville, the part that was urban" might cause offence, Suggs chose "turban" simply because he "thought it would make a nice rhyme with 'urban,'" and was "abashed to find out that the turban is actually religious apparel" (emails to author, 16 and 17 June 2003).[7] Suggs's poem goes on to tell of how "The Binch stole some U airplanes in U morning hours, / And crashed them right into the Uville Twin Towers." In the end, the Binch succeeds in destroying the buildings themselves but cannot destroy "Hope and [. . .] Pride" because "you can't smash the towers we hold deep inside." The poem concludes that "America means a bit more than tall towers, / It means more than wealth or political powers, / It's more than our enemies ever could guess, / So may God bless America! Bless us! God bless!" Here, the Grinch becomes a cardboard villain whose actions unify Americans with a buoyant sense of national pride.

These various appropriations of Seuss's *How the Grinch Stole Christmas!* bring to mind Barthes's claim that "Men do not have with myth a relationship based on truth but on use: they depoliticize according to their needs" (144). In each story, the Grinch has been emptied of his original political content and given new meanings, according to the needs of the fable. Whether he is Newt Gingrich, George W. Bush, Al Gore, or Osama Bin Laden, the Grinch character always serves to dramatize the baseless villainy of the bad guy. In so doing, these myths remove not only the Grinch but these political figures from history. That is, "The Binch" no more explains the root causes of terrorism than "How the Grinch Stole the Election" explains Florida's chaotic (some would say "corrupt") voting processes. Instead, these stories offer up a cultural imaginary—the Grinch—in order to satirize and to simplify political events. Not surprisingly, they are more successful as propaganda than they are as cogent political analysis.

Re-Elect the Cat in the Hat

The Cat in the Hat, very likely Seuss's most famous character, is also the one put to the widest array of uses. However, while cultural appropriations of the Grinch inevitably sever any link to the character's primary meanings, cultural appropriations of the Cat in the Hat do not inevitably do the same. Even though the Cat is used in many, many more ways than the Grinch, the Cat's very nature is malleable. He is, in some senses, a character without a fixed center. The Cat is a con artist, a trickster, a character of possibility, aggressively adaptable to the occasion. In Robert Coover's "The Cat in the Hat for President," the Cat is a revolutionary, disrupting the electoral process. This same Cat is an establishment figure when Supreme Court Justice Stephen Breyer wears the Cat's hat and necktie in honor of the National Education Association's "Read Across America" campaign (1997–), which features the Cat as its figurehead. This array of meanings makes sense: the Cat made his debut as a wily subversive in *The Cat in the Hat* in 1957, but in 1958 he became the logo of Random House's Beginner Books division. Since then, the Cat has always been both anarchist and corporate symbol, and the many roles he has assumed in American public life suit his adaptable personae.

Robert Coover's "The Cat in the Hat for President" offers the most darkly satirical use of Seuss's character. Published in the *New American Review* in August of 1968, the story is populated by variations on characters from Seuss's Beginner Books: the Cat's running mate Sam gains the nickname "Sam-I-Am," after the character from *Green Eggs and Ham*; Ned, one of the Cat's advocates, and Mr. Brown, the party chairman, come from *Hop on Pop*;[8] and Clark, the political visionary behind the Cat's rise, has emerged from *One fish two fish red fish blue fish*. Appropriately, a Cat promoted by "Beginner Books" characters bases his campaign buttons on the "Beginner Books" logo and its slogan, "I CAN READ IT ALL BY MYSELF." As Mr. Brown tells us, "'I CAN LEAD IT ALL BY MYSELF' was the legend on the Cat's campaign buttons. His button portrait was the familiar one: tall floppy red-and-white striped hat, red bow tie, white-gloved hands clasped decorously over his chest, thumbs pressed together, grinning that idiot grin" (12). Riding on the clean-up machine that appears at the end of *The Cat in the Hat*, the Cat magically scrambles the posters of Boone, his opponent, to read "Eat a prune at noon with Boone!" (15); rigs a microphone "through a tape recorder so that everything came out backwards" (17); and either floods the convention hall or causes mass hallucinations—the delegates aren't sure (26). "Now you see / What I can do! / I can give you / Something new! / Something true / And impromptu! / I can give you / A new view!" the Cat proclaims (26). Inspired and bewildered by the Cat's charismatic, surreal behavior at the convention, the delegates nominate the Cat as their presidential candidate.

Written only a decade after the first appearance of the Cat, Coover's story predicts how and why the Cat will become Seuss's most famous and most adaptable character: the Cat's power resides in his ambiguity. Trying to convince a skeptical party chairman of the Cat's electability, Clark asks, "Mr. Brown, what would you say was a politician's greatest asset?" Brown replies, "I don't know. [. . .] Ambiguity, I guess. Meaningful or potent ambiguity." Clark says, "Wonderful!" and adds, "And what do we know about the Cat in the Hat?" Brown concedes, "Two hundred twenty-three different words," and then Clark offers a variety of interpretations, demonstrating how these stories mean different things to different people (21). Interpreting *The Cat in the Hat Comes Back*—in which the Cat uses "Voom!" as the last resort in getting rid of a rapidly spreading pink stain—Joe sees "Voom" as "The Bomb." As Clark explains, "For Joe, the two stories are parables of the foibles of diplomacy, the first being about the effectiveness of air power, followed by technological recovery, the second about the eradication of the, uh, Red menace by atomic power" (22). Ned, in contrast, sees the Cat as an "agent of the absurd" (22).[9] Clark concludes,

> remember, Mr. Brown: ambiguity! *Ambiguity!* Why must it [Voom] be nuclear power? All the Cat says about it is that it is too small to see, yet enormously effective. Why not Reason? Or Love? God? Perception of Infinity and Zero, or the Void? It rhymes with Womb and Tomb: Being and Nonbeing. It suggests Doom or Bloom, Vow or [. . .] simply OM, the final linguistic reduction of the universe. (23)

Coover does to the Cat in the Hat what Frederick Crews did to Winnie-the-Pooh in *The Pooh Perplex* (1963)—he parodies literary criticism. However, Coover's parody is prophetic: the Cat is a classic trickster character, and adaptability is at the core of his appeal.

In his trickster guise, the Cat returned to presidential politics during Republicans' attempts to impeach President Bill Clinton in January of 1999. Pulitzer Prize-winning cartoonist Signe Wilkinson drew Clinton as the Cat in the Hat, balanced on a ball, energetically trying to hold up too many items: "I can hold up a thong / And the dress with the stain! / I can send off a bomb / On this cool fighter plane! / I can make up a speech / While you try to impeach! / But that is not all! / Oh, no. / That is not all! . . ." (figure 6.4). Two years later, Ward Sutton drew "The Cat in the Chad," in which the Cat and Katherine Harris (who is drawn to resemble the Grinch) conspire to confuse the votes in Florida. The Cat implores two retirees, "Let's have us some fun! / Let's have a surprise! / Let's mix up the voting! / Let's use butterflies!" In both cartoons, the Cat behaves much as Coover imagined him in "The Cat in the Hat for President" and as Seuss imagined him in the first two books about the Cat in the Hat. As Coover's narrator Mr. Brown says after the Cat has left the convention hall, his "disruptive spirit lingered on" (17).

Ward Sutton's "Cat in the Chad" ends with the Cat leaving "the Supremes to figure it out," and a couple of months after his cartoon appeared, U.S. Supreme Court Justice Stephen Breyer donned the Cat's hat and bow tie—not as an embodiment of juridical anarchy, but to celebrate the National Education Association's "Read Across America Day." Held annually on March 2 (Dr. Seuss's birthday) since 1997, "Read Across America Day" encourages adults to read with children, and features the Cat in the Hat as its mascot. The Cat has also appeared on a 33-cent U.S. stamp, as a balloon in Macy's Thanksgiving Day Parade, and as a mural above New York's 42nd Street "in a public art project as 'the ringmaster of your imagination . . . saying 42nd Street

Figure 6.4. "I can hold up a thong . . ." by Signe Wilkinson

can be magical'" (Morgan and Morgan 292). In these public appearances, the Cat acts not as the embodiment of subversiveness but as a celebration of reading, the imagination, childhood, or, simply, fun. In his role as a figure of fun, the Cat could become "affirmative culture" in an Althusserian sense, part of the "bread and circuses" that distract people from genuine grievances. As Clark says in Coover's tale, "the Cat is funny. And dramatic. We have a terrible need for the extraordinary. We are weary of war, weary of the misery under our supposed prosperity, weary of dullness and routine, weary of all the old ideas, weary of all the masks we wear, the roles we play, the foolish games we sustain. The Cat cuts through all of this. We laugh. For a moment, we are free" (20). However, while the Cat may bear some of this ideological baggage in public, he shrugs it off in the classroom, in the library, or at home, when he is simply an ambassador to the written word.

Like the Cat, Sam-I-am gets appropriated by people of quite different political persuasions. In this sense, Coover's idea to have Sam-I-am as the Vice Presidential candidate on the Cat's ticket is exactly right. The only Dr. Seuss book to sell more copies than *The Cat in the Hat* is *Green Eggs and Ham*. Seuss's Sam-I-am—unlike Coover's—is in many senses another version of the Cat in the Hat. Like the Cat, Sam-I-am is a combination of the optimist, con man, and trickster. To advance his goal of promoting green cuisine, Sam-I-am conjures up a mouse in a house, a fox in a box, a car, a train, a tree, a goat, and a boat. Not only does he convince the reluctant black-hatted character to try (and to like) green eggs and ham, but Sam-I-am does not even have to clean up the mess he makes. Sam-I-am is also a character of possibility, which has enabled him to serve multiple and contradictory purposes. For example, in February of 1998, Tom Tomorrow's "This Modern World" imagined Special Prosecutor Kenneth Starr as Starr-I-Are, and President Clinton as the subject of his rhyming assault: "DID YOU GROPE HER / IN YOUR HOUSE? / DID YOU GROPE / BENEATH HER BLOUSE?" (figure 6.5). Weary of such questions, Clinton at last answers, "I DO NOT LIKE YOU / STARR-YOU-ARE—/ I THINK THAT YOU / HAVE GONE TO FAR! // I WILL NOT ANSWER ANY MORE—/—PERHAPS I WILL GO START A WAR! / THE PUBLIC'S EASY TO DISTRACT—/—WHEN BOMBS ARE FALLING ON IRAQ!" Where Tom Tomorrow's cartoon is equally critical of both Starr and Clinton, Bruce Kluger and David Slavin's Seussian version of Clinton's memoirs targets Clinton alone. Ostensibly inspired by two summer 2001

Figure 6.5. "This Modern World" by Tom Tomorrow

news stories—plans for the Dr. Seuss National Memorial, and Clinton's selling his memoirs—appearing in close proximity, Kluger and Slavin write, "I did not see her in that dress / I did not start this tawdry mess / I did not own a cheap cigar / (I do not like this Kenneth Starr) / I asked myself, 'Am I a sham?' / Myself responded, 'Damn, I am'"[10] As the narrative progresses, Kluger and Slavin come across as reactionary and bigoted, notably when their rather racist description of Clinton's cabinet echoes the language of President Reagan's Secretary of the Interior James Watt, who in 1983 characterized the makeup of his coal-leasing commission by saying, "We have every kind of mix you can have. I have a black, I have a woman, two Jews and a cripple." Similarly, Kluger and Slavin write, "My team was America, red, white and bluish / A black, a Latino (and one who was Jewish!) / A pack led by Babbitt and Rubin and Reno / (the only thing missing was Sammy and Dino) / I also had Reich and Shalala on call / For a wonk is a wonk, sir, no matter how small." Sam-I-am inspires verse satire from divergent political perspec-

tives because Sam—like his predecessor, the Cat—is a mercurial character whose ambiguity leaves him vulnerable to appropriation.[11]

Of Aphorisms and Icons

For all of their accumulated political meanings, the Cat, Sam-I-am, and
Dr. Seuss have become icons of Children's Literature. As such, they have
come to represent a moral good to people of many difficult political
persuasions. Ronald Reagan, whose foreign policy Seuss's *The Butter Battle
Book* openly criticized in 1984, nonetheless honored Seuss as a "living
American treasure" in 1986. "For nearly half a century, children have
learned the joys of reading and language through your books," Reagan
wrote. "Though your latest work may be called *You're Only Old Once*, you,
like your unforgettable characters and your inimitable style, will remain
forever young." In a speech promoting his "Early Childhood Initiative,"
George W. Bush, said, "Ever since our twins, our twin daughters were
toddlers, we would read to them at every possible opportunity. Sometimes when I sleep at night I think of *Hop on Pop*." The audience
laughed, then Bush continued, "We found it to be fun. And it's important for parents to understand that it's a part of the responsibility for
being a good mom or dad to read to your children." And, at the end of
the speech, Bush said, "As we try to serve our children better, we ought
to keep in mind the wise words of Theodor Geisel—he, better-known
as Dr. Seuss, the guy who wrote *Hop on Pop*." After more laughs, Bush
then offered the quotation from Seuss—"Children want the same things
we want, to laugh, to be challenged, to be entertained and delighted"[12]—and aligned himself with Seuss by adding, "We want our
children, even the youngest children in America, to be challenged and
entertained and delighted by learning." Because we identify Seuss with
his Beginner Books, he can easily be deployed as a benign, apolitical
children's author.

Bush is hardly alone in alluding to this version of Seuss. For at least
the past forty years, one meaning of "Dr. Seuss" has been a classic—and
therefore politically neutral—children's writer. For instance, in January
1962, the *New York Times* reported that "Two hundred books, ranging
from the *History of the English-Speaking Peoples* to *The Cat in the Hat*, were
added today to the White House Library by the American Booksellers

Association." That was the opening sentence. Later, the article also tells us which children's books John F. Kennedy's daughter might like: "Caroline is his 4-year-old daughter, and there were plenty of other books on the list that she might find interesting, including *Early Moon*, by Carl Sandburg, *You Come Too*, by Robert Frost, and the one about Dr. Seuss's well-known cat" ("200 Books . . ."). To this *Times* writer, Seuss is a well-known writer of popular books for children. In 1989, U.S. Games Systems Incorporated offered up a similar version of Dr. Seuss in its "Childrens [*sic*] Authors Card Game," featuring Seuss on all the Aces, A.A. Milne on the deuces, Meindert DeJong on the threes, Rudyard Kipling on the fours, Hans Christian Andersen on the fives, Lewis Carroll on the sixes, Charles Perrault on the sevens, Laura Ingalls Wilder on the eights, Brothers Grimm on the nines, Joel Chandler Harris on the tens, Isaac Bashevis Singer on the Jacks, Beatrix Potter on the Queens, and J. M. Barrie on the Kings. The deck—which, curiously, lacks Jokers—describes Seuss as having "written more than 50 children's books noted for nonsense words, tongue-twisting rhymes, and cartoon-like characters." While the statement is accurate, it also elides the subversive morals for which Seuss is known. During May of 2002, Paul O'Neill confirmed the perception of an apolitical Seuss. Traveling with U2's Bono on a tour of poverty in Africa, O'Neill felt that aid programs were too ensnared by bureaucracy to achieve maximum results: people from wealthy nations ought to " 'in effect, adopt children' by sending copies of children's books like those by Dr. Seuss." He added, "We need to make this into an individual people thing, and not some cosmic stuff about billions of dollars" (Blustein C2). (For the record, Bono disagreed, arguing that wealthy governments should send billions of dollars.) To O'Neill, Seuss is a benign figure he can use to support his argument that individuals and not governments can change the world. Famous for teaching children how to read—an activity presumed to be free of ideology—Seuss appears to be dissociated from any specific political or social content.

While most of Seuss's "Beginner Books" do not intend to promote particular messages about equality or activism (for example), Seuss's message books and non-message books both display a knack for the pithy phrase. Irrespective of a work's political bent, this penchant for aphorisms also makes Seuss susceptible to being co-opted by different people. Though George W. Bush's quotation (which is in fact a slight misquotation) comes not from one of Seuss's books, the comment that "Children want the same things we want, to laugh, to be challenged, to be entertained and delighted" brings the aphoristic Seuss into view. On her daytime television show, Oprah Winfrey (who does not share George W. Bush's political convictions) also felt comfortable invoking the aphoristic Seuss. During a July 2001 *Oprah Winfrey Show*, Oprah quoted a sentence from Seuss's *I Can Read with My Eyes Shut!* as the introduction to a segment on children's books: "The more that you read, / the more things you will know. / The more that you'll learn, / The more places you'll go." The popularity of *Oh, the Places You'll Go!* has done much to promote the axiomatic Seuss. Invoking this book's reputation as popular graduation gift, Al Franken published *Oh, the Things I Know! A Guide to Success, or, Failing That, Happiness* in time for 2002 graduations. With a cover featuring the author dressed in a cap and gown, the book's chapter titles spin variations on *Oh the Places You'll Go!*, such as: "Oh, Are You Going to Hate Your First Job!", "Oh, the Politicians Who Will Disappoint You!", "Oh, the People You'll Sue!", and "Oh, the Nursing Home You'll Wind Up In!" Anne Raver's "Oh, the Things I Have Left Undone," a *New York Times* article about New Year's Resolutions for gardeners, never mentions Seuss but invokes the book in its title. C. R. Snyder and Kimberly Mann Pulvers's "Dr. Seuss, the Coping Machine, and 'Oh, the Places You'll Go',", the opening essay in Snyder's *Coping With Stress: Effective People and Practices* (2001), claims Seuss as "one of the major children's book authors who offered early instruction about the coping process" (3). When perceived as advice-giver or as literacy advocate, Seuss appears to many people as a man without politics, a sage whose advice applies to all people and all situations.

However, these apolitical versions of Seuss can never be fully extricated from Seuss the political fabulist. Inspired by Bush's claim that he thinks of *Hop on Pop* when he sleeps at night, the website *SatireWire* reclaimed the satirical Seuss by suggesting that Bush not only dreams of Dr. Seuss but consults his books for advice. The piece imagines Bush, in dreams and in bed, conferring with Vice President Dick Cheney, Secretary of State Colin Powell, and Attorney General John Ashcroft, all of whom are lying in bed next to him:

> GEORGE: I don't have to tell y'all how many times "Hop on Pop" has saved my bacon. Like during the campaign, I couldn't figure

out how to get support from minorities. Then I dreamed about that one part in "Hop on Pop" . . .

DICK: Yes sir. "Snack snack. Eat a snack. Eat a snack with Brown and Black."

GEORGE: Those minority brunches went over big.

COLIN: Suckered me in.

GEORGE: So last night I'm dreaming about "Hop on Pop," and the solution for the middle East hits me: Vroom.

ASHCROFT: Vroom, sir?

GEORGE: Vroom. You know, it's that powerful stuff Little Cat Z has under his hat. Cleans up snowspots just like that. 'Cause, you know, all that pink snow had to go.

DICK: Sir, that's not "Hop on Pop." That's from "The Cat in the Hat Comes Back."

GEORGE: Really? Strange, I haven't read that one yet.

ASHCROFT: That's probably my fault, sir. I talk in my sleep.

GEORGE: Ah, well, good thing you did. Vroom, boys, will fix everything. We just find this Little Cat Z, send him over to Israel, have him take off his hat, and Vroom! Everything's cleaned up before mother gets home.

COLIN: Mr. President, I don't believe Vroom actually exists.

GEORGE: So, we'll make some. We got a big defense budget, and if we need more money, we'll just cut taxes again.

Among other things, this satire demonstrates how difficult it is to separate Seuss the literacy advocate from Seuss the sharp satirist. Tellingly, like Coover's "The Cat in the Hat for President," the tale mocks politicians by suggesting that they rely on Dr. Seuss as a political sage.

The impossibility of separating Seuss-the-reading-teacher from Seuss-the-satirist explains why Seuss appeals to people of such different ideological positions. Seuss is that peculiarly American combination of icon and iconoclast, embraced by and critical of the establishment, a lifelong Democrat who won praise from Republican presidents. Perhaps the contradictory uses of Seuss's characters exemplify the contradictions within the American character. We are in many respects a paradoxical people. Americans identify with the revolutionary, the rebel. After all, we celebrate July 4, 1776, to honor the Declaration of Independence. We do not celebrate September 17, 1787, to honor the Constitutional

Convention delegates signing the Constitution—or even June 1788, when New Hampshire ratified the U.S. Constitution, establishing the legal foundations for the United States. And though we celebrate Independence Day and not Constitutional Convention Day, we are not in a constant state of revolt; we live by laws and aggressively prosecute people who do not. Seuss embodies these paradoxes. As official symbol *and* subversive radical, children's poet *and* political activist, Dr. Seuss offers a distorted mirror in which Americans can see themselves.

American Icon, American Iconoclast

In America, the iconoclast is iconic. Americans of many backgrounds are inclined to imagine or to align themselves with rebels, the underdog, or the outsider. Often, a political insider will pose as an outsider to get elected or re-elected; a supporter of the status quo will proclaim him- or herself a rebel; a member of the elite will emerge as a crusader for the people. Though there are both disingenuous and honest reasons for speaking from an iconoclast's position, Dr. Seuss's reasons were genuine. Even when he became a wealthy author, he was still capable of writing a cartoon like "The economic situation clarified," which shows the upwardly mobile ascending on the backs (and heads) of the downwardly mobile (fig. 3.4). He did not forget that opportunity is unequally distributed—and gave much of his money away to help those less fortunate than he.

His characters are iconoclastic because they dare speak truths that others would prefer not to face. A few weeks before he died, Judith and Neil Morgan asked if there were anything he might have left unsaid. Ted smiled and said, "Let me think about that" (Morgan and Morgan 286). A few days later, he gave them a piece of paper that read: "Any message or slogan? Whenever things go a bit sour in a job I'm doing, I always tell myself, 'You can do better than this.' The best slogan I can think of to leave with the kids of the U.S.A. would be 'We can . . . and we've *got* to . . . do better than this.'" Then, the Morgans recall, Ted scratched out "the kids of" (287). Seuss was clearly motivated by the notion that America could do better for its people, adults and children alike. While he certainly opposed the totalitarian communism of the Soviet Union and was no pacifist himself, he also knew that the arms race between the U.S. and U.S.S.R. was dangerous. As Coretta Scott King said of *The Butter Battle Book*, "May the wisdom of this book help parents double their efforts for world peace, and may its wit help children forgive us our foolish antagonisms" (*Butter Battle* press release). That's a tall order for one book, and I doubt that Seuss expected his books would change the world in as profound a way. But he knew that it was worth trying. That is why he wrote *The Sneetches*, *The Lorax*, and *Yertle the Turtle*, but is also why he undertook the task of writing primers for children. Seuss created *The Cat in the Hat* and launched Random House's Beginner Books because he wanted to help children to learn to read. Before they could undertake the critical thinking promoted by his activist books, they first had to be able to read.

Not all of Theodor Seuss Geisel's books are as liberating as they might be. Politically progressive as he was, Geisel was a man of his times and his beliefs were of course shaped by those times. By and large, however, he did gain sensitivity, changing the way that he represented differences in race, ethnicity, and (albeit belatedly) gender. If we assume that boys and girls might identify with Zooie Katzen-bein of the story of "King Looie Katz," this character's behavior shows children how even an apparently powerless character can criticize the powerful. The tale, which appears in *I Can Lick 30 Tigers Today and Other Stories*, stars a King who feels that his tail is so "lovely" that it should never be allowed to drag on the ground behind him. So, he appoints Fooie Katz to carry his tail around, an arrangement that works out fine until Fooie decides that *his* tail also deserves carrying. He gains a tail-carrier, as does his tail-carrier, and on and on until each cat in Katzen-stein is carrying the tail of the cat in front of him, including "last cat in the line," a "most unhappy little cat / Named Zooie Katzen-bein." As Seuss's narrator explains,

His tail would never be held up
And poor old Zooie knew it.
Because holding up a cat's tail
Takes another cat to do it.

Poor Zooie got so awfully mad
So mad he could have spit.
But he did a far, far braver thing. . . .

He simply yelled,
"I QUIT!"

Zooie announces, "I can not, shall not, will not / Lug this stupid thing around!" and then he "slammed the tail of Prooie Katz! / He slammed it on the ground." Just Mack's burp topples Yertle the Turtle, so Zooie's tail-slamming creates a chain reaction, as one by one, each cat slams down the tail of the next cat up the line, until finally, "proud King Looie's" is slammed down, too. Because this is a Dr. Seuss book, Zooie and the other cats suffer no reprisals for challenging authority. Instead, the political culture of Katzen-stein changes. On the final pages, Seuss has an illustration of King Looie and many other cats happily carrying their tails as they walk through town, accompanied by this concluding verse: "And since that day in Katzen-stein, / All cats have been more grown-up. / They're all more demo-catic / Because each cat holds his own up." Or, as he wrote in the original draft of the story, "Old Looie, King of Katzenstein / stopped being autocratic. / And all the cats in Katzen-stein / became more demo-catic." As Jo-Jo's "Yopp!" does, Zooie's "I QUIT!" demonstrates how activists can promote democratic ideals by speaking out and standing up for their rights.

If Seuss's morals frequently affirm the need to challenge injustice, his verse and art offers a liberation of the imagination. As Maurice Sendak put it, Seuss "wrote big noisy books with noisy pictures and noisy language. [. . .] He was a bull in a china closet" (qtd. in Lamb A8). The verve of Seuss's language and the energy of his illustrations affirm the child's need to make noise, to be creative, and to make a mess, if need be. Whether creating My Book About Me (a book which asks the child to write in it) or designing a museum that encourages visitors' participation, Seuss wanted his creativity to inspire the creativity of others. His books tell us to go ahead, imagine a Blogg, create a new alphabet, or try green eggs and ham. Naming Green Eggs and Ham as his favorite children's book, Jon Scieszka says it was the "book that made me realize books could be goofy. The book that made The Stinky Cheese Man possible." In granting children the license to think freely, Seuss shows them that the world is what they make it. Children and adults, Seuss suggests, should use this ability think creatively, participating in the world, learning from it, and when necessary doing what they can to make it better.

Encouraging children to get involved and to think for themselves, Dr. Seuss also reminds adults that we must respect the needs and beliefs of young people. In addition to advocating equal treatment of all people, Horton's "A person's a person no matter how small" could be read more narrowly as a manifesto for the rights of children. Certainly, "no matter how small" may resonate with the child reader more than the adult reader: children's smallness is the most visible mark of their powerlessness in a world governed by adults. But "A person's a person no matter how small" also reminds the grown-ups that because children are a vulnerable group, adults have a responsibility to provide a safe environment in which children can grow up. In an uncharacteristically serious, even religious, poem, Seuss speaks directly to this concern. Published in *Collier's* in December of 1955, Seuss's "Prayer for a Child" (figure E.1) offers the following wish:

From here on earth,
From my small place
I ask of You
Way out in space:
Please tell all men
In every land
What You and I
Both understand . . .
Please tell all men
That Peace is Good.
That's all
That need be understood.
In every world
In Your great sky.
   (*We* understand,
   Both You and I.)

The lines "Peace is good / That's all / That need be understood" are as relevant now as they were fifty years ago. Although Seuss disliked ending his children's books with "Amen's," this poem almost seems to warrant one.

However, rather than end *Dr. Seuss: American Icon* with an "Amen," I would like instead to do what Seuss did in many of his books, and conclude with a question. In the pages that follow the notes, you will find a bibliography of everything (or, at least, everything I could find) written by or about Dr. Seuss. I have gathered this information in the hope that it might encourage others to read, think, and write about Dr.

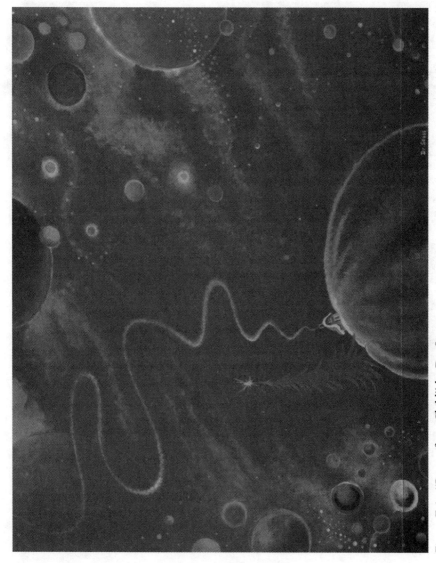

Figure E.1. "Prayer for a Child" by Dr. Seuss

Seuss. So, when you finish this paragraph, move on to the bibliography and begin your investigation: What does Dr. Seuss mean to you? As Scott McCloud says at the end of his *Understanding Comics*, "This book is meant to stimulate debate, not settle it. I've had my say. Now it's *your* turn" (216). So take a turn, and remember what Dr. Seuss says: "Think left and think right / and think low and think high / Oh, the THINKS you can think up if only you try!"

Figure E.2. Photograph of Dr. Seuss by Phyllis Cerf

Notes

Introduction

1. This is by no means a complete list of statuary depicting characters from children's literature. Ramona, Henry Huggins and Ribsy are all in the Beverly Cleary Sculpture Garden of Portland, Oregon. Brooklyn's Prospect Park has Ezra Jack Keats's Peter and Willie. At the Fairport Public Library in Fairport, New York, there is a bronze sculpture of three mice, honoring author-illustrator Ellen Stoll Walsh's *Mouse Paint*. Concrete statues of Eugene Field's Wynken, Blynken, and Nod are in Washington Park of Denver, Colorado. In Washington, D.C., a bronze statue of Uncle Beazley, the triceratops from Oliver Butterworth's *The Enormous Egg*, was on the Smithsonian grounds before it was moved to the National Zoo. Finally, St. Paul, Minnesota plans a bronze statue of Charles Schulz's "Peanuts" characters. And, as Diane G. Kerner points out, there are many castings of the Peter Pan statue around the world: the others are in Parc du Palais d'Egmont in Brussels; Bowring Park in St John's, Newfoundland; Johnson Park in Camden, New Jersey; Queen's Gardens in Perth, Australia; Sefton Park in Liverpool; and the Glenn Gould Park in Toronto.

2. While these monuments are in cemeteries instead of parks, an effigy of John Bunyan lies atop his tomb in Bunhill Fields Burial Ground (London); an obelisk for Daniel Defoe is in the same burial ground. Finally, as Richard Flynn reminded me, a young Randall Jarrell served as the model for Ganymede on Nashville's Parthenon.

3. Theodor Seuss Geisel first gives himself the mock-scholarly title of Dr. Theophrastus Seuss in the *Judge* of 19 November 1927, shortening it to Dr. Seuss in the *Judge* of 12 May 1928.

4. The remaining two Seuss books on the list are board-book versions of *Mr. Brown Can Moo! Can You?* and *Dr. Seuss's ABC* at 98 and 99, respectively (Turvey). It's worth noting here that, as the children's book market has grown more competitive, Seuss is holding his own. In the version of this list published in 1996, Seuss had 15 in the top 100, including *Green Eggs and Ham* (at number 7), *The Cat in the Hat* (8), *One Fish Two Fish Red Fish Blue Fish* (10), *Hop on Pop* (12), *Dr. Seuss's ABC* (13), *The Cat in the Hat Comes Back* (21), *Fox in Socks* (26), *Oh, the Places You'll Go!* (33), *My Book About Me* (35), *How the Grinch Stole Christmas!* (39), *I Can Read with My Eyes Shut!* (50), *Oh, the Thinks You Can Think!* (64), *There's a Wocket in My Pocket!* (81), *Mr. Brown Can Moo! Can You?* (89), *Yertle the Turtle and Other Stories* (95), and *Dr. Seuss's Sleep Book* (99). *Green Eggs and Ham*, *Oh, the Places You'll Go!* and *How the Grinch Stole Christmas!* have risen in their rankings, but the others have fallen slightly. The board-book versions of two Seuss books pushed some of his work off of the list, but Harry Potter has had the largest impact here. In their first appearance on the *Publishers Weekly* list, the *Potter* books occupied the fifth, tenth, eleventh, and nineteenth spots. (Traditionalists will be pleased to note that Janette Sebring Lowrey's *The Poky Little Puppy*, Beatrix Potter's *The Tale of Peter Rabbit*, Gertrude Crampton's *Tootle*, and Dorothy Kunhardt's *Pat the Bunny* have the same positions as they did in 1996: they are, respectively, at 1, 2, 3, and 6.)

5. I here include *Ten Apples Up on Top!*, written under the pseudonym Theo. LeSieg. This book ranks at 130.

6. A minority of contemporary critics still feels that way. In an article praising Chris Van Allsburg's picture books, reviewer Steve Szilagyi wrote "It's a good thing children don't buy picture books. [. . .] Children, it is well known, have terrible taste in pictures. Let them loose in a bookstore, and they'll run past the well-designed artistic picture books, and go straight

to the sub-Hanna-Barbera banalities of the Berenstain Bears, or the sinister cartoons of Dr. Seuss."

7. There have been other books about Seuss, but none can properly be called book-length studies. Helen Younger, Marc Younger, and Daniel Hirsch have assisted book collectors everywhere by compiling *First Editions of Dr. Seuss Books: A Guide to Identification* (2002): it reproduces front and rear dust jackets of almost all first editions, as well as identifying marks. Thomas Fensch edited *Of Sneetches and Whos and the Good Dr. Seuss: Essays on the Life and Writing of Theodor Geisel* (1997), which does Seuss scholars a great service by gathering together a selection of profiles, interviews, and analytical articles. A reference work, Edward Connery Lathem's *Who's Who and What's What in the Books of Dr. Seuss* (2000), offers an alphabetical concordance of people, places, and things in the books written under the pseudonym "Dr. Seuss." Lathem has also edited *Theodor Seuss Geisel: Reminiscences & Tributes* (1996), which collects remarks made at Geisel's memorial service in 1991, including comments by the Morgans, Herb Cheyette, Chuck Jones, and Robert Bernstein. There are also a number of juvenile biographies, the best of which is Maryann Weidt's *Oh, the Places He Went: A Story About Dr. Seuss—Theodor Seuss Geisel* (1994). Other biographies for young readers are Jill Foran's *My Favorite Writer: Dr. Seuss* (2003), Carol Greene's *Dr. Seuss: Writer and Artist for Children* (1993), and Jill C. Wheeler's *Dr. Seuss* (1992). There is a second adult biography—Thomas Fensch's *The Man Who Was Dr. Seuss: The Life and Work of Theodore Geisel* (2001)—but it adds virtually no information that the Morgans have not already provided. Finally, though it had not yet been published when I was writing *Dr. Seuss: American Icon*, Charles Cohen's *The Seuss, the Whole Seuss, and Nothing But the Seuss: A Visual Biography* (2004) should prove a promising entry into the field of Seuss scholarship.

8. The sole exceptions to this claim are myself, John Cech, and Thomas Fensch. If we add the 150+ articles in the "Interviews and Profiles" section of the bibliography, then we must add Michael J. Bandler, Bennett Cerf, Don Freeman, Lee Bennett Hopkins, Hal Humphrey, Stefan Kanfer, Judith Morgan, and Robert Sullivan.

Chapter 1

1. In her reviews of Dr. Seuss's works, Moore consistently focuses on the verse, praising *McElligot's Pool*'s "rhymes, which are sheer delight to read aloud" and adding, "May all halting rhymesters, of whom there are legion, study Dr. Seuss as he in his turn must have studied the best of nonsense poetry before he wrote *Mulberry Street*."

2. The four prose Dr. Seuss books are *The 500 Hats of Bartholomew Cubbins* (1939) and its sequel, *Bartholomew and the Oobleck* (1948); *The King's Stilts* (1939); and the "adult book," *The Seven Lady Godivas* (1939). *My Book About Me* (1969), co-written with and illustrated by Roy McKie, is also in prose.

3. If you look in the "Stories and Poems" section of the bibliography, you'll discover a dozen verse speeches, including: "Pentellic Bilge for Bennett Cerf's Birthday" (1940), "My Uncle Terwilliger on the Art of Eating Popovers" (1977), "To the P.T.A." (1977), "Small Epic Poem (Size 2 3/4 B)" (1978), "Small Epic Poem, Size 3 1/2 B" (1978), "Wilder Award Acceptance Speech" (1980), "Lamentation for Omar Khayyam Who Once Spoke in Praise of Four Great Commodities . . . . . A Book of Verses Underneath the Bough, a Jug of Wine, a Loaf of Bread and Thou" (1982), "Hail to Our Chief! (And I don't mean Ronald Reagan)" (1982), "A Short Epic Birthday Poem entitled 'On occasions such as this I maintain that my late father is of much greater importance than even Robert L. Bernstein'" (1984), and "A Rather Short Epic Poem (Size 6 and 7/8)" (1988). Three notable occasions in which he did not address his audience in verse were his lectures at the University of Utah in 1949 and his appearance on two television specials: "Modern Art on Horseback: TV-Radio Workshop of the Ford Foundation" (1954) and "Omnibus TV-Radio Workshop of the Ford Foundation: Dr.

Seuss Explores the Museum That Ought to Be" (1956). Apart from occasional exceptions such as these, Seuss preferred verse for his public speaking.

4. What I identify as iambs in Horton's verse, Francelia Butler hears as spondees (two syllables of equal weight), and she reads the final line as all spondees (177–78). Scanning poetry is an inexact science; reasonable people may differ on how a line should be scanned.

5. When asked in 1982 what "children's classics" he read as a child, Seuss also named Peter Newell's The Hole Book (1908) and offered a quotation but did not quite get the words verbatim: "It had a die-punched hole through it, and I think some of the words were, let's see: 'Tom Potts was fooling around with a gun, such fooling should not be, when bang! the pesky thing went off accidentally" (Bandler, "Portrait . . ." 2).

6. Don L. F. Nilsen identifies this device as the "polyptoton," in which "a word is repeated throughout a sentence, but each occurrence has a different ending and functions as a different part of speech" (569).

7. Perry Nodelman, too, calls Seuss's verse "accomplished doggerel" (99).

8. In his A Critical Approach to Children's Literature, James Steel Smith also calls Seuss's verse "doggerel": "the doggerel Seuss relies on eventually becomes monotonous" (314).

9. Baring-Gould dates the limerick as far back as Aristophanes (24).

10. Some creatures from Seuss's magazine work do eventually make their way into the children's books. The bird allies of Scrambled Eggs Super!'s Mt. Strookoo Cuckoos resemble the cuckoo-vultures depicted in the early essay "Recent Developments in Cuckoo Clockery" (Tough Coughs . . . 101). Children's-book creatures sometimes get recycled, too. As Ruth K. MacDonald reminds us, many creatures from On Beyond Zebra! have appeared before or since: Floob-Boober-Bab-Boober-Bubs must be cousins of McElligot's fish who go "GLURK!", and the Itch-a-pods may well be cousins of the Whos (91). Finally, as will be mentioned in Chapter Three, On Beyond Zebra!'s Umbus, a many-uddered cow, first appears in a cartoon for Judge titled "Americanizing the Milk Industry" (22 Sept. 1928), and appears again as Hitler's cow, who, with a Nazi insignia on its chest and the names of a conquered country on each of its many hindquarters, reminds the reader: "The head eats . . . . . . the rest gets milked" (PM, 19 May 1941).

11. Francelia Butler appears to concur: comparing Seuss to Lear and Carroll, she writes, "Seuss's imaginative creatures are unsurpassed" (180). In their "Incomplete Glossary of Non-sense Beasticles and Birdles," Anderson and Apseloff include thirty-two different imaginary creatures by Dr. Seuss—a number far greater than any other author on the list—and they add a separate list of twelve "Post-Alphabetical Animals from On Beyond Zebra," bringing Seuss's total up to forty-four (152–60).

12. Significantly, Seuss's second published poem—it appeared in his high-school newspaper just before he turned fifteen—was a nonsensical satire on having to take Latin. In a parody of Walt Whitman's "O Captain! My Captain!" titled "Oh Latin! My Latin!" Seuss (then known as Theodor Geisel) writes in mock-despair about having completed the wrong translation: "My classmates snicker, now they grin, a murmur starts to run, / A fearful class! I'll never pass! My lessons are not done."

13. Though his nonsense poetry is not as widely known as Lear's or Carroll's, it bears mentioning that Gelett Burgess coined the word "blurb," which he defined in his Burgess Unabridged: A New Dictionary of Words You Have Always Needed (1914).

14. Verses like these recall Cammaerts's defense of nonsense poetry: "the technique of good nonsense verse is just as skilful and difficult as that of any other kind of verse. The grotesque impression is produced, not by ignoring the general laws of good poetry, but by upsetting them purposely, and by making them, so to speak, stand on their heads" (40).

15. On the assumption that the first story is more likely to be the true (or truer) story, I lean toward the version Seuss told The Saturday Evening Post's Robert Cahn, since this account appeared the same year that The Cat in the Hat was published. Seuss says, "All I needed, I figured, was to find a whale of an exciting subject which would make the average six-year-old want to read like crazy [. . .] None of the dull old stuff: Dick has a ball. Dick likes the ball. The

ball is red, red, red, red." Cahn then paraphrases Seuss's idea for writing "a book about scaling the peaks of Everest at sixty degrees below zero." The publisher finds the idea "exciting," but tells Seuss, "However, you can't use the word 'scaling,' you can't use the word 'peaks,' you can't use 'Everest,' you can't use 'sixty,' and you can't use 'degrees.'" Six months later, Seuss, unable to come up with anything from such a limited vocabulary, was looking at "[p]age after page of scrawls [. . .] piled in his den. He had accumulated stories which moved along in fine style but got nowhere. One story about a King Cat and a Queen Cat was halfway finished before he realized that the word 'queen' was not on the list." Finally and "when he was almost ready to give up, there emerged from a jumble of sketches a raffish cat wearing a battered stovepipe hat." Seuss "checked his list—both hat and cat were on it" (Cahn 42). Seuss repeated the final part of this story in a 1969 story by Donald Freeman ("Who Thunk You Up . . ." 168), but he often claimed to have come up with the rhyme before the illustration. In 1958, he explained to Edward S. Kitch, "I had cat and the only thing I could think of to rhyme with cat is hat." In 1972, he told Digby Diehl, "People since then have thought that I was brilliant in choosing as my subject the cat and the hat. But I chose them because they were the first two words I found on the list that rhymed" (37). For the rest of his life, Seuss would repeat this version of the story in interviews (Dangaard 1; Lingeman 24; Clark D4; Hopkins, "Stoo-pendous Dr. Seuss!"; Frutig 18; Carlinsky 15; Cott 25; Hacker 8E).

The number of words also varies widely—in part because sometimes Seuss indicates how many words were on the list (348) and other times he says how many words from the list could be included in a book (225). Cahn mentions Seuss working from a list of 348 words; Kitch, Clark and Hopkins report that the book has 223 words. Seuss tells Dan Carlinsky that "there were 223 words to use in this book" (15). In two 1976 interviews, Seuss is said to be working "within the constraints of a 220-word vocabulary" (Lingeman 24; cf. Dangaard 1); in a 1984 interview, Seuss describes "a controlled vocabulary of about 200 words" (Kupferberg 6). Beverly Beyette and Kathy Hacker report that he was "restricted to fewer than 250 words" (Beyette 5; Hacker 8E), but Seuss tells Jonathan Cott of "a list of about three hundred words" (25), and Judith Frutig indicates that Seuss "was given a list of 400 words with instructions to winnow them down to a working list of 220" (18). Finally, Seuss's biographers tell us of the publisher's "insistence that the book's vocabulary be limited to 225 words" (Morgan and Morgan 154).

16. As Cammaerts says, "While the interest in serious poetry is becoming more and more restricted to the so-called intellectual class, nonsense is practically the only type of poetry which is remaining in touch with the great mass of the people" (56). In other words, nonsense is a populist form of poetry.

17. With Seuss's typescript for *Green Eggs and Ham* is a two-page, two-column list, the first column labeled "*WORD*," and the second labeled "*TIMES USED*." According to this list, Seuss's memory was accurate. The statistics also reveal that the third and fourth most-used words are *a* (59 times) and *them* (56 times). The least-used words are *but* and *if*, each of which appears only once in *Green Eggs and Ham*.

18. Wim Tigges usually argues that nonsense should be separated from satire (21, 51, 85) and, as do most scholars of nonsense, he generally considers literary nonsense a nineteenth-century invention (6, 138). He does, however, concede that "playing with language is as old as language itself" (138), and that nonsense may occur within satire (50). My definition of nonsense is somewhat broader than his, and while I would concur that modern literary nonsense is strongly rooted in the nineteenth century (Lear, Carroll), I am persuaded by Noel Malcolm's argument that nonsense dates back to thirteenth-century Germany and seventeenth-century England (Malcolm 4, 53).

Chapter 2

1. As Seuss told an interviewer in 1976, "*McElligot's Pool* was put away in 1941 and finished in 1947" (Clark D4). The original dust jacket to *McElligot's Pool* offers a more dramatic

(but factually identical) version of events: "THIS IS THE FIRST DR. SEUSS BOOK SINCE 1940! There was *Mulberry Street* in 1937. There was *The Five Hundred Hats* in 1938. There was *The King's Stilts* in 1939. And *Horton Hatches the Egg* in 1940. Then the Army found use for the good Doctor's time, and this book, originally scheduled for 1941, had to wait until now for publication" (Younger, Younger, and Hirsch 133).

2. Not that *Horton Hatches the Egg* lacks a political dimension. As Alexander Laing notes in his review, "*Horton Hatches the Egg* is a symbolic parable for our times and its symbolism is as clear as day. The faithful elephant who sits on the egg of the faithless lazy bird has nothing whatever to do with Wendell Willkie. It is a staggering argument, rather, for holding firm to one's faith in first principles, in spite of the devil. It is, among other things, a parable against appeasement. Its crisis comes when Horton, faced by the rifles of the hunters (Munich for Horton) makes his great decision and goes right on sitting on that egg."

3. *Horton Hears a Who!* also inspired one review that Seuss would refer to for the rest of his life. Writing in the *New York Times Book Review*, Jane Cobb said, "It is probably the most moral tale since 'Elsie Dinsmore,' but since it is written and illustrated by Dr. Seuss it is a lot more fun." The "Elsie Dinsmore" part of this remark really stuck in Seuss's craw—he often said, ruefully, that he's been called as moralistic as Elsie Dinsmore, even though one only one reviewer called him this *and* said he was "a lot more fun."

4. As Jules Feiffer writes in *The Great Comic Book Heroes* (1965, repr. 2003), "the unwritten success story of the war was the smash comeback of the Oriental villain. He had failed badly for a few years, losing face to mad scientists—but now he was at the height of his glory. Until the war we always assumed he was Chinese. But now we knew what he was! A Jap; a Yellow-Belly Jap; a Jap-a-Nazi Rat: these being the three major classifications. [. . .] He often sported fanged bicuspids and drooled a lot more than seemed necessary. (If you find the image hard to imagine I refer you to his more recent incarnation in magazines like Dell's *Jungle War Stories* where it turns out he wasn't Japanese at all: He was North Vietnamese. [. . .])" (59–60). Feiffer was writing that in the 1960s. Since the dominant stereotypes shift according to the perceived enemy, I wouldn't be surprised if today's comic-book villain is an Arab terrorist. I hope not, of course. But I wouldn't be surprised.

5. Jenkins reads *Horton Hears a Who!* as "a fable about the decline of the Popular Front" (188). As he says, "Horton's situation encapsulates the dilemmas that many liberals faced in postwar America—torn between the conflicting values of community and individualism, frightened by mob rule and, yet, dedicated to democracy. *Horton* expresses a nostalgia for the Who-ville-like America of the war years, when political differences were forgotten in the name of a common cause" (187).

6. Seuss also felt that, in order to succeed, post-war American foreign policy had to oppose racism. For example, he maintained that Americans must see what they have in common with the Japanese, or else the Japanese may seek alliances with Communist nations. Reviewing Jiro Osaragi's *Homecoming* for the *New York Times Book Review* in 1955, Seuss wrote that advocates of translating Japanese novels include "the groups of Americans and Japanese who have been working together, ever since the war, to promote a healthier interchange of ideas. They feel very strongly that unless we and the Japanese learn to see eye to eye the Japanese may learn to see eye to eye with the Russians. Novels, more than textbooks, help average people see eye to eye" ("The Past Is Nowhere").

7. Seuss also contributed a political cartoon to the cause. A bird in flight approaches a weary bird, perched atop a pole that looks out over buildings as far as the eye can see. The first bird asks, "Pardon me, sir . . . but which way to the nearest park?" Further text adds, "This is what you and your Birds and your Kids will be facing unless You Vote YES on Propositions A and B."

8. Arguably, Seuss's "The economic situation clarified: A prognostic re-evaluation," which appeared in a June 1975 issue of the *New York Times Magazine*, could qualify as a political cartoon, even though it is not as blunt as his other political cartoons.

9. In the opening sentences of the memo, Geisel warned, "All men writing information to troops should be cautioned to steer clear of all German Atrocity Stories unless they have been doubly and triply checked and found *absolutely true*. Many of these stories will backfire on us later, as did the rape of the Belgian Nuns in the last war. The backfiring of last war's over-emphasized atrocity stories did a great deal to whitewash the Germans and made us pretty cynical people about this sort of thing."

Chapter 3

1. For other versions of the story, see "The Other Cool Cat," p. 24; Carlinsky, p. 12; Kupferberg, p. 5. Though the central incident of the tale remains consistent, Seuss's responses to it vary. In one version, he decides he "would never draw again" ("Other Cool Cat" 24). In another, he says, "It's the only reason I went on—to prove that teacher wrong" (Cott 18). In most versions he says that he was then unable to articulate why he was turning the work upside down, but in one version he explains to his teacher that he is "check[ing] the balance of the elements," and she does not believe him (Kupferberg 5). Seuss's claim that he never took another art lesson appears to be hyperbole. His father reports that "Ted did once take a correspondence course in drawing [. . .] He came to me one day with one of those advertisements torn from a magazine. This one showed Uncle Sam and you were supposed to copy it and send it in. Ted did and later I gave him $15.00 to enroll in the course." Confirming his father's story, Seuss adds, "As a matter of fact it wasn't a bad investment. [. . .] I think I picked up a lot of technical points that really helped me get started" (Jordan 25).

2. In her article, "The Mouse in the Corner, the Fly on the Wall: What Very Young Eyes See in Picture Books" (1993), Karla Kuskin argues that the bird in Seuss's *500 Hats* and similar "bit players" in books by other authors are "there to interest younger, sharper eyes than yours [adults']" (Fensch 165). So, perhaps younger readers *do* notice these characters and older readers miss them.

3. Yes, there are a few exceptions. For the curious reader who wishes to know *which* ones, I will tell you. Other readers should resume reading the chapter. Of the forty-four books written and illustrated by Dr. Seuss, nine lack a non-central character observing: *And to Think That I Saw It on Mulberry Street*, *Thidwick the Big-Hearted Moose*, *Horton Hears a Who!*, *Dr. Seuss's ABC*, *I Can Lick 30 Tigers Today!*, *Mr. Brown Can Moo! Can You?*, *Marvin K. Mooney Will You Please Go Now!*, *The Shape of Me and Other Stuff*, *There's a Wocket in My Pocket!* Six other books have "observer" characters who are more central, and so might be added to the list. If the Patrol Cats are main characters, then *The King's Stilts* could be included with the exceptions: on the last page, the Patrol Cats look on as the King and Eric race across the countryside on stilts. Though they have non-speaking roles, the Cats are very important. The dog in *On Beyond Zebra!* acts as silent onlooker, but he also appears in nearly every scene. In *The Cat in the Hat*, the fish is both onlooker and plays the (very vocal) role of the conscience. Norval, another fish, never speaks but both observes and listens throughout *You're Only Old Once!* In *Green Eggs and Ham*, all characters (including minor ones) look on as the black-hatted character tries the food (56–57). *Fox in Socks* has different characters (pigs, tweetle beetles, even the Fox himself) who merely observe at a few moments during the book, but all are more prominent than a mere onlooker would be. Still, even if we add these extra six books to the "exceptions" list, sixty-five percent of all Dr. Seuss books include minor "witness" characters at least once.

4. As Miles Orvell writes, "[W]hen we call an experience or thing 'the real thing,' we are identifying a quality of intensity that is otherwise lacking in the featureless background that constitutes the main hum of experience" (xvi).

5. If we were to include Caldecott Honor books, this list would of course expand to include Maurice Sendak's homage to Winsor McCay, *In the Night Kitchen*; Doreen Cronin's comic parable of unionized farm animals, *Click, Clack, Moo*; and several others.

6. In *White Snow, Bright Snow*, for example, the combination of Duvoisin's images and Tresselt's text recalls some of the best collaborations between Margaret Wise Brown and Leonard Weisgard: poetic language, striking illustrations, brought into relief by an elegant layout.

7. A history of comic art's gradual critical acceptance is beyond the scope of this book, but, clearly, many more names than Eisner and Spiegelman should be mentioned here. Frank Miller's *Batman: The Dark Knight Returns* (1986) Alan Moore and Dave Gibbons' *Watchmen* (1987) also deserve credit here. And the acceptance of Spiegelman, Eisner, et al. was in turn made possible by the serious attention paid to the comics prior to then. Coulton Waugh's *The Comics* appeared in 1947 and Stephen Becker's *Comic Art in America* in 1959. In the 1970s, Bill Blackbeard, Ron Goulart, Maurice Horn, and Richard Marschall all began to publish collections of, histories of, and reference works on the comics. I am certain, too, that the rise of Pop Art—especially Roy Lichtenstein's massive comic-strip canvases—played a role in allowing us to see comics as art. Whether directly or indirectly, Pop Art helped make possible aesthetic appreciation of the comic strip.

8. Seuss's debt to the comic strip may explain his tendency to profess that he was not a serious artist. Even complimentary reviewers of his work seemed to feel that they must apologize for the "comic strip" style. In her favorable review of *Mulberry Street*, Anne Carroll Moore said, "The drawings, in bright color, have the dynamic quality of the comic strip, but are without vulgarity." The *New York Times'* review, also favorable, noted Seuss's debt to "the funny papers," and said that the book's "bright pictures, [. . .] though a bit crude in coloring are as spirited and comic as is the young hero's imagination" (Buell 14, 37).

9. Of *If I Ran the Zoo*'s Gerald McGrew, Ruth MacDonald says, "he invents a Skeeglemobile and a Bad-Animal-Catching-Machine, which look like Rube Goldberg contraptions, flimsy and byzantine in construction, but capable of doing what they were intended to do—catch Gerald's fantasy animals" (MacDonald 68). Reviewing *The Butter Battle Book*, Michael Dirda describes the "increasingly destructive and yet preposterous weapons" as "a mix of Rube Goldberg and Wile E. Coyote contraptions."

10. Among the original finished ink drawings for *Oh, the Places You'll Go!*, this page has no original ink drawing, but instead has a copy of "The economic situation" illustration. Tellingly, this illustration does not appear among the color roughs (an earlier phase of the book), suggesting that Seuss knew he would use "The economic situation" here and so there was no need to attempt to redraw it. I should add here that Seuss usually did not literally photocopy himself. At this point in his life (this was his last book), his line was much shakier, and it would have been very difficult to recreate a drawing as precise as "The economic situation."

11. In 1951, American journals published articles on Escher, a 1954 exhibition in Amsterdam was very successful, and Americans' interest in Escher follows shortly after that (Vermeulen 139).

12. According to Lluís Permanyer, "international awareness of Gaudí's genius did not come until 1952, when American historian George R. Collins presented a major exhibition of his work in New York. The Japanese have since expressed a boundless passion and fascination for Gaudí" (15). Japanese interest in Gaudí suggests that Seuss's 1953 visit to Japan might have provided opportunity to encounter his work, although if Seuss's post-collegiate European travels included a stop in Barcelona, then an acquaintance with Gaudí's architecture might date to the 1920s. Certainly, an interest in Art Nouveau began in Seuss's college days: As Seuss told an interviewer in 1972, "At Dartmouth, [. . .] I went off on an Aubrey Beardsley kick and began buying original copies of the *Yellow Book* and things of that sort" (Bandler, "Portrait of a Man Reading" 2).

13. Of course, *If I Ran the Zoo, Happy Birthday to You!*, and *I Had Trouble in Getting to Solla Sollew* are not the only books with buildings that echo Gaudí's. Who-ville, as represented in *Horton Hears a Who!*, could have been designed by Gaudí. The "underground grotto in Gekko"—where the Yekko lives in *On Beyond Zebra!*—recalls Gaudí's Crypt of the Güell Estate Church, and its design establishes the Yekko's habitat as an alien place.

14. In the exhibit *Springfield Celebrates Seuss!* (2002), its curators point out the Indian Motorcycles appearance in *Mulberry Street* and add that the "names of Seuss characters such as McBean and McElligot were families listed in early twentieth century Springfield phone directories." Also: "In *The Lorax*, the image of Thneeds Factory is reminiscent of a four-towered factory seen in historic images of Springfield." More on this latter point later in the paragraph.

15. As a footnote to Chapter One indicates, there are more examples of Seuss's tendency to recycle than can be adequately catalogued here. That said, here are a few more. *On Beyond Zebra!*'s Wumbus first appears as an Isolationist in "The Isolationist" (*PM*, 16 July 1941). Stacks of turtles appear in "FISH, BEAST, and BIRD: A PISCOZOÖAVISTICAL SURVEY: MAKING THE WORLD SAFE FOR TURTLERY" (*Judge*, 6 Sept. 1930) and return in "You Can't Build A Substantial V Out of Turtles!" (*PM*, 20 Mar. 1942), before making their most famous appearance in *Yertle the Turtle* (1958).

16. Seuss often uses space to create loneliness, using a vast area around the character to underscore how lonely that character is. So, for example, in *Did I Ever Tell You How Lucky You Are?*, the "rusty tin coat hanger" left "all alone in some punkerish place" would be an antecedent for "*All Alone!* / Whether you like it or not, / Alone will be something / you'll be quite a lot." In both scenes, the emptiness around the focal point draws our sympathy—whether it be toward a person or a coat hanger, Seuss (as Edward Gorey does) demonstrates how to create feeling by manipulating the relationship between what is there and what is not.

17. The Escarobus hoax shows that he knew the Cubist style well enough to parody it. In the mid-1950s, Edward Longstreth, a friend of Geisel's and patron of the La Jolla Museum of Art, "launched into a condescending lecture about modern art." Geisel rebelled by tricking his friend into buying some work of "the great Mexican modernist," Escarobus—a fictional painter whom Geisel invented on the spot. Claiming to have five Escarobuses, Geisel then let slip that he had to sell them to raise money to help Escarobus pay his back taxes. Longstreth took the bait, and Geisel "stayed up most of the night creating the world's first Escarobus," the description of which sounds like a parody of modernist art: Geisel "peeled the wood off a soft pencil, scraped the lead lengthwise across art paper, dipped small hunks of bread in the vodka he was drinking, and dragged the soggy bread across the paper. Next he painted [Lady] Godivas on the smudges, bisecting and trisecting them so that it was impossible to tell that they were naked ladies." Later that week, he sold the painting to Longstreth for five hundred dollars. Longstreth was so impressed that he offered to buy the rest: Geisel would have sold him the rest, but Helen stopped him (Morgan and Morgan 142–43). Geisel remarked several years later, "That experience made me suspect that a lot of modern art is malarkey. If I can do it myself, it can't be any good" (Kahn 53). This typically self-deprecatory remark belies his interest in and indebtedness to modern art. As the influence of Surrealism and Dada demonstrate, the Escarobus forgery was by no means Seuss's only entry into modernist styles.

18. This visual style dates back to *Vincent*, Burton's 6-minute directorial debut, from 1982. Asked whether *Vincent*'s "expressionistic set design" was derived from Robert Wiene's *The Cabinet of Dr. Caligari*, Burton replied, "I certainly saw pictures of it, in any monster book there were pictures of it. But I didn't see it until fairly recently. I think it probably has more to do with being inspired by Dr Seuss. It just happens to be shot in black and white, and there's a Vincent Price/Gothic kind of thing that makes it feel that way. I grew up loving Dr Seuss. The rhythm of his stuff spoke to me very clearly. Dr Seuss's books were perfect: right number of words, the right rhythm, great subversive stories. He was incredible, he was the greatest, definitely. He probably saved a bunch of kids who nobody will ever know about" (Salisbury 19).

19. In fact, after Smith met Jon Scieszka, they soon discovered "that they had a similar sense of humor and a great many interests in common. As children they had both loved [Ruth Krauss's] *The Carrot Seed* as well as Dr. Seuss's books, *Mad* magazine and Warner Brothers cartoons" (Marcus).

20. Scieszka says that Dr. Seuss "was the first author that I realized was a different person—that there actually was a person who wrote the book." After reading *Mulberry Street*, he realized, "Wow. Some guy wrote this. He's probably a weird guy, too" (Leipzig).

Chapter 4

1. Not *the* earliest creatures, but some of the earliest ones. In the November 1923 issue of *Jack-o-lantern*, Theodor Seuss Geisel (signing himself "Ted") drew "Who's Who in Bo-Bo," featuring profiles of six imaginary creatures: the Heumkia, the Panifh, the Dinglebläder, the Side Hill Galloper, the Blvgk, and the Pseukeh Snake. The two-page spread does not indicate that any of these were visions brought on by alcohol.

2. There are countless examples of such creativity in Seuss's books. Here is one more of many: *Oh, the Thinks You Can Think!* encourages us to "Think / a race / on a horse / on a ball / with a fish!" Seuss's illustration shows a race, in which each child, balancing a fish bowl on his head, rides a horse which is itself balanced on a large red ball. In the drawing, horse and fish are clearly anxious, and, in the background, one former participant is out of the race, having fallen of the horse, and the horse off of the ball.

3. He told Judith Martin that it was so dirty "that he couldn't even explain in euphemisms what it was about. But it was not intended for publication—only to 'scare the blazes out of' the editors at Random House when he insisted that he wanted it published" (B4).

4. In fact, Seuss first uses Godiva in a cartoon published in an issue of *Judge* from 6 April 1929. As a naked Lady Godiva rides by on an old horse, one man says to the other, "Shameful! Disgraceful! Godiva riding that poor old nag. Why, you can almost see his ribs!"

5. In his introductory essay to Bob Adelman's *Tijuana Bibles: Art and Wit in America's Forbidden Funnies, 1930s-1950s* (1997), Art Spiegelman provides the following thorough and succinct definition: "The Tijuana Bibles probably weren't produced in Tijuana (or in Havana, Paris, or London, as some of the covers imply), and they obviously weren't Bibles. They were clandestinely produced and distributed small booklets that chronicled the explicit sexual adventures of America's beloved comic-strip characters, celebrities, and folk heroes. The standard format consisted of eight poorly printed 4"-wide by 3"-high black (or blue) and white pages with one panel per page and covers of a heavier colored stock" (6). Adelman's book not only reproduces many of these (now) hard-to-find specimens of American erotica but is also the single authoritative source on the genre.

6. Some other examples of Seuss's cartoons which today would be considered racially insensitive but at the time were common stereotypes: "SHE—*Out sportin' again, are yo', nigger? Jest wait 'til I lay hands on yo' tonight!*" (*Judge*, 15 Sept. 1928), "Unusual Philanthropists" (*Judge*, 5 Jan. 1929), "Sorry, sister, but you can't get wholesale baptizin' rates unless you got a minimum of twelve chillun'" (*Judge*, 12 Jan. 1929), "Call me a frothy-mouthed idiot, will ya? Nigger, you must fight me a drool!" (*Judge*, 26 Jan. 1929), and "Africa—Its Social, Religious, and Economical Aspects" (*Judge*, 23 Mar. 1929).

7. On the color roughs for *The Shape of Me and Other Stuff*, the cover page says "By Theo. LeSieg."

8. As he told Digby Diehl in 1972, "*Horton Hatches the Egg* was a lucky accident. I was in my New York studio one day, sketching on transparent tracing paper, and I had the window open. The wind simply took a picture of an elephant that I'd drawn and put it on top of another sheet of paper that had a tree on it. All I had to do was to figure out what the elephant was doing in that tree. I've left my window open for 30 years since that, but nothing's happened" (Diehl 37). For similar versions of this story, see Stewart-Gordon, p. 143; Clark, p. D1; Steinberg, p. 87; Frutig, p. 18. Prior to 1972, Seuss told interviewers a slightly different version of the story—he removes the wind. As he told Lewis Nichols in 1962, " 'Horton' came one day when I drew a picture of an elephant, a sort of doodle. Then I doodled a tree, and in an accidental shuffle, the transparent paper showed an elephant in a tree. Then all I had to do was figure out why an elephant would be sitting in a tree" (Nichols 2). See also Kitch; Kahn, p. 82; Gordon, p. 99; MacEoin, p. 14; Hopkins, *Books Are By People*, p. 256.

9. In the documentary, "An Awfully Big Adventure," Margarita (Peggy) Owens shows this particular Christmas card. As she says, "I have Christmas cards they sent, where they had young

children they practically got off the street come in and pose with them. There was suddenly this family—Ted, Helen and the kiddies."

10. The Morgans' biography underscores the sadness behind Chrysanthemum-Pearl and the other imaginary children: "Ted told his niece, Peggy, who had grown up with Chrysanthemum-Pearl almost as a contemporary, that 'it was not that we didn't *want* to have children. That wasn't it'" (91). However, asked if Ted and Helen's lack of children was "a source of sadness," Audrey Geisel replied, "If it was, it was not a sadness that he chose to share" (Baldacci 33).

11. For more radical, psycho-sexual readings of Seuss, see Emily Stong's "Juvenile Literary Rape in America: A Post-Coital Study of the Writings of Dr. Seuss" (1977), Louis Menand's "Cat People: What Dr. Seuss Really Taught Us" (2002), or Naomi Goldenberg's "A Feminist, Psychoanalytic Exegesis of the Cat in the Hat" (1995, excerpted in Peter Steinfels's "Beliefs"). The first two of these are clearly tongue-in-cheek, but Goldenberg's piece (as reported by Steinfels) appears to be serious.

12. This number varies, although 27, 28, and 29 recur most frequently. For anyone who wishes to keep track, here are some sources for each number: 20 (Kahn 64), 26 ("The 25th Anniversary of Dr. Seuss" 12), 27 (Freeman, "Nonsensical World . . ." 200; Jennings 108; Lathem 21), 28 (Silverman 44; Lindsay 34; Waugh; MacEoin), 29 (Associated Press; Hopkins, "Dr. Seuss [Theodor S. Geisel]" 255–56; Bowman; Berman). In 1982, Glenn Edward Sadler posed the question directly, asking Seuss how many publishers turned down *And to Think That I Saw It on Mulberry Street*. Seuss replied, Twenty-seven or twenty-nine, I forget which. The excuse I got for all those rejections was that there was nothing on the market quite like it, so they didn't know whether it would sell" (248).

13. When E. J. Kahn's profile, "Children's Friend," appeared in the *New Yorker* of 17 December 1960, Ted and Helen both complimented Kahn on the piece (Morgan and Morgan 172–73). However, years later, he told Judith and Neil Morgan, "I don't want you to read that. It got butchered. It was going to be two parts instead of one and they cut it. They took out all the funny stuff" (173). Note that his criticism here is not of the content of the piece, but rather that it isn't as funny as it might have been. The longer version, apparently, would have been more entertaining.

14. Although "Marco Comes Late" (*Redbook*, 1950) does not quite convey the confidence of *McElligot's Pool*, Marco nonetheless has much more faith in his storytelling abilities than he did in *Mulberry Street*. In "Marco Comes Late," Marco concocts an alibis to explain why he is arriving over two hours late for school: a bird laid an egg on top of his "'Rithmetic Book," which was balanced on his head. First worms and then cats argue over whether he should keep still to protect the egg, or move on to arrive at school on time. Finally, the egg hatches, and he rushes off to school. Though his teacher does not seem completely convinced by his story, she does "smile" and tell him, "That's a very good tale, if it's true." Marco admits, "Not *quite* all, I guess. But I *did* see a worm." Though Marco lacks the confidence here that he has in *McElligot's Pool*, he nonetheless does lie with conviction *while* he's doing the lying. Given her smile, Marco's teacher does seem to want to believe him, in spite of her doubts.

15. Dr. T's name is spelled "Terwilliker" on the DVD of *The 5,000 Fingers of Dr. T.* but "Terwilliger" in Seuss's sketches.

Chapter 5

1. Though he never addressed this question (to my knowledge), Seuss was once asked whether toys—then under development—based on his characters would be antithetical to the message of *The Grinch*, given that these toys would be sold during Christmas. Seuss replied, "I see no dualism in purpose. These are not strictly Christmas toys. They will be sold throughout the whole year" (Corwin).

2. This is but a small sampling. In connection with the live-action film (2000), Nabisco sold "Decorate-it-yourself Edible Ornaments," inviting consumers to "Help the Grinch and Cindy Lou Who Finger Paint your edible ornaments and create wacky treats to Hang on your Christmas Tree or to Eat." At Christmastime in 2002, Hallmark was selling a "Keepsake Ornament" titled "Change of Heart": smiling happily as he stands in his Santa outfit, the Grinch holds up an X-ray frame in front of his chest to show his changed heart. That same Christmas, Random House was selling *The Grinch Pops Up!*, a pop-up spin-off of *How the Grinch Stole Christmas!* ("Don't be a GRINCH . . .").

3. I develop this point at greater length in "Dada Knows Best: Growing Up Surreal with Dr. Seuss," the second chapter in *The Avant-Garde and American Postmodernity: Small Incisive Shocks* (2002), and in Chapter Two of this book.

4. John O'Brien's "How The Schnook Stole 'How the Grinch Stole Christmas'" (2000), a verse criticism of the film, casts the movie's producers as "the Schnook" and excoriates them for (as O'Brien sees it) violating the principles of the book. Foreseeing movie versions of other Seuss books supplanting the originals, O'Brien imagines the Schnook saying, "Don't worry, don't fret, don't look so perplexed— / Just wait 'til you see what's coming up next! / Some sneetches will form a star-bellied Aryan nation / While the Lorax is promoting massive deforestation. / The Butter Battle Book's adapted to start a big war— / Just give us some time, and we'll come up with more!" O'Brien's speaker continues, "And so, one by one, our illusions are shattered, / Were we naive to believe that the Doctor still mattered?" In a version of the song, "You're a Mean One, Mr. Grinch," O'Brien writes, "You infuriate me, greedy Schnook / You're an unrepentant crook / You've grasped all you could grasp / And you took all you could took / Greedy Schnook! / I've got just one thing to say to you and I'll say it right now / 'Give . . . back . . . the . . . book!'"

5. Both Herb Cheyette and Karl ZoBell concur that Seuss's business ethic would include marketing plans such as these. Cheyette says that the "implication [. . .] that merchandising and commercialization in all its forms were contrary to Ted's philosophy and offensive to his business ethic [. . .] is simply bunk. [. . .] Dr. Seuss Enterprises has engaged in no activity that Ted did not also engage in. Ted knew the way of the world and was not about to deprive himself of a desirable opportunity for reasons of commercial disdain. The key question, of course, is what was a desirable opportunity? The Christmas commercial of my anecdote was not desirable. A motion picture was, and so was a theme park" (letter, 22 May 2003). ZoBell adds, "I performed legal services for Ted for over 30 years, and was probably his only lawyer for the last 10 or 15 years of his life. Ted also entrusted me to serve as co-executor of his will, and as co-trustee of his trusts. We spent a great deal of time discussing difficult legal matters, business matters, and personal matters, and I found him to be a highly sophisticated person with an acute mind, and a healthy interest in making sound economic decisions. He was, indeed, exceptionally generous with local and national philanthropies, and he did not call his generosity to public attention. He was also keenly aware that generosity (as well as maintaining the lifestyle that he enjoyed) required that he look after his business interests, and protect, preserve and enhance the assets he had created. I am wholly convinced that none of the business decisions which have been made by Dr. Seuss Enterprises since his death are inconsistent in kind from decisions he made during his life time, and/or expected and projected to be taken following his death" (letter to Herb Cheyette, 22 May 2003).

6. As Betty Mensch and Alan Freeman have observed, the anti-racist message of *The Sneetches* "is not to suggest that Dr. Seuss is perfect on the question of racism. In *If I Ran the Zoo* (1950), he failed to rise above his generation, depicting both Asians and Africans with racially stereotypic caricature" (34n).

7. In response to these criticisms, Herb Cheyette writes, "With regard to *The Wubbulous World of Dr. Seuss*, Jim Henson and Ted admired each other. Jim died three weeks before a scheduled meeting with Ted to discuss possible television projects. When Brian Henson, Jim's son, indicated renewed interest on the part of the Muppeteers, Dr. Seuss Enterprises was receptive, especially since the creative head of the project was Michael Frith, a former associate

and collaborator of Ted's at Beginner Books. The affinity was so close, Michael even looked like Ted. Sorry that the completed programs didn't also resemble Ted's work to your satisfaction" (Cheyette, letter, 22 May 2003).

8. The sad irony of the entertainment industry's reliance on Trademark law is that it begets consumption for its own sake. Brian Grazer plans to capitalize on the commercial success he had with *Dr. Seuss's How the Grinch Stole Christmas*, with live-action versions of *The Cat in the Hat* (due fall 2003) and *Curious George*. As Grazer explains, "There's a greater appetite for them [films based on children's books] because when they work, they work in a gigantic way. [. . .] They also generate other byproducts that are natural to the piece. It is natural to have some merchandising and toys" (Abramowitz).

9. Cheyette also notes that Seuss "had completed four drafts of the film script before he died." As for the movie's current status, "[s]even scripts later, this film project is now at Universal" (letter, 22 May 2003).

10. Cheyette adds, "When the opportunity for a Seuss theme park re-presented itself after Ted's death, Audrey, who was present at the previous meeting, welcomed the possibility. Dr. Seuss landing is a work of art. It is tasteful, brilliantly executed and Ted would be proud to have inspired it. It is a lasting addition to Ted's legacy" (letter, 22 May 2003).

Chapter 6

1. Seuss's works have inspired classical pieces, too. At Carnegie Hall in 1943, the New York Philharmonic played Deems Taylor's "set of variations for orchestra" based on *And to Think That I Saw It on Mulberry Street* (Kahn 64). In 1993, the New Jersey Chamber Music Society performed *Dr. Seuss's Green Eggs and Ham*, set to music by Robert Kapilow.

2. The band's "Green Eggs and Swine," from the same album, uses *Green Eggs and Ham* both to assert their street credentials and to distance themselves from false friends: "No no no, green eggs and swine / But they keep edgin' to my plate, I step back and say, / 'Thanks, cause I just ate,' not that I would eat it / even if I was hungry—all the ills of the streets / that could have done me in I stay clear of all the evil all the envy / And ex-homeboys who used to be friendly."

3. As Seuss explained, "The book came from my annoyance over the fact that natural resources were being plundered—not just lumber but land and other things—for dumb reasons like greed" (Glionna).

4. Bill Bailey said of *The Lorax*, "It's a fictionalized account of perceived devastation by the logging industry" (Glionna).

5. In 2002, the Human Life Alliance created an insert for college newspapers, which appeared in Kansas State University's *Collegian* on 22 April 2003. To oppose legal abortions, the insert invoked the line "A person's a person . . . no matter how small," crediting "Dr. Suess [*sic*]" with its authorship (Human Life Alliance 4–5). Though anti-choice groups frequently misuse Horton, he also appears in cartoons about Republicans: in response to the Republican Party's reluctance to pass campaign finance reform in July of 2001, Mike Thompson drew a cartoon captioned "Horton Hears a Clue!" It features Horton, in a suit, wearing a "HOUSE GOP" button. He's holding a soft clover, from which he hears, "This is where you will get booted / if campaign reform is diluted. / It will be a little sore / when voters kick you out the door."

6. The Capitol Steps were not the first to compare Gingrich to the Grinch. According to a report from the *New York Times*, Gingrich's ideological similarity to the Grinch was noticed as early as 1985: "Over the years, politicians to the left of center have often characterized their conservative opponents as mean, stingy and joyless, but few were prepared for the introduction given Representative Newt Gingrich of Georgia, an outspoken conservative, at a recent conference in Dallas. Trammell Crow, the Texas real estate magnate, outlined the Republican's in-

creasingly active role in national and party affairs and concluded: 'Ladies and Gentlemen, I give you Congressman Grinch!'" (Clarity and Warren A16).

7. Suggs adds, "I do wish I had left out the turban, because no one could be more sensitive to cultural differences than me" (email to author, 17 June 2003).

8. *Mr. Brown Can Moo! Can You?* was published in 1970, two years after "The Cat in the Hat for President."

9. In my *The Avant-Garde and American Postmodernity*, I endorse Ned's interpretation: "Although the pink stain and Voom clearly locate the book in the context of anti-Soviet propaganda, *The Cat in the Hat Comes Back* does not endorse such paranoia. True to the radical nature he has shown in *The Cat in the Hat*, the Cat deliberately inverts the dominant logic of the day in order to challenge it. Instead of containing the symbolic Red Menace, he deliberately, even merrily, spreads it" (65). For the full analysis, see pp. 65–66.

10. During the impeachment, several email parodies spun versions along this theme, notably Dale Connelly's "Green Egg on His Face" and "President Clinton's Testimony by Dr. Seuss" (author unknown): the latter began, "I did not do it in a car / I did not do it in a bar / I did not do it in the dark / I did not do it in the park / I did not do it on a date / I did not ever fornicate."

11. Suggestive of their similarity, both the Cat and Sam-I-Am were invoked by parodists responding to the trial of O. J. Simpson. A book titled *The Cat NOT in the Hat*, attributed to Dr. Juice, included verses such as these: "A happy town / Inside L.A. / Where rich folks play / The day away. / But under the moon / The 12th of June. / Two victims flail. / Assault! Assail! / Somebody will go to jail! / Who will it be? / Oh my! Oh me!" (qtd. in Zamorsky). Dr. Seuss Enterprises successfully sued to prevent distribution of this book, but an email parody received no such sanction. Titled "The OJ trial as Told by Dr. Seuss," the parody begins, "I did not kill my lovely wife. / I did not slash her with a knife. / I did not bonk her on the head. / I did not know that she was dead."

12. This is actually a subtle misquotation of Seuss's original words. In "Seuss on Wry" (*Parenting Magazine*, Feb. 1987), David Sheff asked Seuss, "What do kids want from a book?" Seuss replied, "The same things we want. To laugh, to be challenged, to be entertained and delighted" (54). Contrary to Bush's version of this statement, Seuss is *not* saying that children want the same things that adults want; Seuss is instead saying that children want the same things *from a book* that adults want *from a book*.

Annotated Bibliography

This bibliography attempts to list all of Theodor Seuss Geisel's articles, books, stories, cartoons, parodies, as well as secondary sources (including literary criticism, major profiles, books). Because I had to draw the line somewhere, for the most part this bibliography does not include his advertising work. The preceding disclaimers aside, I expect that readers will uncover non-advertising works inadvertently omitted from this list: Geisel was so tremendously prolific a writer and illustrator that I must have missed some. The vastness of his creative output has, I expect, prevented anyone from attempting such a comprehensive bibliography before now. If you find something not included here, please contact me <philnel@ksu.edu> and use "Seuss Bibliography" as your subject line. I will verify and add it to <http://www.ksu.edu/english/nelp/seuss/bib.html>, and to a second edition of this book (should there be one).

For the convenience of scholars, students, and the intellectually curious, I have arranged the bibliography by category. This organization requires you to know what *type* of item you seek. For example, many quotations by Dr. Seuss come from sources in the "Profiles and Interviews" or "Books" sections, both of which are included in with Secondary Sources. Items used exclusively—or nearly exclusively—in individual chapters can be found in Other Works Cited. In addition to providing other sources, Other Works Cited offers a chapter-by-chapter guide to where full citations of main sources may be found.

Works by Theodor Seuss Geisel

Books written and illustrated by Dr. Seuss

And to Think That I Saw It on Mulberry Street. New York: Vanguard Press, 1937.

The 500 Hats of Bartholomew Cubbins. New York: Vanguard Press, 1938.

The Seven Lady Godivas. New York: Random House, 1939. Repr. 1987.

The King's Stilts. New York: Random House, 1939.

Horton Hatches the Egg. New York: Random House, 1940.

McElligot's Pool. New York: Random House, 1947.

Thidwick the Big-Hearted Moose. New York: Random House, 1948.

Bartholomew and the Oobleck. New York: Random House, 1949.

If I Ran the Zoo. New York: Random House, 1950.

Scrambled Eggs Super! New York: Random House, 1953.

Horton Hears a Who! New York: Random House, 1954.

On Beyond Zebra! New York: Random House, 1955.

If I Ran the Circus. New York: Random House, 1956.

The Cat in the Hat. New York: Random House, 1957.

How the Grinch Stole Christmas! New York: Random House, 1957.

The Cat in the Hat Comes Back. New York: Random House, 1958.

Yertle the Turtle and Other Stories. New York: Random House, 1958.

Happy Birthday to You! New York: Random House, 1959.

One fish two fish red fish blue fish. New York: Random House, 1960.

Green Eggs and Ham. New York: Random House, 1960.

The Sneetches and Other Stories. New York: Random House, 1961.

Dr. Seuss's Sleep Book. New York: Random House, 1962.

Dr. Seuss's ABC. New York: Random House, 1963.

Hop on Pop. New York: Random House, 1963.

Fox in Socks. New York: Random House, 1965.

I Had Trouble in Getting to Solla Sollew. New York: Random House, 1965.

The Cat in the Hat Songbook. Piano Score and Guitar Chords by Eugene Poddany. New York: Random House, 1967.

I Can Lick 30 Tigers Today! and Other Stories. New York: Random House, 1969.

I Can Draw It Myself by Me Myself with a Little Help from My Friend Dr. Seuss. New York: Random House, 1970.

Mr. Brown Can Moo! Can You? New York: Random House, 1970.

The Lorax. New York: Random House, 1971.

Did I Ever Tell You How Lucky You Are? New York: Random House, 1973.

The Shape of Me and Other Stuff. New York: Random House, 1973.

There's a Wocket in My Pocket! New York: Random House, 1974.

Marvin K. Mooney Will You Please Go Now! New York: Random House, 1975.

Oh, the Thinks You Can Think! New York: Random House, 1975.
The Cat's Quizzer. New York: Random House, 1976.
I Can Read with My Eyes Shut! New York: Random House, 1978.
Oh Say Can You Say? New York: Random House, 1979.
Hunches in Bunches. New York: Random House, 1982.
The Butter Battle Book. New York: Random House, 1984.
You're Only Old Once! New York: Random House, 1986.
Oh, the Places You'll Go! New York: Random House, 1990.

Books written by Dr. Seuss

Gerald McBoing Boing. Illus. Mel Crawford. New York: Simon & Schuster, 1952. Repr. Random House, 2000.
Great Day for Up! Illus. Quentin Blake. New York: Random House, 1974.
I Am Not Going to Get Up Today! Illus. James Stevenson. New York: Random House, 1987.

Books co-written by Dr. Seuss

With P. D. Eastman. *The Cat in the Hat Beginner Book Dictionary, by the Cat Himself.* Illus. Dr. Seuss. New York: Random House, 1964.
With Roy McKie. *My Book About Me by Me, Myself, with Some Help from My Friends, Dr. Seuss and Roy McKie.* Illus. Roy McKie. New York: Random House, 1969.

Books written by Theo. LeSieg

Ten Apples Up on Top! Illus. Roy McKie. New York: Random House, 1961.
I Wish That I Had Duck Feet. Illus. B. Tobey. New York: Random House, 1965.
Come Over to My House. Illus. Richard Erdoes. New York: Random House, 1966.
The Eye Book. Illus. Roy McKie. New York: Random House, 1968.
I Can Write! A Book By Me, Myself. Illus. Roy McKie. New York: Random House, 1971.
In a People House. Illus. Roy McKie. New York: Random House, 1972.
The Many Mice of Mr. Brice. Illus. Roy McKie. New York: Random House, 1973. Repr. as *The Pop-Up Mice of Mr. Brice.* Random House, 1989.
Wacky Wednesday. Illus. George Booth. New York: Random House, 1974.
Would You Rather Be a Bullfrog? Illus. Roy McKie. New York: Random House, 1975.
Hooper Humperdink . . . Not Him! Illus. Charles E. Martin. New York: Random House, 1976.
Please Try to Remember the First of Octember! Illus. Art Cummings. New York: Random House, 1977.
Maybe You Should Fly a Jet! Maybe You Should Be a Vet! Illus. Michael J. Smollin. New York: Random House, 1980.
The Tooth Book. Illus. Roy McKie. New York: Random House, 1981.

Book written by Rosetta Stone

Because a Little Bug Went Ka-Choo! Illus. Michael Frith. New York: Random House, 1975.

Books by Dr. Seuss published posthumously

Daisy-Head Mayzie. New York: Random House, 1994.
My Many-Colored Days. Paintings by Steve Johnson and Lou Fancher. New York: Alfred A. Knopf, 1996.

Hooray for Diffendoofer Day! Co-written with Jack Prelutsky. Illustrated by Lane Smith. New York: Alfred A. Knopf, 1998.

Books illustrated by Dr. Seuss

Abingdon, Alexander, Compiler. *Boners.* Illustrated by Dr. Seuss. New York: The Viking Press, 1931. 20 illustrations (one each on pp. 5, 7, 10, 13, 21, 25, 31, 35, 39, 43, 49, 54, 57, 63, 67, 71, 77, 83, 94, 97).

————, Compiler. *More Boners.* Illustrated by Dr. Seuss. New York: The Viking Press, 1931. 12 illustrations (one each on pp. 5, 13, 19, 25, 37, 43, 51, 59, 65, 73, 83, 87).

Streeter, Robert A., and Robert G. Hoehn. *Are You a Genius?* Second Series. With six illustrations by Dr. Seuss. New York: Frederick A. Stokes Co., 1933.

Sullivan, Frank. *In One Ear . . . .* New York: Viking, 1933. Cover and frontispiece by Dr. Seuss.

Deane, Albert. *Spelling Bees: The Oldest and the Newest Rage.* Illustrated by Dr. Seuss. New York: Frederick A. Stokes Co., 1937.

Ripley, Austin. *Mystery Puzzles.* With seven full-page illustrations by Dr. Seuss and other decorations by Lloyd Coe. New York: Frederick A. Stokes Co., 1937.

Kaufman, Gerard Lynton. *How's Tricks?: 125 Tricks and Stunts to Amaze Your Friends.* New York: Frederick A. Stokes Co., 1938. Frontispiece by Dr. Seuss.

The Pocket Book of Boners: An Omnibus of Schoolboy Howlers and Unconscious Humor. New York: Pocket Books, 1941. Selections from the first four *Boners* books, reprinting 22 illustrations by Seuss (one each on pp. xviii, 15, 21, 25, 31, 35, 41, 45, 51, 55, 61, 65, 71, 75, 81, 85, 91, 97, 101, 105, 111, 115).

Abingdon, Alexander, Compiler. *Herrings Go About the Sea in Shawls and Other Classic Howlers from Classrooms and Examination Papers.* New York: Viking Press, 1997. New edition of *Boners*, with an abridged introduction, and 19 of the 20 original illustrations by Seuss (one each on pp. 4, 7, 8, 13, 21, 25, 31, 37, 40, 44, 54, 59, 65, 69, 73, 80, 86, 99, 104).

Collections of Dr. Seuss's work

Dr. Seuss' Lost World Revisited: A Forward-looking Backward Glance. New York: Universal Publishing and Distributing Corporation, 1967.

Dr. Seuss Storytime [green cover]. New York: Random House, 1974. Includes *McElligot's Pool, The Zax, The Lorax, Scrambled Eggs Super!*

Dr. Seuss Storytime [purple cover]. New York: Random House, 1974. Includes *Bartholomew and the Oobleck, Yertle the Turtle, Horton Hears a Who!, I Can Lick 30 Tigers Today, What Was I Scared Of?, Gertrude McFuzz* and other stories.

Dr. Seuss Storytime [pink cover]. New York: Random House, 1974. Includes *The King's Stilts, King Looie Katz, Too Many Daves, How the Grinch Stole Christmas!, The Sneetches, Dr. Seuss's Sleep Book.*

Dr. Seuss Storytime [yellow cover]. New York: Random House, 1974. Includes *Thidwick, the Big-Hearted Moose, I Had Trouble in Getting to Solla Sollew, Horton Hatches the Egg, Did I Ever Tell You How Lucky You Are?*

The Tough Coughs As He Ploughs the Dough: Early Cartoons & Articles by Dr. Seuss. Edited by Richard Marschall. New York: William Morrow & Company, 1987.

Dr. Seuss from Then to Now: A Catalogue of the Retrospective Exhibition. Mary Stofflet. Introduction by Steven L. Brezzo. New York: Random House, 1986.

Six by Seuss. Introduction by Clifton Fadiman. New York: Random House, 1991. Includes *And to Think That I Saw It on Mulberry Street, The 500 Hats of Bartholomew Cubbins, Horton Hatches the Egg, Yertle the Turtle and Other Stories, How the Grinch Stole Christmas!* and *The Lorax.*

The Secret Art of Dr. Seuss. Introduction by Maurice Sendak. New York: Random House, 1995.

A Hatful of Seuss. New York: Random House, 1997. Includes *Bartholomew and the Oobleck*, *If I Ran the Zoo*, *Horton Hears a Who!*, *The Sneetches*, and *Dr. Seuss's Sleep Book*.

Dr. Seuss Goes to War: The World War II Editorial Cartoons of Theodor Seuss Geisel. Richard H. Minear. Introduction by Art Spiegelman. New York: New Press, 1999. Reproduces a generous selection of Seuss's *PM* cartoons.

The Art of Dr. Seuss. New York: Random House, 2002. Reprint of *The Secret Art of Dr. Seuss* and *Dr. Seuss from Then to Now* in a single volume.

Pamphlets written and illustrated by Dr. Seuss

Flit Cartoons As they have appeared in Magazines and Newspapers throughout the Country. New York: Stanco Incorporated, 1929. Consists of 18 Flit cartoons, all by Dr. Seuss. UCSD: MSS 0230, MC-121–03.

Flit Cartoons As they have appeared in Magazines and Newspapers throughout the Country. New York: Stanco Incorporated, 1930. Consists of 20 Flit cartoons, all by Dr. Seuss. UCSD: MSS 0230, MC-121–03.

Adventures with a FLIT GUN: A Collection of Flit Cartoons by Dr. Seuss. New York: Stanco Incorporated, 1932. Consists of 17 Flit cartoons, all by Dr. Seuss. UCSD: MSS 0230, MC-121–03.

[Old Captain Taylor.] *Secrets of the Deep; or, The Perfect Yachtsman*. Penola Inc., 1935.

[Old Captain Taylor.] *Secrets of the Deep, Vol. II*. Penola Inc., 1936. "Aquatints by Dr. Seuss."

[Old Captain Taylor.] *The Log of the Good Ship*. c. 1947.

Signs of Civilization. La Jolla, CA: La Jolla Town Council, 1956. Verse repr. in Bennett Cerf's "Trade Winds," *Saturday Review*, 26 Jan. 1957: 6.

Charity Ball 1966. San Diego: San Diego Society for Crippled Children, 1966. "For the benefit of the Children's Hospital Fund." At Hotel del Coronado, 5 Feb. 1966.

Pamphlet illustrated by Dr. Seuss

Leaf, Munro. *This Is Ann*. Washington, DC: War Department (U.S. Govt. Printing Office), 1943.

Hejji

Distributed by the King Features Syndicate, Seuss's comic strip appeared in Hearst's *Sunday American* and other papers. Only 12 strips appeared before it was cancelled: 7 April 1935, 14 April 1935, 21 April 1935, 28 April 1935, 5 May 1935, 12 May, 1935, 19 May 1935, 26 May 1935, 2 June 1935, 9 June 1935, 16 June 1935, and 23 June 1935. *The Smithsonian Collection of Newspaper Comics*, edited by Bill Blackbeard and Martin Williams (see "Reference") reprints 7 April in color (plate 723). Volume 2 of *The Comic Strip Century: Celebrating 100 Years of an American Art Form*, edited by Bill Blackbeard and Dale Crain (Kitchen Sink Press, 1995) reprints all 12 strips, pp. 284–95.

Stories and Poems by Dr. Seuss

All of these are in verse *except* for "A Pupil's Nightmare," "The Class Social of 1945," "The Phantom of El Morocco," the *Judge* stories, the "Royal Housefly and Bartholomew Cubbins" series, and the "King Grimalken and the Wishbones" series.

[T. S. Geisel.] "After the War." *Central Recorder* 17 Jan. 1919.

[Theodor Geisel, '20 1/2] "O Latin! My Latin!" *Central Recorder* 7 Feb. 1919: 8. Parody of Walt Whitman's "O Captain! My Captain!"

[T. S. Lesieg.] "A Pupil's Nightmare." *Central Recorder* 21 Jan. 1921: 16.

[T. S. Geisel.] "The Class Social of 1945." *Central Recorder* 21 Jan. 1921: 17.

[Ted Geisel.] "JAZZ!" *Jack-o-lantern* 8 June 1922: 33.

"To My Grandmother, My 'Buddy' " *Judge* 21 Apr. 1928: 17.

"To the Tallow-Chandler, the Grim Exponent of a Dying Gravy." *Judge* 19 Jan. 1929: 6.

"Apparently, there IS a Santa Claus." greeting card, n.d. c. 1930s. UCSD: MSS 0230.

"A-hunting we must go, my lads. . . ." *College Humor* Jan. 1932: 14–15.

"Dr. Seuss's Poetry Corner." *Jack-o-lantern.* Jackobite Number, 1936: 18–19. Includes two illustrations and six poems: "Pentellic Bilge for Valentine's Birthday"; "HARK!"; "How Was I to Know?"; "Secret Society"; "Salt Spray. . . . Does It Pay?"; and "Square-dance for an Amateur Echo-eater."

"The Phantom of El Morocco." *Stage Magazine* Apr. 1937: 64.

"Quality." *Judge* Mar. 1938: 9–14. Repr. Marschall 49–54.

"Matilda, the Elephant with a Mother Complex: A Dr. Seuss Fable." *Judge* Apr. 1938: 17.

"The Sad, Sad Story of the Obsks." 1938. UCSD: MSS 0230, MC-110–09. Seuss describes this as "An unpublished 4-page Novelette written in 1938 when I was fired by Standard Oil and was looking for a job."

"Pentellic Bilge for Bennett Cerf's Birthday." *An Ode in Commemoration of Bennett Cerf's Thirty-Ninth Birthday written and delivered by Doctor Seuss.* Nov. 14, 1940. Dartmouth, Rauner Library, Alumni G277mi, Box 3, folder titled "Writings and Drawings." This pamphlet was published especially for the occasion, and was delivered "as a feature of Random House Night at the Philadelphia Booksellers' Association."

"King Grimalken and the Wishbones." Part One. *Junior Catholic Messenger* 29 Oct. 1948: 55B–56B.

"King Grimalken and the Wishbones." Part Two. *Junior Catholic Messenger* 5 Nov. 1948: 62B–63B.

"King Grimalken and the Wishbones." Part Three. *Junior Catholic Messenger* 12 Nov. 1948: 70B–71B.

"King Grimalken and the Wishbones." Conclusion. *Junior Catholic Messenger* 19 Nov. 1948: 78B–79B.

"The Royal Housefly and Bartholomew Cubbins." Part One. *Junior Catholic Messenger* 13 Jan. 1950: 126B–127B.

"The Royal Housefly and Bartholomew Cubbins." Part Two. *Junior Catholic Messenger* 20 Jan. 1950: 134B–135B.

"The Royal Housefly and Bartholomew Cubbins." Part Three. *Junior Catholic Messenger* 20 Jan. 1950: 142B–143B.

"The Royal Housefly and Bartholomew Cubbins." Conclusion. *Junior Catholic Messenger* 3 Feb. 1950: 150B–151B.

"Gustav, the Goldfish." *Redbook* June 1950: 48–51.

"If I Ran the Zoo." *Redbook* July 1950: 56–58.

"Tadd and Todd." *Redbook* Aug. 1950: 56–58.

"Marco Comes Late." *Redbook* Sept. 1950: 58–59.

"How Officer Pat Saved the Whole Town." *Redbook* Oct. 1950: 46–48.

"Steak for Supper." *Redbook* Nov. 1950: 44–46.

"The Big Brag." *Redbook* Dec. 1950: 46–47.

"Horton and the Kwuggerbug." *Redbook* Jan. 1951: 46–47.

"The Rabbit, the Bear, and the Zinniga-Zinnaga." *Redbook* Feb. 1951: 46–47.

"Yertle the Turtle." *Redbook* April 1951: 46–47.

"The Bippolo Seed." *Redbook* June 1951: 46–47.

"Gertrude McFuzz." *Redbook* July 1951: 46–47.

"The Strange Shirt Spot." *Redbook* Sept. 1951: 68–69.
"The Great Henry McBride." *Redbook* Nov. 1951: 54–55.
"Wife up a tree." *This Week* 17 May 1953.
"The Sneetches." *Redbook* July 1953: 77.
"The Flustards." *Redbook* Aug. 1953: 65.
"Perfect Present." *Child Life* Dec. 1953: 9.
"The Munkits." *Redbook* Jan. 1954: 67.
"The Zaks." *Redbook* Mar. 1954: 84.
"The Ruckus." *Redbook* July 1954: 84.
"How Gerald McGrew Caught the Filla-ma-Zokk." *Children's Activities* Dec. 1954: 14–15.
"Latest News from Mulberry Street." *Children's Activities* Feb 1955: 12–13.
"The Hoobub and the Grinch." *Redbook* May 1955: 19.
"The Kindly Snather." *Redbook* Dec. 1956: 100.
"Speedy Boy." *Children's Activities* Mar. 1955: 14–15.
"The Great McGrew Milk Farm." *Children's Activities* Apr. 1955: 12–13.
"If I Ran the Circus." *Children's Activities* June 1955: 14–15.
"A Prayer for a Child." *Collier's* Dec. 1955: 86.
"How the Grinch Stole Christmas." *Redbook* Dec. 1957: 53–64.
"The Zode (Split Pants)." c. 1950s. UCSD: MSS 0230, MC-123–02.
"The Glunk that got Thunk." *Woman's Day* July 1969: 45–50.
"Mr. Brown Can Moo Like a Cow! Can You? Dr. Seuss's Book of Wonderful Noises." *McCall's* Oct. 1970: 78–81.
[The Dr. Seuss Surveys.] "The economic situation clarified: A prognostic re-evaluation." *New York Times Magazine* 15 June 1975: 71.
"My Uncle Terwilliger on the Art of Eating Popovers." Published, with introduction, as "Dr. Seuss Speaks Out." *New York Times* 30 June 1977: 25. Repr. in *Seuss-isms* (1997).
"To the P.T.A." Oct. 1977. Dartmouth, Rauner Library: Manuscript 977590/.1.
"Small Epic Poem (Size 2 3/4 B)." *San Diego Union* 19 June 1978: B1.
"Small Epic Poem, Size 3 1/2 B." *Publishers Weekly* 26 June 1978: 93.
"Dr. Seuss's Verse." *San Diego Union* 15 Oct. 1978: E-7. Brief verse in acceptance of Emmy Award.
"Wilder Award Acceptance Speech." 1980. UCSD: MSS 0230, Box 19, Folder 1.
"A Short Condensed Poem in Praise of Reader's Digest Condensed Books." *Reader's Digest Condensed Books*, Vol. 1. Reader's Digest, 1980. Back cover.
"Lamentation for Omar Khayyam Who Once Spoke in Praise of Four Great Commodities. . . . . A Book of Verses Underneath the Bough, a Jug of Wine, a Loaf of Bread and Thou." California Reading Association. Young Reader Medal Award. 6 Nov. 1982. UCSD: MSS 0230, Box 19, Folder 1.
"Hail to Our Chief! (And I don't mean Ronald Reagan)." 13 Dec. 1982. Broadside for birthday celebration of Robert Bernstein, President of Random House. UCSD: MSS 0230, Box 18, Folder 66.
"A Short Epic Birthday Poem entitled 'On occasions such as this I maintain that my late father is of much greater importance than even Robert L. Bernstein.'" 1984. *Theodor Seuss Geisel: Reminiscences & Tributes*, ed. Edward Connery Lathem. Hanover, NH: Dartmouth College, 1996. 43–45.
"A Rather Short Epic Poem (Size 6 and 7/8)." 1988. *Theodor Seuss Geisel: Reminiscences & Tributes*, ed. Lathem: 45–47.
"An Unsolicited Ode to the Teachers of Our Language." n.d. UCSD: MSS 0230, Box 18, Folder 71.

Essays by Dr. Seuss

[T.S. Geisel.] "Prophecy on the Prophets." *The Pnalka* 1920 1/2. The *Pnalka* was Central High School's yearbook.

[T.S. Geisel.] "An Essay on Toleration." *The Dartmouth Bema* Mar. 1925: 7.

[Theodor S. Geisel.] "On the Firing Line." *Springfield Union* 7 July 1925, 8 July 1925, 9 July 1925, 13 July 1925.

". . . But for Grown-Ups Laughing Isn't Any Fun." *New York Times Book Review* 16 Nov. 1952: 2.

"Japan's Young Dreams: Children's drawings show how Occupation has changed their aspirations." *Life* 29 March 1954: 89–95. This article was so thoroughly rewritten by *Life*'s editors that Seuss disowned it (see Morgan and Morgan 137).

"Signs of Civilization." *Saturday Review* 26 Jan. 1957: 6.

"How Orlo Got His Book." *New York Times Book Review* 17 Nov. 1957: 2, 60. Repr. in abridged form as "How to Write a Book for Beginning Readers . . ." *Education Summary* 5 Mar. 1958: 5.

"My Hassle with the First Grade Language." *Chicago Tribune* 17 Nov. 1957. Repr. *Education* 78.6 (Feb. 1958): 323–25.

"Making Children Want to Read." *Book Chat* Fall 1958: 29.

"Writing for Children: A Mission." *Los Angeles Times* 27 Nov. 1960: 11.

"Fan Mail: An Author's Occupation." *Authors League* Apr. 1963.

Foreword. *Neil Morgan's San Diego.* San Diego, 1963.

"If at First You Don't Succeed—Quit!" *Saturday Evening Post* 28 Nov. 1964: 8–9.

"Benfield Pressey: 'He Seemed to Like the Stuff I Wrote.' " *Mentors: Noted Dartmouth alumni reflect on the teachers who changed their lives.* Ed. James Collins. Hanover, NH: Dartmouth College, 1991. 3–4.

"Dr. Seuss." *Pauses: Autobiographical Reflections of 101 Creators of Children's Books.* Ed. Lee Bennett Hopkins. New York: HarperCollins, 1995. 111–14.

Essays illustrated by Dr. Seuss

Laing, A[lexander] K. "Introducing the Hippocrass" and "The Hippocrass at the White House." n.d. c. 1927. Dartmouth, Rauner Library, Alumni G277mi, Box 3, folder titled "Writings and Drawings." Originals in Rauner Iconography, 1342.

Riddell, John. "The science of everything." *Vanity Fair* June 1931: 76–77.

Ford, Corey. "Static City." *Vanity Fair* Aug. 1931: 50–51.

———. "The Game Preserve." *College Humor* Sept. 1931. Repr. Feb. 1932: 73.

———. "Santa Claus's beard through the ages." *Vanity Fair* Dec. 1931: 68–69.

———. "Laying out the garden." *Vanity Fair* June 1932: 43, 71.

Riddell, John. "Van Loon's Catalogue." *Vanity Fair* Jan. 1933: 34–35.

Williams, Gurney. "Queerespondence." *Life* May 1934: 34.

Goodman, J. Eckert Jr. "And They Call It Golf!" *Sports Illustrated and the American Golfer* Apr. 1936: 20–21, 45.

———. "And They Call It Golf!" Part Two. *Sports Illustrated and the American Golfer* May 1936: 32–33, 39.

Jackson, Davis. "Life of a Class Agent." *Dartmouth Alumni Magazine* Apr. 1939: 23–24. On p. 23 are three cartoons by Seuss: "I Hate to do This Johnnie Boy. . . . but the Alumni Fund Must Go On!", "JUST TO REMIND YOU THAT YOU STILL LOVE THE COLLEGE!", "CLASS AGENT."

"The Advertising Business at a Glance." *Redbook.* Date and page unknown.

Reviews by Dr. Seuss

"Harpooner with a Gentle Barb." *New York Times Book Review* 12 Sept. 1954: 3. Review of *The Benchley Roundup: A Selection by Nathaniel Benchley of His Favorites*.

"The Past Is Nowhere." *New York Times Book Review* 16 Jan. 1955: 4. Review of *Homecoming* by Jiro Osaragi.

TSG's Short Pieces in The Central Recorder

The Central Recorder is the newspaper of Central High School in Springfield, Massachusetts. TSG's stories and poems are listed with "Stories and Poems by Dr. Seuss."

[T. G.] "House Debate." *Central Recorder* April 1919.

[T. S. G.] "Pete the Pessimist." *Central Recorder* 24 Oct. 1919

[T. S. G.] "A Pupil's Union." *Central Recorder* 26 Nov. 1919.

[T. S. G.] "Pete the Pessimist." *Central Recorder* Nov. or Dec. 1919. UCSD: MSS 0230, Box 17, Folder 37.

[T. S. G.] "I hear you are very interested in war work." *Central Recorder* 5 Dec. 1919.

[T. S. G.] "A Prize Contest!!" *Central Recorder* 19 Dec. 1919.

[unsigned.] "Pete the Peptimist." *Central Recorder* 16 Jan. 1920.

TSG's Cartoons and Parodies in Jack-o-lantern

Jack-o-lantern is Dartmouth College's humor magazine. TSG's poems are listed with "Stories and Poems by Dr. Seuss." All pieces are signed "Ted G." unless otherwise noted.

"Two Arguments Against Matrimony." *Jack-o-lantern* Oct. 1921: 20.

[Ted Geisel.] "The Pied Piper." *Jack-o-lantern* Oct. 1921: 24.

[Ted Geisel.] "Soc-cer!" *Jack-o-lantern* Oct. 1921: 26.

[T. Geisel.] "For the Love o' Mike." *Jack-o-lantern* 17 Dec. 1921: 19.

"The Fatted Calf." *Jack-o-lantern* 24 Jan. 1922: 29.

[Ted Geisel.] " 'O, clerk, there's something the matter with the keyhole in the door to my room.' 'That so? I'll look into that tonight.' " *Jack-o-lantern* 9 Feb. 1922: 23.

Jack-o-lantern 8 June 1922:

[Ted Geisel.] "Aftermath!!" *Jack-o-lantern* 21 Sept. 1922: 18.

[Ted Geisel.] "So This Is Hanover!?" *Jack-o-lantern* 21 Sept. 1922: 25.

[Ted Geisel.] "Kitten on the Keys." *Jack-o-lantern* 25 Oct. 1922: 21.

[Ted Geisel.] " 'This life's dull. How's to go over and get shot at?' 'I'm game.' " *Jack-o-lantern* 25 Oct. 1922: 22.

[Ted Geisel.] "Jones Ripped Five Yards off Right End." *Jack-o-lantern* 25 Oct. 1922: 28.

[Ted Geisel.] "Sparking Plugs." *Jack-o-lantern* 25 Oct. 1922: 29.

"Tucked in Tight." *Jack-o-lantern* 23 Nov. 1922: 29.

[Ted Geisel.] "A Sailor With His Slicker." *Jack-o-lantern* 23 Nov. 1922: 29.

"The Cat's Own." *Jack-o-lantern* 8 Jan. 1923: 24.

[Geisel.] " 'You've got to quit knockin' your neighbors.' 'I notice you roast a few yourself.' " *Jack-o-lantern* 8 Jan. 1923: 24.

" 'So you've taken up fencing?' 'Oh, I make a stab at it." *Jack-o-lantern* 8 Feb. 1923: 21.

[Ted Geisel.] "Pity the poor sailors on a night like this." *Jack-o-lantern* 8 Feb. 1923: 24.

"Nice Cohen." *Jack-o-lantern* 26 Apr. 1923: 26.

[Ted.] "Highball Thompson wins from Kid Sambo by a shade." *Jack-o-lantern* 26 Apr. 1923: 30.

"After being sent for three extra years to Exeter—to become educated up to College Life—Sylvester de Pestyr—arrives at Dartmouth." *Jack-o-lantern* 26 Sept. 1923: 19.

"VACANT." *Jack-o-lantern* 26 Sept. 1923: 21.

ANNOTATED BIBLIOGRAPHY

[unsigned.] "The Rolling Stone Gathers No Moss But Picks Up A Good Deal of Soil." *Jack-o-lantern* 26 Sept. 1923: 23.

"BEAVER." *Jack-o-lantern* 25 Oct. 1923: 30.

[unsigned.] "Do You Rate Big with the Folks at Home? Or do they realize how lazy you are?" *Jack-o-lantern* 25 Oct. 1923: 32.

[Ted.] "The Height of Disillusionment." *Jack-o-lantern* 26 Nov. 1923: 21

[Ted.] "Who's Who in Bo-Bo." *Jack-o-lantern* 26 Nov. 1923: 24–25.

[unsigned.] "Lecture Notes Taken the Morning of a Peerade." *Jack-o-lantern* 26 Nov. 1923: 27.

[Ted.] "Art for Art's Sake. The aesthetic steeple-jack, in falling thirteen stories to his death, decides to go down in a swan-dive." *Jack-o-lantern* 18 Dec. 1923: 23.

[unsigned.] "The Wearing Out of the Green." *Jack-o-lantern* 18 Dec. 1923: 33.

[T.G.] "He Studied Under Webster." *Jack-o-lantern* 22 Jan. 1924: 19.

[unsigned.] "Frat Club Badges." *Jack-o-lantern* 22 Jan. 1924: 26.

[Apologies to T.G.] "Summer Ski Practice." *Jack-o-lantern* 7 Feb. 1924: 20.

[unsigned.] "Presidential Possibilities." *Jack-o-lantern* 20 Mar. 1924: 24–25.

"The Old Order Changeth, Giving Place To The New." *Jack-o-lantern* 20 Mar. 1924: 31.

[unsigned.] "Pre-Season Rushing Results." *Jack-o-lantern* 21 Apr. 1924: 25.

"THE INITIATION BANQUET." *Jack-o-lantern* 21 Apr. 1924: 28–29.

[unsigned.] "Mr. Mullik Begs to Introduce His Three Checks to Matrimony." *Jack-o-lantern* 8 May 1924: 28–29.

[unsigned.] "The B. and M. Timetable—A Book Review." *Jack-o-lantern* 2 Jun 1924: 33.

[unsigned.] "APOLOGIA PRO VITA SUA." *Jack-o-lantern* 30 Sept. 1924: 15.

[Ted.] "Wanta match pennies?" *Jack-o-lantern* 30 Sept. 1924: 19. Repr. *Jack-o-lantern* 5 Feb. 1925: 25.

[Ted.] "Anything serious Doctor?" *Jack-o-lantern* 30 Sept. 1924: 19.

[unsigned.] "GERMAN MADE EASY." *Jack-o-lantern* 30 Sept. 1924: 21.

[T.G.] "THE OLD ONE BACKWARDS." *Jack-o-lantern* 30 Sept. 1924: 27.

"1st Outing-Clubber:————'I went up to Armington over the McGill game. The week-end of the Vermont game saw me atop Mt. Washington. And I'm going to do the entire White Mountains when the team goes down to Harvard." *Jack-o-lantern* 22 Oct. 1924: 16.

[unsigned.] "ALAS, POOR YORICK—." *Jack-o-lantern* 22 Oct. 1924: 19.

[V. Appia—56 B.C.] "Signalium—II, IV, XII, XXI, XV, IIX, VII, III." *Jack-o-lantern* 22 Oct. 1924: 20.

[unsigned.] "The Referee—'Hey there, you! Quit crawling with that ball!" *Jack-o-lantern* 22 Oct. 1924: 33.

[unsigned.] "Why is it when one sees animals like this one never has a gun along?" *Jack-o-lantern* 24 Nov. 1924: 17.

[unsigned.] "The Veteran Soccer Player Forgets Himself while Playing Baseball." *Jack-o-lantern* 24 Nov. 1924: 28.

[Ted.] "Kindly Visitor, 'I'd like to see convict 515, please, if he's in.'" *Jack-o-lantern* 20 Jan. 1925: 16.

[T.G.] "Mr. Elman, you fool, you're off the key!" *Jack-o-lantern* 20 Jan. 1925: 22.

[Geisel.] "Incidentally, I have neglected to study tomorrow's Eccy." *Jack-o-lantern* 20 Jan. 1925: 23.

[T.G.] "Would you care to skate with me?" *Jack-o-lantern* 20 Jan. 1925: 30.

[Ted.] "Sometimes we wonder if the chorus 'girls' in the Carnival Shows have men up to the house parties." *Jack-o-lantern* 5 Feb. 1925: 29.

[T.G.] "O, Jack, I forgot to bring my skis." *Jack-o-lantern* 5 Feb. 1925: 30.

[T.G.] "He took his girl to the movies so she could see the boys throw peanuts." *Jack-o-lantern* 5 Feb. 1925: 32.

[unsigned.] "Do you smell anything?" *Jack-o-lantern* 5 Feb. 1925: 38.

[Geisel.] "Say, who's the goddess of dawn?" *Jack-o-lantern* 5 Feb. 1925: 42.

[T.G.] "How're your hens doing, Zeb?" *Jack-o-lantern* 5 Feb. 1925: 46.

[unsigned.] "Really, now, we all ought to get together more often at Carnival. Why not this?" *Jack-o-lantern* 5 Feb. 1925: 48.

[unsigned.] "SKIJAWING." *Jack-o-lantern* 5 Feb. 1925: 52.

[L. Burbank.] "PEINTURE SANS FARD." *Jack-o-lantern* 24 Mar. 1925: 22.

[unsigned.] "1st Ghost: One side there, brother. 2nd Ghost: Pipe down, Henry, or I'll knock you for a ghoul." *Jack-o-lantern* 24 Mar. 1925: 28.

[unsigned.] "Mr. John Keats sees the Elgin Marbles for the first time." *Jack-o-lantern* 24 Mar. 1925: 28.

[unsigned.] "PROMINENT PUGLISTS PERFORM." *Jack-o-lantern* 24 Mar. 1925: 32.

[unsigned.] "Concreting the Abstract." *Jack-o-lantern* 24 Mar. 1925: 37.

[L. Pasteur.] "SPRING NUMBER." *Jack-o-lantern* 22 Apr. 1925: 17.

[Thos. Mott Osborne '27] " 'Sure is a tight jail, this.' 'There's no getting out of it.' " *Jack-o-lantern* 22 Apr. 1925: 21.

[T. Seuss.] "FINANCIAL NOTE—Goat's milk is higher than ever." *Jack-o-lantern* 22 Apr. 1925: 24.

[Anton Lang.] " 'Have you gotten your year book yet?' 'Oh, Aegis and Aegis ago.' " *Jack-o-lantern* 22 Apr. 1925: 28.

[D. G. Rossetti, '25.] "(Note: there is a slight discrepancy between the details of this picture and those of the story. But, obviously, one cannot publish pictures of unclothed men in a magazine of this standing.)" *Jack-o-lantern* 22 Apr. 1925: 33.

[Seuss.] "Kiss Me. Whaddaya think this is—a taxi?" *Jack-o-lantern* 22 Apr. 1925: 34.

[unsigned.] " '1st Chimney-sweep: 'Shall I go down first?' 2nd Chimney-sweep: 'Soot yourself.' " *Jack-o-lantern* 7 May 1925: 33.

Dr. Seuss's Cartoons and Parodies in Judge

The early pieces (22 Oct. 1927—30 June 1928) are credited to Dr. Theophrastus Seuss unless otherwise noted; all other pieces are credited to Dr. Seuss unless otherwise noted. TSG's stories and poems are listed with "Stories and Poems by Dr. Seuss." All items with incomplete information are from Dartmouth's Rauner Alumni Library or UCSD's Dr. Seuss Collection (MSS 0230).

[Seuss.] "DISSATISFIED WIFE—*And to think that today I could have been the wife of a six-day bike racer—if I hadn't listened to your rot about Higher Art!*" *Judge* 22 Oct. 1927: 5. Repr. Marschall 10.

[Seuss.] " 'Curse you, Mr. Whitmann, once more you are off your Beethoven!' 'And again, my dear Gershwitz, you have flown off the Handel' " *Judge* 29 Oct. 1927: 3. Repr. Marschall 11.

"Boids and Beasties." *Judge* 19 Nov. 1927: 9. Includes "Turtle Week," "Do Your Turtles Sing?," "Tom Thibbert, 3rd, Tells One," "A Strange Case."

"Boids and Beasties." *Judge* 26 Nov. 1927: 14. Includes "Poetical Contribution," "Who Is This Morose Little Rascal?"

"Christmas Sprits and Their Effects." *Judge* 3 Dec. 1927: 9.

"One moment, Mr. Sutton! Is it really ME you love, or have you only been carried away by my physical attraction?" *Judge* 3 Dec. 1927: 23.

"Boids and Beasties." *Judge* 10 Dec. 1927: 15. Includes "Why Spend Money on Guns, When There Is PSYCHOLOGY?," "The Dachs-Deer," "The Reindeer Season is On!"

"Our Own Mail Order Department." *Judge* 17 Dec. 1927: 9.

"THE FEMALE PARTNER—*After all, it ain't so much of an act, but between my figure and the American flag I think we can put it across.*" *Judge* 24 Dec. 1927: 3.

"Boids and Beasties." *Judge* 24 Dec. 1927: 7. Includes "Paul Jerman's First Whale," "Is Your Whale Grouchy?," "Hieronomos Is Drunk Again!," "Don't Let the Shooting Galleries Bleed You!"

[Theo. Seuss, 2nd.] "FAMOUS PRESIDENTIAL CAMPAIGNS: The Republican Split of 1867." *Judge* 31 Dec. 1927: 5. Repr. Marschall 17.

"Gee! I didn't know I was as tight as all this!" *Judge* 31 Dec. 1927: 8.

"Boids and Beasties." *Judge* 7 Jan. 1928: 20. Includes "A Novel Idea," "Editorial."

[Seuss.] "A SUGGESTION TO THE DRYS." *Judge* 14 Jan. 1928: 9.

"MEDIÑVAL TENANT—*Darn it all, another dragon. And just after I'd sprayed the whole castle with Flit!*" *Judge* 14 Jan. 1928: 16. Repr. Marschall 13.

"Modern Melodrama and the Early Greeks." *Judge* 28 Jan. 1928: 18.

"Gee, this is fun, Ethel. From now on, we're going to spend *all* our vacations in Canada!" *Judge* 4 Feb. 1928: 2.

"Do you think that a woman should support her husband?" *Judge* 4 Feb. 1928: 9.

"Boids and Beasties." *Judge* 4 Feb. 1928: 16. Includes "What Does Your Kangaroo Know About Life?," "Scene in a Fifth Ave. Prairie Dog Clinic," "Canary Lovers, Attention!," "One Way of Cheating the Veterinarian."

"Bridge? A wretched game. I have never played—and what is more, I never shall." *Judge* 11 Feb. 1928: 3.

"If we had some more lemons we could play a game of gin." *Judge* 11 Feb. 1928: 6.

"THE ORIGIN OF CONTRACT BRIDGE." *Judge* 11 Feb. 1928: 8. Repr. Marschall 20–21.

"Boids and Beasties." *Judge* 18 Feb. 1928: 20. On sea-lions.

[Antoinette Seuss.] "Somebody's a-Comin' to Our House." *Judge* 25 Feb. 1928: 20.

[Seuss.] "Young man, what do you know about the Companionate Marriage?" *Judge* 3 Mar. 1928: 2.

"Boids and Beasties." *Judge* 3 Mar. 1928: 14. Includes the Bird of Paradise, the Unglump Bobolink, cross-eyed purple-grackles.

[Seuss.] " 'Poor Henry! They say the creditors took away his high-powered Salmon.' 'Yes, indeed. Only yesterday I saw him driving around on a second-hand smelt.' " *Judge* 10 Mar. 1928: 3.

[Seuss.] "SHOTGUN WEDDING." *Judge* 10 Mar. 1928: 9.

[Seuss.] "FIRST VICTIM—*Lordy, Lordy, but I feel awful, Eddie. Where the dickens is this thing taking us?* SECOND VICTIM—*Just hang on tight, Williams. He always goes back to the speak-easy. I've taken these canters before.*" *Judge* 17 Mar. 1928: 2.

[Seuss.] "REVENGE." *Judge* 17 Mar. 1928: 7.

"Quaffling with the Pachyderms OR Why I Prefer the West Side Speak-easies." *Judge* 17 Mar. 1928: 16–17.

"Boids and Beasties." *Judge* 24 Mar. 1928: 14. Includes "Martyrs to a Great Cause," "A Hitherto Unpublished Fact," "Can a Horse on Snow-shoes Beat a Horse on Skis?," "The Origin of an Old Saying."

[Seuss.] "The exterminator man forgets himself at the flea-circus." *Judge* 31 Mar. 1928: 9. Repr. Marschall 12.

"How Kyng Arthur *Really* Got His Sword, Excalibur." *Judge* 31 Mar. 1928: 16–17. First in the series, "Ye Knights of the Table Round; Being ye Inside Dope on King Arthur's Court."

"Senator Heflin and the Presidency." *Judge* 7 Apr. 1928: 8.

"Sir Galahad's Reforms." *Judge* 7 Apr. 1928: 14, 29. Second in the "Ye Knights of the Table Round" series.

[Seuss.] "They say that Ford has put out a new fish with a twelve-inch fin base." *Judge* 14 Apr. 1928: 5.

"How Launcelot Did Pull a Fast One on the Kyng." *Judge* 14 Apr. 1928: 15. Third in the "Ye Knights of the Table Round" series.

[Seuss.] "The deep breathing champs go into the vacuum cleaning business." *Judge* 14 Apr. 1928: 18.

[Seuss (via Joe Butler).] "Sponging off the Old Man." *Judge* 14 Apr. 1928: 18.

"How Arthur's Gobs Will Check ye Yellow Peril." *Judge* 21 Apr. 1928: 15, 25. Fourth in the "Ye Knights of the Table Round" series.

"PARENTS! Why Not Tell Your Children the Truth!" *Judge* 28 Apr. 1928: 15.

"How a Sorcerer, named Do-Dee-Oh-Do, did Cast a Spell Upon ye Younger Generation." *Judge* 5 May 1928: 15. Fourth in the "Ye Knights of the Table Round" series.

"Ye Greate Real Estate Boome." *Judge* 12 May 1928: 15. Fifth in the "Ye Knights of the Table Round" series.

[unsigned.] "A new invention which makes it possible for you to leave home for a week. The kitten is shown waiting for Tuesday's meal." *Judge* 12 May 1928: 17.

[Dr. Seuss] "Judge's Fifty-Fifty Contest No. 7." *Judge* 12 May 1928: 32.

[Rube Goldbrick.] "LAUGH IS LIKE THAT!" *Judge* 19 May 1928: 21, 26.

"Sir Parchesi's Vow." *Judge* 26 May 1928: 15. Sixth in the "Ye Knights of the Table Round" series.

"How Arthur Saved His Moustache." *Judge* 2 June 1928: 15, 29. Seventh in the "Ye Knights of the Table Round" series.

[Theophrastus Seuss, 4th (Class Whimsey).] "HOOEYANA———— A REVERIE." *Judge* 9 June 1928: 17. Repr. Marschall 24–25.

"THE CUTTING OF THE WEDDING CNOUTH or, Divorce Among the Druids." *Judge* 16 June 1928: 14, 24.

[Dr. S.] "His divorce having been refused him because of insufficient grounds, the Unscrupulous Ventriloquist pulls a fast one on his wife and her attorney." *Judge* 16 June 1928: 17.

[Dr. Seuss.] Mr. I.R.T., the great subway magnate, throws a party in his private swimming pool." *Judge* 23 June 1928: 2.

"Ye Generals of Industrie in Camelot." *Judge* 23 June 1928: 18, 32. Eighth in the "Ye Knights of the Table Round" series.

"Winner of Judge's 50–50 Contest No. 7." *Judge* 23 June 1928: 2.

"THEN WISE OLD DOBBIN GALLOPED TO THE PARSON'S." *Judge* 30 June 1928: 2.

"HE—*A fine sort of a lover you are! Here we hike six miles out of town so's we can hold hands . . . and what do you do but forget to bring your muff!.*" *Judge* 30 June 1928: 4.

"VOCAL TRAINING BEFORE THE DAYS OF LUCKIES." *Judge* 30 June 1928: 8.

[Seuss.] "THE HEIGHT OF DECEPTION." *Judge* 30 June 1928: 9.

[Seuss.] "OUR EMPLOYEES AND THEIR PETS." *Judge* 7 July 1928: 6.

[Seuss.] "Trickery on the high seas or why fish are cynical." *Judge* 14 July 1928: 6.

[Dr. S.] "Weighing in at the House of David." *Judge* 14 July 1928: 16.

[Dr. S.] "Showing musician Fritz Reynolds, the first man to design a Xylophone made entirely of cats." *Judge* 21 July 1928: 3.

"A Gentleman in the Case" *Judge* 21 July 1928: 14. Repr. Marschall 27–28.

"She—*Tell me now, honest and truly, are you really the Yale Fulback? It's so seldom we Follies girls meet men like you, it's hard for us to know.*" *Judge* 28 July 1928: 2.

"ANGRY GOLFER—Now how in Blazes do I get out of this?" *Judge* 28 July 1928: 3.

[Yogi Seuss.] "My Three Best Tricks and How I Do Them." *Judge* 4 Aug. 1928: 6. Repr. Marschall 60.

"SEX AND THE SEA GOD: A Frothy Novelette by Dr. Seuss." *Judge* 11 Aug. 1928: 15, 25.

"MILE AFTER MILE UNDER THE SWAYING PALMS." *Judge* 11 Aug. 1928: 21.

[Dr. Seuss, the Alienist.] "The Tragic Tale of the Turnbull Triplets, *or*, An Urgent Warning to the American Mother." *Judge* 18 Aug. 1928: 8.

[Seuss.] "GUSTAAV SCHLESWIGH, 3rd, 'HOPS OFF.'" *Judge* 25 Aug. 1928: 6.

"DOING ENGLAND ON NINETY CENTS." *Judge* 1 Sept. 1928: 9. Repr. Marschall 31–32.

[Dr. S.] "'Thin? Why, my dear, you look as though you'd been dragged through a knot hole.' What stout person does not yearn to hear those melodious words? The Seuss System of Reduction actually does draw you through a knot hole. Satisfaction guaranteed. No splinters." *Judge* 8 Sept. 1928: 5.

"The Great Diet Derby." *Judge* 8 Sept. 1928: 16, 24.

"SHE—*Out sportin' again, are yo', nigger? Jest wait 'til I lay hands on yo' tonight!*" *Judge* 15 Sept. 1928: 2.

"The Waiting Room at Dang-Dang." *Judge* 15 Sept. 1928: 9. Repr. Marschall 33.

[Dr. S.] "THE SUPREME TEST OF COORDINATION." *Judge* 22 Sept. 1928: 2.

"Americanizing the Milk Industry." *Judge* 22 Sept. 1928: 14.

[Dr. S.] " 'Stand aside, woman! I'se on mah way to the three hundred and fifty-second semi-annual conclave and gatherance of the Antiquated Order of Loyal and Diversified True-blue Ravens, of which organism ah am a sixty-seventh degree Mahoot, to say nothing at all of may exalted and revered position and office as corresponding scribe and *ex post facto* protector and guardian of the sacred scrolls and parchments!' 'My, my, nigger, what an inspiration youse goin' to make when you deliver this here wash to my clients.' " *Judge* 22 Sept. 1928: 16.

[Dr. S.] " 'Oh, Mr. Pong, do you think you can win/? I've just heard that your opponents have also been smoking that strength-giving Strikes's Toasted Mixture.' 'Calm your fears, my dear madam. My pipe is the largest in town.' " *Judge* 20 Sept. 1928: 15.

[Dr. Theophrastus Seuss.] "The Appalling Increase in Animal Smuggling." *Judge* 6 Oct. 1928: 9.

"How Janitor Hemingway Capitalized a Liability." *Judge* 6 Oct. 1928: 20.

"The Harassing of Habbakuk." *Judge* 13 Oct. 1928: 8. Repr. Marschall 34–35.

"A Glimpse Into the Lives of Our Human-Tees." *Judge* 20 Oct. 1928: 9.

"Why I Turned Democrat." *Judge* 27 Oct. 1928: 8. Repr. Marschall 90.

[Dr. S.] "Dispossessed by their landlord, the juggler's family starts out in quest of a new apartment." *Judge* 27 Oct. 1928: 9.

"Fish Racing Growing as Fad." *Judge* 3 Nov. 1928: 6. Repr. Marschall 94.

"Curator of Dime Museum—*And here, ladies and gentlemen, we have the most minute piece of microscopic engraving in the world . . . the Lord's Prayer on the Head of a Pin!* Athiest (to son)—*Don't read a word of it, Robert! It's all propaganda!*" *Judge* 3 Nov. 1928: 7.

"These Small Bronx Apartments." *Judge* 3 Nov. 1928: 14.

"Unsung Heroes of the Gridiron." *Judge* 10 Nov. 1928: 6. Incl. "Mittelmeyer College of Pawnbroking Too Long Ignored," "Map Showing Intersectional Games on Mittelmeyer Schedule," "A Unique Signal System."

[Dr. Theophrastus Seuss.] "The Strangest Game I Ever Refereed." *Judge* 10 Nov. 1928: 14. Repr. Marschall 62.

"A Few Subtle Pleasures." *Judge* 17 Nov. 1928: 6. Repr. Marschall 61.

[Dr. S.] "The Burglar—*Now what th' devil are you doing with that gun?* Timid House-holder—*I-I-I'm only the exterminator man. Have you s-s-seen any m-m-mice?*" *Judge* 24 Nov. 1928: 4.

Barker—*See the dance of the seven veils, young feller?* Sport—*Small-town stuff,* brother, *small-town stuff. Many's the time I've seen 'em do it with eight.*" *Judge* 24 Nov. 1928: 5.

"Making Our Daughters Less Irritating." *Judge* 24 Nov. 1928: 8. Repr. Marschall 59.

The Sultan's Chef—*What! Two more covers stolen from my kettles? Darn those dancing girls, anyhow!*" *Judge* 1 Dec. 1928: 2.

"Let Experts Do Your Insulting For You!" *Judge* 1 Dec. 1928: 6.

"Notes on the Canine Renaissance." *Judge* 29 Dec. 1928: 6.

[Dr. Theophrastus Seuss.] "Our Emotional Apparati and How They are Controlled." *Judge* 22 Dec 1928: 15. Repr. Marschall 88.

"The Seussial Register." *Judge* 15 Dec. 1928: 6.

"Unusual Philanthropists." *Judge* 5 Jan. 1929: 16.

"Sorry, sister, but you can't get wholesale baptizin' rates unless you got a minimum of twelve chillun' " *Judge* 12 Jan. 1929: 2.

"THE WAGER." *Judge* 12 Jan. 1929: 6. Repr. Marschall 119.

"How High Can You Knock Yourself?" *Judge* 19 Jan. 1929: 8.

"Call me a frothy-mouthed idiot, will ya? Nigger, you must fight me a drool!" *Judge* 26 Jan. 1929: 11.

"A Few Bed-Bettering Suggestions." *Judge* 26 Jan. 1929: 19.

"No More Breaks Before the Guests! The 'Multifold Under-the-Table-Kicker' brings the whole family within the range of your silencing boot." *Judge* 2 Feb. 1929: 5.

[Dr. Theophrastus Seuss.] "Encouraging Higher Morality Among the Bulls." *Judge* 2 Feb. 1929: 17.

[Dr. Theophrastus Seuss.] "A Brief Résumé of the Eyebrow Situation." *Judge* 9 Feb. 1929: 9. Repr. Marschall 81.

[Dr. S.] "Another pet!!—as if I ain't got enough work caring for the canary." *Judge* 16 Feb. 1929: 7.

[Dr. Theophrastus Seuss.] "Somnambulists (and Some Don't)." *Judge* 16 Feb. 1929: 18. Repr. Marschall 70.

[Dr. Theophrastus Seuss.] "The Humphrey Brisket School for Barbers." *Judge* 23 Feb. 1929: 10.

[Dr. Theophrastus Seuss.] "Introducing Nature to the City-Bred Child." *Judge* 2 Mar. 1929: 17.

[Dr. Theophrastus Seuss.] "Three More Burning Problems Solved!" *Judge* 9 Mar. 1929: 20. Repr. Marschall 71.

[Dr. Theophrastus Seuss.] "Our Lamentable Misuse of Certain Fine Old Terms." *Judge* 16 Mar. 1929: 16. Repr. Marschall 76.

"Excuse my butting in, boys, but your middle 'C' is just a wee mite Flat!" *Judge* 16 Mar. 1929: 24.

JUNGLE NUMBER. *Judge* 23 Mar. 1929: cover.

[Dr. Theo. Seuss.] "Africa—Its Social, Religious, and Economical Aspects." *Judge* 23 Mar. 1929: 14.

[S + F.H.] "No, thanks; we don't need a taxi!" *Judge* 23 Mar. 1929: 15. Co-written with F. H.

[Dr. Theo. Seuss.] "Adam's Apples Are Coming Back." *Judge* 30 Mar. 1929: 22. Repr. Marschall 74.

[Dr. S.] "Shameful! Disgraceful! Godiva riding that poor old nag. Why, you can almost see his ribs!" *Judge* 6 Apr. 1929: 4.

"Three New Uses for Obsolete Objects." *Judge* 6 Apr. 1929: 14. Repr. Marschall 73.

[Dr. S.] " 'But Mrs. Chong, why is this child so different from your others?' 'Oh, well . . . Occidents will happen.' " *Judge* 13 Apr. 1929: 7.

[unsigned.] " 'What d'ye mean—an Einstein dog?' 'There's no explaining his relativity.' " *Judge* 20 Apr. 1929: 5.

"Now a FIFTH Dimension. . . . . . . 'Billiardescence'!!" *Judge* 20 Apr. 1929: 15.

[Dr. S.] "The Botanist plays 'Ups-a-Daisy' with his offspring." *Judge* 27 Apr. 1929: 15.

"Ough! Ough!" *Judge* 13 April 1929: 18. Repr. Marschall 57.

"Monosyllabic Ejaculations." 27 April 1929: 10. Repr. Marschall 80.

"Some Recent Developments in Criminal Accessories." *Judge* 4 May 1929: 11.

"The Subterfuge of High Finance." *Judge* 11 May 1929: 11.

[Dr. S.] "The Scotch cupid cuts down on his arrow expense." *Judge* 18 May 1929: 8.

" 'Left in the Lurch' and Just What Does It Mean?" *Judge* 18 May 1929: 22. Repr. Marschall 77.

"Punish Your Offspring Scientifically!" *Judge* 25 May 1929: 14. Repr. Marschall 58.

"The 'Wet-Paint Valet' For gentlemen who have uncontrollable curiosity, but hate to get their fingers mussy." *Judge* 1 June 1929: 12.

"Cross-section of the World's Most Prosperous Department Store." *Judge* 1 June 1929: 24.

"Going Abroad? Let the Seuss Travel Bureau Arrange Your Transportation!" *Judge* 8 June 1929: 18. Repr. Marschall 63.

"By Gad, ain't it the truth? Those rascals will eat most anything!" *Judge* 15 June 1929: 11. Repr. Marschall 21.

"Vacationists! Are You Taking Your Pets Along?" *Judge* 15 June 1929: 16. Repr. Marschall 102.

[Dr. S.] "How to Play a Joke on Your Dog." *Judge* 6 July 1929: 2.

"What if I did make it out of proportion? A guy's got to have a place to sit down, ain't he?" *Judge* 13 July 1929: 10.

"'JAB THE DOT'. . . . A GREAT GAME FOR THE KIDDIES!" *Judge* 17 Aug. 1929: 10.

[Dr. Theophrastus Seuss.] "FISH, BEAST, and BIRD: A PISCOZOÖAVISTICAL SURVEY: THE LAP-DOG SITUATION." *Judge* 16 Aug. 1930: 20. Repr. Marschall 98.

[Dr. Theophrastus Seuss.] "FISH, BEAST, and BIRD: A PISCOZOÖAVISTICAL SURVEY: THE ANIMALS' PART IN THE HISTORY OF SLUMBER." *Judge* 23 Aug. 1930: 8.

[Dr. Theophrastus Seuss.] "FISH, BEAST, and BIRD: A PISCOZOÖAVISTICAL SURVEY: SOME RECENT DEVELOPMENTS IN CUCKOO CLOCKERY." *Judge* 30 Aug. 1930: 18. Repr. Marschall 100.

[Dr. Theophrastus Seuss.] "FISH, BEAST, and BIRD: A PISCOZOÖAVISTICAL SURVEY: MAKING THE WORLD SAFE FOR TURTLERY." *Judge* 6 Sept. 1930: 20.

[Dr. Theophrastus Seuss.] "FISH, BEAST, and BIRD: A PISCOZOÖAVISTICAL SURVEY. WELL-MEANING BEASTS AS AN INDUSTRIAL MENACE." *Judge* 20 Sept. 1930: 19.

[Dr. Theophrastus Seuss.] "FISH, BEAST, and BIRD: A PISCOZOÖAVISTICAL SURVEY: THE ANIMALS' PART IN DISHONEST ATHLETICS." *Judge* 27 Sept. 1930: 14.

"Three Fine Social Arts We Are Prone to Neglect." *Judge* 18 Oct. 1930: 20. Repr. Marschall 82.

"The Pitfalls That Beset Our Infant Prodigies." *Judge* 25 Oct. 1930: 20. Repr. Marschall 89.

"The Hole-Testing Department in a Bowling Ball Factory." *Judge* 15 Nov. 1930: 20.

"Some Common-Sense Safety-First Devices." *Judge* 22 Nov. 1930: 10. Repr. Marschall 72.

"The Seuss Foundation Discovers a Beast Whose Tears Will Eradicate the Stain That a Cheap Collar Button Leaves on Your Adam's Apple." *Judge* 29 Nov. 1930: 21.

"Make Christmas More Meaningful. And Save 35,000,000 Hours Yearly!!" *Judge* 27 Dec. 1930: 10. Repr. Marschall 96.

Top-hatted man in bed with striped creature. *Judge* 3 Jan. 1931: cover.

"CROSS SECTION OF THE IZAAK WALTON CLUB." *Judge* 10 Jan. 1931: 18.

"Animals That are Making Our Land a Better Place to Live." *Judge* 17 Jan. 1931: 9. Repr. Marschall 101.

"THE ANIMAL AS A PRACTICAL JOKER." *Judge* 31 Jan. 1931: 9. Repr. Marschall 103.

"TARDY LAURELS FOR FORGOTTEN BROWS." *Judge* 7 Feb. 1931: 8. Incl. "THE JACQUES BRIOCHE MEMORIAL MEDAL," "A STATUE TO BUNG," "THE GREAT ZAKKX PAGEANT." Repr. Marschall 85.

"THE WICKERSHAM REPORT." *Judge* 14 Feb. 1931: 14.

"Tardy Laurels for Forgotten Brows." *Judge* 21 Feb. 1931: 15. Incl. "THE ORIGINAL 'UPS-A-DAISY BABY," "THE JACK ROBINSON FRAUD," "THE INVENTOR OF UP-YOUR-SLEEVE LAUGHING." Repr. Marschall 83.

"Tardy Laurels for Forgotten Brows." *Judge* 28 Feb. 1931: 11. Incl. "THE ORIGINATOR OF THE DITTO," "B-P-HOT WIZARD AT LAST REVEALED," "KELP THE CRUSADER." Repr. Marschall 86.

"SCIENCE GIVES THREE NEW BOONS TO SOCIETY." *Judge* 14 Mar. 1931: 15.

"RECENT DEVELOPMENTS IN THE FIELD OF CLOTHING." *Judge* 11 April 1931: 15. Repr. Marschall 78.

"TARDY LAURELS FOR FORGOTTEN BROWS." *Judge* 18 April 1931: 14. Incl. "A PIONEER IN CHILD-UPBRINGING," "VOLUNTARY MARTYRS TO SPOT-MARKING," "UNSUNG ENRICHERS OF THE TONGUE." Repr. Marschall 84.

"SOME NOTES ON BEATING-UPS." *Judge* 25 April 1931: 20.

"SOME NOTES ON SUB-DEB EDUCATION." *Judge* 9 May 1931: 23.

"THE TRULY-DUMB ANIMAL SHOPPE." *Judge* 30 May 1931: 21. Repr. Marschall 109.

"Willie! Don't you dare touch your desert until both you and Gertrude have finished your spinach!" *Judge* 6 June 1931: 18.

"Joe Spozzuli, the Organ Grinder, Makes Good." *Judge* 13 June 1931: 19.

"THE SUBTLETIES OF PET TRAINING." *Judge* 11 July 1931: 19.

"Scram!" *Judge* 18 July 1931: 8. Repr. Marschall 122.

"F'goshsake, Birdie, Spit it back! Spit it back!" *Judge* 25 July 1931: 10. Repr. Marschall 121.

"Ahh—Haaa-a-a! And she said she was going to spend the weekend at her mother's!" *Judge* 8 Aug. 1931: 14. Repr. Marschall 127.

"Hey, Mama! Kitty's come back!" *Judge* 15 Aug. 1931: 11. Repr. Marschall 113.

"Quit blowing those damn bubbles! You're driving me crazy!" *Judge* 22 Aug. 1931: 5. Repr. Marschall 125.

"G'wan, sit back in the water, big boy! That's a deuce of a place to get sunburned!" *Judge* 22 Aug. 1931: 19. Repr. Marschall 32.

"Cross-eyed Diver:—*Gawd! He thinks I'm making fun of him!*" *Judge* 29 Aug. 1931: 6. Repr. Marschall 126.

"Financial Note—Goat's Milk is higher than ever." *Judge* 29 Aug. 1931: 19.

"Swim for your lives! It's Bosko, the Sword-Swallower!" *Judge* 5 Sept. 1931: 15. Repr. Marschall 117.

"Hey, Mama! Willie's back!" *Judge* 12 Sept. 1931: 11. Repr. Marschall 120.

"Hang the luck! This would happen with that darned sardine looking on!" *Judge* 31 Oct. 1931: 11.

"How many times must I tell you, Kiwi, not to gape when the master is cheating at solitaire." *Judge* 5 Dec. 1931: 8. Repr. Marschall 116.

"Cripes! And she promised to marry me after the very first thaw!" *Judge* 19 Dec. 1931: 6. Repr. Marschall 133.

"Good Gracious, Matilda!—You, Too?" *Judge* 26 Dec. 1931: 10. Repr. Marschall 118. Note: on Seuss's copy (UCSD: MSS 230, Box 17, Folder 45), he has penciled in a subtitle: "or The Penalty of Ignorance."

"Incidental Music for a New Year's Eve Party." *Judge* 2 Jan. 1932: 16–17. Repr. in color as "Musikken bør reformeres," *Illustreret Familie-Journal* Nr. 40 (c. 1932): 15. UCSD MSS 0230, Box 17, Folder 39.

"W.C.T.U." *Judge* 9 Jan. 1932: cover.

"Incidental Music for a New Year's Eve Party." *Judge* 2 Jan. 1932: 16–17.

"Hey, Ma, put on the Kettle! Pop's froze onto it again!" *Judge* 16 Jan. 1932: 8.

"BLOW!" *Judge* 30 Jan. 1932: 9. Repr. Marschall 124.

"What! Stop the wheel and spoil the Five-Year Plan? No! Let him ride it out for two more years!" *Judge* 13 Feb. 1932: 8. Repr. Marschall 131.

"You're a fine host! Always giving me the bike with the little handlebars!" *Judge* 12 Mar. 1932: 19. Repr. Marschall 115.

"HOLDING THE BAG: A Projected Monument to the Great American Public." *Judge* 19 Mar. 1932: 4.

"As I've always said, my good fellow, I'd a darn sight rather be a big man in a little city than a little man in a big city!" *Judge* 16 April 1932: 6.

"So, you're the ———— who fouled me!" *Judge* 30 April 1932: 25.

"If we could find a fourth, we could at least play some bridge." *Judge* Jan. 1933: 12. Repr. Marschall 114.

"Technocracy Number of Judge." *Judge* Mar. 1933: cover.

"It says here, Oh Most Exalted One, that under Technocracy one man shall do the work of many." *Judge* Mar. 1933: 9.

Judge June 1933: cover.

"What Does This Tableau Represent?" *Judge* July 1933: 29. Advert for subscribing to *Judge*.

"This Summer Travel on a Budget!" *Judge* Aug. 1933: 32. Advert for subscribing to *Judge*.

"Boys, wait till you see these breech-clouts—'Tailored with Talon'!" *Judge* Dec. 1936: 31.

"No thanks! Last New Year's I got so plastered I thought I saw a horse!" *Judge* Jan. 1937: 20.

"This is a fine time to find out we're in love!" *Judge* Feb. 1938: 9.

[Dr. Theophrastus Seuss.] "HOW I SPIED ON GENERAL GRANT IN '61." *Judge*. Date unknown. 10, 28. Repr. Marschall 18–19.

[Henry McSeuss Webster.] "The Clock Strikes 13!" Picture by Jack Rose. *Judge*. Date unknown. 8, 16. From the Liberty Number of *Judge*. Repr. Marschall 22–23.

"Next Week DR. XAVIER RUPPZKNOPF Official Tonsil Snatcher of Europe, will tell . . ." *Judge*. Date and page unknown.

[S.] "Art Competition for Amateurs!" *Judge*. Date and page unknown.

Dr. Seuss's Cartoons and Parodies in Life

The earliest pieces (5 July 1929—25 Oct. 1929) are credited to Dr. S. After that date, all pieces credited to Dr. Seuss unless otherwise noted. All items with incomplete information are from Dartmouth's Rauner Alumni Library or UCSD's Dr. Seuss Collection (MSS 0230).

"LIFE's Little Educational Charts: The French Language at a Glance." *Life* 5 July 1929: 13.

"LIFE's Little Educational Charts: The Chinese Language at a Glance." *Life* 12 July 1929: 16.

"LIFE's Little Educational Charts: The German Language at a Glance." *Life* 19 July 1929: 10.

"LIFE's Little Educational Charts: The Idioms of Iceland at a Glance." *Life* 26 July 1929: 12.

"LIFE's Little Educational Charts: The Language of the Congo at a Glance." *Life* 2 Aug. 1929: 10.

"For the immaculate dresser." *Life* 9 Aug. 1929: 2.

"LIFE's Little Educational Charts: The Language of Egypt at a Glance." *Life* 9 Aug. 1929: 18.

"LIFE's Little Educational Charts: The Principal Nouns of the Stone Age at a Glance." *Life* 16 Aug. 1929: 19.

"LIFE's Little Educational Charts: The Slang of Brooklyn at a Glance." *Life* 23 Aug. 1929: 19.

"Just a small chop, loining the pork business." *Life* 30 Aug. 1929: 13.

"LIFE's Little Educational Charts: How to construct a prize-winning float." *Life* 30 Aug. 1929: 19.

"LIFE's Little Educational Charts: The Mediaeval Art of Catapulting." *Life* 6 Sept. 1929: 18. Repr. Marschall 107.

"LIFE's Little Educational Charts: Showing how soap-bubble blowing may be made a truly fascinating pastime." *Life* 13 Sept. 1929: 20. Repr. Marschall 87.

"Nice donkey-wonkey! Now make me a ducky, daddy!" *Life* 13 Sept. 1929: 30.

"LIFE's Little Educational Charts: The Language of Scotland at a Glance." *Life* 20 Sept. 1929: 10.

"LIFE's Little Educational Charts: The Swiss Language Made Easy." *Life* 27 Sept. 1929: 15.

"LIFE's Little Educational Charts: The Latvian Language at a Glance." *Life* 4 Oct. 1929: 16.

"LIFE's Little Educational Charts: How to Construct a 'Pachyderm Compressor.'" *Life* 18 Oct. 1929: 21.

"LIFE's Little Educational Charts: The nautical slang of Montenegro at a Glance." *Life* 25 Oct. 1929: 14.

"LIFE's Little Educational Charts: HOW TO CONSTRUCT A CHEAP BUT RELIABLE—GNORFER -." *Life* 1 Nov. 1929: 15. Repr. Marschall 105.

"LIFE's Little Educational Charts: A Foolproof System for Cheating at Solitaire." *Life* 8 Nov. 1929: 20. Repr. Marschall 106.

[Dr. S.] "THE MULTIPLEX BOOT." *Life* 15 Nov. 1929: 16.

"Four Places Not To Hide While Growing Your Beard." *Life* 15 Nov. 1929: 19.

"LIFE's Little Educational Charts: A Lesson in Connoisseurship." *Life* 22 Nov. 1929: 19. Repr. Marschall 66.

[Dr. S.] "New Invention." *Life* 29 Nov. 1929: 8.

"LIFE's Little Educational Charts: Some New and Better Superstitions!" *Life* 29 Nov. 1929: 15. Repr. Marschall 65.

"LIFE'S LITTLE EDUCATIONAL CHARTS: SOME UNUSUAL SUBSTITUTES FOR MISTLETOE." *Life* 6 Dec. 1929: 35.

[Dr. S.] "HEAD TRAINER *(to new assistant): And, mind you, if I ever catch you smoking on the job, why you're through!" Life* 13 Dec. 1929: 9.

"LIFE'S LITTLE EDUCATIONAL CHARTS: JUST WHAT IS A VERNACULAR, ANYWAY?" *Life* 13 Dec. 1929: 15. Repr. Marschall 79.

"LIFE'S LITTLE EDUCATIONAL CHARTS: How to Play Phrugmhumnb la!" *Life* 20 Dec. 1929: 14. Repr. Marschall 104.

"I'm all for dawgs as a rule, Bill, but a dame sure does make a sap of herself draggin' around one of them little yapping society mutts." *Life* 27 Dec. 1929: 8.

"LIFE'S LITTLE EDUCATIONAL CHARTS: Medicine, Highly Developed in the Day of Pnolioch, Still a Growing Science!" *Life* 3 Jan. 1930: 15. Repr. Marschall 75.

"NONCHALANCE. HIGHLY BLASE VICTIM: *When!" Life* 10 Jan. 1930: 11.

"LIFE'S LITTLE EDUCATIONAL CHARTS: How Certain Fine Dumb Creatures Have Fostered the Noble Cause of Justice." *Life* 10 Jan. 1930: 15. Repr. Marschall 95.

"LIFE'S LITTLE EDUCATIONAL CHARTS: A Critical Survey of the Custom of Hat-Doffing." *Life* 17 Jan. 1930: 14. Repr. Marschall 64.

"W-a-a-h!! He stole my animal cracker!" *Life* 24 Jan. 1930: 7.

"LIFE'S LITTLE EDUCATIONAL CHARTS: The Beast and Bird as an Aid in Habit-Breaking." *Life* 24 Jan. 1930: 16.

"LIFE'S LITTLE EDUCATIONAL CHARTS: The Beast as Man's Best Parlor Companion." *Life* 31 Jan. 1930: 14. Repr. Marschall 97.

"LIFE'S LITTLE EDUCATIONAL CHARTS: Some New Treats for the Noise Connoisseur." *Life* 7 Feb. 1930: 21.

"Portrait of a statistician who plans to be Exactly Right when in later years he says: 'I knew you when you were that high.'" *Life* 14 Feb. 1930: 13.

"LIFE'S LITTLE EDUCATIONAL CHARTS: How Animals Served Us Before the Advent of Science." *Life* 14 Feb. 1930: 23. Repr. Marschall 93.

"LIFE'S LITTLE EDUCATIONAL CHARTS: The Animal-Trainers' Jargon." *Life* 21 Feb. 1930: 19.

"LIFE'S LITTLE EDUCATIONAL CHARTS: The Present Scientific Situation in Europe." *Life* 28 Feb. 1930: 21.

"LIFE'S LITTLE EDUCATIONAL CHARTS: The Latest Developments in Vocal Education." *Life* 7 Mar. 1930: 21. Repr. Marschall 67.

"Note the undulating subtleties of this baby's stride, Eddie, and then try and tell me three dollars a quart was extravagant." *Life* 7 Mar. 1930: 23.

"LIFE'S LITTLE EDUCATIONAL CHARTS: THE WISDOM OF COMPLETE INSURANCE." *Life* 14 Mar. 1930: 21.

"REPRESSED COUNTRY YOUTH: *Whoopee, Henry—Look! The Dance of the Seven Veals!" Life* 21 Mar. 1930: 10.

"LIFE'S LITTLE EDUCATIONAL CHARTS: Static in its More Subtle Forms." *Life* 21 Mar. 1930: 21. Repr. Marschall 68.

"LIFE'S LITTLE EDUCATIONAL CHARTS: THE DANGEROUS SPORT OF ANIMAL NAVIGATION." *Life* 28 Mar. 1930: 22.

"LIFE'S LITTLE EDUCATIONAL CHARTS: The Perplexing Problem of Household Terminology." *Life* 4 Apr. 1930: 19. Repr. Marschall 69.

"EXASPERATED HOUSEWIFE: *Say—is there any way to get rid of you brush peddlers?* INDEFATIGABLE SALESMAN: *Ah, madam, here's just the thing! Our special club-handed model retails for a mere $1.98." Life* 11 Apr. 1930: 2.

"Portrait of a perfect wife." *Life* 11 Apr. 1930: 16.

"LIFE'S LITTLE EDUCATIONAL CHARTS: A study of the unusual systems of transportation running between 'Zelli's' and the 'Dead Rat' in the Montmartre District of Paris." *Life* 11 Apr. 1930: 27.

"LIFE'S LITTLE EDUCATIONAL CHARTS: Connoisseur of Silence." *Life* 18 Apr. 1930: 15.

"LIFE'S LITTLE EDUCATIONAL CHARTS: A few notes on morality among the animals." *Life* 25 Apr. 1930: 13.

"Life's LITTLE EDUCATIONAL CHARTS: A Few Notes on Heredity Among the Animals." *Life* 2 May 1930: 23.

"Life's LITTLE EDUCATIONAL CHARTS: On the Horns of a Dilemma." *Life* 9 May 1930: 13.

"Life's LITTLE EDUCATIONAL CHARTS: Beautifying the Science of Time Telling." *Life* 16 May 1930: 21. Repr. Marschall 99.

"Life's LITTLE EDUCATIONAL CHARTS: SOME UNUSUAL USES FOR HOUSEHOLD PETS." *Life* 23 May 1930: 21.

"AN UNSUNG HERO IN THE HISTORY OF SPORT. GUS PLODOPLUD (*who threw in the ball for the first game of polo*): *Now boys, let's have some action!*" *Life* 30 May 1930: 15. Repr. Marschall 128.

"Now, don't worry there, guide old man. All you've got to do is eat eight or ten pounds of food out of that knapsack, and when the added weight hoists me up, I'll haul you up after!" *Life* 6 June 1930: 10.

"UNSUNG ANIMALS WHO MADE GREAT HISTORICAL EVENTS POSSIBLE: The cat who furnished the strings so Nero might fiddle while Rome burned." *Life* 6 June 1930: 15.

"UNSUNG BEASTS WHO MADE GREAT HISTORICAL EVENTS POSSIBLE: The mule, with whose jawbone Samson slew the Philistines." *Life* 13 June 1930: 15.

"FAMOUS INITIATIONS OF HISTORY: Neophytes of Ye Round Table Take the Test Terrible." *Life* 20 June 1930: 13. Repr. Marschall 130.

"UNSUNG BEASTS WHO MADE HISTORICAL EVENTS POSSIBLE: The stork is persuaded to reveal the facts of life to little Cain." *Life* 27 June 1930: 9.

"FORGOTTEN EVENTS OF HISTORY. *Noah's dissolute brother, Goah, preserves the D.T. beasts of his day for posterity.*" *Life* 4 July 1930: 9. Repr. Marschall 129.

[Dr. S.] [Two men fencing with their noses.] *Life* 4 July 1930: 32.

"UNSUNG BEASTS WHO HAVE MADE BIG BUSINESS POSSIBLE: The Models in the Animal Cracker Factory." *Life* 11 July 1930: 6. Repr. Marschall 123.

"The Yawnsboro Hunt Club (for willing but weary sportsmen) Walking to Hounds." *Life* 25 July 1930: 7.

"THE YAWNSBORO C.C. (FOR WILLING BUT WEARY SPORTSMEN)" *Life* 8 Aug. 1930: 11.

[Dr. S.] "The Teasmellers fight it out." *Life* 8 Aug. 1930: 26.

"Who wouldn't look cynical, I ask you? After working thirty years in this here act, last night I get blackballed by the Elks." *Life* 24 Oct. 1930: 3.

"It's all my own fault. Ma's told me a hundred times not to throw stones at sparrows." *Life* May 1932: 36–37.

"Pshaw—they'll all say I took it from a tree!" *Life* Jan. 1933: 7.

"The Changing Fauna of the Arctic: Some Recent Developments in Adaptation." *Life* Feb. 1933: 21.

"Oh, shoot! It's Sunday and not a plumber to be had." *Life* Feb. 1933: 28.

"*NEW* NEW JERSEY: The Great New Jersey Rehabilitation Plan." *Life* Mar. 1933: 24–25.

"We're lost if we steer by the Great North Bear; steer by the Small South Whoosis!" *Life* May 1933: 24.

"My Three Best Tricks and How I Do Them." *Life* June 1933: 11.

"THE FARM RELIEF SITUATION AT A GLANCE." *Life* July 1933: 19.

"Marching On With Dr. Seuss." *Life* Nov. 1933: 24.

"'Guess Who' Revived as National Pastime!" *Life* Jan. 1934: 20.

"THE FACTS OF LIFE Or, How Should I Tell My Child?" Part I. *Life* Feb. 1934: 22–23, 37, 46–47. Repr. Marschall 36–41.

"THE FACTS OF LIFE Or, How Should I Tell My Child?" Part II. *Life* Mar. 1934: 18, 42. Repr. Marschall 41–43.

"THE FACTS OF LIFE Or, How Should I Tell My Child?" Part III. *Life* Apr. 1934: 24, 28. Repr. Marschall 43–44.

"THE FACTS OF LIFE Or, How Should I Tell My Child?" Part IV. *Life* May. 1934 [?]. Repr. Marschall 45–48.

"I know, my dear, but that's NOTHING compared to having an egg!" *Life* May 1934: cover.

"A Few Notes on the Shameful Paucity of American Words." *Life* July 1934: 13.

"The tangled yarn problem (see text above) as pictured by Dr. Seuss. These members of the Engineers Club lost their lives in an attempt to unsnarl 200 yards of fishing line. The practice is now prohibited by the Anti-Untangle legislation of 1928." *Life* Date unknown. 34.

"Look, Abdulla! Spaghetti for supper!" *Life*. Date and page unknown.

"HISTORY OF ADVERTISING" *Life*. Date and page unknown.

"HISTORY OF ADVERTISING—II" *Life*. Date and page unknown.

"HISTORY OF ADVERTISING—III" *Life*. Date and page unknown.

Dr. Seuss's Cartoons and Parodies in College Humor

All items with incomplete information are from Dartmouth's Rauner Alumni Library or UCSD's Dr. Seuss Collection (MSS 0230).

"*Professor of Phenomena Frumenta:* On the other hand, gentlemen, if we had used Bacardi instead of Applejack in that last batch, these fuzzy little top-knots would all have been horns." *College Humor* Sept. 1930: 29.

[Doctor Theodophilus Seuss, Ph.D., I.Q., S.O.L.] "ANIMALS EVERY STUDENT LOVES." *College Humor* Oct. 1930: 33. Includes "Poker-Conscious Moose," "Abbacadabbi as a Mathematical Asset," "Himalayan Hummer as an Air Carrier."

[Doctor Theodophilus Seuss, Ph.D., I.Q., S.O.L.] "ANIMALS EVERY STUDENT LOVES." *College Humor* Nov. 1930: 27. Includes "Pledging at the U. of Mombjanika," "Blackballing in the Arctic," "Frosh Paddling at the U. of Yien-Chow."

[Doctor Theodophilus Seuss, Ph.D., I.Q., H_2SO_4.] "ANIMALS EVERY STUDENT LOVES." *College Humor* Dec. 1930: 35. Includes "Habit Formation and the Felines," "Study in Auditory Stimulus," "Transmission of Evil Characteristics by Birds."

[Doctor Theodophilus Seuss, Ph.D., I.Q., H_2SO_4.] "ANIMALS EVERY STUDENT LOVES." *College Humor* Jan. 1931: 35. Includes "Bird as an Aid to Theology Students," "Walrus as a Memory Trainer," "Beasts of the Davey School."

[Doctor Theodophilus Seuss, Ph.D., I.Q., H_2SO_4.] "ANIMALS EVERY STUDENT LOVES." *College Humor* Feb. 1931: 45. Includes "Gosling as a Tester of Balance," "Turkish Nightingale as an Elocution Aid," "Goat as an Educational Pioneer."

[Doctor Theodophilus Seuss, Ph.D., I.Q., H_2SO_4.] "ANIMALS EVERY STUDENT LOVES." *College Humor* Mar. 1931: 27. Includes "Serpent as a Grader," "Chickadee as a Soother," "Gweek as a Consoler."

[Doctor Theodophilus Seuss, Ph.D., I.Q., H_2SO_4.] "ANIMALS EVERY STUDENT LOVES." *College Humor* Apr. 1931: 45. Includes "Pigeon as a Dean Deceiver," "Cambrubian Crane as a Graph Inspirer," "Kitten as an Emphasis Tester."

[Doctor Theodophilus Seuss, Ph.D., I.Q., H_2SO_4.] "ANIMALS EVERY STUDENT LOVES." *College Humor* May 1931: 33. Includes "Primate as Telephonic Helpmeet," "Auk as a Freshman Protector," "Pisces as an Animated Insignia."

"Saved at last—here come the St. Bernards!" *College Humor* June 1931: 38–39.

"AT THE SEUSS SCHOOL OF GRAPHIC SCIENCES." *College Humor* July 1931: 27.

[two top-hatted drunken men firing rifle at imaginary creatures.] *College Humor* Aug. 1931: 31, 32, 33, 35.

"Conserving the Energy of Our Soda Drinkers." *College Humor* Sept. 1931: 31.

"Rounding Up the Practice Goats in the Edelweiss-Switzer Barber School." *Maple Leaves* (Maplewood, N.H.) 11 July 1931: 7. Repr. *College Humor* Oct. 1931: 20.

"In quest of a Turkish nightingale, you must first go to the Lake of the Clouds. . . ." *College Humor* Nov. 1931: 33.

"Annual Directors' Meeting of the Gilloppy Safety Razor Company." *College Humor* Dec. 1931: 30. Note: on TSG's personal copy, he crossed out this title and wrote, "Many Bearded Men with Hands folded over Bellies." UCSD: MSS 0230, Box 17, Folder 33.

"Ah Lieut. Calza! Just in time to join us in a little game of strip poker!" *College Humor* Mar. 1932: 13.

"Look, Abdulla! Spaghetti for supper!" *College Humor* Mar. 1932: 67.

"Good gracious! That bull in the china shop is just about as destructive as a bull in a china shop!" *College Humor* June 1932: 56.

"I tell you, Pete, this rolling off a log is just as simple as rolling off a log!" *College Humor* June 1932: 57.

"The Skunk: Gosh—a skunk at a picnic is just about as popular as a skunk at a picnic!" *College Humor* June 1932: 58.

"The Duck: Oh, pooh! This water rolls off my back just like water off a duck's back." *College Humor* June 1932: 59.

"BONERS from the Indiana Bored Walk." *College Humor* Aug. 1932: 50–53.

[4-part cartoon of African sticking thorn in lion's paw and then removing it.] *College Humor* Sept. 1932.

"Poly. Sci. I. at the U. of N.C. Training Future Governors of North Carolina What to Say to the Future Governors of South Carolina." *College Humor* Oct. 1932: 44–45.

[unsigned.] [3-panel cartoon of Persian man fishing.] *College Humor*. Date unknown. UCSD: MSS 0230, Box 17, Folder 33.

Dr. Seuss's Cartoons and Parodies in Liberty Magazine

Dr. Seuss's Lost World Revisited (1967) collects most of these cartoons, with the exceptions of "A Few Notes on Fires," "A Few Notes on Navigation," and all of the "Few Notes on Games" and "Some New Aids to Better Living" (for these latter two items, *Dr. Seuss's Lost World Revisited* reprints only two cartoons for each).

"Goofy Olympics." *Liberty* 4 June 1932: 44–45.

"Some Recent Developments in Zoölogy: Four Beasts Who Are Making This a Better World to Live In." *Liberty* 11 June 1932: 19.

"A Few Notes on Birds." *Liberty* 18 June 1932: 33.

"A Few Notes on the Coming Election." *Liberty* 25 June 1932: 29

"A New Idea in Taxation." *Liberty* 2 July 1932: 40.

"Three Summer Problems And How to Solve Them." *Liberty* 9 July 1932: 47

"A Few Notes on Torture: Three Unique Forms Worked Entirely Through Birds." *Liberty* 16 July 1932: 56.

"Some Recent Inventions in the Offspring Field." *Liberty* 23 July 1932: 23.

"Three Praiseworthy Educational Projects." *Liberty* 30 July 1932: 11.

"A Few Bright Spots on the Business Horizon." *Liberty* 6 Aug. 1932: 23.

"Three Glorious Movements in the Clothing Field." *Liberty* 27 Aug. 1932: 11.

"The Rough Road to International Harmony." *Liberty* 3 Sept. 1932: 39.

"A Few Notes on Games." *Liberty* 10 Sept. 1932: 11.

"Housecleaning the English Language." *Liberty* 17 Sept. 1932: 35.

"A Few Hints on Hypnotism." *Liberty* 24 Sept. 1932: 43.

"Some New Aids to Better Living." *Liberty* 1 Oct. 1932: 47.

"A Few Notes on Origins." *Liberty* 8 Oct. 1932: 54.

"A Few Notes on Fires." *Liberty* 22 Oct. 1932: 45.

"A Few Hints on Navigation." *Liberty* 29 Oct. 1932: 45.

"Is the Bird in Hand REALLY Worth Two in the Bush?" Part I. *Liberty* 5 Nov. 1932: 43.

"Is the Bird in Hand REALLY Worth Two in the Bush?" Part II. *Liberty* 12 Nov. 1932: 39.

"A Few Notes on Facial Foliage." *Liberty* 26 Nov. 1932: 51.
"A Few Notes on Sleep." *Liberty* 3 Dec. 1932: 51.

Dr. Seuss's Cartoons and Parodies in Other Publications

All items with incomplete information are from UCSD's Dr. Seuss Collection (MSS 0230).

"I am So Thrilled, My Dear! At Last I Can Understand the Ecstasy Lawrence Experienced When He Raced Posthaste Across the Sands of Arabia in Pursuit of the Fleeting Arab." *Saturday Evening Post.* Date and page unknown.
"Triumphant return of Mermaid Delegate No. 1, after fixing a twelve-hour day code for the sailor-luring trades." *University Magazine* Sept. 1933: 49.
"A large family of Dilemmas, the assorted horns of which the wayward student finds himself on." *University Magazine* Oct. 1933: 47.
"Some Mooses I Have Known." *University Magazine* c. 1933: 60–61.
[Indian and papoose.] *University Magazine* c. 1933: 49.
"I've a Darned Good Mind to Get Caught—Just to Go Up and See the Argument." *This Week* 3 Mar., probably 1935.
"See Dr. Seuss for Social Publicity!" *New York Woman* 7 Oct. 1936: 40.
"Maternity Marches On!" *New York Woman* 4 Nov. 1936: 40.
"Gad, Emma, This Stuff's Dynamite!" *Ballyhoo* [month unknown] 1937: cover. This is Vol. 12, No. 6.
"Bring 'em Buck Alive!" *Ballyhoo* Sept [year unknown]: 16–17.
"Remember that harum-scarum Sammy Ichthyosaurus? I hear they finally dug him up out in Arizona somewhere." *Collier's* 17 Apr. 1937.
[sea serpent cozying up to inflatable creature] . *Collier's* 31 July 1937.
"We use the honor system around here!" *Collier's* 18 Sept. 1937: 68.
"Fancy Meeting You Here!" *Saturday Evening Post.* Date and page unknown.
"Thidwick Asleep." *Dartmouth Alumni Magazine* Jan. 1949: 58.

Dr. Seuss's Cartoons (sources unknown)

All are from UCSD's Dr. Seuss Collection (MSS 0230).

"Personally, Mr. Belknap, I prefer riding astride, but you know how these things are." Source and date unknown. 34.
"An intimate portrait of Frank Sullivan by Dr. Seuss." Source, date and page unknown. Below caption is "From 'In One Ear' "; on other side of page, there is a reference to "Rexford G. Tugwell, Secretary of Agriculture and member of the President's 'brain trust.' " Also: it's on newsprint.
"It Can't Happen Here!" source and date unknown. 60.
"Even If She Does Lay an Egg, What Sort of Meal Is That?" Source, date and page unknown. It's on newsprint.
"U.S. NAZIS FASCISTS COMMUNISTS." Source, date and page unknown. Possibly between March and June of 1941. It's clearly prior to U.S. entry into the war. In a nearby article, we learn that New York's National Youth Administration (head: Miss Helen H. Harris) had "to lay off 7,000 young people of the 26,000 it employed." Several stories have the theme of supporting the president's foreign policy of aiding Britain.
"MAJORING IN FASHION with Dr. Seuss." Source, date and page unknown. "Gad, Emma! This stuff's dynamite!" Source and date unknown. 43. On p. 44 is "gal about town," which includes a reference to Garbo and to Radio City, Ritz Carlton, La Coq Rouge.

PM *Cartoons by Dr. Seuss*

208 of these 400 cartoons have been reproduced in Minear's *Dr. Seuss Goes to War* (listed above), and all are available at this on-line exhibit: "Dr. Seuss Went to War," Dr. Seuss Collection, Mandeville Special Collections Library, University of San Diego <http://orpheus-1.ucsd.edu/speccoll/dspolitic/index.htm>, 2000-present.

"VIRGINIO GAYDA Says:" *PM* 30 Jan. 1941: 2. Includes letter to the editor. Repr. Minear 11.

"IT'S SMART TO SHOP AT ADOLF'S." *PM* 25 Apr. 1941: 19.

" 'Since when did we swap our ego for an ostrich?' " *PM* 28 Apr. 1941: 22. Repr. Minear 29

"We Always Were Suckers for Ridiculous Hats . . ." *PM* 29 Apr. 1941: 20. Repr. Special Issue [circa 30 May 1941]: 19. Repr. Minear 30.

" 'Sometimes I wonder—would we speed things up if we used turtles instead of snails?' " *PM* 4 May 1941: 1. Repr. Minear 172.

"HAF YOU A MATCH, JA?" *PM* 7 May 1941: 20.

"TALK TALK TALK TALK TALK TALK TALK." *PM* 8 May 1941: 1. Repr. Minear 200.

"How're We Doing?" *PM* 9 May 1941: 9.

"Gad, if we could only harness that jaw-power!" *PM* 11 May 1941: 1.

"Portrait of a man on the horns of a dilemma." *PM* 12 May 1941: 6.

"IT'S ALL YOURS, DEAR LADS!" *PM* 13 May 1941: 17. Repr. Minear 173.

"Ho Hum! No chance of contagion." *PM* 15 May 1941: 21. Repr. Minear 31.

"Hey! It's your NOSE you're supposed to keep to the grindstone!" *PM* 16 May 1941: 21.

"The head eats . . . . . . the rest get milked." *PM* 19 May 1941: 5. Repr. Minear 81.

" 'Put your arm up like this, and your troubles are over . . .' " *PM* 20 May 1941: 5. Repr. Minear 155.

" 'Ho hum! When he's finished pecking down that last tree he'll quite likely be tired.' " *PM* 22 May 1941: 3. Repr. Minear 32.

"Yes—By All Means—Listen, and Think!" *PM* 23 May 1941: 9. Repr. Minear 19.

"The Cloud Climbers." *PM* 25 May 1941: 19.

"She embarrasses Ma and Pa a bit, but Fraulein sure can push!" *PM* 26 May 1941: 10.

"The old Family bath tub is plenty safe for me!" *PM* 27 May 1941: 12. Repr. Minear 33.

"BOY! Is His Face Red Today!" *PM* 28 May 1941: 14.

" 'Now, Adolf, Just Forget What Franklin Said. 80 Per Cent of Us Here Want to Let You Have Your Fling.' " *PM* 29 May 1941: 7.

" ''Tis Roosevelt, Not Hitler, that the World Should Really Fear.' " *PM* 2 June 1941: 20. Repr. Minear 34.

" 'Gad! What a pair of lungs for a sparrow!' " *PM* 3 June 1941: 13.

"Speaking of Blockaders . . ." *PM* 4 June 1941: 21.

" 'Great news, Francois! We've signed you to fight Kid Britain!' " *PM* 6 June 1941: 21. Repr. Minear 156.

" 'There is no Allah but Hitler and Adolf is his Prophet!' " *PM* 8 June 1941: 11.

" 'There You Are, Johnny . . . Sell THAT to the Suckers in the U.S.A.' " *PM* 9 June 1941: 14. Repr. Minear 35.

" 'By the Way . . . Did Anyone Send that Aid to Britain?' " *PM* 10 June 1941 : 15. Repr. Minear 36.

" 'Salute to thee, Italia, for thy most victorious year!' " *PM* 11 June 1941: 2. Repr. Minear 127.

" 'Please push bit harder. Hon. feet still slightly holding back!' " *PM* 13 June 1941: 21. Repr. Minear 138.

"The Appeaser." *PM* 16 June 1941: 11.

" 'Relatives? Naw . . . Just three fellers going along for the ride!' " *PM* 18 June 1941: 18. Repr. Minear 222.

"'Why do I deliver this stuff by fish-back when I own so many good boats?'" *PM* 19 June 1941: 14.

"'In other words, gentlemen, Togo won't hit Joe and Joe won't hit Togo . . . unless they take a poke at each other when I start socking Joe.'" *PM* 20 June 1941: 21. Repr. 22 June 1941: 18. Repr. Minear 166.

Hitler breaking Russia off of his stilts. *PM* 22 June 1941: 10. Note: the original (or an earlier?) sketch (UCSD: MSS 0230, MC-128–09) bears the caption, "Nice stilts, ja . . . but better soon mit der British, Russian und American extensions!" In this version, Russia was clearly part of the stilts, but then was cut out of the drawing and placed at an angle, to show it breaking off.

"Said a bird in the midst of a Blitz . . ." *PM* 23 June 1941: 9.

"A. HITLER, TAXIDERMIST." *PM* 25 June 1941: 21. Repr. Minear 163.

"'Dear me . . . such spines! Someone's apt to get hurt!'" *PM* 27 June 1941: 22. Repr. Minear 37.

"'Gosh, I wonder how easy this Tattoo Stuff comes off . . .!'" *PM* 30 June 1941: 21.

"'Yoo hoo, Adolf! Lookee! I'm attacking 'em too'" *PM* 1 July 1941: 22. Repr. Minear 128.

"The Great U.S. Sideshow." *PM* 3 July 1941: 11. Rpt. with Rose P. Schuyler's letter to the editor, "Guts Is an Ugly Word, but Good" 9 July 1941: 21.

"The Unexpected Target." *PM* 4 July 1941: 3. Repr. Minear 164.

"Keep your eye on the bum that's tagging along behind!" *PM* 4 July 1941: 23.

"'It's just Hamilton Fish, Sir, talking back to Knox!'" *PM* 7 July 1941: 21.

"'And on this platform, folks, those most perplexing people . . . the Lads with the Siamese Beard! Unrelated by blood, they are joined in a manner that mystifies the mightiest minds in the land!'" *PM* 8 July 1941: 20. Repr. Minear 38.

"'Sis! Boom! Bah! Rah! . . .'" *PM* 10 July 1941: 21. Repr. Minear 165.

"'So you don't like my new Eskimo suit, SO WHAT!'" *PM* 11 July 1941: 11.

"'Mighty pretty sunset . . . *unless*, of course, Roosevelt thinks so, in which case the thing simply stinks!'" *PM* 14 July 1941: 21.

"Virginio Gayda Says:" *PM* 15 July 1941: 5.

"The Isolationist." *PM* 16 July 1941: 20. Repr. Minear 39.

"We Clams Can't Be Too Careful." *PM* 17 July 1941: 11.

"'Time to knock off, boys. Our year is up!'" *PM* 20 July 1941: 9.

"'Atta boy, Lindy! Keep me under control!'" *PM* 21 July 1941: 21.

"What you need to do is get away from your worries. I recommend a little excursion up Vladivostok way." *PM* 23 July 1941: 9. Repr. Minear 139.

"Crisis in Berchtesgaden." *PM* 24 July 1941: 21. Repr. Minear 82.

"'How do you like your army . . . well done or half-baked?'" *PM* 25 July 1941: 12.

"'Such nice boats we buy our leetle boy Benito . . . and so mean the big boys treat him over at the pond!'" *PM* 27 July 1941: 7.

"ADOLF: Wipe Your Feet on our Door Mat and come right in!" *PM* 28 July 1941: 21.

"Subversive Activity." *PM* 30 July 1941: 5.

"All Set to Answer the Bell." *PM* 31 July 1941: 11.

"Virginio Gayda Says:" *PM* 1 Aug. 1941: 4.

"As I was saying when we were so rudely interrupted, I am taking a poll of public opinion. You don't think this country will ever be attacked, do you?" *PM* 1 Aug. 1941: 8.

"'If you were smart enough to make silk, it ought to be a cinch to whip up a little gun cotton.'" *PM* 4 Aug. 1941: 21.

"'And with new WAR Taxes, mind you, we'll soon be going THREES on our dollar cigars!'" *PM* 5 Aug. 1941: 8. Repr. Minear 237.

"Communique: 'The anihilation is proceeding according to schedule.'" *PM* 6 Aug. 1941: 1. Repr. Minear 161.

"The Bird." *PM* 8 Aug. 1941: 20.

"In Russia a chap, so we're told, . . ." *PM* 11 Aug. 1941: 20. Repr. Minear 167.

" 'Remember . . . One More Lollypop, and Then You All Go Home!' " *PM* 13 Aug 1941: 1. Repr. Minear 40.

" 'Confidentially . . . how much Hell do you think these Japs will raise?' " *PM* 14 Aug. 1941: 5.

"Uncle Adolf's Cigars." *PM* 15 Aug. 1941: 7.

"RETALIATION." *PM* 17 Aug. 1941: 8.

" 'Quite dead I shoot him . . . unt still, by Himmel, he bites!' " *PM* 18 Aug. 1941: 21. Repr. Minear 83.

" 'Training . . . There's some talk he may have to spend the winter up in Russia!' " *PM* 20 Aug. 1941: 6.

" 'Pssst . . . Adolf! How am I doin'?' " *PM* 22 Aug. 1941: 20.

"Sail on, Sail on, Oh, Ship of State!" *PM* 24 Aug. 1941: 20.

" 'He has *Pursis Emptosis*, or Empty Purse . . . a disease that's very very bad for Morale!' " *PM* 25 Aug. 1941: 19. Repr. Minear 201.

" 'Himmel! How much thumbs it takes fur dis leaky dike!' " *PM* 28 Aug. 1941: 21.

" 'Don't waste a torpedo, Fritz, we can take this gang with a butterfly net!' " *PM* 31 Aug. 1941: 4. Repr. Minear 223.

"SCIENCE MARCHES ON: 'Fellow experimenters, we are gathered here today to mate the Eagle and the Jellyfish!' " *PM* 2 Sept. 1941: 22. Repr. Minear 41.

"Man who draw his bath too hot, sit down in same velly slow." *PM* 4 Sept. 1941: 5.

" 'Hey! Hide if you have to, but by thunder, stop nibbling!' " *PM* 5 Sept. 1941: 21.

" 'What's the cheery word from Russia?' " *PM* 7 Sept. 1941: 4.

" 'Relax, Sam, I assure you the express turns off right here!' " *PM* 9 Sept. 1941: 10. Repr. Minear 42.

" 'It's truly encouraging how much of this stuff drifts into British ports!' " *PM* 10 Sept. 1941: 1. Repr. Minear 174.

" 'Just *whose* time are we biding . . . ours or Mr. Hitler's?' " *PM* 11 Sept. 1941: 7.

" 'But let this warning be clear. . . .' " *PM* 12 Sept. 1941: 2.

"A Costume He Found in the Kaiser's Attic . . ." *PM* 17 Sept. 1941: 21.

"Spreading the Lovely Goebbels Stuff." *PM* 18 Sept. 1941: 10. Repr. Minear 43.

"Velly Scary Jap-in-the-Box . . . Wasn't It?" *PM* 19 Sept. 1941: 21.

"I AM PART JEWISH." *PM* 22 Sept. 1941: 1. Repr. Minear 62.

"Stop Wringing the Hands That Should Wring Hitler's Neck!" *PM* 25 Sept. 1941: 9. Repr. Minear 202.

" 'Jeepers! Is that *Me*' " *PM* 26 Sept 1941: 21. Repr. Minear 44.

"The Old Man of the Sea." *PM* 28 Sept. 1941: 8.

"A Symphony of Catcalls." *PM* 29 Sept. 1941: 8.

" '*JUNIOR! No shadow movies!* You'll get caught in the Nye Investigation!' " *PM* 30 Sept. 1941: 7.

" . . . and the Wolf chewed up the children and spit out their bones . . . But those were *Foreign Children* and it really didn't matter.' " *PM* 1 Oct. 1941: 12. Repr. Minear 45.

"I WAS WEAK AND RUN-DOWN . . ." *PM* 5 Oct. 1941: 11. Repr. Minear 46.

" 'Remember . . . no punting . . . no passing . . . no plunging. Just dig in on your One Inch Line and WIN!' " *PM* 9 Oct. 1941: 20.

"ALL-OUT AID TO OUR ALLIES." *PM* 10 Oct. 1941: 6. Repr. Minear 175.

"Nursing an Old Grudge." *PM* 12 Oct. 1941: 12.

" 'Shall we let out some more? We can always wind it back.' " *PM* 13 Oct. 1941: 4.

"BAD NEWS," "GOOD NEWS." *PM* 15 Oct. 1941: 1.

" 'Looks Like the Boys Are Changing Their Game Laws' " *PM* 17 Oct. 1941: 6.

" 'No . . . YOU'RE supposed to shove him over MY back!' " *PM* 19 Oct. 1941: 5. Repr. Minear 105.

" 'Now what in blazes am I going to use for Jews?' " *PM* 20 Oct. 1941: 19.

"The End of the Trail." *PM* 21 Oct. 1941: 7.

"GOPSTRICH: 'He's a noisy little so-and-so, but, sweetheart, he's all ours!'" *PM* 22 Oct. 1941: 4.

"GOPSTRICH: STOP ALL U.S. PROGRESS." *PM* 24 Oct. 1941: 9.

"'Atta Boy, Sam-Bird! Keep Your Sword at Splitting Hairs!'" *PM* 27 Oct. 1941: 21.

"A Brave Knight and True *(But a darn poor judge of horses)*." *PM* 28 Oct. 1941: 21.

"'The Lord Giveth, and the Lord Taketh Away . . .'" *PM* 30 Oct. 1941: 21.

"*AND NOW, KIDDIE-WIDDIES, WE TAKE YOU TO MADISON SQUARE GARDEN WHERE UNCLE LINDY-WINDY WILL SING 'THERE AIN'T NO BOGEY MAN NOW!'*" *PM* 31 Oct. 1941: 21.

"WINDBAGS OF AMERICA: '. . . and speaking of Fires, ladies and gentlemen, reminds me of a couple dozen rather lengthy stories . . .'" *PM* 3 Nov. 1941: 10. Repr. Minear 203.

"'Today's the Big Day, Folks. Vote Early and Often!'" *PM* 4 Nov. 1941: 18.

"'So help me Gott, I was aggressed against! He blitzed mein Fist mit his Eye!'" *PM* 5 Nov. 1941: 21.

"'You may fire when I am damn good and ready, Gridley!'" *PM* 7 Nov. 1941: 5. Repr. Minear 47.

"It's a Cinch, Adolf . . . Once You Learn to Play It." *PM* 10 Nov. 1941: 20. Repr. Minear 84.

"'Gimme some kerosene, some excelsior and a blow torch. Ma wants to bake a cake.'" *PM* 11 Nov. 1941: 4. Repr. Minear 140.

"'Well, It Looks Like the Mighty Hunter Has Us Convinced.'" *PM* 12 Nov. 1941: 1. Repr. Minear 176.

"'Write a piece called *Mare Nostrum*, and make it good and strong!'" *PM* 14 Nov. 1941: 20. Repr. Minear 129.

"BLITZ BUGGY DE LUXE." *PM* 18 Nov. 1941: 22. Repr. Minear 238.

"'I'll uncork your ears for this news any day, Fritz!'" *PM* 19 Nov. 1941: 19. Repr. *Town Meeting: Bulletin of America's Town Meeting of the Air* (Columbia University Press), 1 Dec. 1941: 8. Repr. Minear 66.

"A Toast to *Next* Thanksgiving: '*Here's hoping we're not the bird!*'" *PM* 20 Nov. 1941: 21.

"The New Fuehrer." *PM* 23 Nov. 1941: 4.

"'Don't look now . . . but I think there's a new exhibit!'" *PM* 25 Nov. 1941: 8. Repr. Minear 48.

"'Presenting a symphony of artists assembled from the twelve great capitals of the world!'" *PM* 27 Nov. 1941: 20. Repr. Minear 85.

"Final Warning: '*You gimme a brick to bean you with, or I'll paste you with a pie!*'" *PM* 28 Nov. 1941: 20. Repr. Minear 141.

"'If I chew you up, honey, it's only to save you from the British!'" *PM* 30 Nov. 1941: 1.

"GOOD NEWS." *PM* 1 Dec. 1941: 1.

"BEWARE! I CAN BE VELLY DANGEROUS WHEN AROUSED!" *PM* 1 Dec. 1941: 20. Repr. Minear 142.

"'. . . anyhow, we're capturing the most Foreign Correspondents!'" *PM* 2 Dec. 1941: 20.

"'Vote with care in November '42, and you'll never get hurt in a war!'" *PM* 3 Dec. 1941: 20.

"'Master! What do I do when they won't come across?'" *PM* 5 Dec. 1941: 20. Repr. Minear 143.

"He Never Knew What Hit Him." *PM* 8 Dec. 1941: 20. Repr. Minear 28.

"The End of the Nap." *PM* 9 Dec. 1941: 14. Repr. Minear 144.

"'Maybe only alley cats, but Jeepers! a hell of a lot of 'em!'" *PM* 10 Dec. 1941: 14. Repr. Minear 145.

"GOOD NEWS," "GOOD NEWS," "GOOD NEWS." *PM* 12 Dec. 1941: 1.

"Don't Let Them Carve THOSE Faces on Our Mountains!: BUY UNITED STATES SAVINGS BONDS AND STAMPS!" *PM* 12 Dec. 1941: 22. Repr. Minear 146.

"CAGES COST MONEY! Buy More U.S. Savings Bonds and Stamps!" *PM* 15 Dec. 1941: 1.

"You Can't Kill Japs Just by Shooting Off Your Mouth!" *PM* 16 Dec. 1941: 22. Repr. Minear 204.

"Please, Uncle Henri . . . won't you take this up with Santa?'" *PM* 17 Dec. 1941: 22.

Seuss's American Bird. Repr. with Thomas Campbell's letter to the editor, "A Mighty Bird in Any Guise." *PM* 18 Dec. 1941: 22. Repr. Minear 23.

"'Quick, Henry, THE FLIT!': U.S. DEFENSE BONDS + STAMPS." *PM* 19 Dec. 1941: 1. Repr. Minear 106.

"BUNDLES FOR BENITO." *PM* 22 Dec. 1941: 22. Repr. Minear 130.

"The Latest Self-Portrait." *PM* 23 Dec. 1941: 22. Repr. Minear 86.

"They're serving Roast Adolf at Joe's House tonight!'" *PM* 24 Dec. 1941: 22. Repr. Minear 168.

"'Boss, maybe you'd better hock me and buy more U.S. Defense Bonds and Stamps!'" *PM* 26 Dec. 1941: 22. Repr. Minear 239.

"ADOLF FRANKENSTEIN, M.D.: 'Patience! The table is just a wee mite crowded!'" *PM* 29 Dec. 1941: 22.

"Time to swap the old book for a set of Brass Knuckles!" *PM* 30 Dec. 1941: 22. Repr. Minear 107.

"The Battle of the Easy Chair." *PM* 31 Dec. 1941: 22. Repr. Minear 205.

"HAPPY NEW YEAR! But, Boy! What a Hangover!" *PM* 1 Jan. 1942: 23. Repr. Minear 108.

"'Doktor! I got frozen up here, and sunburned down here . . . all at the very same time!'" *PM* 2 Jan. 1942: 22. Rpt. in "Malice in Wonderland," *Newsweek* 9 Feb. 1942: 58.

"WAR MONUMENTS No. 1: JOHN F. HINDSIGHT . . ." *PM* 5 Jan. 1942: 22. Repr. in "Malice in Wonderland," *Newsweek* 9 Feb. 1942: 58. Repr. in *Town Meeting: Bulletin of America's Town Meeting of the Air* (published by Columbia University Press), 23 Mar. 1942: 28. Repr. Minear 195.

"WAR MONUMENTS No. 2: WATER WEEPER . . ." *PM* 6 Jan. 1942: 22. Repr. Minear 196.

"Tire Shortage Solved." *PM* 7 Jan. 1942: 22. Repr. Minear 131.

"WAR MONUMENTS No. 3: DAME RUMOR . . ." *PM* 8 Jan. 1942: 22. Repr. Minear 197.

"ROLL HIM FLAT WITH THE OLD PAY-ROLLER." *PM* 9 Jan. 1942: 22. Repr. Minear 240.

"Girdle Shortage." *PM* 12 Jan. 1942: 22. Repr. Minear 241.

"WAR MONUMENTS No. 4: TO JOHN HAYNES HOLMES." *PM* 13 Jan. 1942: 22. Repr. Minear 198.

"'Scram! We're busy listening to Sumner Welles!'" *PM* 15 Jan. 1942: 22.

"The Wonders of Russian Science." *PM* 16 Jan. 1942: 22.

"WAR MONUMENTS No. 5: ERECTED IN HONOR OF The WISHFUL LISTENERS." *PM* 18 Jan. 1942: 19. Repr. Minear 199.

"'Champ, Ain't It About Time We Tied on the Other Glove?'" *PM* 19 Jan. 1942: 22.

"Mein Early Kampf: I give the hotfoot to the stork that brings me." *PM* 20 Jan. 1942: 22. Repr. Minear 87.

"Mein Early Kampf: I reject milk from Holstein cows as Non-Aryan." *PM* 21 Jan. 1942: 22.

"Dr. Seuss's Rebuttal." [letter from Dr. Seuss.] *PM* 21 Jan. 1942: 22.

"Latest Modern Home Convenience: Hot and Cold Running Subs." *PM* 22 Jan. 1942: 22.

"Still Two More Daisies to Go . . ." *PM* 23 Jan. 1942: 22.

"The Stench of the Scented Isles." *PM* 26 Jan. 1942: 22.

"The Tail of the Boxing Kangaroo." *PM* 27 Jan. 1942: 22.

"Mein Early Kampf: I cut my first tooth on a Bust of Bismark." *PM* 29 Jan. 1942: 21.

"'How'd I get into this danged thing?'" *PM* 30 Jan. 1942: 21.

"Fly Him Out of the Sky!" *PM* 2 Feb. 1942: 21. Repr. Minear 206.

"Red Tape." *PM* 3 Feb. 1942: 21. Repr. Minear 207.

"'Knots in my tail . . . !'" *PM* 4 Feb. 1942: 21.

"That Man is Back Again." *PM* 5 Feb. 1942: 21.

"'Yeah . . . but who takes over when the big guy's time is up?'" *PM* 6 Feb. 1942: 21. Repr. Minear 162.

"Still Cooking With Goebbels Gas." *PM* 9 Feb. 1942: 21. Repr. Minear 49.

"Complacency." *PM* 10 Feb. 1942: 23. Repr. Minear 208.

" 'Those Americans sure can attack . . . themselves!' " *PM* 11 Feb. 1942: 22. Repr. Minear 224.

" 'Hm-m! Can't Understand It!' " *PM* 12 Feb. 1942: 21.

"Waiting for the Signal From Home . . ." *PM* 13 Feb. 1942: 21. Repr. Minear 65.

" 'Funny . . . Some people never learn to keep their barn doors locked.' " *PM* 16 Feb. 1942: 21.

"*Keep count of those foxholes!* YOU'RE the guy Who's got to win 'em back!" *PM* 17 Feb. 1942: 21. Repr. Minear 147.

"Our Big Bertha." *PM* 18 Feb. 1942: 21. Repr. Minear 209.

" 'Now don't tip the red cap too much! You know how I hate Russians.' " *PM* 19 Feb. 1942: 21. Repr. Minear 169.

"SHUX! WE CAN WHIP THE JAPS WITH ONE HAND TIED BEHIND US!" *PM* 20 Feb. 1942: 21.

" 'Hurry Up With That Ark!' " *PM* 23 Feb. 1942: 21. Repr. Minear 178.

"Time to get up and Face the new day!" *PM* 24 Feb. 1942: 23. Repr. Minear 210.

" 'I don't like the color of that guy's tie!' " *PM* 25 Feb. 1942: 21. Repr. Minear 225.

"Our 42d Street MacArthurs" *PM* 26 Feb. 1942: 21.

"Are We Mice or Are We Men?" *PM* 27 Feb. 1942: 21.

"SQUAWK! AGAINST BRITAIN." *PM* 2 Mar. 1942: 21.

"*No More Scorched Earth!* LET'S BLISTER THEIR BRITCHES!" *PM* 4 Mar. 1942: 21. Repr. Minear 242.

"WHAT HAVE YOU DONE TODAY TO HELP SAVE YOUR COUNTRY FROM THEM?" *PM* 5 Mar. 1942: 21. Repr. Minear 148.

"WHAT HAVE YOU DONE TODAY TO SPEED UP?" *PM* 6 Mar. 1942: 21. Repr. Minear 243.

"Why Do We Sit and Take It?" *PM* 9 Mar. 1942: 21. Repr. Minear 226.

"Mighty Trapper . . . But He Misses the Big Ones." *PM* 10 Mar. 1942: 21. Repr. Minear 227.

"Gnawing at Our Life Line." *PM* 11 Mar. 1942: 21. Repr. Minear 177.

"Measuring Up a Couple of Prospects." *PM* 12 Mar. 1942: 21. Repr. Minear 109.

"Patty-Cake on a Time Bomb." *PM* 13 Mar. 1942: 23.

"Awkward Predicament . . . For YOU to Solve." *PM* 16 Mar. 1942: 21.

"Sure an' one day while you celebrate . . ." *PM* 17 Mar. 1942: 21. [note: island labelled IRELAND] Repr. Minear 88.

"Stopping Will Never Save the House . . *You Gotta Smash Those Pots!*" *PM* 18 Mar. 1942: 21.

"What do YOU expect to be working at after the war?" *PM* 19 Mar. 1942: 21. Repr. Minear 89.

"You Can't Build A Substantial V Out of Turtles!" *PM* 20 Mar. 1942: 21. Repr. Minear 244.

"Berlin Repeats a Berlin Story . . . And Laughs." *PM* 24 Mar. 1942: 19. Repr. Minear 75.

"Speaking of Railroads . . . *Here's* One to Take Over!" *PM* 23 Mar. 1942: 21. Repr. Minear 50.

" 'I Hear the Americans Are Stripping Their Gears Again!' " *PM* 24 Mar. 1942: 21. Repr. Minear 228.

"Gassing the Troops on Our Own Front Line." *PM* 26 Mar. 1942: 22. Repr. Minear 67.

"EXACTLY ONE YEAR AGO TODAY the people of JUGOSLAVIA STOOD UP AGAINST HITLER!" *PM* 27 Mar. 1942: 21.

" 'Not bad, Coughlin . . . but when are you going to start printing it in German?' " *PM* 30 Mar. 1942: 6. Repr. Minear 51.

"A Chance to Fight for His OWN Freedom." *PM* 31 Mar. 1942: 22. Repr. Minear 179.

" 'Come on, Sam . . . Try the Great German Manicure!' " *PM* 1 Apr. 1942: 21.

"Awkward Place to Be Arguing About Contracts" *PM* 2 Apr. 1942: 21. Repr. Minear 180.

"Second Creation." *PM* 3 Apr. 1942: 21. Repr. Minear 90.

"Do YOU Belong to One of These Groups?" *PM* 6 Apr. 1942: 21. Repr. Minear 211.

"THE GAS YOU BURN UP IN YOUR CAR IN ONE WHOLE YEAR. . . . WOULD ONLY TAKE A LIGHT TANK 653 MILES!" *PM* 7 Apr. 1942: 21.

"Beware the Man Who Makes a Fortune in a Flood!" *PM* 8 Apr. 1942: 21. Repr. Minear 245.

"The One Thing You Can't Hoard Is TIME!" *PM* 9 Apr. 1942: 22.

"'Hold her, Newt! Get her down on the road!'" *PM* 13 Apr. 1942: 22.

"'*I'll* run Democracy's War. *You* stay In your Jim Crow Tanks!'" *PM* 14 Apr. 1942: 21. Repr. Minear 56.

"'Marianne . . . look what the cat brought back!'" *PM* 15 Apr. 1942: 22. Repr. Minear 157.

"'Don't look now, pal, but you'll be needing a bigger Flute!'" *PM* 16 Apr. 1942: 20.

"Don't Kid Yourself. If He Shoots The Works You're Sunk!" *PM* 19 Apr. 1942: 19.

"The Old Tobacco Juice Where It Counts!" *PM* 20 Apr. 1942: 21. Repr. Minear 149.

"'Just a harmless little game we call Popping the Commander-in-Chief!'" *PM* 21 Apr. 1942: 22. Repr. Minear 229.

"'Doc, give my eyes a bit of a slant. I've joined the Japanese Navy.'" *PM* 22 Apr. 1942: 20.

"When the Sucker Season Opens, Don't You Bite!" *PM* 23 Apr. 1942: 21.

"'GOD MADE ME A RABBLE-ROUSER!'" *PM* 26 Apr. 1942: 19.

"The OLD GRUDGE of 42d Street." *PM* 28 Apr. 1942: 21.

"'He thinks we oughta save his cash register, too!'" *PM* 29 Apr. 1942: 14. Repr. Minear 246.

"The OLD GRUDGE of 42d Street: *Sauerkraut Symphony*." *PM* 30 Apr. 1942: 21. Repr. Minear 230.

"ONE BUCK OUT OF EVERY 10!" *PM* 1 May 1942: 21.

"The Gateway to India." *PM* 4 May 1942: 21. Repr. Minear 181.

"At Last, a New Weapon . . . Our Counteroctopus." *PM* 6 May 1942: 15.

"'LOOK! I weep for the Honor of France!'" *PM* 7 May 1942: 19.

"Then there was a man who was SO LOW, he could walk under a Dachshund's belly." *PM* 8 May 1942: 21. Repr. Minear 111.

"Giving the Axis a Lift." *PM* 11 May 1942: 13. Repr. Minear 110.

"'ME . . . ? Oh, I'm the Climax of the Act!'" *PM* 12 May 1942: 21. Repr. Minear 150.

"When the Punching Bag Socks the Champ—That's NEWS." *PM* 13 May 1942: 22.

"SO LONG AS MEN CAN DO THIS THEY'RE FREE!" *PM* 14 May 1942: 22. Repr. Minear 221.

"'*Nuts!* We drive 50 miles for the view, and now look at that ugly smoke!'" *PM* 17 May 1942: 19.

"'We're just going to knock out the Unnecessary Floors designed by F.D.R!'" *PM* 18 May 1942: 21. Repr. Minear 68.

"Designed Exclusively for Going UP." *PM* 19 May 1942: 22.

"THESE ARE YOUR LIGHTS, MISTER!" *PM* 20 May 1942: 21. Repr. Minear 247.

"'I might drive here. I might drive there. Or I MIGHT just drive around the corner for an aspirin!'" *PM* 21 May 1942: 19.

"'Isn't it just swell about the War being over!'" *PM* 22 May 1942: 18. Repr. Minear 212.

"YOU, TOO, CAN SINK U-BOATS" *PM* 24 May 1942: 20. Repr. Minear 15.

"Society of Red Tape Cutters Elects Roosevelt." *PM* 25 May 1942: 3. Repr. Minear 188.

"The Optimist's Picnic." *PM* 25 May 1942: 21. Repr. Minear 213.

"Attention, Voters of the 26th N.Y. District:" *PM* 26 May 1942: 21.

"Saber Rattling (By Remote Control)." *PM* 28 May 1942: 21. Repr. Minear 69.

"Assure you, this is merely *tail* of snake. Fang part is in other direction." *PM* 29 May 1942: 21.

"'Yes, I guess as people go, he's just about the smallest!'" *PM* 1 June 1942: 21.

"Biddle: '. . . and protect my beddie from the Communist Boogey Man!'" *PM* 2 June 1942: 4.

"'Yeah, but Bub, I'm still queen of your Eastern seaboard!'" *PM* 3 June 1942: 21. Repr. Minear 91.

"*THIS* GUN'S FOR YOU, JOE, TO PROTECT ME FROM THE NAZIS . . ." *PM* 4 June 1942: 21.

"More Red Tape Cutters Honored." *PM* 5 June 1942: 12.

"No Sign Yet of Sagging Morale." *PM* 5 June 1942: 21. Repr. Minear 92.

"Hey, You Talent Scouts, Give a Look Down!" *PM* 8 June 1942: 21. Repr. Minear 70.

"'Well, well! Seems to be a slight shifting of the Japanese current!'" *PM* 9 June 1942: 14.

"What This Country Needs Is a Good Mental Insecticide." *PM* 10 June 1942: 22. Repr. Minear 57.

" 'Schmidt, I want you should 5th-Column a bit around Hell. A lot of us may be going there one of these fine days.' " *PM* 11 June 1942: 22. Repr. Minear 93.

" 'All I'm doing, pal, is converting you birds of paradise into working carrier pigeons!' " *PM* 12 June 1942: 13.

" 'Me? Why I'm just going my own independent American way!' " *PM* 15 June 1942: 22. Repr. Minear 231.

"Stretching for Every Autograph in Town!" *PM* 16 June 1942: 21.

" 'As one cockroach to another . . . don't you think Laval goes a bit too far?' " *PM* 17 June 1942: 19.

"Many Happy Returns!" *PM* 18 June 1942: 21.

" 'Not a bad tone, pal, but what I want is more volume!' " *PM* 19 June 1942: 21. Repr. Minear 158.

"Churchill Joins Red Tape Cutters" *PM* 22 June 1942: 14.

" 'Himmel! We've been standing here exactly one year!' " *PM* 22 June 1942: 21.

" 'NEWS NOTE: War production drives report sick and injured war workers lose 6,000,000 work days every month." *PM* 23 June 1942: 21. Repr. Minear 248.

" 'A balloon barrage . . . but not against bombs. It's designed to protect the mind against facts!' " *PM* 24 June 1942: 21. Repr. Minear 249.

"Neutrality Mixture . . . Guaranteed to Bite the Tongue!" *PM* 25 June 1942: 21.

"The Old Run-Around." *PM* 26 June 1942: 20. Repr. Minear 58.

" 'After him, Sam! It's a Robin RED-Breast!' " *PM* 28 June 1942: 12.

" 'Listen, maestro . . . if you want to get *real* harmony, use the black keys as well as the white!' " *PM* 29 June 1942: 22. Repr. Minear 59.

" 'Say, isn't it about time you obstructionists turned that old rubber in?' " *PM* 30 June 1942: 21.

" '. . . and although I obstructed the purchase of a fire engine, I'm really the type of leader you ought to elect again!' " *PM* 1 July 1942: 22.

"G-Man Hoover Joins Red Tape Cutters." *PM* 2 July 1942: 12.

"No Shortage." *PM* 2 July 1942: 21.

"With Adolf in Egypt: 'Stop them praying with heads toward Mecca!' " *PM* 3 July 1942: 21. Repr. Minear 94.

"Caesar and Cleopatra." *PM* 6 July 1942: 21.

" 'End of the line, sir. From here on you walk.' " *PM* 7 July 1942: 14. Repr. Minear 214.

" 'There seems to be a white man in the woodpile!' " *PM* 8 July 1942: 22. Repr. Minear 60.

" 'Remember, now . . . you can come up *so* high, but *no* higher!' " *PM* 9 July 1942: 22.

"Warming Up the Springboard." *PM* 10 July 1942: 21.

" 'Fascinating Problem . . . how'll we Yanks cut the world up after we win the war?' " *PM* 13 July 1942: 21.

"The ALIBI BOYS: 'You know . . . their act is beginning to strike me as a trifle corny.' " *PM* 14 July 1942: 23. Repr. Minear 215.

" 'If you expect me to win this war, Mr. Voter, keep your Katzenjammer kids at home!' " *PM* 15 July 1942: 22. Repr. Minear 232.

" 'Easy, There, EASY! *No Acrobat Is Fall-Proof!*' " *PM* 16 July 1942: 14. Repr. Minear 233.

" 'Strange . . . with all the priorities . . . that they still let us run full-blast!' " *PM* 17 July 1942: 21.

" 'Only God can make a tree . . .' " *PM* 20 July 1942: 21. Repr. Minear 101.

" 'Carry on, my faithful dogs, and you shall each share equally!' " *PM* 21 July 1942: 22. Repr. Minear 132.

"THE KNOTTY PROBLEM OF CAPITOL HILL." *PM* 22 July 1942: 22. Repr. Minear 216.

" 'Jeepers! It's time I took this problem *seriously!*' " *PM* 23 July 1942: 21. Repr. Minear 250.

"What Are You Chasing Most, Pal . . . Butterflies or Skunks?" *PM* 24 July 1942: 22.

"'Aw, relax! I'm a guide you can lean on heavily!'" *PM* 27 July 1942: 21.

"INSURE YOUR HOME AGAINST HITLER!" *PM* 28 July 1942: 30. Repr. Minear 14.

"With Adolf in Egypt: 'The New Humped-Dachshund you ordered . . .'" *PM* 28 July 1942: 21. Repr. Minear 112.

"The Guy Who Makes a Mock of Democracy." *PM* 29 July 1942: 22.

"In the Bottom of the Hour Glass." *PM* 30 July 1942: 21.

"'You know, it might be I'm just not destined to soar!'" *PM* 31 July 1942: 19.

"The Tiller of the Soil." *PM* 3 Aug. 1942: 21.

"ROME TOWN BOY MAKES GOOD." *PM* 4 Aug. 1942: 22. Repr. Minear 133.

"Speaking of Giant Transports . . ." *PM* 5 Aug. 1942: 21. Repr. Minear 217.

"Velvet Carpet to the Oil Well." *PM* 6 Aug. 1942: 20. Repr. Minear 170.

"'But, mein lieber louse Laval . . . it isn't how many Frenchmen you *bite*, it's how many you really *infect!*'" *PM* 7 Aug. 1942: 19. Repr. Minear 102.

"Still Spraying Our Side With Disunity Gas!" *PM* 10 Aug. 1942: 22. Repr. Minear 234.

"It Won't Be Long Now Before He Trots THIS Out Again!" *PM* 11 Aug. 1942: 22. Repr. Minear 218.

"'Could you lend us some of that energy, pal? We'd really like to win this war!'" *PM* 12 Aug. 1942: 22.

"Playing Musical Chairs . . . For Keeps and With Experts." *PM* 13 Aug. 1942: 21. Repr. Minear 151.

"Man Power That *Could* Be Winning the War . . ." *PM* 14 Aug. 1942: 21.

"'I don't like to brag, boys . . . but when I bit Col McCormick it established the greatest all-time itch on record!'" *PM* 17 Aug. 1942: 21. Repr. Minear 235.

"'If we had some ham, we could have a Real Production Omelette right now . . . if we had some eggs . . .'" *PM* 18 Aug. 1942: 22. Repr. Minear 251.

"'You can keep your American eagle. I got a bird all my own!'" *PM* 19 Aug. 1942: 22. Repr. Minear 61.

"'But nobody wants to attack the scrap right in his own back yard!'" *PM* 20 Aug. 1942: 22. Repr. Minear 252.

"We'll Need Changes in the Old Victory Band Before We Parade in Berlin." *PM* 21 Aug. 1942: 21. Repr. Minear 219.

"'The Pattersons 'n' McCormick is keepin' it warm so's we can crawl back inta it after the war.'" *PM* 24 Aug. 1942: 22. Repr. Minear 52.

"'Gee, It's All Very Exciting . . . But It *Doesn't Kill Nazi Rats.*'" *PM* 26 Aug. 1942: 21. Repr. Minear 236.

"'Tck! Tck! Now he writes it looks like he'll need dot Historical Underwear back!'" *PM* 27 Aug. 1942: 21. Repr. Minear 171.

"'Gif a quick look, Schultz, for fingerprints. Der guilty one must be punished!'" *PM* 28 Aug. 1942: 21.

"'Yeah . . . but 10% of his income for War Bonds. That's a different matter." *PM* 31 Aug. 1942: 22.

"'Between you and me, what this country needs is a Beefless Day!'" *PM* 1 Sept. 1942: 22.

"Society of Red Tape Cutters: Maj. Gen. Alexander A. Vandergrift." *PM* 2 Sept. 1942: 18.

"'Boy, am *I* having trouble with *Me!*'" *PM* 2 Sept. 1942: 21.

"Hershey Awarded Tape Cutters Scroll." *PM* 4 Sept. 1942: 11.

"INSURE YOUR HOME AGAINST HITLER! Buy WAR SAVINGS BONDS & STAMPS." *PM* 4 Sept. 1942: 18.

"Cheer up, boys! Your Congress is going to declare an all-out war . . . after those November elections.'" *PM* 4 Sept. 1942: 21.

"On Guard [Tape Cutters: Admiral Stanley V. Parker]." *PM* 7 Sept. 1942: 21.

"Randolph Paul Gets Tape Cutter Award." *PM* 10 Sept. 1942: 13.

"OWI Official Given Tape Cutter Award [Paul C. Smith]." *PM* 13 Sept. 1942: 11.

"Tape Cutter Diploma Goes to Rep. Ramsay" *PM* 14 Sept. 1942: 13.

"Speaking of Decorations . . ." *PM* 22 Sept. 1942: 22.

" 'Don't worry pal. We plan to raise or lower you from time to time, so you'll always hang, nicely, at parity!' " *PM* 23 Sept. 1942: 21.

" 'How's *Your* Scrap Drive? *Mine*'s doing fine!' " *PM* 24 Sept. 1942: 21.

" 'You see it's like this . . . Congress simply abolishes the ceiling, and from now on we say it's a floor.' " *PM* 25 Sept. 1942: 21. Repr. Minear 253.

"Pledge of Allegiance." *PM* 28 Sept. 1942: 22.

" 'Come on, you. Get in there and fight!' " *PM* 29 Sept. 1942: 21.

"Can't Pound It Into His Head!" *PM* 30 Sept. 1942: 21. Repr. Minear 220.

" 'She Says the Government Can Have Her Zipper, If the Government Can Get It Unjammed!' " *PM* 1 Oct. 1942: 21. Repr. Minear 254.

"**IF** ALL OF US WERE FIGHTING AS HARD AS **YOU** ARE . . . **WHO** WOULD WIN THE WAR, AND HOW SOON?" *PM* 2 Oct. 1942: 21.

"WHAT? Roosevelt went all the way to the Coast and he didn't tell *ME*?" *PM* 5 Oct. 1942: 21.

" 'Now for Pete's sake, if you want to *keep* things within reach, keep plenty of knots in that rope!' " *PM* 6 Oct. 1942: 21.

" 'Food? We Germans don't eat *food*! We Germans eat countries!' " *PM* 7 Oct. 1942: 21. Repr. Minear 95.

" 'Instead of the Stalingrad Victory Parade, originally scheduled for this time, we bring you a talk by Colonel Schmaltz of the Gestapo on his recent experiences in Norway!' " *PM* 8 Oct. 1942: 21. Repr. Minear 96.

"Down the River." *PM* 9 Oct. 1942: 21. Repr. Minear 159.

"Democracy's Turnstile." *PM* 12 Oct. 1942: 21. Repr. Minear 71.

"WIPE THAT SNEER OFF HIS FACE!" PM 13 Oct. 1942: 19. Repr. Minear 16.

"Crisis in the High Command" *PM* 13 Oct. 1942: 22. Repr. Minear 104.

"Beware the Vendor of Breakable Toys!" *PM* 14 Oct. 1942: 21.

"He's testing das new secret weapon for 1943 . . ." *PM* 15 Oct. 1942: 21. Repr. Minear 97.

"Times are certainly getting hard. No Ruffles on our Lamb Chops!" *PM* 16 Oct. 1942: 21.

" 'Another little trip back through the wringer, and man, you'll be yourself again!' " *PM* 19 Oct. 1942: 21. Repr. Minear 160.

" 'This new Victory Spaghetti, gentlemen, contains 100% of Hole . . . our resources for the production of which are practically inexhaustible!' " *PM* 20 Oct. 1942: 21. Repr. Minear 134.

"Your Nutty Aunt Carrie Is Loose Again!" *PM* 22 Oct. 1942: 21.

" 'I appeal to the civilized world in righteous protest. . . . . . against American barbarism and inhumanity!' " *PM* 23 Oct. 1942: 21. Repr. Minear 152.

" 'Training again . . . There's a rumor the '44 Olympics might be held right here in Rome!' " *PM* 26 Oct. 1942: 21.

"HOW DOES THIS AFFECT YOU AND ME?" *PM* 1 Nov. 1942: 18. Rpt. 18 Feb. 1943: 8.

"YOU, Too, CAN SINK U-BOATS. BUY U.S. WAR SAVINGS, BONDS & STAMPS." *PM* 1 Nov. 1942: 19.

"Unexpected Meeting in Darkest Africa." *PM* 9 Nov. 1942: 5.

"A New Pet from the Sewers of Paris." *PM* 10 Nov. 1942: 15.

"Try and Pull the Wings Off These Butterflies, Benito!" *PM* 11 Nov. 1942: 21. Repr. Minear 135.

"Tin Can for the Tail of the Soaring Dachshund." *PM* 12 Nov. 1942: 22.

"Slightly Diverted." *PM* 13 Nov. 1942: 21. Repr. Minear 98.

"Buck Bilbo Rides Again." *PM* 16 Nov. 1942: 13. Repr. Minear 72.

"Jitters a la Duce." *PM* 17 Nov. 1942: 21. Repr. Minear 136.

" 'Truly embarrassing, O Son of Heaven . . . 40,000 men lose face with body unfortunately attached thereto!' " *PM* 18 Nov. 1942: 21. Repr. Minear 153.

" 'Be calm, BE CALM! One way or another, I'll pull you through!' " *PM* 19 Nov. 1942: 21. Repr. Minear 99.

" 'Lose your way, bud?' " *PM* 20 Nov. 1942: 7.

" 'Hold tight, I'm switching to reverse! . . . Remember the gear we used so much last winter?' " *PM* 24 Nov. 1942: 21. Repr. Minear 113.

"Darlan announces ze program is sponsored by Petain. But Petain announces HE is sponsored by ze Consolidated Berlin Wurst Works!" *PM* 25 Nov. 1942: 21.

"Thanksgiving, 1942." *PM* 26 Nov. 1942: 21.

" 'Did you have turkey at your house? I had dachshund at mine." *PM* 27 Nov. 1942: 20. Repr. Minear 114.

"Piping the New Admiral Abroad." *PM* 30 Nov. 1942: 21.

"He's still strong on the Luft . . . but where's the Waffe?" *PM* 1 Dec. 1942: 21.

" 'Are your bags packed, Sir? They're exhibiting you in the Museum.' " *PM* 2 Dec. 1942: 21. Repr. Minear 137.

"Don't Lean on It Too Hard, Pal!" *PM* 3 Dec. 1942: 21.

"I would like to take this opportunity to prophesy a white Christmas!" *PM* 4 Dec. 1942: 21. Repr. Minear 100.

"Married Exactly One Year Today." *PM* 7 Dec. 1942: 21. Repr. Minear 154.

"We *could* move back into this one . . . or shall we look for something else?" *PM* 8 Dec. 1942: 21.

"Helium-Filled Easy Chair." *PM* 9 Dec. 1942: 20.

" 'If peace ever breaks out, we might be caught short with too-little-and-too-late!' " *PM* 10 Dec. 1942: 21.

"Busy as Beavers!" *PM* 14 Dec. 1942: 22. Repr. Minear 53.

" 'This year I'm afraid my kiddies suspect who I really am!' " *PM* 15 Dec. 1942: 18.

" 'Put your finger here, pal . . .' " *PM* 16 Dec. 1942: 18. Repr. Minear 63.

"WHO . . . ME?" *PM* 16 Dec. 1942: 18. Repr. Minear 106.

" 'Crawl Out and Round Me Up Another 400,000 Frenchmen!' " *PM* 17 Dec. 1942: 18. Repr. Minear 103.

"A Peculiar Family Is Economics." *PM* 18 Dec. 1942: 18.

" 'We may not be reaching the End of the End, but it may be the Beginning of the Beginning!' " *PM* 21 Dec. 1942: 18.

"Maybe it's none of our business . . . but How much are YOU giving This Christmas in U. S. War Bonds and Stamps?" *PM* 22 Dec. 1942: 18. Repr. Minear 255.

" 'ALL ABOARD . . . if you insist! But if you really want to help the Army, *stay at home!*'" *PM* 23 Dec. 1942: 18. Repr. Minear 256.

" 'Jeepers! Just what we asked Santa Claus not for!' " *PM* 24 Dec. 1942: 18.

"With a Whole World to Rebuild . . ." *PM* 25 Dec. 1942: 2. Repr. Minear 54.

"The Man Who Wears His Flag Upon His Belly." *PM* 28 Dec. 1942: 18. Repr. Minear 257.

"We'll Have to Clean a Lot of Stuff Out Before We Put Peace Thoughts In!" *PM* 30 Dec. 1942: 18. Repr. Minear 64.

"Blow, Benito! You Remember . . . B-L-O-W . . . BLOW!" *PM* 31 Dec. 1942: 18.

"The Kidnapper." *PM* 1 Jan. 1943: 18. Repr. Minear 55.

"But the Piper Must Pay." *PM* 4 Jan. 1943: 18.

"The Veteran Recalls the Battle of 1943." *PM* 5 Jan 1943: 18. Repr. Minear 258.

" 'It's hard for a guy to make out what's going on when the sandstorms keep getting in his eyes!' " *PM* 6 Jan. 1943: 18.

"The Oil Burning Dragon," or "Joe Stalin's GAS STATION Plenty Miles Ahead." n.d. UCSD: MSS 0230, MC-128–09.

"Just because I use your umbrella, don't get the idea we're friends." Feb. 1942. UCSD: MSS 0230, MC-128–09.

"You know, sometimes I'm tempted to chuck it all and take up my music again." 1942. UCSD: MSS 0230, MC-128–09.

"Choking only *this* chicken, and *she* say she does not mind!" Jan. 1942. UCSD: MSS 0230, MC-128–09. Note: written at bottom of cartoon is "Sorry! 20 minutes late." Presumably, the cartoon was not used because it arrived 20 minutes after *PM*'s deadline.

"The Old Gun on the Wall Goes Off!" n.d. UCSD: MSS 0230, MC-128–09.
"His first letter in almost a year. . ." June 1942. UCSD: MSS 0230, MC-128–09.

Other Political Cartoons

"OVER THE HILLS." *New York Sun* 13 Oct. 1937: 25.
"THE FORGOTTEN MAN." *New York Sun* 18 Oct. 1937: 21
"And last night Col. Lindbergh said. . . ." *SOS [Share Our Strength]* 16 May 1941: 2.
"Ceiling? Heck! She's growing through the *ROOF!*" *Victory* 28 Apr. 1942: 5.
"TO WIN THIS WAR . . . MORE PEOPLE HAVE GOT TO ENJOY RIDING IN FEWER CARS." *Victory* 19 May 1942: 17.
"YEAH, BUT THINK OF THOSE UNFORTUNATE PEOPLE AT HOME WHO'LL HAVE TO WALK TO THE MOVIES!" *Victory* 26 May 1942: 17.
"YOU KNOW, DEAR. . . . SOMETIMES I WISH WE'D GONE EASY ON OUR TIRES BACK IN 1942!" *Victory* 16 June 1942: 17.
"ARE YOU ACCEPTING DOUBLE CHINS?" *Victory* 14 July 1942: 9.
"ONE FACTORY, ONE UNION, ONE GUARD." *Victory* 11 Aug. 1942: 17.
"Don't YOU Work too hard, now . . . It's bad for MY Health!" *Highway Traveler* Feb.–Mar. 1943: 30.
"Dr. Seuss, brilliant prewar political cartoonist, came out of retirement, looked at the current American scene, and temporarily retired again." [a.k.a. "COMMUNIST!"] *New Republic* 28 July 1947: 7.
"Leave Something Green." *San Diego Magazine* Dec. 1972: cover.
"Pardon me, sir . . . but which way to the nearest park?" *San Diego Union*, c. 1972–1973. UCSD: MSS 0230, Box 18, Folder 54.
"Dope! You Need It Like You Need a Hole in the Head!" *San Diego Tribune* c. 1986.

Art not *in* The Secret Art of Dr. Seuss

The Happy Grasshopper. 1928. Pencil and watercolor. Collection of Audrey Geisel. Reproduced in "The Art of Dr. Seuss: A Retrospective on the Artistic Talent of Theodor Seuss Geisel" (2003).
The Rape of the Sabine Women. c. 1930. Painting originally displayed above the Dartmouth Club bar, 37th Street, New York. Reproduced on cover of *Dartmouth Alumni Magazine*, Feb, 1975.
The Kangaroo Bird. c. 1930s. Sculpture featured in "Unusual Occupations" (Paramount, 1940; full citation with "Profiles and Interviews") and on PBS' *Antiques Roadshow*. <http://www.pbs.org/wgbh/pages/roadshow/appraiseit/game64/1a.html>. 2003.
The Flowerpot Walrus. c. late 1930s. Sculpture featured in "Unusual Occupations" (Paramount, 1940; full citation with "Profiles and Interviews") .
The Seagoing Hornswaggle. c. late 1930s. Sculpture featured in "Unusual Occupations" (Paramount, 1940; full citation with "Profiles and Interviews") .
Two in the Bush. n.d. Painting. Caption is "The two in the bush that the one in the hand is worth more than." Reproduced in "The Art of Dr. Seuss: A Retrospective on the Artistic Talent of Theodor Seuss Geisel" (2003).

Play by Theodor Geisel

"Chicopee Surprised." Described on the program as "A one-act Comedy," this piece was performed at Springfield's Central High School Auditorium, 29 April 1921, 8 p.m. No manuscript survives. Program is at UCSD, MSS 0230, Box 1, Folder 12.

Animated Short Films

The character of Private SNAFU was created by Theodor Geisel (Dr. Seuss), P. D. Eastman, and Chuck Jones. Authorship of individual scripts is not known, but Geisel is considered the author of "The Home Front" and all eight verse cartoons: "Gripes," "Spies," "The Gold-brick," "The Infantry Blues," "Fighting Tools," "Rumors," "Going Home," and "The Chow Hound." He and Munro Leaf are believed to be co-authors of "It's Murder, She Says . . ." See Morgan and Morgan (pp. 109–11) and Eric O. Costello's "Private SNAFU and Mr. Hook" (*ANiMATO!* 37, pp. 44–57).

"Coming SNAFU." Dir. Chuck Jones. Warner Bros., June 1943.
"Private SNAFU: Gripes." Dir. Friz Freleng. Warner Bros., July 1943.
"Private SNAFU: Spies." Dir. Chuck Jones. Warner Bros., Aug. 1943.
"Private SNAFU: The Goldbrick." Dir. Frank Tashlin. Warner Bros., Sept. 1943.
"Private SNAFU: The Infantry Blues." Dir. Chuck Jones. Warner Bros., Sept. 1943.
"Private SNAFU: Fighting Tools." Dir. Bob Clampett. Warner Bros., Oct. 1943.
"Private SNAFU: The Home Front." Dir. Frank Tashlin. Warner Bros., Nov. 1943.
"Private SNAFU: Rumors." Dir. Friz Freleng. Warner Bros., Dec. 1943.
"Private SNAFU: Booby Traps." Dir. Bob Clampett. Warner Bros., Jan. 1944.
"Private SNAFU: SNAFUperman." Dir. Friz Freleng. Warner Bros., Mar. 1944.
"Private SNAFU: SNAFU vs. Malaria Mike." Dir. Chuck Jones. Warner Bros., Mar. 1944.
"Private SNAFU: A Lecture on Camouflage." Dir. Chuck Jones. Warner Bros., Apr. 1944.
"Private SNAFU: Gas." Dir. Chuck Jones. Warner Bros., May 1944.
"Private SNAFU: Going Home." Dir. Chuck Jones. Warner Bros., May 1944.
"Private SNAFU: The Chow Hound." Dir. Frank Tashlin. Warner Bros., June 1944.
"Private SNAFU: Censored." Dir. Frank Tashlin. Warner Bros., July 1944.
"Private SNAFU: Outpost." Dir. Chuck Jones. Warner Bros., Aug. 1944.
"Private SNAFU: Payday." Dir. Friz Freleng. Warner Bros., Sept. 1944.
"Private SNAFU: Target SNAFU." Dir. Friz Freleng. Warner Bros., Oct. 1944.
"Private SNAFU: A Few Quick Facts: Inflation." Dir. Osmond Evans. UPA, Nov. 1944.
"Private SNAFU: Three Brothers." Dir. Friz Freleng. Warner Bros., Dec. 1944.
"Private SNAFU: In the Aleutians." Dir. Chuck Jones. Warner Bros., Feb. 1945.
"Private SNAFU: A Few Quick Facts: Fear." Dir. Zack Schwartz. UPA, Apr. 1945.
"Private SNAFU: It's Murder, She Says." Dir. Chuck Jones. Warner Bros., May 1945.
"Private SNAFU: Hot Spot." Dir. Friz Freleng. Warner Bros., July 1945.
"Private SNAFU: No Buddy Atoll." Dir. Chuck Jones. Warner Bros., Oct. 1945.
"Private SNAFU Presents Seaman TARFU." Dir. George Gorman. Harman-Ising, Jan. 1946.
"Gerald Mc Boing-Boing." UPA, 1950.

Film Scripts

Your Job in Germany. Dir. Frank Capra. 1945. Later released as *Hitler Lives?* Warner Bros., 1945.
With Helen Palmer Geisel. *Design for Death*. Narr. Kent Smith, Hans Conried. RKO Radio Pictures, 1947.
The 5,000 Fingers of Dr. T. Dir. Roy Rowland. Screenplay by Dr. Seuss and Allan Scott. Story, conception, and lyrics by Dr. Seuss. Music by Frederick Hollander. Perf. Peter Lind Hayes, Mary Healy, Hans Conried, Tommy Rettig. Columbia Pictures Corp., 1953.

Television Scripts

"Modern Art on Horseback: TV-Radio Workshop of the Ford Foundation" Excursion #19. NBC-TV. 31 Jan. 1954, 4:00–4:30 p.m., EST.

"Omnibus TV-Radio Workshop of the Ford Foundation: Dr. Seuss Explores the Museum That Ought to Be." Dir. Lee Rothberg. Perf. Dr. Seuss. Mar. 1956.

Animated Television Specials

"How the Grinch Stole Christmas." 1966.
"Horton Hears a Who." 1969.
"The Cat in the Hat." 1971.
"The Lorax." 1972.
"Dr. Seuss on the Loose." 1973
"Hoober Bloob Highway." 1975.
"Halloween Is Grinch Night." 1977.
"Pontoffel Pock Where Are You?" 1980.
"The Grinch Grinches the Cat in the Hat." 1982.
"The Butter Battle Book." 1989.

Secondary Sources about Dr. Seuss

Books

See also the collections of Dr. Seuss's work (listed above), especially Marschall in *The Tough Coughs as He Ploughs the Dough*, Stofflet and Brezzo in *Dr. Seuss from Then to Now*, Fadiman in *Six By Seuss*, Sendak in *The Secret Art of Dr. Seuss*, Minear and Spiegelman in *Dr. Seuss Goes to War*.

Cohen, Charles D. *The Seuss, the Whole Seuss, and Nothing But the Seuss: A Visual Biography.* New York: Random House. Forthcoming in February, 2004.

Fensch, Thomas. *The Man Who Was Dr. Seuss: The Life and Work of Theodore Geisel.* Xlibris Corp, 2001. Biography, but adds little to the information provided by the Morgans.

———, ed. *Of Sneetches and Whos and the Good Dr. Seuss: Essays on the Life and Writing of Theodor Geisel.* Jefferson, North Carolina, and London: McFarland & Company, 1997. This useful volume gathers a selection of profiles, interviews, and analytical articles.

Foran, Jill. *My Favorite Writer: Dr. Seuss.* Mankato, MN: Weigl Publishers, 2003. Brief, illustrated juvenile biography.

Greene, Carol. *Dr. Seuss: Writer and Artist for Children.* Chicago: Children's Press, 1993. Juvenile biography.

Lathem, Edward Connery. *Who's Who and What's What in the Books of Dr. Seuss.* Hanover, NH: Dartmouth College, 2000. Repr. <http://www.dartmouth.edu/~drseuss/whoswho.pdf>. Alphabetically arranged concordance of people, places and things in the "Dr. Seuss Books of Theodor Seuss Geisel" (i.e., it does not cover the books written under other names).

———, ed. *Theodor Seuss Geisel: Reminiscences & Tributes.* Introductory note by Audrey S. Geisel. Hanover, NH: Dartmouth College, 1996. Published in a limited edition of 2,000 copies. From 1991 memorial service, remarks made by Victor H. Krulak, Jed Mattes, Judith & Neil Morgan, Herbert Cheyette, Chuck Jones, and Robert L. Bernstein.

MacDonald, Ruth K. *Dr. Seuss.* New York: Twayne, 1988. The first book-length critical study analyzes Seuss's books through 1987.

Morgan, Judith, and Neil Morgan. *Dr. Seuss and Mr. Geisel.* New York: Random House, 1995. The definitive biography and the single best secondary source on Seuss. Any discussion of Seuss's life and work must begin with this book.

Nel, Philip. *Dr. Seuss: American Icon*. New York and London: Continuum Publishing, 2004. The second book-length critical study (MacDonald's is the first).

Weidt, Maryann. *Oh, the Places He Went: A Story About Dr. Seuss—Theodor Seuss Geisel*. Minneapolis: Carolrhoda, 1994. Thorough juvenile biography, based on original research.

Wheeler, Jill C. *Dr. Seuss*. Edina, Minn.: Abdo & Daughters, 1992. Brief juvenile biography, illustrated with five photos of Seuss and photos of other people and events.

Younger, Helen, Marc Younger, and Daniel Hirsch. *First Editions of Dr. Seuss Books: A guide to identification*. Saco, Maine: Custom Communications, 2002. The book reproduces front and rear dust jackets of almost all first editions.

Films

"In Search of Dr. Seuss." Directed by Vincent Patterson. Perf. Kathy Najimy, Matt Frewer, Robin Williams, Christopher Lloyd. Turner Pictures, 1994.

"An Awfully Big Adventure: The Making of Modern Children's Literature. [Dr. Seuss.]" Produced and directed by Roger Parsons. Narrated by Connie Booth. Feat. Christopher Cerf, Herb Cheyette, Bernice Cullinan, Michael Frith, Audrey Geisel, Chuck Jones, Judith Morgan, Neil Morgan, Peggy Owens, Robert Sullivan, Phyllis Cerf Wagner. London: BBC, 1998.

"A&E Biography: Dr. Seuss." A&E. 16 Nov. 2003.

Exhibition Catalogues

"The Art of Dr. Seuss: A Retrospective on the Artistic Talent of Theodor Seuss Geisel." Chicago, IL: The Chase Group, 2003.

Cohen, Charles D. "The Seuss, the Whole Seuss, and Nothing But the Seuss." Exhibition catalogue. Springfield, Mass.: Connecticut Valley Historical Museum, 2002.

Minear, Richard H. "The Political Dr. Seuss." Exhibition catalogue. Springfield, Mass.: Connecticut Valley Historical Museum, 2000.

Literary Criticism

In addition to literary-critical articles and chapters, this section includes selected essays, essay-reviews and editorials.

Arakelian, Paul G. "Minnows into Whales: Integration Across Scales in the Early Styles of Dr. Seuss." *Children's Literature Association Quarterly* 18.1 (Spring 1993): 18–22. Analyzing the relationship between words and pictures, contends that *Mulberry Street* and *McElligot's Pool* deploy "an aesthetic based on accretion."

Bader, Barbara. "Dr. Seuss." *American Picturebooks from Noah's ark to the Beast Within*. New York: Macmillan, 1976. 302–12. Overview and analyses, focusing on *Mulberry Street*, *500 Hats*, *Bartholomew and the Oobleck*, *Horton Hatches the Egg*, *Thidwick*, *Horton Hears a Who!*, *If I Ran the Circus*, *On Beyond Zebra*, and *The Cat in the Hat*.

Bailey, John P. Jr. "Three Decades of Dr. Seuss." *Elementary English* 42 (Jan. 1965): 7–12. Sees Seuss's work as falling into three periods: pre-war ("a period of initial experimentation in the children's story field"), 1947–1957 (Seuss's highly inventive "middle period"), and the "crass marketing approach" of works produced since then.

Barrs, Myra. "Laughing Your Way to Literacy." *Times Educational Supplement* 23 Jan. 1976: 20–21. A Briton's perspective on Seuss's appeals, which include humor, "comic strip pictures," and wordplay. Also speculates on why the books took time to catch on in Britain.

Begak, Boris. "Gora idet k Magometu." *Detskaya Literatura* Oct. 1976: 34–37. In Russian.

Benzel, Jan. "Dr. Seuss Finally Transcended the Gender Barrier." *New York Times* 20 Jan. 1995. Repr. Fensch 181–83. On reading *Daisy-Head Mayzie*, the author reflects on gender in Dr. Seuss.

Bodmer, George R. "The Post-Modern Alphabet: Extending the Limits of the Contemporary Alphabet Book, from Seuss to Gorey." *Children's Literature Association Quarterly* 14.3 (Fall 1989): 115–17. Considers *Dr. Seuss's ABC, The Cat in the Hat Comes Back* and *On Beyond Zebra!* among "anti-alphabet books" that "reflect the anti-didactic mood of our time."

Boyd, Brian. "The Origin of Stories: *Horton Hears a Who.*" *Philosophy and Literature* 25.2 (2001): 197–214. Offering an "evolutionary analysis," the eminent scholar and biographer of Nabokov argues that *Horton* is a "timeless tale" that appeals to the shared interests of all humankind.

Bracey, Earnest N. "American Popular Culture and the Politics of Race in Dr. Seuss' The Sneetches." *Popular Culture Review* 10.2 (Aug. 1999): 131–37. Points out that *The Sneetches* suggests ways in which Americans might overcome prejudice.

Burns, Thomas A. "Dr. Seuss's *How the Grinch Stole Christmas:* Its Recent Acceptance into the American Popular Christmas Tradition." *New York Folklore* 2:3–4 (Winter 1976): 191–204. First surveys major literary criticism to date, then examines how the Grinch has become a Christmas tradition: its symbolism is always "positively associated with the Whos" and largely avoids explicit references to Christian symbols; the Grinch combines the themes of Scrooge, Santa Claus, and materialism.

Butler, Francelia. "Seuss as a Creator of Folklore." *Children's Literature in Education* 20.3 (1989): 175–81. Focuses on folk rhymes, poetry, and satire in *The Lorax, Horton Hatches the Egg, Butter Battle Book, Fox in Socks, Cat in the Hat, Hop on Pop,* and others.

Cech, John. "Pictures and Picture Books on the Wall." *Children's Literature* 19 (1991): 179–88. Review of *Dr. Seuss From Then to Now* offers insightful comments on Seuss's art, and the genres in which he works.

———. "Some Leading, Blurred, and Violent Edges of the Contemporary Picture Book." *Children's Literature* 15 (1987): 197–206. Considers *The Butter Battle Book* in the context of such works as Raymond Briggs's *The Tin-Pot Foreign General and the Old Iron Woman*, David Macaulay's *Baaa*, and Roberto Innocenti's *Rose Blanche*.

Chénetier, Marc. "Robert Coover for President! (A turning of the tables, 'flaunting the rules of the game')." *Delta: Revue du Centre d'Etudes et de Recherche sur les Ecrivains du Sud aux Etats Unis* 28 (June 1989): 53–62. In French: treats Robert Coover's "The Cat in the Hat for President."

Cianciolo, Patricia. *Illustrations in Children's Books.* Second Edition. Dubuque, IA: Wm. C. Brown Company Publishers, 1976. 50, 99. Brief discussion of *Horton Hatches the Egg*, mention of *Mulberry Street, King's Stilts, 500 Hats, Cat in the Hat*.

Cobb, Clay. "Script Comments: The Grinch Who Stole Christmas." *Creative Screenwriting* 7.6 (Nov.–Dec. 2000): 10. Favorable review of the screenplay of Ron Howard's film.

Costello, Eric O. "Private SNAFU & Mr. Hook." *ANiMATO!: The Animation Fan's Magazine* 37 (Spring 1997): 44–57. The single best source on Private SNAFU, includes production history, as well as analyses, synopses and running times.

Deans, Jill R. "Horton's Irony: Reading the Culture of Embryo Adoption." *Interdisciplinary Literary Studies: A Journal of Criticism and Theory* 2.1 (Fall 2000): 1–20. Sees "Horton's irony—the desire for the adopted and the biogenetic hybrid—as an expression of the conflict between cultural values that influence the American family."

Disch, Thomas M. "The Essential Dr. Seuss." *Entertainment Weekly* 31 May 1991: 68–70. Brief comments on "10 of Dr. Seuss' best books."

Dohm, Janice H. "The Curious Case of Dr. Seuss: A Minority Report from America." *Junior Bookshelf* 27 (Dec. 1963): 323–29. As Seuss's books are being published in Britain, the article thinks them unworthy of their popularity: they have a "facile sort of knock-about word play," "most of the pictures are downright ugly and the texts are often tiresome and sometimes vulgar." Also finds the morals "heavy-handed." However, considers the Beginner Books "a welcome change from 'See funny, funny baby'" and wonders if Seuss will "prove the all-American Lear."

Fadiman, Clifton. "Professionals and Confessionals: Dr. Seuss and Kenneth Grahame." *Only Connect: Readings on Children's Literature*. Ed. Sheila Egoff, G. T. Stubbs, and L. F. Ashley. Toronto: Oxford UP, 1980. Sees Grahame as a "confessional writer" of children's books, and Seuss as a "professional writer" of children's books: that is, Grahame's life emerges in his art, and Seuss's does not.

Flesch, Rudolf. "The Lilting World of Mr. Ted Geisel." *Los Angeles Times* 19 July 1959. The author of *Why Can't Johnny Read?* calls Dr. Seuss "a genius pure and simple."

Galbraith, Mary. "Agony in the Kindergarten: Indelible German Images in American Picture Books." *Text, Culture and National Identity in Children's Literature: International Seminar on Children's Literature, Pure and Applied*. University College Worcester, England, June 14th–19th, 1999. Ed. Jean Webb. Helsinki: Edita Ltd., 2000. 124–43. Reads *Mulberry Street* and H. A. Rey's *Curious George* in terms of intersections between the author-illustrators' lives and "German and American history and identity."

Gough, John. "The Unsung Dr. Seuss: Theo LeSieg." *Children's Literature Association Quarterly* 11.4 (Winter 1986–87): 183–86. Includes a letter from Seuss on the origins of his other alias, Theo. LeSieg. Surveys the LeSieg books, finding resonances between them and some Seuss books.

Greenleaf, Warren T. "How the Grinch Stole Reading: The Serious Nonsense of Dr. Seuss." *Principal* 61 (1982): 6–9. Repr. Fensch 91–97. With "a serious though sketchy theory of reading behind them," Seuss's books appeal to both children and adults because the "bump-biddy-bump meter" is fun to read aloud, and the "daffy" plots are enjoyable. Also provides a biography.

Hearn, Michael Patrick, Trinkett Clark, and H. Nicholas B. Clark. *Myth, Magic, and Mystery: One Hundred Years of American Children's Book Illustration*. Norfolk (VA), Boulder (CO), and Dublin (Ireland): Roberts Rinehart Publishers and the Chrysler Museum of Art, 1996. 47, 49, 76, 96, 97, 101, 108, 121, 122. Offers brief analyses of and reprints manuscript pages from *On Beyond Zebra!*, *The Cat in the Hat*, the Grinch, *Horton Hatches the Egg*, *500 Hats*, and *Yertle the Turtle*.

Jenkins, Henry. "'No Matter How Small': The Democratic Imagination of Dr. Seuss." *Hop on Pop: The Politics and Pleasures of Popular Culture*. Ed. Jenkins, Tara McPherson, Jane Shattuc. Durham and London: Duke UP, 2002. 187–208. Focuses on the Popular Front politics of Seuss's books, and how they fostered democratic ideals. Required reading for anyone interested in Chapter 2 of *Dr. Seuss: American Icon*.

Kidd, Sue Monk. "Turning Loose." *Guideposts* Sept. 1991. Repr. Fensch 177–80. The memoirist and novelist offers a sentimental reflection on Dr. Seuss, as her son heads off to college.

Lanes, Selma G. "Seuss for the Goose Is Seuss for the Gander." *Down the Rabbit Hole: Realism and Misadventures in the Realm of Children's Literature*. New York: Atheneum, 1971. 79–89. Repr. Fensch 45–51. Argues that Seuss's books provide "a safety valve" for children's anxieties, and says that Seuss himself is always allied "with the child's free spirit." Focuses on *The Cat in the Hat*, *Mulberry Street*, "King Louis Katz," *500 Hats*, *Yertle the Turtle*, *The King's Stilts*, and *On Beyond Zebra*.

Lebduska, Lisa. "Rethinking Human Need: Seuss's *The Lorax*." *Children's Literature Association Quarterly* 19.4 (Winter 1994–95): 170–76. Argues that *The Lorax* dramatizes a conflict between environmentalism and consumer culture, and asks us to examine which need (nature or economics) is greater. Article also provides "overview of anthropocentrism's role in children's culture."

Lurie, Alison. "The Cabinet of Dr. Seuss." *The New York Review of Books* 20 Dec. 1990: 50–52. Repr. Fensch 155–64. Notes that Seuss's books address both children and adults, promote the imagination, and often offer an "anti-establishment moral"; however, the books lack female protagonists, and presents what few female characters there are in an unflattering light. Concludes with a reading of *Oh, the Places You'll Go!*, claiming that it departs from earlier works by suggesting that happiness "is equated with wealth."

Lystad, Mary. "The Cat in the Hat." *From Mother Goose to Dr. Seuss: 200 Years of American Books for Children.* Boston: G. K. Hall, 1980. 196–201. Brief overview of Seuss's life, followed by extensive quotation from and short explication of *The Cat in the Hat.*

Marshall, Ian. "The Lorax and the Ecopolice." *ISLE: Interdisciplinary Studies in Literature and Environment* 2.2 (Winter 1996): 85–92. Suggests that the Once-ler may in fact be a more sympathetic character than the Lorax: the Once-ler has good qualities (inventive, shares wealth with family), and the Lorax (failed spokesman for nature).

May, Jill P. "Dr. Seuss and *The 500 Hats of Bartholomew Cubbins.*" *The Bulletin: Newsletter of The Children's Literature Assembly of National Council of Teachers of English* 11.3 (1985): 8–9. Argues that Seuss's contribution to children's literature resides not in his Beginner Books but in his earlier folkloric tales, such as *500 Hats.* Reads book in context of folklore conventions, and compares it to Carroll's *Alice's Adventures in Wonderland*, Leaf's *The Story of Ferdinand*, and Sendak's *Where the Wild Things Are.*

McArthur, Tom. "English to Order." *English Today* 5 (Jan. 1986): 27–29. Includes Seuss among those writers who create works intended to help beginning readers, non-English speakers, or people with learning disabilities.

Menand, Louis. "Cat People: What Dr. Seuss Really Taught Us." *New Yorker* 23 & 30 Dec. 2002: 148–54. Rehearses biographical details from Morgans' biography, and offers psychoanalytic readings of *The Cat in the Hat* and *The Cat in the Cat Comes Back.* Analyzes both *Cat* books and, more generally, the Beginner Books in the context of the Cold War.

Mensch, Betty, and Alan Freeman. "Getting to Solla Sollew: The Existential Politics of Dr. Seuss." *Tikkun* 2.2 (1987): 30–34, 113–17. Argues that the books' "discourse of resistance" empowers children to develop "new selves, liberated from orthodox assumptions" and forms of oppression. Examines Freudian and religious themes of *The Cat in the Hat*, reads *Solla Sollew* as advocating struggle against adversity, and interprets "political stories" *Yertle, The Sneetches, The Lorax,* and *The Butter Battle Book.* Also discusses lessons of *Horton Hatches the Egg, Thidwick, Horton Hears a Who!, The Grinch,* and *You're Only Old Once!*

Moje, Elizabeth B., and Woan-Ru Shyu. "Oh, the Places You've Taken Us: *The Reading Teacher's* Tribute to Dr. Seuss." *Reading Teacher* May 1992. Repr. Fensch 191–98. Assembles biographical details from various sources, offers general praise of Dr. Seuss.

Moynihan, Ruth B. "Ideologies in Children's Literature: Some Preliminary Notes." *Children's Literature* 2 (1973): 166–72. Examines the ways in which Baum's *The Wizard of Oz*, Milne's *Winnie-the-Pooh*, Piper's *The Little Engine that Could*, Burton's *The Little House*, and Seuss's *Horton Hears a Who!* reflect the political ideologies of their time.

Nel, Philip. "Dada Knows Best: Growing Up 'Surreal' with Dr. Seuss." *The Avant-Garde and American Postmodernity: Small Incisive Shocks.* Jackson and London: UP of Mississippi, 2002. 41–72. A revised version of an article that first appeared in *Children's Literature* 27 (1999): 150–84. On modernism, postmodernism, nonsense, and the political uses of the avant-garde in many books, notably *The Cat in the Hat, The Cat in the Hat Comes Back, The Butter Battle Book, The Lorax,* and *On Beyond Zebra!*

———. "The Disneyfication of Dr. Seuss: Faithful to Profit, One Hundred Percent?" *Cultural Studies* 17.5 (Sept. 2003). An earlier version of Chapter 5 of *Dr. Seuss: American Icon.*

———. "'Said a Bird in the Midst of a Blitz . . .': How World War II Created Dr. Seuss." *Mosaic: A Journal for the Interdisciplinary Study of Literature* 34.2 (June 2001): 65–85. <http://www.umanitoba.ca/publications/mosaic/backlist/2001/June/nelessay34–2 .html>. An earlier version of Chapter 2 of *Dr. Seuss: American Icon.*

Nikolajeva, Maria, and Carole Scott. *How Picturebooks Work.* New York: Garland Publishing, 2001. 29, 78, 214–17, 242. Emphasis on how Seuss exploits the gap between signifier and signified.

Nilsen, Don L. F. "Dr. Seuss as Grammar Consultant." *Language Arts* 54 (May 1977): 567–72. This analysis of "grammatical deviations in thirty-four Seuss books written between 1937 and 1973" argues that Seuss violates the rules of grammar on purpose, praising his "innovative" morphology, syntax, and neologisms.

Nodelman, Perry. *Words About Pictures: The Narrative Art of Children's Picture Books*. Athens and London: Georgia UP, 1988. 44, 47, 60–61, 99, 113–114, 127, 142–144, 149, 255. Focuses on aspects of *Horton Hatches the Egg*, especially design, color, and perspective.

Ort, Lorrene Love. "Theodore [*sic*] Seuss Geisel—The Children's Dr. Seuss." *Elementary English* 32 (March 1955): 135–42. Enthusiastic biography (mostly paraphrasing stories TSG tells of himself) and enthusiastic analysis of books up to 1954. Touches on art, layout, movement, satire, and language.

Quindlen, Anna. "The One Who Had Fun." *New York Times* 28 Sept. 1991: 19. Posthumous tribute offers perceptive analysis of Seuss's poetry.

Raymo, Chet. "Dr. Seuss and Dr. Einstein: Children's Books and Scientific Imagination." *The Horn Book* Sept.–Oct. 1992. Repr. Fensch 169–75. Points out that Seussian plants are animals are no stranger than those found in nature, and suggests that books such as Seuss's help children to cultivate "a scientific attitude towards the world." They do so because childhood is the best time to learn the "habits of mind crucial for science," which Raymo identifies as "[c]uriosity, voracious seeing, sensitivity to rules and variations within the rules, and fantasy."

Reimer, Mavis. "Dr. Seuss' *The 500 Hats of Bartholomew Cubbins*: Of Hats and Kings." *Touchstones: Reflections on the Best in Children's Literature. Volume 3: Picture Books*. Ed. Perry Nodelman. West Lafayette, IN: Children's Literature Association, 1989. 132–42. Speculates on lack of literary criticism on Seuss, suggests Seuss's connections to fairy tales, and investigates deeper meanings of *500 Hats*.

Renthal, Helen. "25 Years of Working Wonder with Words." *Chicago Tribune* 11 Nov. 1962. Repr. Fensch 37–39. Praises Dr. Seuss for creating characters that "express a kind of freedom from conventional ways of thinking."

Ross, Suzanne. "Response to 'The Lorax and the Ecopolice' by Ian Marshall." *ISLE: Interdisciplinary Studies in Literature and Environment* 2.2 (Winter 1996): 99–104. Suggests that the Lorax would be more persuasive if his rhetoric made use of Kenneth Burke's notion of the poetic metaphor.

Roth, Rita. "On Beyond Zebra with Dr. Seuss." *New Advocate* Fall 1989. Repr. Fensch 141–53. Influenced by Mensch and Freeman, sees Seuss's books as offering "a cultural discourse about power relations, as a kind of rhetoric of opposition and possibility." Also examines prejudice against Seuss within "children's literature establishment," and provides classroom applications for teachers.

"Rx From Dr. Seuss." *New Republic* 26 Mar. 1984: 4, 42. A Republican interpretation of Seuss's political books claims that *The King's Stilts* "is unabashedly Reaganite," *Horton Hatches the Egg* has a "theme of welfare dependency," *Thidwick* is about "big government," and *The Butter Battle Book* provides a "defective" analysis of the Cold War.

Sale, Roger. *Fairy Tales and After: From Snow White to E. B. White*. Cambridge, MA: Harvard UP, 1978. 8–12. Sees *The 500 Hats* as somewhere between realism and the fairy tale, and suggests that the pleasure of the story resides in the tension between control (we know that the hats will stop at 500) and mystery ("how did all these hats get on Bartholomew's head?").

Schichler, Robert L. "Understanding the Outsider: Grendel, Geisel, and the Grinch." *Popular Culture Review* 11.1 (Feb. 2000): 99–105. Compares Seuss's Grinch to *Beowulf*'s Grendel, and explores TSG's identification with the Grinch.

Schroth, Evelyn. "Dr. Seuss and Language Use." *Reading Teacher* 31 (April 1978): 748–50. Catalogues the ways in which Seuss plays with language.

Smith, James Steel. "The Comic Style of Dr. Seuss." *A Critical Approach to Children's Literature*. New York: McGraw-Hill Book Company, 1967. 313–14. Discusses Seuss's "comic art," dismisses his verse. On pp. 209–10, offers a brief analysis of Seuss's humor. Other references occur on pp. 49, 74, 125–26, 176, 182, 187, 190, 204, 211, 221–222, 310, 326–27, and 346–48.

Snyder, C. R. and Kimberley Mann Pulvers. "Dr. Seuss, the coping machine, and 'Oh the Places You'll Go.'" *Coping with Stress: Effective People and Processes*. Ed. C. R. Snyder. Oxford and New York: Oxford University Press, 2001. 3–29. In context of psychological research on coping (to which most of the article is devoted), shows how *Oh, the Places You'll Go!* and *Oh, the Thinks You Can Think* teach the coping process.

Spiegelman, Art. "Horton Hears a Heil." *New Yorker* 12 July 1999: 62–63. A shorter version of his introduction to Minear's *Dr. Seuss Goes to War*.

Steig, Michael. "Dr. Seuss's Attack on Imagination: *I Wish That I Had Duck Feet* and the Cautionary Tale." *Proceedings of the Ninth Annual Conference of the Children's Literature Association*. Boston, MA: Northeastern University, 1983. 137–41. Freudian reading of *I Wish That I Had Duck Feet*, seen as a cautionary tale "more oppressive" than Heinrich Hoffmann's *Struwwelpeter*. *Duck Feet* encourages "acculturation to a society where imagination is often an object of distrust."

Steinfels, Peter. "Beliefs." *New York Times* 19 Aug. 1995: 9. Description of Naomi Goldenberg's lecture, "A Feminist, Psychoanalytic Exegesis of *The Cat in the Hat*," which reads *The Cat in the Hat Comes Back* as a masculine attempt to overcome womb envy: the Cat gives birth to little alphabetic cats (invents language) in order to erase the role of the mother (removing a menstrual stain from mother's dress and bed).

Stong, Emily. "Juvenile Literary Rape in America: A Post-Coital Study of the Writings of Dr. Seuss." *Studies in Contemporary Satire* 4 (1977): 34–40. Tongue-in-cheek examination of sexual and/or perverse subtexts of *Hop on Pop*, "What Was I Scared Of?", *Dr. Seuss's Sleep Book*, *One Fish*, *The Lorax*, *On Beyond Zebra!*, *Thidwick*, and *500 Hats*.

Sutton, Roger. "Children's Books: Yooks, Zooks and the Bomb." *New York Times* 22 Feb. 1987: 22. Finds all children's books about nuclear war to be overly simplistic, except for Judith Vigna's *Nobody Wants a Nuclear War*.

Touponce, William F. "Children's Literature and the Pleasures of the Text." *Children's Literature Association Quarterly* 20.4 (1995–96): 175–82. Brief discussion of *Mulberry Street* in final paragraphs.

Vandergrift, Kay E. "Planning Encounters with Story." *Child and Story: The Literary Connection*. New York: Neal Schuman, 1980. 180–211. Recounts 5-year-old children graphing the transition "from believe to make-believe" in *And to Think That I Saw It on Mulberry Street*, pp. 189–93.

Wilson, Robert. "Call Your Muse, Dr. Seuss." *Washington Post Book World* 12 Oct. 1980: 8. Says Seuss's imagination does not lead beyond "the pleasures of the moment," and disputes the claim that Seuss's books are classics.

Wolf, Tim. "Imagination, Rejection, and Rescue: Recurrent Themes in Dr. Seuss." *Children's Literature* 23 (1995): 137–64. In *Mulberry Street*, *500 Hats*, *The King's Stilts*, and *Green Eggs and Ham*, Seuss explores a theme of children's imagination provoking parents and children internalizing responsibility for their parents' behavior. Notably, views Sam-I-Am as androgynous.

Wolosky, Shira. "Democracy in America: By Dr. Seuss." *Southwest Review* 85.2 (Spring 2000): 167–83. Seuss "initiates young Americans into their cultural heritage" while "register[ing] tensions lurking within it." In particular, Seuss's work endorses "classic American liberal individualism" while exploring the dangers of extreme individualism. Sees Seuss as heir to Walt Whitman in his "liberal vision of individual integrity as the basis for communal commitment." Works analyzed include the *Horton* books, *The Sneetches*, *Yertle the Turtle*, *Thidwick*, *The Cat in the Hat*, and others.

Zicht, Jennifer. "In Pursuit of the Lorax: Who's in charge of the last Truffula seed?" *EPA Journal* Sept./Oct. 1991: 27–30. Describing *The Lorax* as an "amusing," "thought-provoking," "wholesome and unbiased" book, the article posits it as a model for educating young children about environmental problems. Also reviews other books and resources.

Zornado, Joseph. "Swaddling the Child in Children's Literature." *Children's Literature Association Quarterly* 22.3 (1997): 105–12. In the film of *The Wizard of Oz* and the animated version of *How the Grinch Stole Christmas*, Glinda and the Grinch serve as manipulative, predatory parent figures who inflict traumas upon children (Dorothy, the Whos) and then force children to repress their emotional experience.

Profiles and Interviews

Alderson, Brian. "A perfect 'parent's assistant.'" *Times* (London) 23 Aug. 1972: 16. TSG on sexism in his books.

Associated Press. "Grinch Steals in to Christmas." *Register* (Torrington, Conn.) 20 Dec. 1968. TSG on creating *The Grinch*, animating *The Grinch*, naming his creations, writing *Mulberry Street*.

Bandler, Michael J. "Dr. Seuss: Still a Drawing Card." *American Way* Dec. 1977: 23–26, 28. TSG on TV vs. fantasy, momentum in children's books, writing *The Cat in the Hat*, Theo. LeSieg, graduate school adventures, his cataract operation, his paintings, his drawing style, writing for children, on the kid (Gus) who could draw better than he, the Hearst dictum, and "obsolete children."

————. "For Kids Over the Age of 70." *Newsday* 3 Mar. 1986. 2: 4–5.

————. "Portrait of a Man Reading." *Washington Post Book World* 7 May 1972: 2. TSG on his early reading, favorite children's books, books he read in college, books he reads for fun, the Great American Novel, disappointing books, and humor.

————. "Seuss on the Loose." *Parents* Sept. 1987: 116–20+.

Baldacci, Leslie. "The Dr. Is In." *Chicago Sun-Times* 15 Oct. 1998: 33, 36. On the Chicago Children's Museum's Dr. Seuss exhibit. Comments from Audrey on meeting TSG, Helen, Ted and Helen's lack of children, TSG as sharp even in his final days, and the Grinch.

"Beginner Books: New Trade Learn-to-Read Juveniles." *Publishers Weekly* 2 June 1958. Phyllis Cerf on Beginner Books, TSG, and others.

"Beginner Books." *Publishers Weekly* 4 Jul. 1960: 174, 176. Phyllis Cerf on Beginner Books.

Bell, Terry. "The Saga of Dr Seuss." *N.Z.W.W.* [*New Zealand Weekly?*] 7 June 1976: 20–21. UCSD: MSS 230, Box 36, Folder 22. TSG on Flit, starting to write for children, writing for *PM*, his "bawdy" manuscripts, Yertle as Hitler, *Horton Hears a Who!*, and *Life*'s disastrous revisions to his "Japan's Young Dreams" article (1954),

Berman, Susan. "The Real Dr. Seuss." *Boston Globe* 8 Oct. 1971. TSG on meeting his fans, writing *The Lorax*, publishing *Mulberry Street*, rhyming, and the creative process.

Bernstein, Peter W. "Epitaph: Green Eggs and Me." *U.S. News and World Report* 7 Oct. 1991. Repr. Fensch 201–03. Reminiscences, incl. a drawing based on a childhood remark, TSG using nonsense to get a plumber, and writing to his father (Bob Bernstein) regarding Clarence Thomas being nominated to the Supreme Court.

Beyette, Beverly. "Seuss: New Book on the Tip of His Tongue." *Los Angeles Times* 29 May 1979. Sec. 5: 1, 5. TSG on "Pontoffel Poc," fan mail, the end of "a certain type of fantasy," graduate school, writing *Mulberry Street*, feminism, *The Cat in the Hat*, his books as "escapist," getting rid of Richard Nixon, incompetence in financial matters, *Oh, Say Can You Say?*, dislike of public appearances, and meeting President Theodore Roosevelt.

Bowman, Dick. "Dr. Seuss in La Jolla." *Sentinel* 11 July 1971. TSG on publishing *Mulberry Street*, writing for *PM*, his name, not writing down to kids, his inability to draw, translations of his books, New Zealand, writing for still-younger readers.

"Brief Biographies, 1925—Number 2. Theodor Seuss Geisel." *Dartmouth Alumni Magazine* Mar. 1938. No direct quotations from TSG, but paraphrased stories about graduate school, the Great American Novel, mummy-digging in South America.

Brown, A. S. "When Dr. Seuss did his stuff for Exxon." *The Lamp* Spring 1987: 28–29. TSG on his advertising work.

Bunzel, Peter. "The Wacky World of Dr. Seuss Delights the Child—and Adult—Readers of His Books." *Life* 6 Apr. 1959: 107, 109, 110, 113. Repr. Fensch, 11–13. TSG on drawing, Beginner Books, the Multi-Beasts, visiting a school, drawing animals, morals, logical nonsense, fan mail, fan who claims "Dr. Seuss has an imagination with a big long tail."

Burchell, Sam. "Architectural Digest Visits Dr. Seuss." *Architectural Digest* Dec. 1978: 88–93. Audrey on fans' birthday greetings, TSG on his paintings, house, and work ethic.

"Business at Work." *Investor's Reader* 22 Dec. 1959: 16–17.

Butters, Patrick. "Dr. Seuss' secret series. Whimsical artworks are product of renowned creator's late-night playtime." *Washington Times* 28 Mar. 1999. Audrey on TSG and his art.

Cahn, Robert. "The Wonderful World of Dr. Seuss." *Saturday Evening Post* 6 July 1957: 17–19, 42, 46. TSG on his inability to draw, writing *The Cat in the Hat*, meeting Helen, Flit, the Infantograph, writing and publishing *Mulberry Street*, the Whos, morals, Chrysanthemum-Pearl, "obsolete children"; Helen on TSG's animals, hiding in Grand Central Station to avoid public speaking, and the Whos.

Callan, Louise. "Dr. Seuss' Laundry Once Upon a Time." *Thursday Magazine* [New Zealand] 24 May 1976: 28. On finding a publisher for *Mulberry Street*, writing *Mulberry Street*, and *The Seven Lady Godivas*.

Carlinsky, Dan. "The Wily Ruse of Doctor Seuss." *The Magazine of the Boston Herald American* 4 Mar. 1979: 12–15. TSG on smoking, his early work, drawing animals, teacher criticizing him for turning his paper upside-down, his graduate work, Flit, his novel, *The Seven Lady Godivas*, the business of writing children's books, book-signings, writing *The Cat in the Hat*, *Dr. Seuss's ABC*, fantasy vs. TV, and the causes of illiteracy.

Cerf, Bennett. *At Random: The Reminiscences of Bennett Cerf*. New York: Random House, 153–55. Includes a royalty statement from *The Seven Lady Godivas*, annotated by Seuss; also has a photograph of Cerf and Seuss.

———. "Hilarity in Hollywood." *This Week Magazine* 27 Nov. 1960. TSG, visiting Mexico City "a short while back," is duped by a "fish story."

———. Untitled column. *Saturday Review* 17 July 1954. Neil Morgan relates story of child who, inspired by *Scrambled Eggs Super!*, creates his own inedible dish and gives it to TSG as a present.

Christy, Marian. "A Muse on the Loose." *Boston Globe* 20 July 1980: C1, C5.

Clark, Diane. "He Is Waking Children to a World of Words." *San Diego Union* 19 Dec. 1976: D1, D4. TSG on his name, work habits, inventing words (obsk) and borrowing names (McElligot, Marvin K. Mooney), origin of *Horton Hatches the Egg*, *The Grinch*, *500 Hats*, morals, writing *The Cat in the Hat*, Beginner Books vs. Big Books, art teacher critical of his turning paper upside-down, *Seven Lady Godivas*, audience, and meeting his fans.

Clifford, Jane. "A farewell to Dr. Seuss." *San Diego Tribune* 25 Sept. 1991: C1–C2. TSG on drawing flies, writing for children, fans who visit him, child (Gus) who could draw better than he, Cerf's claim that he was a genius, favoring his "devious" characters, being "part Grinch" himself, not condescending to children, *The Lorax* as "propaganda with a plot," and children's ability to laugh.

Corwin, Miles. "Author Isn't Just a Cat in the Hat." *Los Angeles Times* 27 Nov. 1983. Sec. Metro: 1, 3. First half repr. as Associated Press, "Dr. Seuss contends his books are for all people, not just kids." *Leesburg Commercial* 14 Dec. 1983: 10B. TSG on writing for children, audience, *The Lorax*, *The Butter Battle Book*, nonsense, humor, *The Grinch*, marketing, work habits, writing *The Lorax*, not writing for Hollywood (anymore), his unpublished novel. Also includes comments from Peter Neumeyer and Carol Christ.

Cott, Jonathan. "The Good Dr. Seuss." *Pipers at the Gates of Dawn: The Wisdom of Children's Literature*. New York: Random House, 1983. 1–37. Repr. Fensch 99–123. TSG on success, how his eyesight affected his art, *The Seven Lady Godivas*, his father, Cyril Gaffey Aschenbach, the dinosaur footprint, his inability to draw, the art teacher critical of his turning paper upside-down, *The Travels of Sir John Mandeville*, his graduate work, *Mulberry Street* and "The Erl-King," books he read as a child, the creative process, his responses to Kornei

Chukovsky's rules for composing verse for children, art, *The Cat in the Hat*, killing off Dick and Jane, Beginner Books, being subversive, Hilaire Belloc, *Yertle the Turtle*, *The Sneetches*, *The Lorax*, Includes remarks from Brian Sutton-Smith and Howard Gardner, with quotations from Lanes, Kuskin, Bandler, Lurie and others.

Crichton, Jennifer. "Dr. Seuss Turns Eighty." *Publishers Weekly* 10 Feb. 1984: 22–23. TSG on avoiding birthday well-wishers, *The Butter Battle Book*, morals, audience, reality "viewed through the wrong end of the telescope," accidentally inventing an atomic bomb during WWII, real people as nuttier than him or his books.

"Currents." *Publishers Weekly* 24 Aug. 1959: 23. TSG recalls receiving a letter, with a dollar bill enclosed, from Mrs. Jean C. Brown, whose three-year-old "had just sprinkled merhiolate on the living room rug and forestalled a scolding by telling her that 'Voom' [. . .] would surely clean it off." Mrs. Brown writes to ask for a dollar's worth of Voom or Oobleck, if he's out of Voom. TSG repllies that he is "frightfully embarrassed and terribly upset" but "The transportation of 'Voom' or 'Oobleck,' whether in liquid, solid or gaseous form, across state borders is to be discontinued immediately as a result of a Supreme Court decision (Justice Douglas dissenting)."

"Czar of the Insect World." *Vanity Fair* Dec. 1931. While working on murals for Harkness Edwards's home, TSG spins fanciful stories of his post-secondary education.

Dangaard, Colin. "Dr. Seuss reigns supreme as king of the kids." *Boston Herald American* 21 Nov. 1976. Sec. 5: 1, 3. Dangaard on Seuss books selling in Australia and New Zealand. TSG on "You make 'em, and I'll amuse 'em," audience, not testing his books on children, *Dr. Seuss's ABC*, writing *The Cat in the Hat*, writing for children, teaching reading, his hats, *The Lorax*, the creative process, "obsolete children"; Audrey on living with TSG, TSG's sense of humor.

Dempsey, David. "The Significance of Dr. Seuss." *New York Times Book Review* 11 May 1958: 30. TSG on Beginner Books, teaching children to read, *Yertle the Turtle*, "logical preposterosity," using "implausible facts to create a plausible world."

Diehl, Digby. "Q & A 'Dr. Seuss.'" *Los Angeles Times WEST Magazine* 17 Sept. 1972: 36–39. Repr. *Supertalk*. Garden City, NY: Doubleday & Company, Inc., 1974. 169–79. TSG on advertising, the origins of *Horton Hatches the Egg* and *The Lorax*, his work habits, conflict as key to storytelling, Hearst's "Tears, Laughs, Loves and Thrills" dictum, writing *The Cat in the Hat*, Beginner Books, feminism, racial integration, teaching children to read, Ph.D. theses on his work, *Hitler Lives!*, *The Seven Lady Godivas*, writing children's books as "a sweat-and-blood thing," audience.

"Dr. Seuss." *Wilson Library Bulletin* Nov. 1939: A1. TSG on Dartmouth, Oxford, unpublished novel, cartooning, "Dr. Seuss School of Unorthodox Taxidermy," and *Seven Lady Godivas*.

Dowd, Maureen. "Novel 'Ironweed' and Mamet Play Are Awarded 1984 Pulitzer Prizes." *New York Times* 17 April 1984: A1, B4.

"Dr. Seuss Remembered." *Publishers Weekly* 25 Oct. 1991: 32–33. Repr. Fensch 185–88. Recollections by Gerald Harrison, Janet Schulman, Cathy Goldsmith, Robert Bernstein, Christopher Cerf, Stan and Jan Berenstain.

Duffy, Mike. "Q. Dr. Seuss." *Detroit Free Press* 22 Nov. 1979. TSG on his pseudonym, his great American novel, creating *The Cat in the Hat*, attitudes towards children's writers, rhyme, being interviewed by Dick Cavett on TV, and not condescending to children.

Dummit, Chris. "The Man Behind the Cat in the Hat." *Los Angeles Times* 18 Aug. 1983. Part IB: 7. TSG on meeting his fans, his hat collection, work habits, his ideas, *The Lorax*, verse, his drawing ability, his unfinished novel, children as "smarter than they used to be," *Green Eggs and Ham*, morals, the musical of *The Seven Lady Godivas*.

Dunlap, David W. "Waiting in Fotta-fa-Zee." *New York Times Book Review* 23 Mar. 1986: 39. TSG on *You're Only Old Once!*

Engel, Leigh. "Hats of to special cat on his 80th birthday." *La Jolla Light* 1 Mar. 1984: A1, A3. Features comments by Everett Raymond Kinstler, Kenneth Montgomery, Chuck Jones,

Audrey Geisel, Maurice Sendak, Beatrix Potter (from her 1940s letter), and several TSG quotations from Lathem's interview.

Fleischer, Leonore. "Authors and Editors: Theodor Seuss Geisel." *Publishers Weekly* 2 Dec. 1968: 7–8. TSG on education, Beginner Books, and humor.

Freedman, Jonathan. "Nearing 80, Dr. Seuss still thrills young, old." *San Diego Tribune* 24 Feb. 1984: A1, A12. TSG on graduate school, his unfinished novel, Hemingway, Joyce, magazine work, Flit, origin of *Mulberry Street*, writing for *PM*, the Battle of the Bulge, his documentary films, the baby boom, Beginner Books, and the *Butter Battle Book*.

Freeman, Donald. "The Nonsensical World of Dr. Seuss." *McCall's* Nov. 1964:115 + . TSG on his radish-seed pipe, *Mulberry Street*, his work habits, his paintings, Beginner Books, "obsolete children," where he gets his ideas (Zyblknov), Helen as manager, being Democrats in a Republican city, fan mail, morals, *Horton Hears A Who*.

———. "Who Thunk You Up, Dr. Seuss?" *Authors and Illustrators of Children's Books: Writings on Their Lives and Works*. Ed. Miriam Hoffman and Eva Samuels. New York and London: R. R. Bowker Company, 1972. 165–71. Repr. from *San Jose Mercury News* 15 June 1969. Sec. Parade. 12–13. Fan's "Who thunk you up, Dr. Seuss?" letter; TSG on the creative process, where he gets his ideas (Zybliknov), morals, inability to draw dogs, writing *The Cat in the Hat*, his pseudonyms, his unfinished novel, "obsolete children," *Seven Lady Godivas*, meeting President Theodore Roosevelt, meeting his fans, "You make 'em and I'll amuse 'em,"

Freeman, Don. "Dr. Seuss from Then to Now." *San Diego Magazine* May 1986: 132–39, 242–43. Fan's "Who thunk you up, Dr. Seuss?" letter; TSG on age, *You're Only Old Once!*, meeting child fan with wet hand (George), book-signings in London and Boston where no children show up, not appearing on U.S. TV, New Zealand, meeting President Theodore Roosevelt, his name, his unpublished novel, carrying a bronzed Flit gun on a plane, morals, *The Sneetches*, the Zax, *Green Eggs and Ham*, genius, the creative process, and his next book. Also includes remarks from Steven Brezzo, Sebastian Adler, and Bennett Cerf's "genius" quotation. Lavishly illustrated, including photos, draft manuscript pages.

———. Untitled column. *San Diego Union* 15 Oct. 1973: A-8. Child's letter that asked "Who thunk you up, Dr. Seuss?"; TSG on writing *Green Eggs and Ham*, the Zax, and *The Sneetches*.

———. Untitled column. *San Diego Union* 17 Dec. 1976: B-8. TSG on his inability to draw dogs, TV, being on TV, New Zealand, and eye surgery.

" 'Friends' Visits Dr. Seuss—The Man Who Hatched Thornton and Thidwick." *Friends* Mar. 1962: 8–9. TSG on not being able to fool kids, and on not being able to draw.

Frith, Michael. "Dr. Seuss at Home." *Children's Book Crannie* Jan–Apr. 1973. TSG on his health, sleep habits, and "obsolete children." Frith on TSG's house, work habits, and hat collection.

Frutig, Judith. "Dr. Seuss's green-eggs-and-ham world." *Christian Science Monitor* 12 May 1978: 18–19. Repr. Fensch 77–81. TSG on eating green eggs and ham, his paintings, writing *The Cat in the Hat*, writing for children, his unfinished novel, *I Can Read with My Eyes Shut*, audience, writing for children, TV, teaching children to read, work habits, the creative process, origin of *Horton Hatches the Egg*, *The Lorax*, and *Green Eggs and Ham*.

Fuller, John G. "Trade Winds." *Saturday Review* 14 Dec. 1957: 7–8. TSG on *The Cat in the Hat*.

"Gay Menagerie of Queer Animals Fills the Apartment of Dr Seuss." *Springfield Sunday Union and Republican* 28 Nov. 1937: 5E. Margaretha Dahmen (TSG's sister) offers anecdotes about her brother's early life and current activities.

Gelber, Carol. "A Few Well-Chosen Words for Children Make Dr. Seuss' New Book a Delight." *Philadelphia Bulletin* 14 Nov. 1958. TSG on being an "obsolete child," *The Cat in the Hat*, graduate school, writing *Mulberry Street*, humor, and writing for children.

Georgatos, Dennis. "Dr. Seuss Sets Sights on Adults." *Sunday Rutland Herald*. No date on clipping, but story is a reprint of "Books and Authors: An Adult's Book in a Child Format." *Associated Press* 5 July 1985. Dartmouth, Rauner Library: Alumni G277mi. TSG on *You're Only Old Once!*, work habits, *The Seven Lady Godivas*, adults and children.

Girson, Rochelle. "Juvenile Authors: Some Bows & Encores." *Saturday Review* 11 Nov. 1950: 34–36. TSG on Flit and "mummy digging in Peru." Also brief profiles of William Pène du Bois and others.

———. Profile of Dr. Seuss. *Saturday Review* 11 May 1957: 52. TSG on writing *The Cat in the Hat*, children's sense of humor, and "realizing [his] latent desire to be a professor."

Gordon, Arthur. "The Wonderful World of Soledad Hill." *Woman's Day* Sept. 1965: 74–75, 99–100. "You have 'em, I'll amuse 'em," his paintings, his work habits, his drawing ability, taking children seriously, origin of *Horton Hatches the Egg*, morals, books in translation, Helen on TSG's "instinct for what kids like."

Gorney, Cynthia. "Grinch, Hippo-heimer, Cat in Hat, Wocket, He's Got Generations of Kids in His Pocket." *Washington Post* 21 May 1979: B1, B3. Repr. Fensch 83–89. TSG on *Yertle the Turtle*, turning 75, *Mulberry Street*, books in translation, his Grinch license plate, fan mail, his paintings, his reading habits, "Bunny-bunny books," taking children seriously, the origin of *500 Hats of Bartholomew Cubbins*, fairy tales, *The Lorax*, *The Seven Lady Godivas*, *Oh Say Can You Say?*; Grace Clark on TSG's "sophisticated" color sense.

"The Grinch . . . Now he's someone you can love to hate." *San Diego Union* 23 Dec. 1967: 3. TSG on children's talent for "expressing total disdain," and the Grinch as "pure Bad Guy."

Hacker, Kathy. "Happy 80th Birthday, Dr. Seuss." *Philadelphia Inquirer* 7 Mar. 1984: E1, E8. Repr. as "The ordinary guise of the extraordinary Dr. Seuss." *San Francisco Examiner* 18 Apr. 1984: E9. TSG on meeting his fans, the child (Gus) who could draw better than he, *Yertle the Turtle*, *The Butter Battle Book*, *The Lady and the Tiger*, *Mulberry Street*, *The Cat in the Hat*, writing for children, the musical of *The Seven Lady Godivas*, and his creative process.

Hammond, Sally. "Dr. Seuss: The Man Who Stole Boredom." c. Dec. 1969, Section 3. Dartmouth, Rauner Library: Alumni G277mi. TSG on writing *The Grinch*, identifying with the Grinch, drawing ability, teaching reading, "treating kids as adults," "logical preposterosity," his grandfather and father, the Springfield Zoo, the unpublished novel, graduate school, magazine work, Flit, writing for *PM*, and life in La Jolla.

"A Happy Accident." *Newsweek* 21 Feb. 1972: 100, 103. TSG on *The Lorax*, its TV version, why he got into children's books, children, his drawing style, and his desire to write "a great musical."

Harper, Hilliard. "The Private World of Dr. Seuss: A Visit to Theodor Geisel's La Jolla Mountaintop." *Los Angeles Times Magazine* 25 May 1986. Repr. Fensch 129–34. TSG on politics, seeing things "through the wrong end of the telescope," his inadequacies as an artist, writing in verse, *Seven Lady Godivas*, and getting rid of Dick and Jane. Audrey on TSG's inspiration, work habits.

Hart, William B. "Between the Lines." *Redbook* Dec. 1957: 4. TSG on the Grinch. Includes a self-portrait of Seuss looking in the mirror and seeing a Grinch.

"He makes C-A-T spell big money." *Business Week* 18 July 1964.

Hopkins, Lee Bennett. "Dr. Seuss (Theodor S. Geisel)." *Books Are By People*. New York: Citation Press, 1969. TSG on writing *Mulberry Street*, origin of *Horton Hatches the Egg*, conflict as key to storytelling, writing *The Cat in the Hat*, and "You have 'em, I'll amuse 'em."

———. "Mother Goose's Sons and Daughters." *Teacher* 95 (1978): 36–38.

———. "Stoo-pendous Dr. Seuss!" *Family Weekly* 9 Apr. 1978: 16. TSG on writing *Mulberry Street*, writing *The Cat in the Hat*, writing for children, teaching children that "reading is fun," "You have 'em, I'll amuse 'em," meeting his fans, and TV.

Humphrey, Hal. "Skeptical Dr. Seuss." *Miami Herald TV Preview* 11 Dec. 1966: 18. Chuck Jones on drawing Seuss's characters, and the cost of the *Grinch* TV special.

———. "Special Visit with the Whos." *TV Times: Los Angeles Times' Weekly TV Magazine* 18–24 Dec. 1966: 2. TSG on TV and the *Grinch*.

———. "Zoo's Who? Dr. Seuss, That's Who." *Coronet* Dec. 1964: 114–120. Returned from New Zealand, TSG on Beginner Books, educators, *Fox in Socks*, TV, art, *PM*, the Nye-as-horse's-ass story, the nuclear-fission story.

Hutshing, Ed. "Seuss' Ribs Tickle Ids of All Kids." *San Diego Union* 20 May 1979. Books: 1, 10. TSG on contemporary illustrations, book sales, the relationship between words and pictures, writing for children, Beginner Books, his reading habits, TV, and *Oh Say Can You Say?*

"I can't draw—I just doodle claims Dr Seuss in city." *Christchurch Star* [New Zealand] 6 May 1976. TSG on his inability to draw, late-night inspiration, writing the *Grinch*, advertising work, the zoo, and trying to "supplant [. . . .] Dick and Jane."

Jacoby, Alfred. "Dr. Seuss & Mr. Geisel: How to Capture a Child's Fancy." *San Diego Union* 3 June 1956: E1, E3. Jacoby paraphrases TSG, provides brief history of career to date. TSG on Flit, children's sense of humor, and simplicity.

Jennings, C. Robert. "Doctor Seuss: What Am I Doing Here?" *Saturday Evening Post* 23 Oct. 1965: 105–9. Fan's "Who thunk you up, Dr. Seuss" letter; TSG on meeting his fans, meeting President Theodore Roosevelt, his characters' appearance, "logical insanity," "bunny-bunny" books, morals, childhood visits to the zoo, inability to "draw the world as it is," graduate school, meeting Helen, his unfinished novel, writing *Mulberry Street*, *Seven Lady Godivas*, writing for *PM*, being unsuited for Hollywood, learning from Hollywood, "You make 'em, I amuse 'em," not "writing down to children," perfectionism, and humor; Helen on TSG's Oxford notebooks and drawing style.

Jordan, Clifford L. "Dr. Seuss." *Dartmouth Alumni Magazine* Oct. 1962: 24–27. Bennett Cerf on TSG as "in tune with the secret world of childhood"; TSG on not test-marketing, work habits, teacher critical of his turning his paper upside-down, Dartmouth, Oxford, Beginner Books, morals; TRG on TSG's correspondence course in drawing; Don Bartlett on TSG's "Rape of the Sabine Women" (painting).

Kahn, E. J. Jr. "Children's Friend." *New Yorker* 17 Dec. 1960, 47–93. Repr. Fensch 15–35. The most thorough article on TSG to date. Highly recommended. TSG on his audience, money, fan mail, his drawing style, modern art (the Escorobus hoax), meeting Theodore Roosevelt, Dartmouth, revisiting Oxford, the Seuss Navy, *Boners*, the early ABC book, origins of *Mulberry Street*, translations, *PM*, World War II, being ordered to burn the *Times*, *The 5,000 Fingers of Dr. T*, meeting his fans, his idea for a children's museum, origins of *Horton Hatches the Egg*, "Mrs. Mulvaney and the Billion-Dollar Bunny, Revell's Multi-Beasts, *Green Eggs and Ham*, *The Seven Lady Godivas*.

Kane, George. "And, Dear Dr. Seuss, the Whole World's in Love with Yeuss." *Rocky Mountain News* 15 Feb. 1976. Repr. Fensch 57–60. TSG on advertising work, higher education, his Great American Novel, his work habits, origins of *The Cat in the Hat*, ending of *The Grinch*, his magazine cartoons.

Kanfer, Stefan. "The Doctor Beloved by All." *Time* 7 Oct. 1991: 7. Repr. Fensch 199–200. TSG on logical insanity, Mack's burp, "obsolete children," and children as products of their environment.

———. "Father of the Lorax Turns 75." *Time* 7 May 1979: 3. TSG on "obsolete children" and preferring animals to humans.

Karlen, Neal, with Hilliard Harper. "Yooks and Zooks from Dr. Seuss." *Newsweek* 16 Jan. 1984: 12. TSG on children's perception of him, audience, "logical insanity"; Audrey on the "wild little kid" in TSG.

Katz, Lee Michael. "Most Kids say Yooks should talk to Zooks." *USA Today* 29 June 1984: 11A. TSG on accidentally inventing an atomic bomb during WWII, *The Butter Battle Book*, audience, computers, reality of his characters, writing for children, *Marvin K. Mooney*, fan mail, and not condescending to children.

Kennedy, Graeme. "Just what the doctor ordered . . . Green eggs and ham for the cat in the hat." *Star Sports & Magazine* [New Zealand] 8 May 1976. TSG on not writing down to children, creating *The Cat in the Hat*, his grandfather's brewery, Prohibition, graduate school, adopting his pseudonym, his Great American Novel, "Quick Henry, the Flit," WWII, and the creative process.

Kitch, Edward S. "Modern Mother Goose: He Deals in Lilliputian Humor." *Long Island Press* [Jamaica, NY] 23 Nov. 1958. TSG on meeting an adult fan, meeting Helen, origins of *Horton Hatches the Egg* and *The Cat in the Hat*, and fan mail.

Kupferberg, Herbert. "A Seussian Celebration." *Parade* 26 Feb. 1984: 4–6. TSG on audience, writing for children, aging, avoiding birthday celebrations, teacher critical of his turning his paper upside-down, magazine work, *Mulberry Street*, not casting Reagan in *Your Job in Germany*, *The Cat in the Hat*, his favorite characters (Horton, the Grinch), his paintings, where he gets his ideas (Retired Thunderbird in Carajo, Arizona).

Kuskin, Karla. "Seuss at 75." *New York Times Book Review*. 29 Apr. 1979. Children's Books: 23, 41–42. TSG on publishing *Mulberry Street*, and the "breathless quality" of his work.

Lamb, John R. "Dr. Seuss Dies: La Jollan was renowned children's author." *San Diego Tribune* 25 Sept. 1991: A1, A8. TSG on where he gets his ideas (Zybilknov), writing *The Cat in the Hat*, La Jolla, the Grinch, *The Lorax*, and Alison Lurie's article. Comments from Glenn Edward Sadler, Clifton Fadiman, Peter Neumeyer, Francelia Butler, Maurice Sendak, Bob Bernstein, Ben Myron, Neil Morgan, Judith Morgan, and Karl ZoBell.

Lathem, Edward Connery. "Words and Pictures Married: The Beginnings of Dr. Seuss." *Dartmouth Alumni Magazine* Apr. 1976: 16–21. Repr. Fensch 61–75. Along with E. J. Kahn's *New Yorker* profile, this is one of the best single articles on TSG. It focuses primarily on his early years (up to 1937).

Lindsay, Cynthia. "The Miracle of Dr. Seuss." *Good Housekeeping* Dec. 1960: 32, 34, 37. TSG on fan mail, Cluny, Chrysanthemum-Pearl, origin of *Mulberry Street*, the Seuss name, Helen as manager, audience, where he gets his ideas (Zyblknov), respecting children.

Lingeman, Richrd R. "Dr. Seuss, Theo. LeSieg. . . ." *New York Times Book Review* 14 Nov. 1976: 24, 48. TSG on sexism in *Mulberry Street*, *The Cat in the Hat*, his artistic style, feminists, and morals.

"Living with People." *McCall's* Oct. 1970: 6. Remarks regarding all major pieces in this month's *McCall's*, including TSG on his child readership.

"The Logical Insanity of Dr. Seuss." *Time* 11 Aug. 1967: 58–59. TSG talking with children, and commenting on imagination, beginning readers, morals, and "logical insanity."

Lyon, Jeff. "Writing for Adults, It Seems, Is One of Dr. Seuss' Dreams." *Chicago Tribune* 15 Apr. 1982. Sec. 3: 1, 10. TSG on his unfinished novel, quitting smoking, the radish pipe, *Hunches in Bunches*, his paintings, morals, the ending of *The Grinch*, fables, *The Lorax*, the child (Gus) who could draw better than he.

Macdonald, Iain. "From fly spray came drum-tum Snumm." *New Zealand Herald* 1 May 1976. TSG on getting the "Flit" job, publishing *Mulberry Street*, adopting "Dr.," and the creative process.

MacEoin, Dottie. "It's on the Loose, It's on the Loose! It's Not a Triple-Crested Swoose, It's Not a Moose—It's Dr. Seuss." *Stars and Stripes* 26 Mar. 1967: 14–16. TSG on morals, logical insanity, origins of *Horton Hatches the Egg* and *Mulberry Street*, the nuclear-fission story, where he gets his ideas (Zyblknov).

Mackin, Tom. "'Grinch' Is Christmas Grouch." *Newark Sunday News* 15 Dec. 1968. Sec. 6, E1. TSG on his name, his unfinished novel, his audience, Bright and Early Books, TV, and *A Charlie Brown Christmas*.

"Malice in Wonderland." *Newsweek* 9 Feb. 1942: 58–59. TSG on his *PM* cartoons and his name.

Marbella, Jean. "At 87, Dr. Seuss is gone but his language lives on." *Baltimore Sun* 26 Sept. 1991: 1A, 6A. TSG on "You make 'em, I amuse 'em," H. L. Mencken, his final message for children.

Marcus, Jon. "Seeking Seuss in Springfield." *Yankee Traveler* Nov.–Dec. 1995: 6. Peggy Owens on TSG's memory; article addresses Springfield's influence on TSG's imagination, and offers directions to 74 Fairfield St. (TSG's childhood home).

Marcus, Leonard. "He Left Us Smiles." *Parenting* Dec.–Jan. 1992. Repr. Fensch 189–90. TSG on what children want, and his books' appeal. Marcus suggests that Seuss's "most lasting impact was his ability to address kids—tenderly and candidly—on their own fiercely imaginative terms."

Martin, Edwin. "Dr. Seuss Has Prolific Pen." *San Diego Union* 30 Aug. 1953: E1-E2. On occasion of *5,000 Fingers of Dr. T*'s release, TSG on his books' popularity and the visit to Japan.

Martin, Judith. "Dr. Seuss: Good Times with Rhymes." *Washington Post* 15 Nov. 1971: B1, B4. Repr. as "Springfield's Dr. Seuss Stumbled Into Success." *Springfield Republican* 28 Nov. 1971. Repr. in abridged form as "Generation Gets Hooked on Dr. Seuss." *Los Angeles Times* 18 May 1972. Part 4, p. 17. TSG on his adventures in graduate school, Flit, *PM* cartoons, his paintings, *The Seven Lady Godivas*, his unfinished novel, "Adults are just obsolete children," and audience.

Mathews, Jay. "Page After Page on the Humor of Age." *Valley News* 4 Mar. 1986: 13, 24. Repr. from *Washington Post*. TSG on *You're Only Old Once!*, *The Butter Battle Book*, and *The Seven Lady Godivas*.

McCabe, Bruce. "Dr. Seuss: Theodor Geisel, 82, publishes his first book specifically for adults." *Boston Globe* 3 Mar. 1986. Sec. Living: 9, 11. TSG on graduate school adventures, Flit, Frank Capra's Army unit, audience, writing for children, teaching reading, *Green Eggs and Ham*, and his creative process.

Mehegan, David. "Dr. Seuss is Dead." *Boston Globe* 26 Sept. 1991: 1, 25. Comments from Ann Flowers and Betsy Schulz.

Monaghan, Charles. "Book Report." Item on TSG's 82nd birthday includes TSG referring to his 80th birthday: "At that time, I called you all together to help abolish nuclear weapons. You all know how that turned out. Now we have a new goal—to abolish old age."

Morgan, Judith. "Golden People." *Signature* Apr. 1984: 59–59, 86–90. Profiles of prominent Californians, including Dianne Feinstein, Peter Uberroth, Jonas Salk, TSG, Cathy Guisewite, and others. TSG's profile appears on pp. 59 & 86. TSG on nonsense, humor, children, where he gets his ideas (Uber Gletsch and Left Field).

———. "Dr. Seuss: A Moral to Every Rhyme." *Valley News* 27 Sept. 1991. Repr. from *Los Angeles Times*. Judith Morgan recalls plotting with TSG to escape noisy parties, TSG's mail; TSG on people who asked him to write their wedding vows, *The Lorax* as "anti-greed," Marvin K. Mooney and Richard M. Nixon.

Nichols, Lewis. "Then I Doodled a Tree." *New York Times Book Review* 11 Nov. 1962: 2, 42. Repr. Fensch 41–43. Nichols on TSG's sales figures, contents of hotel room table; TSG on *The Cat in the Hat*, his favorite characters (the Cat, Horton, and the pair of pants from "What Was I Scared Of?"), *Mulberry Street*, *Horton Hatches the Egg*, on whether words or pictures come first, and fan mail.

Norris, Max. "Seuss (Like Goose) is Sauce for Tots." *Sacramento Bee* 14 Feb. 1976: A3. TSG on books, Flit, WWII, trying to get rid of Dick and Jane, and Bennett Cerf's "genius" remark.

"Nut Stuff." *Sales Management* 1 Jan. 1939. Repr. as "Latest Seussiana." *Dartmouth Alumni Magazine* Mar. 1939: 5. TSG on the Hankey Bird (which he created for Hankey Bannister Scotch Whiskey).

Olten, Carol. "To a living literary legend . . ." *San Diego Union* 17 Apr. 1984: D1 +. TSG on the Pulitzer Prize, *The Butter Battle Book*, and audience. Includes comments by Clifton Fadiman, Glenn Edward Sadler, and others.

"The One and Only Dr. Seuss and His Wonderful Autographing Tour." *Publishers Weekly* 8 Dec. 1958: 12–15. TSG's 10-store tour, attitude towards marketing; TSG on having his books signed by Chief Black Feather, children treating him as if he were Santa Claus.

Osterman, Elsie. "Dr. Seuss expands his audience to include 'obsolete kids.'" *Arizona Daily Star* 9 Feb. 1986: H16. TSG on *You're Only Old Once!*, work habits, "preaching" to children, origin of *Mulberry Street*, his drawing ability, his name, and *The Seven Lady Godivas*.

"The Other Cool Cat." *Early Years: A Magazine for Teachers of Preschool Through Grade 3* Apr. 1973: 22–24. TSG on where he gets his ideas ("noodling around"), how his books are used in schools, fan mail, Beginner Books, *The Shape of Me and Other Stuff*, creativity in children, teacher critical of his turning his paper upside down, and *I Don't Spelk Very Welk*.

Pace, Eric. "Dr. Seuss, Modern Mother Goose, Dies at 87." *New York Times* 26 Sept. 1991: A1, D23. TSG on "logical insanity," "obsolete children," the Springfield Zoo; Helen on TSG's Oxford notebooks. Comments from Jerry Harrison.

"Pied Piper of Bookland." *Philadelphia Inquirer* 12 Nov. 1961. TSG on his artistic ability, where he gets his ideas (Swiss mountaintop), "You have them—I'll entertain them," morals, audience.

Powell, Ronald W. "Multitude pays tribute to late author." *San Diego Union* 18 Nov. 1991: B-1, B-3. Audrey comments on TSG's creative process and legacy.

Raddatz, Leslie. "Dr. Seuss Climbs Down from His Mountain to Bring the Grinch to Television." *TV Guide* 17 Dec. 1966: 12–14. TSG on Hollywood, *Grinch* TV-special, audience, child-who-draws-better-than-TSG story, and Cerf's Faulkner-O'Hara-Capote-genius story.

Redelings, Lowell E. "Man Behind the Scenes." *Hollywood Citizen News* 19 Jan. 1948. UCSD: MSS 0230, Box 9, Folder 5. TSG on meeting Helen, creating the "Flit" campaign, origins of *Mulberry Street*, writing documentaries, and creating films for children.

Richardson, Barbara. "Dr. Seuss: Creator of 'The Cat in the Hat.'" *Book and Magazine Collector* 202 (2001): 44–58. Draws heavily on the Morgans' biography, providing overview of TSG's life as seen from Britain. Touches on British reception of Seuss's books and prices of first editions; has bibliography of U.S. and U.K. editions.

Rohter, Larry. "After 60 Years, Dr. Seuss Goes Home." *New York Times* 21 May 1986: A20. TSG on his style, his characters, and his books as based on "exaggerated truth." Also TSG visits his boyhood home (74 Fairfield St., Springfield).

Sadler, Glenn Edward. "A Conversation with Maurice Sendak and Dr. Seuss." 8 Dec. 1982. Ed. Sadler. *Teaching Children's Literature: Issues, Pedagogy, Resources*. New York: Modern Language Association of America, 1992. 241–50. Excerpts repr. as "Dr. Seuss: An Interview," *Children's Books and Their Creators*, ed. Silvey, 592. Version without Sadler's intro. first published in *Horn Book* and repr. Fensch 135–40. Fascinating conversation between TSG and Sendak on a range of topics, including TSG on where he gets his ideas (Uber Gletch), nonsense words in translation, motivating children to read, the critics, the fairy tale, his characters, *Mulberry Street*, childhood and adolescence, doodling, Yertle as Hitler, and "the wrong end of the telescope." Recommended.

Salzhauer, Mike. "A Carnival Cavort with Dr. Seuss." *Dartmouth Review* 2 Feb. 1981: 6–7. Repr. *Dartmouth Review* 13 Nov. 1991: 8–9. TSG on writing *Mulberry Street*, Dartmouth, *The Lorax*, the creative process, morals, realism "through the wrong end of a telescope," audience, *Thidwick*, his books' popularity, and Dartmouth's Winter Carnival.

See, Carolyn. "Dr. Seuss and the Naked Ladies." *Esquire* June 1974: 118–19, 176. Repr. Fensch 53–56. TSG on Oxford, his unpublished novel, *The Seven Lady Godivas*, Fort Fox, the atomic bomb, and a five-page outline for an unpublished "dirty book."

Seidenbaum, Art. "Muse on the Loose is Dr. Seuss." *Los Angeles Times* 5 Jan. 1964. Sec. Calendar: 1, 14. TSG on his paintings, writing for children, meeting his fans; Helen on TSG's "instinctive knowledge of what a child WOULD like," that TSG is happiest when drawing

"The Seuss and the Suit." *Newsweek* Dec. 1968.

"Seussology: Birds, Beasts, and Creatures of the Deep in Advertising." Publication unknown, but possibly *Sales Management*. c. 1939. Dartmouth, Rauner Library: Alumni G277mi, Box 1, folder titled "Magazine Articles—Undated." TSG on graduate school and painting.

Sheff, David. "Seuss on Wry." *Parenting Magazine* Feb. 1987: 52–57. TSG on fan mail, not condescending to children, what kids want from a book ("The same things we want. To laugh, to be challenged, to be entertained and delighted"), the creative process, origins of *Horton Hatches the Egg*, adults and children, *The Butter Battle Book*, Japan, the botched *Life* article, origins of *Horton Hears a Who!*, WWII experiences, inventing the atom bomb, origins of *The Lorax*, the film of *The Lorax*, writing *The Cat in the Hat*, Richard M. Nixon Will You Please Go Now!, origins of *You're Only Old Once!*.

Shepard, Richard F. "Dr. Seuss Beasts Trample Word Lists." *New York Times* 17 Oct. 1968: 49. TSG on Beginner Books, TV, Theo. LeSieg, billboards, "obsolete children," and his paintings.

Silverman, Betsy Marden. "Dr. Seuss Talks to Parents about Learning to Read and What Makes Children Want to Do It." *Parents* Nov. 1960: 44–45, 134–37. TSG on *Mulberry Street*, teaching children to read, writing Beginner Books, *One fish two fish red fish blue fish*, rhymes, sounds, and *Green Eggs and Ham*.

Smith, Kathleen. "Dr. Seuss battles with butter to drive home a message for children and adults." *The Dartmouth's Weekend Magazine* 18 Jan. 1985: 12–13. TSG on *The Butter Battle Book*, morals, trusting children's intelligence, and *The Lady and the Tiger*.

"Sneetches, Sugar, and Success: The Boom in Books for Children." *Newsweek* 25 Dec. 1961: 73–75. Ludwig Bemelmans praises Dr. Seuss for treating "the child as an adult." TSG on money, the Springfield Zoo, and morals. Phyllis Cerf attributes success to TSG being "a child" and "a genius."

" 'Somebody's Got to Win' in Kids' Books: An Interview with Dr. Seuss on His Books for Children, Young and Old." *U.S. News and World Report* 14 Apr. 1986. Repr. Fensch 125–27. TSG on *You're Only Old Once!*, *Green Eggs and Ham*, *The Cat in the Hat*, rhyming, *The Lorax*, the creative process, Maurice Sendak, and the child with his hand in his mouth told to "shake hands with Dr. Seuss"

Stein, Ruthie. "Dr. Seuss for Grownups." *San Francisco Chronicle*. 11 Mar. 1986. Sec. People: 19, 21. Before and during a book-signing, TSG on book-signings, *Seven Lady Godivas*, *You're Only Old Once!*, Flit, and his books' appeal.

Steinberg, Sybil S. "What Makes a Funny Children's Book?: Five Writers Talk About Their Methods." *Publishers Weekly* 27 Feb. 1978: 87–90. In the section on Seuss (pp. 87–88), TSG discusses his name, writing for children, Saxe Commins, the creative process, the origin of *Horton Hatches the Egg*, naming his characters, the teacher who criticized his turning his paper upside down, and Theo. LeSieg.

Stewart-Gordon, James. "Dr. Seuss: Fanciful Sage of Childhood." *Reader's Digest* Apr. 1972: 141–45. TSG on not being able to draw, "logical insanity," making up words, not writing down to children, rhyme, writing *The Grinch*, origin of *Horton Hatches the Egg*, being encouraged to drop art by his high-school art teacher, graduate school, and deciding to write children's books.

Sullivan, John. "Growing Up with Dr. Seuss." *American Baby* Aug. 1984: 46, 52.

Sullivan, Robert. "The Boy Who Drew Wynmmphs." *Yankee* Dec. 1995: 54–59, 120–21. TSG on drawing animals at the zoo, meeting President Theodore Roosevelt, *Jack-o-lantern*, returning to Springfield in 1986. Generously illustrated with photos and images from books, the article focuses on TSG's life in Springfield.

———. "Oh, the Places He Went!" *Dartmouth Alumni Magazine* Winter 1991: 19–42. Lavishly illustrated, offers many anecdotes from earlier interviews, including: TSG on his name, childhood and laughter, Deegel Trout, parents' responsibility to teach children reading, being encouraged to draw by his parents, not wanting to draw the world as-is, attending Dartmouth, graduate school, his unfinished novel, living in Hell's Kitchen, magazine work, Flit, writing and publishing *Mulberry Street*, *The Seven Lady Godivas*, writing for *PM*, gardening, creating *Horton Hatches the Egg*, writing *The Lorax*, creative process, Dick and Jane, writing *The Cat in the Hat*, fame, meeting fans; Larry Leavitt on Seuss's writing of *Horton Hatches the Egg*; and Sydney Lea on TSG's poetry. Also includes comments from Ann Geisel, and accounts of controversy surrounding *Butter Battle* and *The Lorax*.

"The 25th Anniversary of Dr. Seuss." *Publishers Weekly* 17 Dec. 1962: 10–13. TSG on publishing *Mulberry Street*, writing *The Cat in the Hat*, Beginner Books, his work habits, his work published in England, and Outgo J. Schmierkase.

"Unusual Occupations." Produced by Fairbanks and Carlisle. Written by Walter Anthony. Narrated by Ken Carpenter. Paramount, 1940. This 90-second film clip is in color—"processed in the New Magnacolor," as the credits explain—and features Seuss's sculptures.

"Upfront." *Retail Ad Week* 8 Mar. 1976: 3, 4, 6.

Warren, Bob. "Dr. Seuss, Former Jacko Editor, Tells How Boredom May Lead to Success." *The Dartmouth* 10 May 1934: 9. TSG on his taxidermy, *Jack-o-lantern*, graduate school, travel, drawing animals, designing costumes for a musical show, his novel, and his name.

Waugh, John C. "Kingdom of Seuss." *Christian Science Monitor* 29 Jan. 1964: 9. TSG on the logic of fantasy, writing for children, writing *The Cat in the Hat*, teaching children that reading is fun, the origins of *Mulberry Street*, humor, and imagination; Helen on TSG's Oxford notebooks.

Webb, Jack. "Dr. Seuss also has worn many hats." *San Diego Evening Tribune* 11 Sept. 1974: A-21. Repr. in abridged form as "The delightful world of Dr. Seuss." *Pictorial Living Coloroto Magazine* 5 Jan. 1975: 18. TSG on fans who visit him, being asked to tell stories to an upset child, work habits, the creative process, his graduate school adventures, writing for *PM*, writing for children, and his serious side.

Wheeler, David. "Dr. Seuss Gets Tip of Hat at Top of Hop." *Valley News* 16 Oct. 1982: 1, 14. TSG on where his ideas come from (doodling), the origin of *The Grinch*, New Zealand, sitting for his portrait, work habits; also includes TSG quotations from the Lathem interview.

Wilder, Rob. "Catching Up with Dr. Seuss." *Parents Magazine* June 1979: 60–64. TSG on target shooting, his father and Prohibition, being teased during WWI, fantasy as "an extension of reality," *McElligot's Pool* based on fishing trips with father, Marvin K. Mooney as Richard M. Nixon, Latin, TV, and *Oh Say Can You Say?*

Wintle, Justin, and Emma Fisher. "Two Letters: Dr. Seuss and E. B. White." *The Pied Pipers: Interviews with the Influential Creators of Children's Literature.* New York: Two Continents, 1975. 113–31. In his responses (pp. 113–23) to the authors' questionnaire, TSG offers brief comments on his childhood, Oxford, the origins of *Mulberry Street*, fairy tales, *Horton Hatches the Egg*, "logical nonsense," not pre-testing books on children, lack of formal artistic training, Beginner Books, and money.

Wright, Virginia. Profile of Theodor Seuss Geisel. *L.A. Daily News* 9 Jan. 1948. UCSD MSS 0230, Box 9, Folder 5. TSG on getting involved with *Design for Death*, his father sending him to Oxford "to save face," and the Seuss Navy. Helen on *Design for Death*.

Selected Reference

Blackbeard, Bill, and Martin Williams, eds. *The Smithsonian Collection of Newspaper Comics.* New York and Washington, D.C.: Smithsonian Institution Press and Harry N. Abrams, 1977. 321. Paragraph on "Hejji," reprints first strip in color, plate 723.

Calhoun, Richard. "Geisel, Theodor Seuss." *Contemporary Graphic Artists.* Vol. 3. Ed. Maurice Horn. Detroit, Mich: Gale Resarch. 75–78.

Carpenter, Humphrey, and Mari Prichard. "Seuss, Dr." *Oxford Companion to Children's Literature.* 1984. New York and Oxford: Oxford UP, 1999. 477–78. Profile focuses on first half of his career.

Commire, Anne, ed. "Geisel, Theodor Seuss." *Something About the Author.* Vol. 1. Detroit, MI: Gale Research Company, 1970 [?]. 104–06.

———, ed. "Geisel, Theodor Seuss." *Something About the Author.* Vol. 28. Detroit, MI: Gale Research Company, 1982. 107–116.

Darling, Harold. *From Mother Goose to Dr. Seuss: Children's Book Covers 1860–1960.* San Francisco: Chronicle Books, 1999. 96, 115. Reprints the original covers to *Thidwick* and *If I Ran the Circus*.

Duggan, Anne. "Seuss, Dr." *Oxford Companion to Fairy Tales*. Ed. Jack Zipes. Oxford and New York: Oxford UP, 2000. 460.

Estes, Glenn E., Ed. "Theodor Seuss Geisel." *Dictionary of Literary Biography*. Vol. 61. American Writers for Children Since 1960: Poets, Illustrators, and Nonfiction Authors. Detroit, MI: Gale, 1987. 75–86. Profile follows TSG's life and work through *Butter Battle*.

Fisher, Margery. "Bartholomew Cubbins" and "Marco." *Who's Who in Children's Books: A Treasury of the Familiar Characters of Childhood*. New York: Holt, Rinehart and Winston, 1975. 36, 198.

"Geisel, Theodor Seuss." *Current Biography 1968*. 138–41.

Mass, Wendy. "Dr. Seuss." *Great Authors of Children's Literature*. San Diego, CA: Lucent Books, 2000. 55–64. A good biography, accompanied by four photographs of Geisel. Relies heavily on profiles and interviews by Bunzel, Freeman, Kahn, and Lathem.

Meigs, Cornelia, Anne Eaton, Elizabeth Nesbitt, and Ruth Hill Viguers. *A Critical History of Children's Literature*. New York: MacMillan Company, 1953. 477. Mentions *500 Hats*.

Parravano, Martha V. "Dr. Seuss." *Children's Books and Their Creators*. Ed. Anita Silvey. New York: Houghton Mifflin Company, 1995. 590–93. Biographical profile.

Sadker, Myra Pollack, and David Miller Sadker. *Now Upon a Time: A Contemporary View of Children's Literature*. 274, 322, 340–41, 405. Devotes a paragraph each to *The Lorax* and *500 Hats*, offers another three paragraphs on imaginary creatures and on poetry.

Selected Websites

Since the web is an ephemeral medium, I will strive to keep my own page of Seuss links (listed third in this section) current: <http://www.ksu.edu/english/nelp/seuss/>.

Dr. Seuss Collection. <http://orpheus.ucsd.edu/speccoll/collects/seuss.html>. Mandeville Special Collections Library, University of California at San Diego. Includes *Dr. Seuss Went to War* (all of Seuss's *PM* cartoons) and *The Advertising Artwork of Dr. Seuss* (a selection of Seuss's ads).

Dr. Seuss National Memorial. <http://www.catinthehat.org/>. Official site for the memorial in Springfield, Mass.

Dr. Seuss on the Web. Ed. Philip Nel. <http://www.ksu.edu/english/nelp/seuss/>. My collection of links.

The Dr. Seuss Web Page. Ed. David Bedno. <http://www.seuss.org/>. An unofficial site, notable for its collection of parodies.

Read Across America. <http://www.nea.org/readacross/>. The National Education Association's "Read Across America" features the Cat in the Hat as its mascot.

Seussville. <http://www.seussville.com/seussville/>. Random House's official page.

Selected Reviews

• *And to Think That I Saw It on Mulberry Street* (1937)

C., E. "When It's Time to Read." *Christian Science Monitor* 25 Oct. 1937: 6.

Mack, Elsie M. "The Book Trail for Boys and Girls." *Boston Evening Transcript* 30 Oct. 1937: 4.

Moore, Anne Carroll. "The Three Owls' Notebook." *Horn Book* Nov. 1937: 365–67.

"[Picture Books]." *Horn Book* Nov. 1937: 373–74.

Fadiman, Clifton. "Books. Or Am I Just Being Cranky?" *New Yorker* 6 Nov. 1937: 76–80.

Benét, William Rose. "The Children's Bookshop." *Saturday Review of Literature* 13 Nov. 1937: 22–27.

B[uell]., E[llen]. L[ewis]. "The Startling Parade." *New York Times Book Review* 14 Nov. 1937: 14, 37.

• *The 500 Hats of Bartholomew Cubbins* (1938)

Jordan, Alice M. "For Readers of Children's Books, Including Parents." *Boston Evening Transcript* 29 Oct. 1938. Sec. 3: 1.

Becker, May Lamberton. "The 500 Hats of Bartholomew Cubbins." *New York Herald Tribune Books* 12 Nov. 1938: 22.

B[uell], E[llen] L[ewis]. "A Humorous Tale." *New York Times Book Review* 13 Nov. 1938: 11, 32.

Stanton, Jessie, and Ellen Steele. "The 500 Hats of Bartholomew Cubbins." *New Republic* 7 Dec. 1938: 149.

• *The Seven Lady Godivas* (1939)

Laing, Alexander. Review of *The Seven Lady Godivas* and *The King's Stilts*. *Dartmouth Alumni Magazine* Jan. 1940: 24.

"The Seven Lady Godivas." *Publishers Weekly* 17 July 1987: 51.

Roraback, Dick. "Seven Lady Godivas." *Los Angeles Times Book Review* 30 Aug. 1987: 4.

• *The King's Stilts* (1939)

Buell, Ellen Lewis. "The King's Stilts." *New York Times Book Review* 15 Oct. 1939: 12.

Becker, May Lamberton. "The King's Stilts." *New York Herald Tribune Books* 12 Nov. 1939: 10.

W[hite], K[atharine] S. "The King's Stilts." *New Yorker* 25 Nov. 1939: 75.

• *Horton Hatches the Egg* (1940)

Buell, Ellen Lewis. "Elephant's Egg." *New York Times Book Review* 13 Oct. 1940: 10.

Jordan, Alice M. "Dr. Seuss, Author-Illustrator *Horton Hatches the Egg*." *Horn Book* Nov. 1940: 434.

W[hite], K[atharine] S. "Horton Hatches the Egg." *New Yorker* 7 Dec. 1940: 106–07

Laing, Alexander. "Horton Hatches the Egg." *Dartmouth Alumni Magazine* Dec. 1940: 88.

• *Design for Death* (1947)

"Documentary Shows Nips' Power Plan." *Hollywood Reporter*. 27 Jan. 1948: 3. Dartmouth, Rauner Library: Alumni G277mi.

• *McElligot's Pool* (1947)

"McElligot's Pool." *Virginia Kirkus Bookshop Service Bulletin* 15 Sept. 1947: 502.

Moore, Anne Carroll. "The Three Owls' Notebook." *Horn Book* Nov. 1947: 433–36.

Becker, May Lamberton. "McElligot's Pool." *New York Herald Tribune Weekly Book Review* 16 Nov. 1947: 6.

G, S. C. "McElligot's Pool." *New York Times Book Review* 16 Nov. 1947: 45.

Benét, R. C. "McElligot's Pool." *New Yorker* 6 Dec. 1947: 136.

Jordan, Alice M. "Dr. Seuss, Author-Illustrator *McElligot's Pool*." *Horn Book* Jan. 1948: 34.

* *Thidwick, the Big-Hearted Moose* (1948)

"Thidwick, the Big-Hearted Moose." *Virginia Kirkus Bookshop Service Bulletin* 1 Sept. 1948: 436.

Buell, Ellen Lewis. "Thidwick, the Big-Hearted Moose." *New York Times Book Review* 10 Oct. 1948: 25.

Davis, Mary Gould. "Thidwick, the Big-Hearted Moose." *Saturday Review* 11 Oct. 1948: 35

M., V. H. "Thidwick, the Big-Hearted Moose." *New York Herald Tribune Weekly Book Review* 14 Nov. 1948: 12.

Burr, Elizabeth. Review of *Thidwick, the Big-Hearted Moose. Wisconsin Library Bulletin* Dec. 1948: 214.

* *Bartholomew and the Oobleck* (1949)

"Bartholomew and the Oobleck." *Virginia Kirkus Bookshop Service Bulletin* 1 Sept. 1949: 465.

Castor, Gladys Crofoot. "King and Page." *New York Times Book Review* 13 Nov. 1949: 12.

Burr, Elizabeth. Review of *Bartholomew and the Oobleck. Wisconsin Library Bulletin* Dec. 1949: 12.

* *If I Ran the Zoo* (1950)

Moore, Anne Carroll. "The Three Owls' Notebook." *Horn Book* Sept. 1950: 354–6.

"If I Ran a [*sic*] Zoo." *Virginia Kirkus Bookshop Service Bulletin* 15 Sept. 1950: 558.

Lindquest, Jennie D., and Siri M. Andrews. "Theodor Seuss, Geisel, Author-Illustrator *If I Ran the Zoo*." *Horn Book* Nov. 1950: 466.

Chrystie, Frances. "Ideal Zoo." *New York Times Book Review* 9 Nov. 1950: 42.

Bechtel, Louise S. "If I Ran the Zoo." *New York Herald Tribune Book Review* 12 Nov. 1950: 8.

Kinkead, Katharine T. "If I Ran the Zoo." *New Yorker* 2 Dec. 1950: 175.

* *Scrambled Eggs Super!* (1953)

"Scrambled Eggs Super." *Virginia Kirkus Bookshop Service Bulletin* 1 Apr. 1953: 216.

Kelly, Walt. "A La Peter T. Hooper." *New York Times Book Review* 5 Apr. 1953: 21

Burr, Elizabeth. Review of *Scrambled Eggs Super! Wisconsin Library Bulletin* May 1953: 130.

Bechel, Louise S. "Fine New Picture Books." *New York Herald Tribune Book Review* 17 May 1953: 10.

* *The 5,000 Fingers of Dr. T.* (1953)

Berg, Louis. "Dr. Seuss' 5,000 Fingers." *This Week* 10 Aug. 1952.

Rowan, Arthur. "Set Lighting Innovations Mark the Photography of '5,000 Fingers of Dr. T.'" *American Cinematographer* Jan. 1953: 16, 17, 42.

"The 5,000 Fingers of Dr. T." *Films in Review* Mar. 1953: 151, 54.

"The New Pictures." *Time* 22 June 1953: 84.

• *Horton Hears a Who!* (1954)

"Horton Hears a Who!" *Virginia Kirkus Bookshop Service Bulletin* 1 Sept. 1954: 581.

Buell, Ellen Lewis. "New Books for the Younger Readers' Library." *New York Times Book Review* 12 Sept 1954: 32.

Kinkead, Katharine T. "Picture Books." New Yorker 27 Nov. 1954: 207.

• *On Beyond Zebra* (1955)

Bechtel, Louise S. "On Beyond Zebra!" *New York Herald Tribune Book Review* 31 Nov. 1955: 3.

Cobb, Jane. "Transalphabetica." *New York Times Book Review* 13 Nov. 1955: 45.

Moore, Anne Carroll. "The Three Owls' Notebook." *Horn Book* Dec. 1955: 443–45.

• *If I Ran the Circus* (1956)

"If I Ran the Circus." *Kirkus Service* 1 Oct. 1956: 750.

Cobb, Jane. "Snumms, Foons & Jotts." *New York Times Book Review*, Part 2. 18 Nov. 1956: 47.

Libby, M[argaret] S. "If I Ran the Circus." *New York Herald Tribune Book Review* 18 Nov. 1956: 4.

• *The Cat in the Hat* (1957)

"The Cat in the Hat." *Kirkus Service* 15 Mar. 1957: 216.

"The Cat in the Hat." *Kirkus Service* 1 Apr. 1957: 276.

Buell, Ellen Lewis. "High Jinks at Home." *New York Times Book Review* 17 Mar. 1957: 40.

Libby, M[argaret] S. "The Cat in the Hat." *New York Herald Tribune Book Review* 12 May 1957: 24.

Hines, L.G. "The Cat and the Hat." *Dartmouth Alumni Magazine* June 1957: 6.

Burr, Elizabeth. [Review of *The Cat in the Hat*.] *Wisconsin Library Bulletin* July 1957: 455.

• *How the Grinch Stole Christmas!* (1957)

"How the Grinch Stole Christmas." *Kirkus Reviews* 15 Sept. 1957: 687

B[uell]., E[llen]. L[ewis]. "Yuletide in Who-Ville." *New York Times Book Review* 6 Oct. 1957: 40.

Libby, Margaret S. "Three Threats to Christmas." *New York Herald Tribune Book Review* 17 Nov. 1957: 30.

Maxwell, Emily. "Books: Christmas for First and Second Readers." Review of both *How the Grinch . . .* and *The Cat in the Hat. New Yorker* 23 Nov. 1957: 232, 234.

"The Grinch & Co." *Time* 23 Dec. 1957: 74–76.

• *Yertle the Turtle and Other Stories* (1958)

"Yertle the Turtle and Other Stories." *Kirkus Service* 1 May 1958: 335.

Review of *Yertle the Turtle and Other Stories. Wisconsin Library Bulletin* July 1958: 298.

Doak, Elizabeth. "Geisel, Theodor Seuss, Author-Illustrator *Yertle the Turtle and Other Stories.*" *Horn Book* Aug. 1958: 262.

• *The Cat in the Hat Comes Back* (1958)

Buell, Ellen Lewis. "A Few New Books for All the New Readers." *New York Times Book Review* 5 Oct. 1958: 36.

Review of *The Cat in the Hat Comes Back*. *Wisconsin Library Bulletin* Nov. 1958: 525.

"Beginner Books Series." *Kirkus Service* 1 Nov. 1958: 824.

* *Happy Birthday to You!* (1959)

Libby, Margaret S. "Happy Birthday to You!" *New York Herald Tribune Book Review* 1 Nov. 1959: 4.

"Joys for Many Days." *Christian Century* 2 Dec. 1959: 1405.

Childs, Nancy B. "Seuss, Dr. Happy Birthday to You!" *Library Journal* 15 Jan. 1960: 349.

* *One fish two fish red fish blue fish* (1960)

Buell, Ellen Lewis. "A Nook for Others." *New York Times Book Review* 20 Mar. 1960: 42.

Libby, M[argaret] S. "One Fish Two Fish Red Fish Blue Fish." *New York Herald Tribune Book Review* 8 May 1960: 21.

Marsh, Pamela. "One Fish, Two Fish, Red Fish, Blue Fish." *Christian Science Monitor* 12 May 1960: 4B

Childs, Nancy. "Seuss, Dr. One Fish, Two Fish, Red Fish, Blue Fish." *Library Journal* 15 May 1960: 50.

[Review of *One fish two fish red fish blue fish*.] *Wisconsin Library Bulletin* May 1960: 171.

* *Green Eggs and Ham* (1960)

"Green Eggs and Ham." *Kirkus Service* 15 Aug. 1960: 679.

Lavender, Carolyn H. "New Books for the Younger Readers' Library." *New York Times Book Review* 2 Oct. 1960: 44.

Libby, Margaret S. "Few Words, but Lively Ones." *New York Herald Tribune Book Review* 13 Nov. 1960: 16.

Maxwell, Emily. Review of *Green Eggs and Ham*. *New Yorker* 19 Nov. 1960: 226.

* *Ten Apples Up on Top!* (1961)

Lavender, Carolyn H. "High-Jinks." *New York Times Book Review* 19 Mar. 1961: 42.

* *The Sneetches and Other Stories* (1961)

Woods, George. "The Sneetches and Other Stories." *New York Times Book Review*, Part 2. 22 Nov. 1961: 54.

Skahill, Helen. "Seuss, Dr. The Sneetches and Other Stories." *Library Journal* 15 Dec. 1961: 45.

* *Dr. Seuss's Sleep Book* (1962)

Buell, Ellen Lewis. "For the Youngest Reader: Picture Books." *New York Times Book Review* 9 Sept. 1962: 30.

Libby, M[argaret] S. "Dr. Seuss's Sleep Book." *New York Herald Tribune Books* 11 Nov. 1962: 30.

Foell, Earl W. "Quiet Please." *Christian Science Monitor* 15 Nov. 1962: 2B.

Brown, Margaret Warren. "Dr. Seuss, Author-Illustrator *Dr. Seuss's Sleep Book*." *Horn Book* Feb. 1963: 52.

* *Dr. Seuss's ABC* (1963)

Eiseman, Alberta. "Dr. Seuss's ABC." *New York Times Book Review*, Part 2. 10 Nov. 1963: 52.

Libby, M.S. "F for First Steps." *Book Week*. Fall Children's Issue. 10 Nov. 1963: 43.

Jackson, Charlotte. "A Christmas List." *Atlantic Monthly* Dec. 1963: 170.

- *The Cat in the Hat Beginner Book Dictionary, by the Cat Himself (1964)*

  Woods, George A. "The Cat in the Hat Beginner Book Dictionary." *New York Times Book Review* 25 Oct. 1964: 36.

  Gilbert, Christine B. [Review of *The Cat in the Hat Beginner Book Dictionary.*] *Library Journal* 15 Nov. 1964: 56.
- *Fox in Socks* (1965)

  Woods, George A. "Fox in Socks." *New York Times Book Review* 18 April 1965: 16.

  Harmon, Elva. "Seuss, Dr. Fox in Socks." *Library Journal* 15 May 1965: 96.
- *I Had Trouble in Getting to Solla Sollew* (1965)

  Kluger, Richard. "Hi-jinks, and low." *Book Week* [*New York Herald Tribune Book Review*] 31 Oct. 1965: 6, 12, 16.

  Woods, George A. "The Fun of Picture Books." *New York Times Book Review* 31 Oct. 1965: 56.
- *Come Over to My House* (1966)

  "LeSieg, Theo. *Come Over to My House.*" *Bulletin of the Center for Children's Books* June 1967: 155.
- *Dr. Seuss's Lost World Revisited* (1967)

  "Dr. Seuss's Lost World Revisited." *Publishers Weekly* 19 June 1967: 86.
- *Horton Hears a Who!* (TV, 1970)

  Gould, Jack. "TV: Dr. Seuss's Horton." *New York Times* 20 Mar. 1970: 95.
- *The Lorax* (1971)

  Smith, Jennifer Farley. "Under the shade of the Truffula Trees." *Christian Science Monitor* 11 Nov. 1971: B4.

  Bandler, M. J. Review of *The Lorax*. *Washington Post Children's Book World* 7 Nov. 1971: 3.

  Furnas, Gail Abbott. "Seuss, Dr. The Lorax." *Library Journal* 15 Nov. 1971: 109.
- *The Lorax* (TV, 1972)

  Mitchell, Henry. "Dr. Seuss on Ecology: Lorax and Thneeds." *Washington Post* 14 Feb. 1972: B11.
- *Did I Ever Tell You How Lucky You Are?* (1973)

  Chatfield, Carol. "Dr. Seuss. Did I Ever Tell You How Lucky You Are?" *Library Journal* 15 Dec. 1973: 41–42.
- *"Who Is Dr. Seuss?"* (exhibition, 1976)

  Reilly, Richard. "Geisel's Work Imaginative." *San Diego Union* 11 Dec. 1976: D1.
- *The Cat's Quizzer* (1976)

  Weeks, Brigitte. "Young Bookshelf." *Book World* 10 Oct. 1976: E6.

  Sheehan, Ethna. "The Cat's Quizzer." *America* 11 Dec. 1976: 428.

  Sutherland, Zena. "Seuss, Dr. The Cat's Quizzer." *Bulletin of the Center for Children's Books* March 1977: 114.

  Wiener, Suzanne. "Pachyderms." *Times Educational Supplement* 25 Nov. 1977: 25.
- *The Butter Battle Book* (1984)

  Ferguson, Margaret. "Dr. Seuss Is Back—With a Surprise." *San Francisco Chronicle* 2 Mar. 1984: 63.

  Goodale, Gloria. "From Dr. Seuss, an arms race allegory about Yooks and Zooks." *Christian Science Monitor* 2 Mar. 1984: 20.

Curley, Suzanne. "Dr. Seuss At 80: There's No Happy Ending This Time." *Valley News* 10 Mar. 1984: 13. Repr. of "The Nuclear Dr. Seuss," *Newsday* 5 March 1984: 3.

Dirda, Michael. "The Butter Battle Book." *Washington Post Book World* 11 Mar. 1984: 11.

"People." *Time* 12 Mar. 1984: 67.

Goodman, Ellen. "Dr. Seuss and the Bomb." *Washington Post* 24 Apr. 1984: A13.

Killan, Michael. "The Big-Boy Boomeroo race." *Chicago Tribune* 1 May 1984.

• *You're Only Old Once!* (1986)

Henig, Robin Marantz. "The Age of the Sage." *Washington Post Book World* 9 Mar. 1986: 1, 11.

Smith, Jack. "You're Only Old Once!" *Los Angeles Times Book Review* 19 Mar. 1986: 1.

Sorel, Edward. "The Shape That He's In." *New York Times Book Review* 23 Mar. 1986: 39.

• *Oh, the Places You'll Go!* (1990)

Dirda, Michael. "Young Bookshelf." *Washington Post Book World* 14 Jan. 1990: 10.

Gregory, Kristiana. "A. Nonny Mouse and Other Children's Poets." *Los Angeles Times Book Review* 28 Jan. 1990: 15.

Manuel, Diane. "Oh, the Places You'll Go!" *New York Times Book Review* 11 Mar. 1990: 29.

Flowers, Ann A. "Dr. Seuss, Author-Illustrator *Oh, the Places You'll Go!*" *Horn Book* May–June 1990: 329.

• *The Secret Art of Dr. Seuss* (1995)

Agee, Jon. "The 500 Cats Of Theodor Geisel." *Los Angeles Times Book Review* 3 Dec. 1995: 22.

Spiegelman, Art. "The Doc in the Smock." *Village Voice* 26 Dec. 1995: 49.

Other Works Cited

Reminder: this section only provides full bibliographic listings for items used exclusively—or nearly exclusively—in individual chapters. To find other full citations, when the source is *first* used I have provided the author's name (or the title of the source, if no author is given) and the relevant section of the bibliography. Sections are abbreviated as follows: B = Books, C = Collections of Dr. Seuss's Work, E = Essays by Dr. Seuss, EC = Exhibition Catalogues, F = Films, LC = Literary Criticism, PI = Profiles and Interviews, R = Selected Reviews, Ref = Selected Reference, SP = Stories and Poems by Dr. Seuss, W = Selected Websites. All are in "Secondary Sources about Dr. Seuss" except C, E, and SP, which are in "Primary Sources." I have consistently supplied such labels for Secondary Sources; however, I have provided them for Primary Sources only when a failure to do so may have led to confusion.

Introduction

"An Awfully Big Adventure: The Making of Modern Children's Literature": F.
Arakelian: LC.
Bailey: LC.

ANNOTATED BIBLIOGRAPHY

Barrs: LC.
Butler: LC.
Cech: LC.
"Children's Best Sellers." *New York Times Book Review* 2 Nov. 1958.
Cott: PI.
Deans: LC.
DeLillo, Don. *Libra.* New York: Viking, 1988.
Dohm: LC.
Fadiman: R.
Fensch, *Of Sneetches and Whos . . .* : B.
Flesch: LC.
Georgatos: PI.
Hackett, Alice Payne. *50 Years of Best Sellers 1895–1945.* New York: R. R. Bowker Co., 1945.
———. *70 Years of Best Sellers 1895–1965.* New York and London: R. R. Bowker Co., 1967.
———. *60 Years of Best Sellers 1895–1955.* New York: R. R. Bowker Company, 1956.
Hackett, Alice Payne, and James Henry Burke. *80 Years of Best Sellers 1895–1975.* New York and London: R. R. Bowker Company.
Lanes: B.
Lebduska: LC.
Lurie: LC.
MacDonald: B.
Marschall: C.
Marshall: LC.
Menand: LC.
Mensch and Freeman: LC.
Minear: C.
Morgan and Morgan: B.
Murray, Thomas E. "Re: dialect and Dr. Seuss." Email to author. 29 June 2003, 5:15:03 pm Central Time.
Nikolajeva and Scott: LC.
Moynihan: LC.
Nel: LC.
Nodelman: LC.
Nichols: PI.
Ort: LC.
Potter, Beatrix. Letter to Anne Carroll Moore. 18 Dec. 1937. *Beatrix Potter's Americans: Selected Letters.* Ed. Jane Crowell Morse. Boston, Mass.: The Horn Book, 1982. 83–85.
Raymo: LC.
Reimer: LC.
Ross: LC.
Roth: LC.
Safire, William. "Quick, Henry, the emollient!" *New York Times Magazine* 1 July 2001: 26–27.
Seuss, Dr. *Oh, the Places You'll Go!*: "Bone pile" holograph. UCSD: MSS 0230, MC-106–14.
"Springfield Celebrates Seuss: The Making of the Dr. Seuss National Memorial Sculpture Garden." Exhibit. Museum of Fine Arts. The Quadrangle. Springfield, Mass. 1 June 2002.
Steig: LC.
Stong: LC.
Sutton: LC.
Szilagyi, Steve. "Holiday Favorite Still Appealing." *The Plain Dealer* 1 Dec. 1996: 11.
Turvey, Debbie Hochman. "All-Time Bestselling Children's Books." Edited by Diane Roback and Jason Britton. *Publishers Weekly* 17 Dec. 2001: 24–27.
Wolf: LC.
Wolosky: LC.
Zornado: LC.

Chapter 1

Abrams, M. H. *A Glossary of Literary Terms*. Sixth Edition. New York: Harcourt Brace Jovanovich, 1993.

Anderson, Celia Catlett, and Marilyn Fain Apseloff. *Nonsense Literature for Children: Aesop to Seuss*. Hamden, Conn.: Library Professional Pub., 1989.

Bandler: PI.

Baring-Gould, William S. *The Lure of the Limerick: An Uninhibited History*. New York: Clarkson N. Potter, 1967

Beyette: PI.

Boynton, Sandra. *Hey, Wake Up!* New York: Workman Publishing, 2000.

————. *Oh My Oh My Oh Dinosaurs!* New York: Workman Publishing, 1993.

————. *Pajama Time!* New York: Workman Publishing, 2000.

————. *Snoozers: 7 Short Short Bedtime Stories for Lively Little Kids*. New York: Simon and Schuster, 1997.

Brown, Calef. *Dutch Sneakers and Flea-Keepers*. Boston: Houghton Mifflin, 2000.

————. *Polka-Bats and Octopus Slacks*. Boston: Houghton Mifflin, 1998.

Burgess, Gelett. *Burgess Unabridged: A New Dictionary of Words you have always Needed*. With cover designs and illustrations by Herb Roth. New York: Frederick A. Stokes Company, 1914.

Cammaerts, Emile. *The Poetry of Nonsense*. 1925. Folcroft, PA: Folcroft Library Editions, 1974.

Carlinsky: PI.

Carroll, Lewis. *The Annotated Alice: The Definitive Edition*. Introduction and Notes by Martin Gardner. Original Illustrations by John Tenniel. New York: W. W. Norton & Co., 2000.

Clark: PI.

Corwin: PI.

Couric, Katie. *The Brand New Kid*. Illus. Marjorie Priceman. New York: Doubleday, 2000.

Dangaard: PI.

Diehl: PI.

Freeman: PI.

Frutig: PI.

Gorey, Edward. *Amphigorey*. 1975. New York: Penguin Putnam, 1991.

Gopnik, Adam. "Grim Fairy Tales." *New Yorker* 18 Nov. 1996: 96–102.

"grinch, v." *Oxford English Dictionary*. Ed. J. A. Simpson and E. S. C. Weiner. 2nd ed. Oxford: Clarendon Press, 1989. *OED Online*. Oxford University Press. 29 June 2003. <http://dictionary.oed.com/cgi/entry/00098886>.

"grinched, ppl. a." *Oxford English Dictionary*. Ed. J. A. Simpson and E. S. C. Weiner. 2nd ed. Oxford: Clarendon Press, 1989. *OED Online*. Oxford University Press. 29 June 2003. <http://dictionary.oed.com/cgi/entry/00098887>.

Hacker: PI.

Hall, Donald. *Oxford Book of Children's Verse in America* New York: Oxford UP, 1985.

Heller, Steven. "Children's Books: Captain Slaughterboard Drops Anchor." *New York Times Book Review* 10 Feb. 2002: 21.

Hersey, John. "Why Do Students Bog Down on First R?" *Life* 24 May 1954: 136–50.

Hopkins: PI.

Kitch: PI.

Kupferberg: PI.

Lear, Edward. *The Complete Nonsense of Edward Lear*. 1947. Collected and Introduced by Holbrook Jackson. New York: Dover Publications, 1951.

"Limerick." *Oxford English Dictionary*. Ed. J. A. Simpson and E. S. C. Weiner. 2nd ed. Oxford: Clarendon Press, 1989. *OED Online*. Oxford University Press. 29 June 2003. <http://dictionary.oed.com/cgi/entry/00133409>.

Lingeman: PI.

Lithgow, John. *Marsupial Sue*. Illus. Jack E. Davis. New York: Simon & Schuster, 2001.

———. *Micawber*. Illus. C. F. Payne. New York: Simon & Schuster, 2002.

———. *The Remarkable Farkle McBride*. Illus. C. F. Payne. New York: Simon & Schuster, 2000.

"nerd." *Oxford English Dictionary*. Ed. J. A. Simpson and E. S. C. Weiner. 2nd ed. Oxford: Clarendon Press, 1989. *OED Online*. Oxford University Press. 29 June 2003. <http://dictionary.oed.com/cgi/entry/00157015>.

Malcolm, Noel. *The Origins of English Nonsense*. 1997. London: Fontana Press (HarperCollins), 1998.

Maxwell: R.

Moore: R.

Newell, Peter. *The Hole Book*. 1908. Boston, Rutland, and Tokyo: Tuttle Publishing, 1985.

———. *The Slant Book*. 1910. Boston, Rutland, and Tokyo: Tuttle Publishing, 1967.

———. *The Rocket Book*. 1912. Boston, Rutland, and Tokyo: Tuttle Publishing, 1969.

Nilson: LC.

Peake, Mervyn. *Captain Slaughterboard Drops Anchor*. 1939. Cambridge, MA: Candlewick Press, 2001.

Perec, Georges. *A Void*. Trans. Gilbert Adair. London: Harvill, 1994.

Prelutsky, Jack. *The Snopp on the Sidewalk*. New York : Greenwillow Books, 1977.

Quindlen: LC.

R.E.M. "The Sidewinder Sleeps Tonite" *Automatic for the People*. Warner Brothers,1992.

Rowling, J. K. *Harry Potter and the Chamber of Secrets*. New York: Scholastic, 1999.

Schroth: LC.

Seuss, Dr. "Cat in the Hat—original sketches. Pencil and crayon on paper with typescript captions." UCSD: MSS 0230, MC-079–01.

———. "Dr. Seuss": E.

———. "Green Eggs and Ham—Rough sketches." UCSD: MSS 0230, MC-089–02.

———. "Green Eggs and Ham—Typescript." UCSD: MSS 0230, MC-089–01.

———. "Small Epic Poem, Size 3 1/2 B": SP.

Sewell, Elizabeth. *The Field of Nonsense*. London: Chatto and Windus, 1952.

Silverstein, Shel. *Where the Sidewalk Ends*. New York: HarperCollins, 1974.

Smith, James Steel: LC.

"Somebody's Got to Win": PI.

Speed, Toby. *Brave Potatoes*. Illus. Barry Root. New York: G. P. Putnam's Sons, 2000.

Steiner, Wendy. *The Colors of Rhetoric*. Chicago: University of Chicago Press, 1982.

Stewart, Garrett. *Reading Voices: Literature and the Phonotext*. Berkeley: U of California P, 1990.

They Might Be Giants. *No!* Idlewild/Rounder, 2002.

Tigges, Wim. *An Anatomy of Literary Nonsense*. Amsterdam: Rodopi, 1988.

Valentine: See Chapter 6.

West, Mark I. "Edward Lear's *Book of Nonsense*: A Scroobious Classic." *Touchstones: Reflections on the Best in Children's Literature*. Volume Two. Ed. Perry Nodelman. West Lafayette, IN: Children's Literature Association, 1987. 150–56.

Wilder: PI.

"Would you, could you, find that book?" Advertisement. *New York Times Book Review* 19 May 2002: 19.

Zahn, Paula. "People in the News [Michael Stipe]." CNN. 23 Feb. 2002, 2:50 p.m CST.

Chapter 2

Cobb: R.

Feiffer: See Chapter 3.

Freedman: PI.

Galbraith: LC.

Geisel, Theodor. Notebook describing war experiences. Nov. 1944—Jan. 1945. UCSD: MSS 0230, Box 1, Folder 30.

——. "Atrocities." Memo, 1945. UCSD: MSS 0230, Box 1, Folder 34.

——. Letter to Bill. Monday, n.d. but probably Dec. 1947. Dartmouth, Rauner Library: Alumni G277mi.

Hollenbeck, Don. "Lindbergh's Dirtiest Speech: Attack on Jews." *PM* 12 Sept. 1941: 14.

Hoopes, Roy. *Ralph Ingersoll: A Biography*. New York: Atheneum, 1985.

Jeansonne, Glen. *Gerald L. K. Smith: Minister of Hate*. New Haven: Yale University Press, 1988.

Jenkins: LC.

"Jew-Baiter Lindbergh Puts America Firsters on Spot." *PM* 14 Sept. 1941: 7.

Laing: R.

Low, David. *Years of Wrath. A Cartoon History: 1931–1945*. With a Chronology and Text by Quincy Howe. New York: Simon and Schuster, 1946.

Kahn: PI.

Margolick, David. "*PM*'s Impossible Dream." *Vanity Fair* Jan. 1999: 116–132.

Minear, "The Political Dr. Seuss": EC.

Milkman, Paul. *PM: A New Deal in Journalism, 1940–1948*. New Brunswick, NJ: Rutgers University Press, 1997.

Mosley, Leonard. *Lindbergh: A Biography*. Garden City, NY: Doubleday & Co., 1976.

"Pied Piper of Bookland": PI.

Schuyler, Rose P. Letter to the Editor. *PM* 9 July 1941: 21.

Seuss, Dr. Lecture notes. Delivered at University of Utah, July 1949. UCSD: MSS 0230, Box 19, Folder 6.

——. Letter to Americus Vesputius Fepp. UCSD: MSS 0230, Box 18, Folder 28.

——. "Japan's Young Dreams": E.

——. "The Past Is Nowhere": See "Reviews by Dr. Seuss."

——. "Writing for Children: A Mission": E.

Sheff: PI.

Spiegelman: LC.

Stenehjem, Michelle Flynn. *An American First: John T. Flynn and the America First Committee*. New Rochelle, NY: Arlington House Publishers, 1976.

"Suckers for The Senators." *PM* 20 Nov. 1942: 2.

Webb: PI.

"Who Is the No. 1 Lollipop of the U.S. Senate?" *PM* 20 Nov. 1942: 3.

Younger, Younger, and Hirsch: B.

Chapter 3

Agee, Jon. *Milo's Hat Trick*. 2001. New York: Michael di Capua, 2002.

Agee: R.

Bang, Molly. *Picture This: How Pictures Work*. New York: SeaStar Books, 2000.

Beane, Douglas Carter. *As Bees in Honey Drown*. Garden City, NY: Stage & Screen, 1997.

Becker, Stephen. *Comic Art in America: A Social History of the Funnies, the Political Cartoons, Magazine Humor, Sporting Cartoons and Animated Cartoons*. With an Introduction by Rube Goldberg. New York: Simon and Schuster, 1959.

Blackbeard, Bill, and Martin Williams. *The Smithsonian Collection of Newspaper Comics*. Washington and New York: Smithsonian Institution Press and Harry N. Abrams, 1977.

Buell: R.

Burchell: PI.

Cox, Palmer. *The Brownies: Their Book*. 1887. New York and London: D. Appleton-Century Company, 1915.

Crichton: PI.

Cronin, Doreen. *Click, Clack, Moo: Cows That Type*. Pictures by Betsy Lewin. New York: Simon & Schuster, 2000.

Dirda: R.

Duncan, Alastair. *Art Nouveau*. London: Thames and Hudson, 1994.

Eisner, Will. *A Contract with God and Other Tenement Stories: A Graphic Novel*. 1978. Kitchen Sink Press, 1998.

————. *Comics and Sequential Art*. 1985, Expanded 1990. Tamarac, FL: Poorhouse Press, 2001.

Escher, M[aurits] C[ornelis]. *Escher on Escher: Exploring the Infinite*. With a contribution by J. W. Vermeulen. Translated from the Dutch by Karin Ford. Japan: Harry N. Abrams, 1989.

Feiffer, Jules. *The Great Comic Book Heroes*. 1965. Seattle, WA: Fantagraphics Books, 2003.

Goulart, Ron, ed. *The Encyclopedia of American Comics*. New York: Facts on File, 1990.

————. *Great History of Comic Books*. Chicago and New York: Contemporary Books, 1986.

Hammond: PI.

Hines: R.

Horn, Maurice, ed. *The World Encyclopedia of Comics*. New York: Chelsea House, 1976.

Johnson, Crockett. *Harold and the Purple Crayon*. New York: Harper & Row, 1955.

Jordan: PI.

Kuskin, Karla. "The Mouse in the Corner, the Fly on the Wall: What Very Young Eyes See in Picture Books." *New York Times Book Review* 14 Nov. 1993. Repr. Fensch 165–68.

Lear, Edward. *The Pelican Chorus and Other Nonsense*. Illus. Fred Marcellino. New York: Harper-Collins, 1995.

Leipzig, Diane. "Reading Rockets Interview with Jon Scieszka." *Reading Rockets*. 2003. <www.-readingrockets.org/transcript.php?ID＝42>. 22 March 2003.

"The Logical Insanity of Dr. Seuss": PI.

Lyon: PI.

Marcus, Leonard S. "A Collaborative Effort: Two children's book teams talk about their working methods." *Publishers Weekly* 16 July 2001: 84.

Marschall, Richard. *America's Great Comic-Strip Artists: From the Yellow Kid to Peanuts*. 1989. New York: Stewart, Tabori & Chang, 1997.

————. *Sunday Funnies*. New York: MacMillan, 1978.

McCloud, Scott. *Understanding Comics: The Invisible Art*. 1993. New York: HarperCollins, 1994.

Milhous, Katherine. *The Egg Tree*. New York: Charles Scribner's Sons, 1950.

Miller, Frank, with Klaus Janson and Lynn Varley. *Batman: The Dark Knight Returns*. 1986. New York: DC Comics, 2002.

Moore, Alan, and Dave Gibbons. *Watchmen*. New York: DC Comics, 1987.

Orvell, Miles. *The Real Thing: Imitation and Authenticity in American Culture, 1880–1940*. Chapel Hill and London: U of North Carolina P, 1989.

"The Other Cool Cat": PI.

Permanyer, Lluís. *Gaudí of Barcelona*. Photographs by Melba Levick. English text adapted and edited by Sarah Underhill. New York: Rizzoli, 1997.

Politi, Leo. *Song of the Swallows*. New York: Charles Scribner's Sons, 1949.

Rohmann, Eric. *My Friend Rabbit*. Brookfield, Conn.: Roaring Brook Press, 2002.

Salisbury, Mark, ed. *Burton on Burton*. Foreword by Johnny Depp. London: Faber and Faber, 2000.

Scieszka, Jon. *The Stinky Cheese Man and Other Fairly Stupid Tales*. Illus. Lane Smith. New York: Viking, 1992.

————. *The True Story of the Three Little Pigs! by A. Wolf*. Illus. Lane Smith. 1989. New York: Puffin Books, 1996.

Seldes, Gilbert. "The Krazy Kat That Walks by Himself." 1924. *Krazy Kat: The Comic Art of George Herriman*. By Patrick McDonnell, Karen O'Connell, and Georgia Riley de Havenon. New York: Harry N. Abrams, 1986. 15–22.

Sendak, Maurice. *Caldecott & Co.: Notes on Books and Pictures*. 1988. Noonday Press, 1990.

————. *In the Night Kitchen*.

Seuss, Dr. "All I want to do is to build the museum-workshop." UCSD, MSS 0230, Box 19, Folder 24.

———. "The Dr. Seuss: Museum: A Creative Workshop for Beginners of All Ages." UCSD, MSS 0230, Box 19, Folder 12.

———. "Kids' Participation in Building the Museum." UCSD, MSS 0230, Box 19, Folder 21.

———. Letter to Andy Gump Fepp. UCSD, MSS 0230, Box MC-127, Folder 29.

———. Oh the Places You'll Go!: Color Roughs. UCSD: MSS 230, MC-106–16.

———. Oh the Places You'll Go!: Original finished ink drawings. UCSD: MSS 230, MC-106–18.

———. "Purposes." UCSD, MSS 0230, Box 19, Folder 24.

Shepard: PI.

Smith: R.

Spiegelman, Art. MAUS I: A Survivor's Tale. My Father Bleeds History. New York: Pantheon Books, 1986.

———. MAUS II: A Survivor's Tale. And Here My Troubles Began. New York: Pantheon Books, 1991.

Spiegelman: R.

Springfield Celebrates Seuss!: The Making of the National Memorial Sculpture Garden. Museum of Fine Arts, Quadrangle, Springfield, Mass. 1 June—8 Sept. 2002.

Steig, William. Sylvester and the Magic Pebble. 1969. New York: Aladdin, 1980.

Steinberg: PI.

St. George, Judith. So You Want to Be President? Illus. David Small. New York: Philomel Books, 2000.

"The Making of Tim Burton's The Nightmare Before Christmas." Tim Burton's The Nightmare Before Christmas. Special Edition. DVD. Touchstone Home Video, no. 20102.

Tim Burton's The Nightmare Before Christmas. Dir. Henry Selick. Music, lyrics and score by Danny Elfman. Story by Tim Burton. Screenplay by Caroline Thompson. Disney, 1993. DVD. Touchstone Home Video, no. 20102.

Tresselt, Alvin. White Snow, Bright Snow. Illus. Roger Duvoisin. New York: Lothrop, Lee & Shepard Co., 1947.

Van Allsburg, Chris. The Mysteries of Harris Burdick. Boston: Houghton Mifflin Company, 1984.

Vermeulen, J. W. "I'm Walking Around All By Myself Here." Escher on Escher: Exploring the Infinite. Translated from the Dutch by Karin Ford. Japan: Harry N. Abrams, 1989. 139–53.

Waugh, Coulton. The Comics. 1947. With an introduction by M. Thomas Inge. Jackson and London: University Press of Mississippi, 1991.

Wiesner, David. Free Fall. 1988. New York: Mulberry Books, 1991.

———. Tuesday. New York: Clarion Books, 1991.

The Wizard of Oz. Dir. Victor Fleming. Perf. Judy Garland, Frank Morgan, Ray Bolger, Bert Lahr, Jack Haley, Billie Burke, Margaret Hamilton. MGM, 1939.

Chapter 4

Adelman, Bob. Tijuana Bibles: Art and Wit in America's Forbidden Funnies, 1930s-1950s. Introductory Essay by Art Spiegelman. Commentary by Richard Merkin. Essay by Madeline Kripke. New York: Simon & Schuster, 1997.

Associated Press: PI.

Baldacci: PI.

Baum, L. Frank. The Wonderful Wizard of Oz. Pictures by W. W. Denslow. 1900. New York: Dover, 1960.

Berman: PI.

Bowman, David. Bunny Modern. Boston: Little, Brown & Company, 1998.

————. "Re: Seuss and Bunny Modern and . . ." Email to the author. 23 Sep. 2002, 12:08:22 EDT.

Bowman, Dick: PI.

"Dr. Seuss": PI.

Faulkner, William. *The Hamlet.* 1940. New York: Vintage, 1964.

————. *The Mansion.* 1959. New York: Vintage, 1965.

————. *The Town.* New York: Random House, 1957.

Freeman: PI.

Fuller, R. B. "OH, BOY, THAT WASH POTENT SHTUFF!" *Judge* 23 Apr. 1927: 4.

Geisel, Theodor Seuss. Vanguard Press correspondence. Box 53. Rare Book and Manuscript Library, Columbia University.

Gelber: PI.

Gordon: PI.

Gorney: PI.

Gough: LC.

Grimsley: See Chapter 5.

Hart: PI.

Jennings: PI.

Knoepflmacher, U. C., and Mitzi Myers. " 'Cross-Writing' and the Reconceptualization of Children's Literary Studies." *Children's Literature* 25 (1997): vii–xvii.

Kuskin: PI.

Laing: PI.

Lanes, Selma G. *The Art of Maurice Sendak.* 1980. New York: Abradale Press/Harry N. Abrams, 1993.

Lathem: PI.

Lindberg, Gary. *The Confidence Man in American Literature.* New York and Oxford: Oxford UP, 1982.

Lindsay: PI.

MacEoin: PI.

Martin: PI.

Melville, Herman. *The Confidence Man.* 1857. New York: Oxford University Press, 1991.

The Music Man. Music by Meredith Willson. Book by Willson and Frank Lacey. Screenplay by Marion Hargrove. Dir. Morton DaCosta. Perf. Robert Preston, Shirley Jones, Buddy Hackett, Hermione Gingold. Warner Bros., 1962.

Osterman: PI.

Pace: PI.

Sadler: PI.

Salzhauer: PI.

Schuman, Michael. "Cat in the Hat a lark in the park." *Kansas City Star* 23 June 2002: I1, I5.

Seuss, Dr. "The Hoobub and the Grinch": Original finished ink drawings. UCSD: MSS 0230, MC-126–04.

————. Lecture notes. Delivered at University of Utah, July 1949. UCSD: MSS 0230, Box 19, Folder 6.

————. *Maybe You Should Fly A Jet!*: Rough sketches. UCSD: MSS 0230, MC-103–11.

————. *The Shape of Me and Other Stuff*: Color roughs. UCSD: MSS 0230, MC-113–06.

Seuss, Dr., and Allan Scott. *The 5,000 Fingers of Dr. T.* Screenplay. Final Draft. 30 Jan. 1952. UCSD: MSS 0230, Box 8, Folder 4.

Seinfeld. Perf. Jerry Seinfeld, Julia Louis-Dreyfus, Michael Richards, Jason Alexander. NBC-TV, 1990–98.

Silverman: PI.

Smith: See Chapter 5.

"Sneetches, Sugar, and Success": PI.

Spiegelman, Art, and Maurice Sendak. "In the Dumps." *New Yorker* 27 Sept. 1993: 80–81.

Steinfels: PI.
Stewart-Gordon: PI.
Sullivan: PI.
Wadler, Joyce. "Mrs. Seuss Hears a Who, and Tells About It." *New York Times* 29 Nov. 2000.
Warren: PI.
Waugh: PI.

Chapter 5

Abramowitz, Rachel. "Kids' Stories, Grown-Up Business." *L.A. Times* 4 Aug. 2002. Calendar.
<http://www.calendarlive.com/movies/cl-ca-abramowitz4aug04.story>.
Bartlett, John. *Familiar Quotations*. Ed. Justin Kaplan. 16th Edition. Boston: Little, Brown and
Co., 1992.
Brantley, Ben. " 'Seussical: The Musical!': The Cat! The Whos! The Places They Go!" *New York
Times* 1 Dec. 2000: <http://www.nytimes.com/2000/12/01/arts/01SEUS.html?pagewan-
ted=1>. 1 Dec. 2000.
Bryan, Antonia D. *Grinch Meets His Max*. New York: Random House, 1998.
Cheyette, Herb. Letter to the author. 3 October 2001.
———. Letter to the author. 15 October 2001.
———. Letter to the author. 22 May 2003.
Clueless. Dir. Amy Heckerling. Feat. Alicia Silverstone, Paul Rudd. Paramount Pictures, 1995.
Cohen: EC.
Copyright Law of the United States of America. Chapter 1, Section 102. Revised to July 2001.
<http://www.loc.gov/copyright/title17/92chap1.html>. 6 Feb. 2002.
Cross, Gary. *Kids' Stuff: Toys and the Changing World of American Childhood*. Cambridge, Mass., and
London, England: Harvard UP, 1997.
Del Vecchio, Gene. *Creating Ever-Cool: A Marketer's Guide to a Kid's Heart*. Gretna, Louisiana:
Pelican Publishing Company, 1998.
"Don't be a GRINCH . . . Give the Gift of SEUSS!" Advertisement. *New York Times Book Review*
8 Dec. 2002: 65.
Dorfman, Ariel, and Armand Mattelart. *How to Read Donald Duck: Imperialist Ideology in the Disney
Comic*. Translation and Introduction by David Kunzle. 1975. New York: International Gen-
eral, 1984.
Dr. Seuss's How the Grinch Stole Christmas! Directed by Ron Howard. Performers: Jim Carrey,
Taylor Momsen, Jeffrey Tambor, Christine Baranski, Molly Shannon, Bill Irwin. Universal,
2000.
Dr. Seuss Went to War. Incl. in the *Dr. Seuss Collection*: W.
Gaines, Jane M. *Contested Culture: The Image, the Voice, and the Law*. Chapel Hill and London:
University of North Carolina Press, 1991.
Geisel, Ted. Letter to Mrs. Phyllis Jackson. 13 Sept. 1973. UCSD, MSS 230, Box MC-106,
Folder 22.
*Geisel v. Poynter Products Inc., Alabe Crafts Inc., Linder, Nathan & Heide Inc., and Liberty Library
Corporation*. U.S. District Court for the Southern District of New York. 158 USPQ. April
1968.
*Geisel v. Poynter Products Inc., Alabe Crafts Inc., Linder, Nathan & Heide Inc., and Liberty Library
Corporation*. U.S. District Court for the Southern District of New York. 160 USPQ. Dec.
1968.
Giroux, Henry A. "Are Disney Movies Good for Your Kids?" *Kinderculture: The Corporate Construc-
tion of Childhood*. Ed. Shirley R. Steinberg and Joe Kincheloe. Boulder, Colorado: Westview
Press, 1997. 53–67.
"Giving a Grinch for the Holidays." *Chronicle of Philanthropy* 17 Dec. 1998: 7.

Grimsley, Kirstin D. "To Thing That I Bought It From the Clothier, Esprit." *Valley News* 27 March 1994.

Handelman, David. "Curiouser and Curiouser." *New York Times Book Review* 16 May 1999: 39 <http://www.nytimes.com/books/99/05/16/bookend/bookend.html>.

Hiltbrand, David. "Flat in the Hat," *TV Guide* 21 Mar. 1998: 66.

Jameson, Fredric. *Postmodernism; or, the Cultural Logic of Late Capitalism.* Durham and London: Duke UP, 1991.

Kline, Stephen. *Out of the Garden: Toys, TV, and Children's Culture in the Age of Marketing.* London and New York: Verso, 1993.

Klugman, Karen. "Under the Influence." *Inside the Mouse: Work and Play at Disney World.* The Project on Disney. Durham and London: Duke UP, 1995. 98–109.

Kuenz, Jane. "It's a Small World After All." *Inside the Mouse: Work and Play at Disney World.* The Project on Disney. Durham and London: Duke UP, 1995. 54–78.

Lanham Act. Title 15, Chapter 22, Subchapter III. Sec. 1125. Repr. Legal Information Institute <http://www4.law.cornell.edu/uscode/15/1125.html>.

Lathem: B.

Lessig, Lawrence. *The Future of Ideas: The Fate of the Commons in a Connected World.* New York: Random House, 2001.

Morgan, Judith. "RE: Seuss chapter attached." Email to author. 30 July 2002, 17:00:46.

O'Brien, John. "How The Schnook Stole 'How the Grinch Stole Christmas.' " 2000. *The Dr. Seuss Parody Page*, ed. David Bedno. <http://www.seuss.org/seuss/schnook.html> 23 Apr. 2002.

"The One and Only Dr. Seuss . . .": PI.

Palmer, Debra. "Audrey Geisel: On Top of the World of Dr. Seuss." *San Diego County [619]* 2 Nov. 2000: 7–8.

Rabe, Tish. *The Song of the Zubble-Wump.* Adapted from a script by David Stephen Cohen. Illustrated by Tom Brannon. New York: Random House, 1996.

———. *The King's Beard.* Adapted from a script by Will Ryan. Illustrated by Joe Mathieu. New York: Random House, 1997.

———. *Oh, the Things You Can Do That Are Good for You!* Illustrated by Aristides Ruiz. New York: Random House, 2001.

"Revell, Inc." *Publishers Weekly* 31 Aug. 1959: 53.

Scott, A. O. "Sense and Nonsense." *New York Times Magazine* 26 Nov. 2000: 48–52, 105. <http://www.nytimes.com/library/magazine/home/20001126mag-seuss.html>.

Seuss, Dr. *The Cat in the Hat's Great Big Flap Book.* New York: Random House, 1999.

———. *Daisy-Head Mayzie*: Rough sketches, photographs of an early version by Geisel. UCSD: MSS 0230, MC-083–19.

———. *Dr. Seuss's ABC: An Amazing Alphabet Book.* New York: Random House, 1996.

———. *The Foot Book : Dr. Seuss's Wacky Book of Opposites.* New York: Random House, 1996.

———. *Green Eggs and Ham: With Fabulous Flaps and Peel-Off Stickers.* Adapted by Aristides Ruiz. New York: Random House, 2001. "Adapted from *Green Eggs and Ham.*"

———. *Mr. Brown Can Moo! Can You?: Dr. Seuss's Book of Wonderful Noises.* New York: Random House, 1996.

———. *Oh, Baby, the Places You'll Go!: A Book to Be Read in Utero.* Adapted by Tish Rabe from the works of Dr. Seuss. New York: Random House, 1997.

———. *Seuss-isms for Success: Insider Tips on Economic Health from the Good Doctor.* With an Introduction by Tom Peters. New York: Random House, 1999.

———. *Seuss-isms: Wise and Witty Prescriptions for Living from the Good Doctor.* New York: Random House, 1997.

"Seuss Creations Inspire Furniture." *La Jolla Light* 27 Aug. 1970: 6.

Seussical. Original Broadway Cast Album. Decca Broadway, 2001.

Small, David. *Imogene's Antlers.* New York: Crown Publishers, 1985.

Smith, Dinitia. "A Purist's Creatures Go Commercial," *New York Times*, 13 Feb. 1997, B1.

Updike, Nancy. "Green Eggs and Lawsuits." *LA Weekly* 20–26 July 2001: <http://www.la-weekly.com/printme.php3?eid=26588>. 19 June 2002.

U.S. Copyright Office. "Circular 1: Copyright Basics." Dec. 2000. <http://www.loc.gov/copyright/circs/circ1.html>. 10 Jan. 2002.

U.S. Copyright Office. "Circular 14: Copyright Registration for Derivative Works." June 1999. <http://www.loc.gov/copyright/circs/circ14.pdf>. 27 Mar. 2002.

U.S. Copyright Office. "Questions Frequently Asked in the Copyright Office Public Information Section." 5 Dec. 2001. <http://www.loc.gov/copyright/faq.html>. 6 Feb. 2002.

U.S. Patent and Trademark Office. "Trademark Information." <http://www.uspto.gov/web/menu/tm.html>. 27 Mar. 2002.

U.S. Patent and Trademark Office. "What Are Patents, Trademarks, Servicemarks, and Copyrights?" 24 Apr. 2001. <http://www.uspto.gov/web/offices/pac/doc/general/whatis.htm>. 10 Jan. 2002.

Wadley, James. "Re: Query about Dr. Seuss, Copyright, and Trademark." Email to author. 8 Feb. 2002, 10:47:59.

"We All Dream of Oz." Written, produced, and directed by David M. Bryant and Pamela Kerlin. Turner Network Television, 2000. TNT. Dec. 2001.

Weber, Jonathan. "The Ever-Expanding, Profit-Maximising, Cultural-Imperialist, Wonderful World of Disney." *Wired* 10.02 (Feb. 2002): 70–79.

Wintle and Fisher: PI.

Worth, Bonnie. *Oh, Say Can You Seed?* Illustrated by Aristides Ruiz. New York: Random House, 2001.

"You Will Love It on a Page, or on CD, or on a Stage." *Inside Borders* May 2001.

Zipes, Jack. *Sticks and Stones: The Troublesome Success of Children's Literature from Slovenly Peter to Harry Potter.* New York and London: Routledge, 2001.

ZoBell, Karl. Letter to Herb Cheyette. 22 May 2003.

Chapter 6

"Anti-Litter Organization Gives Award to Dr. Seuss." Press release. New York. Keep America Beautiful, Inc. 12 Nov. 1971. Dartmouth, Rauner Library, Alumni G277mi, Box 3, folder titled "Fan Mail."

Arias, Ron, and Liz McNeil. "A Boy Sides with Dr. Seuss's Lorax, and Puts a Town at Loggerheads." *People Weekly* 23 Oct. 1989: 67–68.

Arzt, George. "Mayor in Astonishing Blast at Carol Bellamy." *New York Post* 8 Dec. 1981: 4, 8.

"At the Court of King Edward." *New York Times* 10 Dec. 1981: A30.

Barthes, Roland. *Mythologies.* 1957. Translated by Annette Lavers. 1972. New York: Hill and Wang, 1994.

"Be a Lorax Helper—Help Build the Dr. Seuss Lorax Forest." Advertisement. Healdsburg, CA: Green Gems USA, 1997.

Birkett, Terri. *Truax.* 1995. Illus. Orrin Lundgren. Memphis, TN: National Oak Flooring Manufacturers' Association, 1997. <http://www.nofma.org/truax.htm>.

Blustein, Paul. "Treasury Bonds with Bono." *Washington Post* 4 June 2002: C1-C2.

Bulworth. Dir. Warren Beatty. Screenplay Warren Beatty and Jeremy Pikser. Feat. Warren Beatty, Halle Berry, Don Cheadle, Oliver Platt.

Bush, Barbara. Letter to "Friends" who organized tribute to TSG. 12 Nov. 1991. UCSD: MSS 0230, AB-009-C.

Bush, George W. "President Announces Early Childhood Initiative." Speech. Pennsylvania State University, Media, Pennsylvania. 2 Apr. 2002. Official transcript. <http://www.whitehouse.gov/news/releases/2002/04/20020402–9.html>.

"Carol: Ed's just playing a shell game!" *New York Post* 8 Dec. 1981: 4.

Clarity, James F. and Warren Weaver Jr. "Dr. Seuss Persists." *New York Times* 5 Apr. 1985: A16.

Connelly, Dale. "Green Egg on His Face." 1998. Repr. <http://www.seuss.org/seuss/gd.star.e-xpl.html>.

Coover, Robert. "The Cat in the Hat for President." *New American Review* 4 (Aug. 1968): 7–45.

Crews, Frederick. *The Pooh Perplex*. New York, Dutton, 1963.

Deee-Lite. "Groove Is in the Heart" *World Clique*. Elektra, 1990.

Dr. Seuss's Green Eggs and Ham. Text by Dr. Seuss. Music by Robert Kapilow. Chester, NY: G. Schirmer, 1995 (Dist. by Hal Leonard).

Dr. Seuss's Green Eggs and Ham. Text by Dr. Seuss. Music by Robert Kapilow. Perf. Angelina Réaux, Brett Tabisel, Robert Kapilow, and the New Jersey Chamber Music Society. Koch International Classics, 3–8900–2 H1.

Ellis, Bill. "Making a Big Apple Crumble: The Role of Humor in Constructing a Global Response to Disaster." *New Directions in Folklore* 6 (June 2002): <http://www.temple.edu/isllc/newfolk/bigapple/bigapple1.html>.

"Gale Norton, Keeper of All Things Wild." *Washington Post Weekly Edition* 24 Jan. 2001.

Gates, Henry Louis, Jr. "The White Negro." *New Yorker* 11 May 1998: 62–65.

Glionna, John M. "Timber Town Split to Roots; Child's Tale by Dr. Seuss Lays Bare Tensions That Threaten to Topple Reign of Loggers." *Los Angeles Times* 18 Sept. 1989.

Haberman, Clyde. "Koch Taking Steps to Consolidate His Control Over City Government." *New York Times* 30 Dec. 1981: A1 + .

Holland, Carol. Letter to Dr. Seuss. 15 Feb. 1972. Dartmouth, Rauner Library, Alumni G277mi, Box 3, folder titled "Fan Mail."

Hornaday, Ann. " 'Bulworth' tells it like it is hilariously." *Baltimore Sun* 22 May 1998: 1E.

Human Life Alliance. "The Silent Epidemic." 12-page insert. St. Paul, Minnesota: Human Life Alliance, 2002.

Kluger, Bruce and David Slavin. "If Clinton memoir has Seuss-like passages . . ." *Manhattan Mercury* 19 Aug. 2001: C9. Repr. from *L.A. Times*.

Levine, Richard, and Carlyle C. Douglas. "Mayor Rants, Then Recants." *New York Times* 13 Dec. 1981. Sec. 4: 6.

Maher, Bill. "How the Grinch Stole the Election." *Politically Incorrect* Nov. 2000. Repr. <http://www.seuss.org/seuss/pi-grinch.html>.

Morello, Carol. "Message Received, Dr. Seuss: Holt Children Unite as 'Loraxes' to Save Their Trees." *State Journal* (Lansing, Michigan). 20 May 1973.

Moxy Früvous. "Green Eggs and Ham" *Moxy Früvous*. Self-released cassette, 1990.

Raver, Anne. "Oh, the Things I Have Left Undone." *New York Times* 29 Dec. 2002: 13.

Reagan, Ronald. Letter to Theodor Geisel. 25 Apr. 1986. UCSD: MSS 0230, AB-0009-F.

Renko, Nancy. "How Al Sore Stole the Election by Dr. Ruse." 2000. Repr. <http://www.seuss.org/seuss/alsore.html>.

Romanowski, Patricia, and Holly George-Warren, editors. *The New Rolling Stone Encyclopedia of Rock & Roll*. Jon Pareles, Consulting Editor. New York & London: A Rolling Stone Press Book, 1995.

Rushdie, Salman. "How the Grinch Stole America." *The Guardian* 4 Jan. 2001. <http://www.-guardian.co.uk/Archive/Article/0,4273,4112192,00.html>.

Sheff: PI.

"Sometimes, when I sleep at night, I think of 'Hop on Pop.'" *Satire Wire*. April 2002 <http://www.satirewire.com/news/april02/hoponpop.shtml>.

Strauss and Newport. "How the Gingrinch Stole Congress." 1996. Repr. <http://www.seuss.org/seuss/gingrinch.html>.

Suggs, Rob. "The Binch." 14 Sep. 2001. Repr. in Laura Hoffart, "Fwd: The Binch." Email to the author. 18 Sep. 2001. This has also been reprinted in Bill Ellis, "Making a Big Apple Crumble: The Role of Humor in Constructing a Global Response to Disaster," *New Directions in Folklore* 6 (June 2002), Appendix D: <http://www.temple.edu/isllc/newfolk/bigapple/bigappleappd.html>.

————. "Re: Quoting you re: 'The Binch.'" Email to the author. 16 June 2003, 6:56:25 pm Central Time.

————. "Re: Quoting you re: 'The Binch.'" Email to the author. 17 June 2003, 12:31:34 pm Central Time.

————. "RE: The Binch." Email to Bill Ellis. 12 June 2002, 13:53:23.

Sutton, Ward. "The Cat in the Chad." *TV Guide* 6 Jan. 2001.

3rd Bass. "Pop Goes the Weasel" and "Green Eggs and Slime." *Derelicts of Dialect.* Def Jam, 1991.

Thompson, Mike. "Horton Hears a Clue!" *Manhattan Mercury* 11 July 2001.

"200 Books Given to White House." *New York Times* 19 Jan. 1962.

Valentine, Johnny. *One Dad Two Dads Brown Dad Blue Dads.* Illus. Melody Sarecky. Boston: Alyson Wonderland, 1994.

————. *Two Moms, the Zark, and Me.* Illus. Angelo Lopez. Boston, MA: Alyson Wonderland, 1993.

Wilkinson, Signe. "I can hold up a thong . . ." *New York Times* 24 Jan. 1999. Section 4.

Winfrey, Oprah. *The Oprah Winfrey Show* 6 July 2001.

Zamorsky, Tania. "The Parody is NOT in the Bag." *The Author's Guild Bulletin* Summer 1997. <http://www.webcom.com/guild/casenotes/cns971.html>. 2 July 2002.

Epilogue

Butter Battle Book press release. Dartmouth, Rauner Library: Alumni G277mi, Box 3.

Lamb: PI.

Seuss, Dr. *I Can Lick 30 Tigers Today and Other Stories*: King Looie Katz, Rough sketches and notes [151–153, 155]. UCSD: MSS 230, MC-096–18.

Scieszka, Jon. "Jon Scieszka." *Salon.com* 16 Dec. 1995: <http://www.salon.com/16dec1995/features/kids4.html>. 24 Jan. 2002.

Index

"Oh Latin! My Latin!", 201n.12

Oh Say Can You Say?, 4, 23–24, 27, 101

Oh, the Places You'll Go!, 4, 6, 14, 77, 80, 86–87, 134, 154, 158, 164, 190, 199n.4, 205n.10

Oh, the Thinks You Can Think!, 4, 10, 22, 86, 100, 158, 199n.4, 207n.2

Ohio Farm Bureau Children's Literature Award, 136

Ohio Sea Grant Program, 108

Old Globe Theatre (San Diego), 139

"Omnibus TV-Radio Workshop of the Ford Foundation: Dr. Seuss Explores the Museum That Ought to Be," 93, 200n.3

On Beyond Zebra!, 22, 24, 26–28, 67, 76, 86, 121–122, 154, 201n.10, 201n.11, 204n.3, 205n.13, 206n.15

Once-ler (character), 10, 26, 46, 68–69, 82, 123, 154, 165, 174, 178

One fish two fish red fish blue fish, 4–6, 22, 26, 36–37, 66, 153, 171–172, 183, 199n.4

O'Neill, Paul, 189

Oprah. See Winfrey, Oprah.

Oregon. See Portland.

Orlando (Florida), 131, 133

Ort, Lorrene Love, 12

Orvell, Miles, 204n.4

Osaragi, Jiro, 203n.6

"Ough! Ough! Or Why I Believe in Simplified Spelling," 25–26

Oursler, Fulton, 141

Outcault, R. F., 155

Owens, Peggy, 207n.9, 208n.10

Oxford, 110

Oxford English Dictionary, 21, 25

Ozarks, 10

"Quick, Henry, the Flit!" See Flit.

Pacific Ocean, 39, 56

Paddington Bear, 1

Parents, 121

Paris, 39

Peake, Mervyn, 21–23; *Captain Slaughterboard Drops Anchor*, 21

Pennsylvania. See Philadelphia.

"Pentellic Bilge for Bennett Cerf's Birthday," 200n.3

Perec, Georges, 29

Perkins, Dan. See Tomorrow, Tom.

Permanyer, Lluís, 205n.12

Perrault, Charles, 189

Perth (Australia), 199n.1

Peter Pan, 1, 199n.1. See also Barrie, J. M.

Philadelphia, 2

Picasso, 89–90

Pinocchio, 1

Plath, Sylvia, 35

PM, 3, 39, 41–42, 46, 51–52, 54, 57–58, 60–62, 86, 105–106, 108, 206n.15. See also cartoons, political; *Private SNAFU*; World War II.

Politi, Leo, 70

"Politically Incorrect," 180

politics, 11–14, 38–62, 98, 105–110, 125–128, 130, 132–134, 136, 138–139, 153, 168–192, 194–197, 203n.2, 209n.6. See also cartoons, political; Seuss, Dr., politics.

poll tax, 41. See also racism.

Pop Art, 97, 205n.7

Porter, Gene Stratton, 5

Portland (Oregon), 199n.1

Post-Impressionism, 89

Potter, Beatrix, 4, 71, 129, 189, 199n.4; *The Tale of Peter Rabbit*, 4, 199n.4

Potter, Harry. See Rowling, J. K.

Powell, Colin, 190–191

Poynter, Don, 142

Poynter Products Inc., 141–142, 145

"Prayer for a Child," 196–197

Prelutsky, Jack, 21, 23, 95, 151

Price, Vincent, 206n.17